Jesus Versus Christianity

Alfred Reynolds

Cambridge International Publishers
London

to A.G.D

First published in 1988 by
Cambridge International Publishers
8 Herbrand St. London WC1

This completely revised and extended edition published in 1993

Copyright © 1988 & 1993 by Cambridge International Publishers

British Library Cataloguing in Publication Data

A catalogue record for this book is available from the British Library

ISBN 0–946101–03–5

Reproduced and Printed by
Halstan & Co. Ltd., Amersham, Bucks., England

Contents

Notes, Acknowledgments, Abbreviations.
Apologia

1	The Man Jesus	1
2	The Lord Jesus Christ	38
3	The God Christ	76
4	The Holy Spirit	91
5	The Blessed Trinity	117
6	The Virgin Birth	156
7	Power and Authority	195
8	Jesus and Riches	236
9	War and Violence	259
10	Jesus and Women	286
11	Jesus lived and Died a Jew	297
12	Geneologies – The Seed of David	320
13	Public Worship Miscellany	338
14	Jesus did not found a Church	349
	Index of Names	361
	Bibliography	374
	Glossary	378
	Index of Biblical Passages	385

Notes

This is the first volume of Jesus versus Christianity, to be followed by a second one considering in detail the theologians of our age: Barth, Brunner, Bultmann, Jeremias, Kung, Niebuhr, Rahner, Schillebeekx, Tillich and others. In that book I will also have more to say about the fashionable talk concerning ecumenical hopes.

The second volume will also contain reflections on authority, the resurrection, slavery, sexuality: all issues which, in the wake of St. Paul's influence, blur the image of the Teacher.

On several occasions I have inserted short passages in the original Greek, wherever I thought that the translations are misleading. In such cases the correct wording is relevant to the argument itself.

The bible passages are taken from the Authorised Versions. Diversions from this translation are frequently indicated.

At the end of this book a glossary of terms used is to be found.

Acknowledgements

My thanks to the following friends whose help in preparing this book has been invaluable: Robert Broadfoot, Sheila Brygman, Marco Cevidalli, David Donlan, John Murphy, Jeremy Reed, Tom Walsh, Colin Wilson and Tim Wilson.

Abbreviations

CC	Catholic Commentary (RC)
JN	Jesus of Nazareth (Klausner)
NGR	The Nazarene Gospel Restored (Graves/Podro)
OVBC	One Volume Bible Commentary (Dummelow)
PC	Peake's Commentary (Protestant)
QB	Question Box (RC)
RC	Roman Catholic

Apologia

The source is clear.
Its water is cold and refreshing.
A lasting joy.
The river is grey, dirty and full of pollution.
My boat is drifting on its surface, and even the strokes of the
    oars cover my hands and my face with defiling drops.
Sometimes my anger mounts, my indignation.
Unworthy emotions.
Keep calm and let the waves pass.
The waves of today carry waters which differ from
    yesterday's!
Alas, they don't.
Flowing through centuries, they have remained polluted,
    and there is but little hope.
I love truth even if it hurts. But as the pain dies away, my zest and my
    love decline. One day, I, too, will die, though the river continue in
    its course.
There is but little hope.

The pages of this book express indignation and resignation.
A cold wind is blowing through its pages, but what does it matter if it
    can clear away only a little of the dust. the grime of centuries cannot
    be undone. A hundred volumes would be of no avail.
The Augean Stables were covered with the grime of decades. It needed
    a Heracles to clean them up in a day. The day of one generation is
    short. Only years of such days could remove the grime. By then the
    stables are encrusted with more. In the form of learned books. And I
    am not a Heracles.
I am not a theologian either. Nor even a scholar. I am trying to do the
    work of a critic, comparing the living source with the sluggish
    river. In effecting this confrontation I may have made some
    mistakes. All the same, this is a few minutes work in the Augean
    Stables. A small contribution to the great task which coming ages
    might accomplish, perhaps. It may bring the day nearer when we
    can once again drink of the clear water of the source. There is still a
    little hope.

This book will infuriate many. It will help a few. The victims I love. I
am trying to love the deceivers, too. It is difficult.

He who hath ears to hear
                let him hear . . .

                Why call me Lord, Lord,
          and do not the things which I say

                            The kingdom of heaven
                                  is within you

I
The Man Jesus

A man approved by God by mighty works

What do we know of the man Jesus?

If we rely on historical sources, nothing. The New Testament cannot be regarded as a historical record since the extant copies were written by believers, in foreign countries and in Greek, over almost a hundred years after the events they describe. Even the synoptic gospels are too full of mutual contradictions and miraculous stories to be accepted as historical documents. The great Roman historians of the first and second centuries do not know of the man Jesus.

Let us then consider the sources presented by Christian apologists as historical evidence. First of all there is only actual mention of Jesus, made about A.D. 93 and attributed to Josephus, a Jewish priest and historian who is supposed to have written: 'Now there was about this time Jesus, a wise man if it be lawful to call him a man, for he was a doer of wonderful works; a teacher of such men as receive the truth with pleasure. He drew over to him both many of the Jews, and many of the Gentiles. He was the Messiah: and when Pilate, at the suggestion of the principal men amongst us, had condemned him to the cross, those that loved him at the first did not forsake him, for he appeared to them alive again on the third day, as the divine prophets had foretold these and ten thousand other wonderful things concerning him; and the tribe of Christians, so named from him, are not extinct at this day' (*Ant*. 18:3:3).

This is placed between two considerably longer paragraphs, the preceding one dealing with a rising against Pilate because of his attempt to extract temple-money for an aqueduct, and the following one reporting a scandal which at that time affected the Court in Rome, in connection with the worship of the goddess Isis. The short passage was first quoted by Eusebius, but earlier Church Fathers seem to have had no knowledge of it. Origen, for example, twice mentions that Josephus did not admit that Jesus was the Messiah (*Contra Celsum* 1:47 and *Commentary to Matthew* 10:17). Nor did Chrysostom, who had a good knowledge of Josephus, appear to be acquainted with the passage. Many reasons had been advanced to show that *Ant* 18:3:3 is fraudulent. First of all it is not likely that a Jewish historian should accept the Messianic claim of Jesus without being converted to Christianity. If he did accept the claim that the Messiah lived and died in his own century, he would not be content to devote merely one short paragraph to such a momentous event, inserted between two stories completely irrelevant to it. Even if he did not accept the claim, the mere existence of the Christian movement would have prompted this vociferous historian to give it and its alleged founder a more detailed treatment in his thirty-two books of historical reportage. Many scholars, even some Christians, believe that the passage as it now reads, is a Christian fabrication, while the original text was, for certain reasons, expurgated. We do not know who might have been responsible for this manoeuvre, some think that Eusebius himself was the culprit. However, no proof exists for this assumption. Among the authorities who rejected the authenticity of the text in its present form was Gibbon, who wrote: 'The passage concerning Jesus Christ, which was inserted into the text of Josephus between the time of Origen and that of Eusebius, may furnish an example of no vulgar forgery' (*Decline and Fall of the Roman Empire*, II,p.100).

In the *Antiquities* of Josephus we find another short passage which reads:

. . . he (Ananus) assembled the sanhedrin of judges and brought before them the brother of Jesus who was called the Messiah . . . ' (*Ant* 20:9:1).

It seems that, while Josephus cannot be quoted as proof for the historical existence of Jesus, his first, suitably altered text and his second passage increase the probability, that the man Jesus did exist in the period immediately preceding that of Josephus.

This pernicious superstition

Other texts of external evidence for the existence of Jesus undoubtedly reflect Christian beliefs concerning him, since he is never mentioned by his name but as 'Christ', that is, Messiah. This kind of record may indeed be genuine but bears witness to nothing more than the pagan historians' intelligence as regards Christian beliefs.

The most important of these texts is by Tacitus, written between 115 and 120. It reports the Great Fire that ravaged Rome under the Emperor Nero in A.D. 64, and continues: 'But all human efforts, all the lavish gifts of the Emperor, and the propitiation of the gods, did not banish the sinister belief that the conflagration was the result of an order. Consequently, to get rid of the report, Nero fastened the guilt and inflicted the most exquisite tortures on a class, hated for their abominations, called Christians by the populace. Christus, from whom the name had its origin, suffered the extreme penalty during the reign of Tiberius at the hands of one of our procurators, Pontius Pilatus; and a most pernicious superstition, thus checked for the moment, again broke out not only in Judaea, the first source of the evil, but even in Rome, where all things hideous and shameful from every part of the world find their centre and become popular. Accordingly, an arrest was first made of all who pleaded guilty; then, upon their information, an immense multitude was convicted, not so much of the crime of firing the city, as of hatred against mankind. Mockery of every sort was added to their deaths. Covered with the skin of beasts, they were torn by dogs and perished, or were nailed to crosses, or were doomed to the flames and burnt, to serve as a nightly illumination, when daylight had expired . . . Hence, even for criminals who deserved extreme and exemplary punishment, there arose a feeling of compassion; for it was not, as it seemed, for the public good, but to glut one man's cruelty that they were being destroyed' (*Annals* 15:44).

There are, of course, some weighty arguments against the authenticity of the text, although it is difficult to see what the early Christian apologists would have hoped to gain from the interpolation of this passage. The *Annals* were first published at Venice in 1468 by Johannes de Spire, and that publication contains the celebrated text. However, not one of the Church Fathers seems to have been acquainted with it, and even Tertullian, who quotes Tacitus, did not know the passage. Tertullian mentions the cruelty of Nero and says, 'Consult your histories, there you will find that Nero was the first to draw the bloody imperial sword against this sect then rising at Rome' (*Apo.*5) but does not speak of the atrocities Nero was supposed to have committed against the Christians.

Gibbon accepts the passage as authentic but emphasises that Tacitus was born only a few years before the Great Fire, and his information is obtained mainly from reading about these events. 'At the distance of sixty years,' Gibbon says, 'it was the duty of the annalist to adopt the narrative of contemporaries; but it was natural for the philosopher to indulge himself in the description of the origin, the progress and the character of the new sect, not so much according to the knowledge or prejudice of the age of Nero, as according to the time of Hadrian (op. cit.p.II p.101).

It is unlikely that Tacitus, a fairly objective observer, should have used such extravagant language against a 'criminal sect' without describing the crimes of which they were guilty. Furthermore, the text bears traces of exaggeration of which Tacitus should not be accused. On the other hand, if a Christian interpolator fabricated this passage why should he not have attempted to include more 'evidence'? I tend to agree with the Jewish scholar Dr. Klausner who wrote: 'These words would have had considerable value as spontaneous evidence of a Gentile if they had been written earlier than many decades after the event. But we do not need the evidence of Tacitus to know that at the beginning of the second century the belief was widespread that there had been a 'Messiah' or 'Christ' who was condemned to death by Pontius Pilate' (*Jesus of Nazareth, {JN}* p.60).

In any case, if we rely on Tacitus, we should accept his complete testimony with its contempt and hostility for the 'pernicious superstition' or, if we choose to reject it, there is no reason why that part of the testimony which serves the purpose of the Christian apologist should be accepted to the exclusion of the rest.

At the instigation of one Chrestus

Another piece of 'evidence' produced by Christians is a passage in *The Lives of the Twelve Caesars* by Suetonius, which reads: 'Claudius banished from Rome all the Jews who were continually making disturbances at the instigation of one Chrestus . . .' (*Claudius*, XXV p.318). Another reference to Christians, also quoted as 'evidence', is to be found in the same work: '(Nero) likewise inflicted punishments on the Christians, a sort of people who held a new and impious [better translated as 'malevolent' or 'malicious' – AR] superstition' (*Nero*, XVI p.347). These passages, written about A.D. 120, contain little information except that the first one confirms a statement in Acts 18:12. According to Chrysostom, however, Claudius did not expel the Jews from Rome, merely forbade their religious assemblies The name Chrestus, which most authorities take to mean Christus, was a frequent name. Cicero mentions a Chrestus in *Fam. Ep.* 11:8. In Greek χρηστός means 'good' or 'kind' and Justin Martyr, referring to the name of the movement in his address to Emperor Antoninus Pius, about A.D. 150, makes a pun on that name, saying: 'We are called Christians. So then we are the best of men (Chrestians), and it can

THE MAN JESUS

never be just to hate what is good (chrest-) and righteous' (*Justini Apol.*)' This pun was probably quite widespread, and a string of similar puns on the names Christus and Chrestus is attributed to Theophil, the bishop of Antioch, thought to have been the first to compile a concordance of the gospels, but most of whose works have disappeared. We know about him from Jerome (*Epist.* 121:6:15).

The only information of value in the passages from Suetonius is the justifiable view that the Christian movement, whatever its origin, was already active in the Rome of Claudius in the middle of the first century.

Pliny the Younger mentions the Christians in a letter addressed to Emperor Trajan, written during his office as Proconsul of Bithynia, in A.D. 111. He describes them as a popular movement singing hymns to Christ as a god, and refusing to pay homage to the Roman Emperor. Pliny knows little about the beliefs of this strange sect and wonders how to deal with their 'folly' (amentia). The letter shows a certain grudging admiration for them and asks for the Emperor's advice as to what he should be doing with this people.

Such documents merely prove that the second century saw the rise of the Christian movement in the whole realm: a fact no one doubts. They contribute no evidence concerning the life and actions of the man Jesus. For any information on that subject we depend on the contradictory and often garbled accounts of the New Testament, and especially of the synoptic gospels.

Apart from the above, fleeting mentions of the Christian movement are made by the Emperor Hadrian in a letter to his brother-in-law, Servianus, in A.D. 138; by Emperor Marcus Aurelius in his *Meditations* (Book 11); and by the satirist Lucian, in his *Philopatris*, in A.D. 176.

Seneca, Pliny the Elder, the geographers Pausanias and Pomponius Mela, the historians Appianus, Justinus and Curtius Rufus, as well as the famous writer and orator Quintilianus, did not know of the Christians or, if they did, ignored their existence. The main body of Roman legislation, the Corpus Iuris Civilis, does not contain one word about the Christians.

Another Jesus whom we have not preached

This quotation (*2 Cor.* 11:4) applies (it seems to me) to the man Jesus presented by those who, like the Apostle Paul, have preached the 'Lord Jesus Christ'.

Briefly, this is the record we possess about Jesus' life and his ministry pieced together from the often contradictory statements made by not too reliable witnesses. Jesus (Yeshua or Joshua), son of Joseph of the seed of David was the son of a Jewish carpenter and his wife Mary (Miriam). We have no source to establish the origin of his mother. She is said to have been the cousin of Elizabeth, wife to the priest Zachariah – the parents of John the Baptist. Elizabeth was of the seed of Aaron (that is, not of the seed of David); Zachariah was 'of the course of Abia' (*Luke* 1:5) that is, of the seed of David (*Matthew* 1:7), if we follow the genealogy not according to Luke but to Matthew. If we keep to the Gospel according to Luke, Abia is not even mentioned. Thus scripture does not help us to trace the descent of Mary.

Apart from Jesus, their first-born, Joseph and Mary had four sons and at least two daughters (*Matthew* 13:55/6 and *Mark* 6:3). According to Matthew, who was very concerned with the fulfilment of prophesies, and according to Luke, Jesus was born in Bethlehem, a little township in Judaea associated with the origin of King David and with the 'prophecy': 'Thou Bethlehem Ephrata, though thou be little among the thousands of Judah, yet out of thee shall come forth unto me that is to be ruler in Israel . . . ' (*Micah* 5:2). It seems more likely that Jesus was born in Nazareth, the home town of his family. Mark and John make no reference to his place of birth. Some authorities believe that the Galilean Bethlehem, a small village near Nazareth, was the place where Jesus was born (Graetz, Neubauer, Klein, Réville). This village is mentioned in *Joshua* 19:15. Others scholars (Loisy) think that a Galilean town Nazareth did not exist in the days of Jesus, but it is likely that there was a town of homophonous name not far from the present Nazareth. Jesus was probably born about 4 B.C., but the actual date and year of his birth cannot be established.

Like every Jewish child, he was circumcised soon after his birth. At the ceremony, according to age-old custom, Joseph must have declared him to be his child, and Mary, like every Jewish mother, went through the rite of purification (*Luke* 2:21/2).

Schools where children were instructed in the Torah did not exist outside Jerusalem until about A.D. 64. Jesus, who had a very good knowledge of the Law and the scriptures, must have learnt them from his father and in the local synagogue. We read that Galileans were recognisable by their speech (*Erubin* 53b, *Matthew* 26:73 *Mark* 14:70), and indeed the mother-tongue of Jesus was not Hebrew but a closely related language, Aramaic. It was Joseph Justus Scaliger who, in the 16th century, discovered from a few words quoted in the original in the gospels, that Jesus' native language was not Hebrew. Aramaic was an important branch of the Semitic languages, and, linguistically, Aramaic conquered a big part of Syria and Asia Minor. During the first

THE MAN JESUS

millennium B.C. it became the commercial and diplomatic language, as Babylonian had been during the second. It was only the rise of Greek as a universal language which put an end to the spread of Aramaic (quoted from Schweitzer, *The Quest of the Historical Jesus*, p.272).

From the Old Testament we learn that at the time of Ezekiel (about 700 B.C.) Aramaic was not yet understood among Jews (*2 Kings* 18:26), and it must have made rapid progress throughout Syria to become the language of the Galileans. It is of course difficult, if not impossible, to tell to what extent Hebrew and Aramaic interpenetrated one another, and whether Hebrew was used colloquially, or only as liturgical language in Galilee.

It may amuse the reader to learn that after the first shock of discovering that Jesus did not speak the classical language of the Jews, a Viennese Jesuit, Inchofer, maintained that Jesus did not speak Hebrew or Aramaic but Latin! The Lord cannot have used any other on Earth, he argued, since Latin is the language of the Saints in Heaven (ibid., p.270).

We know nothing at all about the childhood and adolescence of Jesus. The New Testament is silent about his development from the age of twelve to his baptism, which occurred at the beginning of his ministry. When he became a wandering teacher in the Jewish land he is said to have been thirty years of age (*Luke* 3:23). From the statement that the Baptist began his activity in the fifteenth year of the reign of Tiberius, we may conclude that Jesus was about that age. Some scholars are inclined to think that towards the end of his ministry he was nearing his fiftieth birthday (*John* 8:57). Be that as it may, it is difficult to compile the circumstances of his ministry so as to cover a period longer than two years, although it is possible that the writers of the gospels tended to condense their story which may have extended over a long stretch of time.

Jesus accepted baptism, a ritual indicative of purification and religious devotion, but it is most unlikely that he commanded his followers to baptise. He renounced power and wealth as it is symbolically presented in the temptation story. His father Joseph is not mentioned during his ministry: it is likely that he had died before his son's mission began. It is also probable that, having left his family, Jesus had very little contact with his relations – he certainly did not pay them a visit while in his home town. He refused to meet his mother and brothers, and apart from a short trip when she joined Jesus' little group, his mother reappears only at the Crucifixion (*John* 19:25-6). Of his brothers, James became a believer after Jesus' death.

During his ministry Jesus was an itinerant preacher, a 'rab' (teacher) who, like many other religious visionaries, travelled through the lands of the Jews. He taught and healed, and liked to refer to himself as 'Son of man' which merely signifies *man* (Klausner, op. cit., p.256). It is possible that Jesus used these words because they were associated with the Messiah in the books of Daniel and Enoch. Klausner believes that it may be an interpolation by the evangelists and, in fact, if Jesus used the expression it was merely a substitution for the first person singular. Perhaps is was his intention both to reveal and at the same time conceal his Messiahship.

He found twelve disciples to accompany him in most of his wanderings. They seem to have been, with few exceptions, unlettered men from menial trades. The significance of the number, apart from the mystical implications of the number twelve, was in the fact that a community of at least ten male Jews could perform their religious duties and functions without having to rely on priestly authority. They constitute a *minneh*, a kind of independent ecclesiastical group.

Jesus wandered over a large part of the Jewish lands. The main places mentioned are Capernaum, Chorazin, Migdal and Nazareth west of the Jordan, and Bethsaida and Gadara east of the river. Later we find him in Tyre, Sidon, Caesarea Philippi, Jericho and Jerusalem.

He is recorded as having visited synagogues; and one of his first public acts was preaching on a sabbath in Nazareth (*Luke* 4:16 ff.). On no occasion is he reported, however, as having taken part in public worship in a synagogue. These buildings were used for a variety of purposes: as centres of public discussion, reading, preaching, meditating, as schools for children, courts of law, and frequently as mere meeting places. There was only one Temple, the Temple in Jerusalem. Jesus is also recorded as having read from the scriptures on the above-mentioned occasion which shows that he was a literate man.

His ministry was ended abruptly when he was denounced by some of his enemies to the Roman authorities. He was condemned to death as a rebel and pretender to the Jewish throne. He suffered crucifixion, one of the most painful forms of execution and the common way of the Romans to deal with political offenders.

The doctrine

Concerning the teaching of Jesus, Klausner makes an interesting observation: 'The three synoptics all preserve one noteworthy saying, "And they were all amazed at his teaching, for he taught them as one that had authority and not as the scribes" (*Matthew* 7:29, *Mark* 1:22, *Luke* 4:32). The words "as one that had authority" shows clearly that

Jesus differed from the scribes in that they taught nothing of themselves but based themselves wholly on Scripture, while he spoke intuitively without this constant reference to the Scriptures' (op.cit.,p.264).

As a teacher he was and remained a Jew. It seems that he often wished to confine his words and his preaching to Jewish audiences. How else could one explain utterances such as: 'Go not the way of the Gentiles [correct translation 'nations'], neither enter any city of the Samaritans; but go unto the lost sheep of Israel' (*Matthew* 10:5-6); 'I am not sent but unto the lost sheep of the house of Israel' (*Matthew* 15:24); 'Let him be unto thee as a heathen [foreigner] and a publican' (*Matthew* 18:17); and 'When ye pray, use not vain repetitions as the heathens [foreigners] do' (*Matthew* 6:7). With their usual skill, the translators of the Authorised Version rendered the term ἐθνικὸς as 'Gentile' (foreigner), or, when it suited them, in a derogatory fashion as 'heathen'. The Revised Version corrects this blatant mistranslation. Jesus continually refers to the Law and impresses upon his listeners the importance of its strict observance.

His brother James went so far as saying: 'For whosoever shall keep the whole Law, and yet stumble in one point, he is become guilty of all' (*James* 2:10). The observance of the Jewish Law as an attempt to do the will of God is the central theme of the teaching of Jesus and his followers.

Yet his teaching also showed points of divergence from traditional Judaism. He discarded the Jewish reluctance to eat, drink and keep company with sinners and publicans who were considered unclean by the faithful. Similarly he rejected the demands of ritual cleanliness which affect the external form without heeding the purity of thought and speech. Klausner remarks: 'When one asked Jesus how to attain eternal life, he enumerated six only of the Ten Commandments, precisely those which embody plain, human, ethical principles, but makes no mention of the four which comprise the known ceremonial religious duties (the first four of the Ten Commandments' (*JN* 3:70). It is certain that he paid little attention to the ritual, ceremonial and outward display of religious sentiments. He discouraged public worship, ostentatious fasting and almsgiving. There is every indication that he disliked any functional or institutional religion: 'The kingdom of heaven is within you' (*Luke* 17:21). We are told by some Christian theologians that the word Jesus used was *among* you and not *within* you. They imply that the saying presages the Church which is *among* us. If the reader takes the trouble to check on this example of superficiality, he will find that the Greek text uses ἐντὸς in Luke and μέσος in

John, but it is clear that Luke *meant* 'within'. Jesus' rejection of ecclesiastical authority was so obvious that perhaps Nietzche's remark is justified: 'The Church is precisely that against which Jesus preached – and against which he taught his disciples to fight' (*Wille zur Macht*, para 168).

Jesus disapproved of judging in any form, whether in condemning a man for his misdeeds, or sentencing a transgressor against the Law, or even mediating unnecessarily between contesting opponents. He taught a voluntary and self-imposed 'moderate poverty' (Nietzche's expression), which alone can cleanse our hearts from greed and malice. He advocated the abandonment of all external and social ambition, both in the political and economic spheres. He deplored family ties if they impeded spiritual growth.

Some authorities believe that the admirable saying 'the Sabbath was made for man, and not man for the Sabbath' (*Mark* 2:27) is original. It is however a traditional saying included in the early Talmud: 'God delivered the Sabbath unto you, not you unto the Sabbath' (*Yoma* 85b).

There are also a few disconcerting injunctions contained in the teaching of Jesus, which I have to count among those of his ideas which are not necessarily based on traditional Jewish thought. He forbade divorce on any grounds whatsoever ('save only for fornication' – and even this might be a later interpolation). He would have us take no interest in politics, production, culture or art. He disapproved of punishment between man and man, but believed in a just God which in his use of language meant a punishing God. He belittled the importance of this life, and emphasised the significance of a life to come. And, finally, he seemed to be in favour of asceticism, in being 'a eunuch for heavens sake.' (*Matthew* 19:12).

Some aspects of his teaching enabled the religious leaders to make him suspect in the eyes of the Roman authorities. This led to his arrest, his appearance before Pilate, and his eventual crucifixion. This unjust sentence and his cruel end added fuel to the influence of his teaching, and the members of his *minneh* were soon joined by powerful personalities who carried his name and fame far beyond the borders of the Jewish lands.

The name

'Jesus' is the grecianized form ('Ιησοῦς) of the Hebrew Yeshu or Joshua. According to the New Testament it was given at the command of the Angel: 'Thou shalt call his name Jesus: for he shall save his people from their sins' (*Matthew* 1:21). In the next verse the evangelist

THE MAN JESUS

refers to *Isaiah* 7:14 in which the prophet said: 'They shall call his name Emmanuel which being interpreted is God with us' (*Matthew* 1:23). The name is also mentioned in The Gospel according to Luke: 'They shall call his name Jesus', the words being spoken by the Angel in the Annunciation (1:31).

The name Yeshua means 'Yahweh is Salvation'. Christian apologists make much of the meaning of the name Jesus, some even use it as proof of his divinity. It is certainly an echo of the words of the Psalmist: 'He shall redeem Israel from all his iniquities' (*Psalm* 130:8).

However, most Hebrew names were connected with God. A short list will show that apart from Yeshua and Emmanuel, the meanings of which are already familiar to us, many well known names contain the syllables Ye (Je)). Ya (Ja) or El, signifying God.

ARIEL	Lion of God
ELIEZER	my God is help
ELISHEBA (ELIZABETH)	to whom God is oath
EZEKIEL	God strengthens me
ELISHA	to whom God is salvation
GABRIEL	man of God
JOAB (JOB)	God is father
JOEL	Jehovah is God
JOHANAN (JOHN)	God is loving
JEREMIAH	exalted by Jehovah
JONATHAN	whom Jehovah gave
MATTHIA (MATTHEW)	gift of God
MICAH (MICHAEL)	likeness of God
NATHANIEL (NATHAN)	gift of God
RAPHAEL	giant of God
RUACHEL (RACHEL)	breath of God
SAMUEL	name of God
ZECHARIAH	whom God remembers

As can be seen there is nothing extraordinary in Jesus bearing the name Yeshua which was very frequent among the sons of Israel.

Emmanuel (imanu El), i.e. 'with us God' was not so common, but then the teacher's name just was *not* Emmanuel.

In the chapter on Genealogies I shall examine the question whether we may consider Jesus as being the son of Joseph and, if we attribute a modicum of authenticity to the gospels, as being of the House of David. His full name then would have been Jesus son of Joseph of the House of David.

His appearance

Of Jesus' physical appearance we know nothing, absolutely nothing. Not one of the evangelists describes his face or figure, and no mention is made of the colour of his hair, his eyes or complexion. The ludicrous attempt to borrow from Isaiah's description of the 'Suffering Servant': 'He hath no form nor comeliness; and when we shall see him, there is no beauty that we should desire him . . . ' (*Isaiah* 53:2) is beneath contempt. My suspicion is that a description of his appearance is lacking because the authors of the gospels, never having seen him, were completely in the dark about his physical attributes.

There are, however, certain negative statements I can safely make. He did *not*, and that is sure, look like the images of him we find in the portraits by many great painters as well as in devotional books and leaflets. The custom of painting a fine-looking tall man with long flowing hair and a golden beard, with blue eyes and a fair complexion, is pure fantasy, introduced by European painters who represented him in the likeness of their most attractive models. True that among the Syrians we find today some blond and blue-eyed people, but this is due to the influx of Greeks in the first few centuries of our era, and of Germanic elements during the crusades. It is likely that the Syrians of Jesus' day resembled Assyrian and Babylonian reliefs; their features were strong and their hair, eyes and complexion dark. Their stature was probably small to medium, and their habits none too clean. It was for this reason that Oriental religions insisted on ritual cleanliness which, one may assume, pious Jews observed with great circumspection. It can be stated without a shadow of a doubt that Jesus did not have long hair, otherwise it would be difficult to explain why we should find in an Epistle attributed to Paul (one among the earliest Christian scriptures) this sentence: 'Doth not even nature itself teach you, that if a man have long hair, it is a shame unto him' (*1 Cor.* 11:14). It is unlikely that the Jews of Jesus' day had long hair, apart from the occasional freak who disregarded all communal custom.

Of course, there has always been a tendency in the Church to attribute breath-taking beauty to Jesus. But if this had been the case it would have become part of verbal tradition and had found its way into the gospels.

'All our pictures of the handsome Jew,' writes Robert Taylor, 'present the closest family likeness to the Indian Krishna, and the Greek Apollo. Had the Jewish text been respected, he would have been exhibited as hideously ugly: "his visage was so marred more than any man, and his form more than the sons of men . . ." (*Isaiah* 52:14). But this would have spoilt the ornaments of the Church as well as of the theatre, and been fatal to the faith of the fair sex. Who would have believed in an ugly son of God?' (*Diegesis*, p. 379).

One of the blatant forgeries, which until the end of the eighteenth century passed as an authentic document, is a report attributed to a certain Publius Lentulus, alleged predecessor of Pontius Pilate. It was supposed to have been written by the Procurator to the Roman Senate, and found its way into the first *History of Christ* written by St. Jerome. This clumsy counterfeit contains a full description of the appearance of Jesus which seems to have been current in the early Church.

'At this time, there hath appeared, and still lives, a man endowed with great powers, whose name is Jesus Christ [sic]. Men say he is a mighty prophet; his disciples call him the Son of God. He restores the dead to life, and heals the sick from all sorts of ailments and diseases. He is a man of stature, proportionately tall, and his cast of countenance has a certain severity in it, so full of effect as to induce beholders to love, and yet still to fear him. His hair is the colour of wine, as far as the bottom of his ears, without curls and straight: from the lower part of his ears it is curled, down to his shoulders [sic] and bright, and hangs downwards from his shoulders; at the top of his head it is parted after the fashion of the Nazarenes. His forehead is smooth and clean, and his face without a pimple (sine macula), adorned by a certain temperate redness (rubor temperatus); his countenance noble and agreeable, his nose and mouth nothing amiss (nulla modo reprehensibilia) his eyes blue [sic] and uncommonly bright. In reproving and rebuking he is formidable; in teaching and exhorting of a bland and friendly tongue. He has a wonderful grace of person combined with seriousness. No one has ever seen him smile, but weeping indeed they have. He has a longish structure of body, his hands are straight and upturned, his arms are delectable; in speaking deliberate and slow; and sparing of his conversation – the most beautiful of countenance among the sons of men' (*Fabricii Cod. Apol.*, 1. p. 302).

Today we know that the predecessor of Pontius Pilate as Procurator of Judaea was *not* Publius Lentulus, but Valerius Gratus, an unpleasant and mercenary official who was only surpassed in cunning and ruthlessness by Pilate himself. As these two procurators covered the whole period of Jesus' manhood (and Pilate the whole period of his ministry), it is certain that neither of them could have been the author of this ornate account. Even before then there was no procurator of the name of Lentulus. The first procurator was Coponius, followed by Marcus Ambibulus and Annius Rufus.

I believe it is fiction which comes nearer to reality than the carefully thought-out speculation of believers. In one of his short stories, *The Procurator of Judaea*, Anatole France describes an encounter between Pontius Pilate and Laelius Lamia, an educated and widely travelled Roman. Now in retirement, they discuss that strange people, the Jews, they both had known so well. Towards the end of their conversation, Laelius mentions Jesus and his trial. 'Pontius Pilate contracted his brows, and his hand rose to his forehead in the attitude of one who probes the depths of his memory. Then, after a silence of some seconds – "Jesus?" he murmured "Jesus – of Nazareth? I cannot call him to mind."' (*Mother of Pearl*, p. 26).

The truth is that, apart from the circle of followers who were deeply impressed by their teacher, and a number of active opponents, nobody noticed the wandering preacher – neither his contemporaries nor the historians of the time. It was only when his memory had faded and merged into the image of the God Christ, the risen Saviour, that the world took notice of his name.

And his own received him not

As I shall show in a later chapter, Jesus was a pious Jew, a devout servant of his God, a conscientious observer of the Law. However, his followers' activities alienated Jewish opinion throughout the ages, and it was not before the 19th century that Jewish voices were raised in the defence of one of the greatest sons of Abraham.

At first, talmudic writers were quite prepared to accept Christian accounts of the doubtful paternity of Joseph. With glee they speculated about the circumstances of Jesus' illegitimate birth. The idea of direct intervention (a frequent pagan myth) as the cause of a woman's conception seemed both ridiculous and blasphemous to the Jewish mind, and it was taken for granted that the Christian story aimed at covering up an adulterous relationship from which Jesus was born. We learn from Origen that in his day the view was current among Jews that Mary had been divorced from her husband, a carpenter, after she was found guilty of adultery. Hiding in shame, she gave birth to Jesus whose father was a Roman soldier called Pantheras. The Jews used to refer to Jesus as Ben Pandera. Nietsch and Black suggest that the name possibly originated from a corruption of the word Παρθενος (virgin) (*Studien und Kritiken*, p. 116). Dr. Klausner concurs (op, cit., p. 24). When they heard that the Christians referred to Jesus as υἱὸς παρθένος (son of a virgin), the Jews may have called him mockingly 'Ben ha-Pandera'.

Direct Jewish sources mention Jesus from the second century

onward. The first baraita of this kind reads: 'On the eve of passover they hanged Yeshu and the herald went before him for forty days saying "[Yeshu of Nazareth] is going forth to be stoned in that he hath practised sorcery and beguiled and led astray Israel. Let anyone knowing aught in his defence come and plead for him." But they found nought in his defence and hanged him on the eve of Passover' (*Sanh.* 43a).

Another talmudic reference tells how someone wanted to 'raise up Jesus by spells and say to him "What is the most important thing in the world?". He answered and said "Seek their good and do not seek their harm; everyone that hurteth them is as if he hurt the apple of God's eye . . ."' (*Gitt.* 57a). The resurrected Jesus is presented as one who cares for his people and acknowledges them as the Chosen of God, although later he is referred to as a transgressor in Israel who 'scoffeth against the words of the Wise'.

There are also completely hostile references to Jesus in the Talmud. Generally, he is not mentioned by name but by the term 'Such-an-One'. A typical passage of this kind reads: 'Rabbi Shimeon ben Azzai said, I have found a genealogical roll in Jerusalem wherein was recorded "Such-an-One is a bastard of an adulteress", (*Yeb.* 4:3, 49a). However, Dr. Klausner observes, and I believe rightly, that 'there is no historical foundation for the tradition of Jesus' illegitimate birth and that the tradition arose from opposition to the Christian view that Jesus was born without a natural father . . . ' (*JN* p. 36).

It seems that the knowledge of the man Jesus is not advanced by the testimony of early Jewish sources – most of those records were mere reaction to Christian assertions: being told of the Christian belief in the Virgin Birth they countered with the allegation that Jesus was born in adultery; to some of the most profound sayings they responded with the accusation that he mocked at the words of the Wise. Yet there appeared to be no open hostility to him, as there was towards those sons of Israel who abandoned their religion to join the Christians.

The Toldoth Yeshu

The 5th century *Toldoth Yeshu* is the first Jewish document which displays open enmity towards both the Christians and the memory of their alleged teacher. From then onward there are a number of similar writings which show the same hostile rejection of the person of Jesus. The extant text of the *Toldoth Yeshu* is probably of later origin (Klausner estimates the 10th century) and its contents have no bearing at all on our knowledge of Jesus' life.

The Toldoth and similar associated texts tell the following tale: Yochanan, a learned man of the house of David was espoused to the Bethlehem virgin, Miriam. However, a certain Joseph ben Pandera deceived her one day into submitting to him. He pretended to be her husband and she, feebly resisting, was surprised at the impious act of Yochanan. The deception came to light when she mentioned her surprise to her husband who, although suspecting Pandera, could not prove anything against him. Miriam brought forth a child whom she named Yehoshua who grew up into an impudent and irreverent boy, a 'son of uncleanness'. The priests soon found out, owing to Yochanan's confidences and Miriam's own confession, that the child was a bastard.

When he grew up, Yeshu went to Jerusalem where he learnt the ineffable name of God and, in order not to forget it, wrote it down on a piece of leather which he sewed into the flesh of his thigh. Then he went and proclaimed himself the Messiah and the Son of God, gathering around him a few young disciples. He committed acts of sorcery and healing by the power of the name in his flesh.

The Queen of Israel summoned him and found him guilty of beguilement. However, Yeshu raised a dead man which so frightened the Queen that she began to believe in him. Once again free he continued his sorcery in Galilee where many people followed him. The sages of Israel then sent Yehuda Iskarioto to try to learn the ineffable name so that he could surpass the signs and wonders of Yeshu. When both appeared before the Queen, Yeshu flew up into the air, but Yehuda flew even higher and caused Yeshu to fall to earth. The Queen now condemned Yeshu and delivered him to the Sages of Israel who imprisoned him in Tiberias. He was freed by his followers and fled to Antioch.

After his escape Yeshu went to Egypt to 'collect spells', but Yehuda mingled among his disciples and eventually succeeded in robbing him of the 'name'. In his despair Yeshu travelled to Jerusalem trying to obtain the 'name' a second time. Yehuda now told the Sages that when Yeshu appears in the Temple, he would give them a sign so that they could arrest Yeshu before he gets hold of the 'name'. And so it happened. Yeshu was hanged on a cabbage stem – he had earlier bewitched all the trees, so that no tree would bear him. The body was taken from the tomb by the gardener Yehuda, and thrown into a canal. When the disciples found no body in the tomb, they declared that Yeshu had been resurrected. The angry Queen would have executed the Sages but the body was found and produced to the Queen as proof that there had been no resurrection.

The disciples of Yeshu fled and dispersed all over the world. Among them were twelve who caused much distress to the Jews. In order to prevent them from confusing the pious and the faithful, one of the Sages of Israel, Shimeon Kepha, sacrificed himself by joining the ranks of the disciples in order to give them their own religious laws and thereby free them from any connection with the Jewish community. After he achieved this end, he went and lived alone in a tower built in his honour, where he composed hymns and psalms, and sent them to all the synagogues of Israel.

This garbled story is quite useless as a source of information. It is obviously a re-hash from Christian accounts about Jesus 'Christ', suitably distorted to fit in with Jewish legends and prejudices. The only historical value it possesses, as Dr. Klausner points out, is that we gain insight into how the Jews of the Middle Ages thought about Jesus, in the same way as we may assess their views in the first five centuries from the testimony of the Talmud (op.cit., p.53).

The choicest treasures of Jewish literature

Many centuries have passed since the *Toldoth Yeshu* was compiled. Modern Jewish writers have an altogether different vision of the man Jesus: it is a revised, detached and reverent approach which regards him as 'a great teacher of morality and an artist in parable'.

It is realised now that he was a Jewish teacher who taught the faith of Israel from which he never deviated. He merely tried to continue the work of the prophets who castigated Israel for its indifference towards the great mission imposed upon it by the Almighty. In this approach C.G. Montefiore sees the possibility of 'a reconciliation or meeting point between the Reformed or Liberal Judaism and frankly unitarian Christianity of the distant future'. *That* Judaism and *that* Christianity may find that they differ in name, in accent and in memories rather than essentially and dogmatically. *That* Judaism and *that* Christianity may both claim Jesus as their own' (*The Synoptic Gospels*, Vol. 1).

'Jesus is,' asserts Klausner, 'for the Jewish nation a great teacher of morality and an artist in parable. He is *the* moralist for whom, in the religious life, morality counts as everything . . . as a consequence of this extremist standpoint his ethical code has become simply an ideal for the isolated few . . . an ideal for "the days of the Messiah when an end shall have been made of this "old world", this present social order. It is no ethical code for the nations and the social order of today, when man are still trying to find the way to . . . "the kingdom of the Almighty" spoken of by the *Talmud*, and ideal which is of "this world" and which, gradually and in the course of generations, is to take shape in this world.'

'But in his ethical code there is a sublimity, distinctiveness and originality in form, unparalleled in any other Hebrew ethical code. Neither is there any parallel to the remarkable art of his parables. The shrewdness and sharpness of his proverbs and his forceful epigrams serve, to an exceptional degree, to make ethical ideas a popular possession. If ever the day should come and this ethical code be stripped of its wrappings or miracles and mysticism, the Book of Ethics of Jesus will be one of the choicest treasures in the literature of Israel for all time' (op.cit.,p.414).

No less outspoken is E.R. Trattner who, in his *As a Jew Sees Jesus* calls the Teacher, 'the most influential Jew the world has ever seen'. He is surprised that, paradoxically, Jewish history has kept 'provokingly silent' on this subject. Among many passages of praise and admiration he says that 'Jesus was in all probability among the greatest of those dynamic apocalyptic preachers who addressed the Palestinian multitudes of the first century . . . Not that Jesus said anything entirely new. With a clearness and simplicity unmatched perhaps by any Jewish teacher, he brought out several aspects of the deeper spiritual significance of the religion of his fathers. More than that: he gave those thoughts a power that they never had before' (quoted from Osborne *Whom Do Men Say That I Am?* p.128).

Some of the most beautiful words ever spoken about Jesus are to be found in the work of another Jewish author, Dr. Paul Winter. In a remarkable book he discusses the question of responsibility for Jesus' trial and execution, and concludes with this epitaph:

'It is not over . . .

Not Pilate's sentence, not the jostling of the soldiers who divided his garments, not even the cry from the cross was the last word.

The accusers of the old are dead. The witnesses have gone home. The judge has left the court. The trial of Jesus goes on. His is a trial that is never finished, and one in which the roles of judge and accused are strangely reversed.

Tribunals assemble. Tribunals disband. The bailiffs, the informers, the accusers, the witnesses, the procurators, the executioners, are still with us.

Many have come in his name, and have joined the accusers; and there arose new false witnesses among them – yet even so, their testimony agrees not. Never spoken when Jesus was tried, the words, "His blood upon us and our children!" have come true – a thousand times. But no valid answer had yet been given to the question, "What will you that I do with the King of the Jews?", only the cry, "Crucify him! Crucify him!" echoes throughout the centuries.

Rabbi Eliezer the Great said of Jesus: "He owns a share in the Age that is Coming . . ."

It was not finished. Sentence was passed, and he was led away. Crucified, dead and buried, he yet rose in the hearts of his disciples who loved him and felt he was near.

Tried by the world, condemned by authority, buried by the Churches that profess his name, he is rising again, today and tomorrow, in the hearts of men who love him and feel: he is near' (*On the Trial of Jesus*, p. 149).

To show how one ought to live

Not only Jewish authors but many great writers and philosophers felt it necessary to express their view on the astounding paradox of a man of outstanding compassion and ethical strength being identified with some of the most ruthless and unprincipled organisations in the world.

The most remarkable attack on Christianity, which often sounds as a defence of Jesus, was launched by Friedrich Nietzsche who unveiled the dangerous trends, inherent in the cherished views and values of the 19th century. He attacked the political institutions of his time with unswerving hostility. It was in Christianity, however, that he found his most challenging target, indeed, that he became a 'philosopher with the hammer'.

Many efforts have been made to reconcile this thinker with organised Christianity. The most impressive of these attempts was that of Karl Jaspers who, in his *Nietzsche and Christianity*, tries to show that it was the philosopher's basically Christian orientation that led to his rebellion against Christianity. Nietzsche opposed a Christian faith largely uncommitted to, and uninvolved in, Jesus' teaching, a Christian religion that paid lip service to his memory. Jaspers argues that the seeming contradictions in Nietzsche's statements concerning Christianity, Christ and the priests, are not contradictions at all, but merely two sides of the same coin. Even the exclamation 'God is dead!' becomes a heart-rending cry in the ears of Jasper, which in fact it would be if it were divorced from that which follows those words, and gives a clue to Nietzsche's philosophy.

There is, of course, a *contradiction* in Nietzsche's approach to Christianity and to the figure of Jesus. However, this contradiction is a conscious one which takes into account the sensitive intelligence that suffers and the intellect which wishes to avoid being hurt. Man cannot be raised through vicarious suffering, only by rising above pity. The weak should be made aware of their potential strength, the shadow of its substance, the mirrored likeness of live flesh and blood. This is Nietzsche's approach to God whose death he welcomes so 'that the Superman may live!' It is also his approach to Jesus who is eternally sacrificed on the altar of human weakness, eternally alienated from his own nature, a Saviour outside his own light and his own life. From Nietzsche's *Antichrist* emerges a Jesus, divested of inhuman attributes and primitive trappings, a real person ready to live that form of existence of which he is the unique expression. It cannot be ignored that Nietzsche hates Christianity as much as he loves that Don Quixote of ideas, Jesus, who is called the Christ.

Nietzsche claims that the question 'Who was Jesus?' cannot be answered. The Jesus of the Christians is a figure full of contradictions and improbabilities. There remains, however, the possible vision of a man who brings *good tidings* because death has no hold on him; because there is no more reason to fight against anything, not even evil; because action can turn away from an unresponsive world to a fulfilling inner expression. These *good tidings* are dissimilar to anything preceding them, they open the kingdom of God, not in the distant future, but now and within us.

Nietzsche's vision of Jesus is at the core of *Antichrist*. It is not the followers of Jesus who arouse his enmity: it is the sight of Jesus' enemies masquerading as his disciples. The picture Nietzsche draws of the Jewish teacher is moving, and has a ring of truth about it. His Jesus is unsophisticated: 'Denying precisely that which is quite impossible to him . . . Dialectics is quite absent as is the idea that any faith, and *truth* can be proved by argument. . . . (his proofs are *inner lights*) . . . Neither can such a doctrine . . . realise the fact that there are, or can be, other doctrines, it is . . . incapable of imagining a contrary judgement . . . Wherever it encounters such things . . . it bemoans such blindness, for it sees the light – but raises no objections' (*Twilight of the Idols*, pp 170/1).

Nietzsche's interpretation of Jesus is not confined to praise: 'The founder of Christianity [Nietzsche thought of Jesus as that – AR] believed that there was nothing from which men suffered so much as from their sins: it was his error, the error of a person who felt himself without sin, to whom experience was lacking in this respect! It was thus that his soul was filled with that fantastic pity which referred to a trouble that even among his own people, the inventors of sin, was rarely a great trouble. But Christianity understood subsequently how to do justice to the Master, and to sanctify his error into a *truth* ' (*The Joyful Wisdom*, para. 138).

Of all the remarkable words Nietzsche spoke about the 'pale Hebrew' whom he revered, I shall quote in conclusion only those which head this sub-chapter: 'This messenger of *good tidings* died as he lived and as he taught – *not* in order to *save mankind*, but in order to show how one ought to live' (*Twilight of the Idols*, p. 174). No higher praise is conceivable from the pen of Nietzsche.

A picture of the Messiah

Among the skeptical critics of Christianity there is perhaps none more important than Bruno Bauer, a German scholar who in the course of his life developed and deepened the theory that Christianity was a literary invention, a product of the disintegrating Roman Empire, born out of a merger of Stoic philosophy and Jewish dogmatism. According to Bauer, Jesus the teacher was a figure of fiction presented by Mark and later by Matthew and Luke, while Jesus the Logos was the brainchild of John who developed his ideas under the influence of the Alexandrian Philo. Paul's Epistles were, claims Bauer, later and not earlier products than the Gospels, and the above-quoted passages of Josephus, Tacitus and Suetonius were crude interpolations perpetrated by Christian forgers. The historicity of Jesus is questioned, although Bauer concedes the possibility that fictitious stories were woven around the memory of a great personality who lived some time before the authors.

This idea prompted Bauer to write: 'We save the honour of Jesus when we restore his person to life from the state of inanition to which the apologists have reduced him, and give him once more a living relation to history, which he certainly possessed – that can no longer be denied. If a conception was to become dominant, which should unite heaven and earth, God and man, nothing more and nothing less was necessary than that a man should appear, the very essence of whose consciousness should be the reconciliation of these antitheses . . . Jesus accomplished this mighty work, but not prematurely pointing to his own person . . . and through the rise of belief in him a clear conception, a definite mental picture of the Messiah became possible . . . ' (Quoted from Schweitzer, *The Quest of the Historical Jesus*, p. 143).

Bauer believed that the expectation of the coming Messiah was not at all as widespread among the Jews in the time of Jesus as the Christian apologists would have us believe. The chronologically last work of the Old Testament, the Wisdom Writings, contains hardly any reference to the Messiah, and even the Septuagint did not try to introduce a Messianic image into its translation. Philo and other contemporary Jewish thinkers ignore the idea and it seems that it became current and crystallised into a definite image only when the early Christians endowed the figure of the Teacher with the attributes of the Messiah. Bauer differs greatly from most well-known critics who preceded him in that he does not take it for granted that 'before the appearance of Jesus the expectation of the Messiah prevailed among the Jews'; and in that he does not regard the history of Jesus as certain.

Bauer has many scathing references to the miracles which he calls 'the maltreatment, mockery and insulting' of Nature. For this reason he considers the Christ of the Gospels a figure which would engender aversion in human hearts if they were not conditioned to revere him.

However, the stories of the miracles were superimposed upon the accounts, and Bauer tries to prove this assertion by showing that the first of the gospels, Mark, recounts the raising from the dead of one person who had just succumbed to an illness; Luke of somewhat later date speaks about the raising of a young woman whose body is being carried to the grave; while John, the last of these writings, tells of the raising of Lazarus who had been in the tomb and subject to corruption for several days.

In brilliantly argued commentaries Bauer presents the many difficulties which confront those who try to reconcile the gospel stories with reason. A staggering miracle occurs during the baptism which should be irrevocable proof for all those present that Jesus was 'he who should come', yet we read of John the Baptist sending emissaries to Jesus asking him 'Art thou he that should come, or do we look for another?' (*Matthew* 11:3).

When Jesus asks the momentous question, 'Whom do men say that I am?' (*Mark* 8:27), not one of the disciples answers that some people thought he was the Messiah. The idea appears only when Peter voices it as his own personal realisation. Even then Jesus forbids his disciples to reveal the thought to the people. Bauer regards that as a further proof that the claim would not have made much sense to the Jewish masses, and it was known to the author of the gospel that the Messianic idea affected mainly the Christian believer. The *Gospel according to John* destroys altogether the nostalgic beauty of *Mark* 8 – in the former the disciples know from the beginning that Jesus *is* the Messiah.

Bauer equally doubts the value of the Mission of the Twelve (*Matthew* 10:5, *Luke* 9:2 and *Mark* 6:7), since it is not preceded in any of the gospels by a coherent doctrine which they could have 'preached'. We may except here the Beatitudes in Matthew, but as we shall see in another chapter, they are mainly reiterations of well-known Jewish blessings which contain very little original teaching. Jesus points out that he speaks in parables which they, the disciples, might comprehend, but the people will not understand. Yet we see that even the disciples are baffled by the parables which Jesus has to explain to them. Meaningless, too, are some of the prohibitions following various instances of healing: of what use can secrecy be when a large multitude has seen the performance of the miracle? Finally, Bauer emphasizes that the Jews never expected the Messiah to perform miracles in any case, and it is not surprising that they did not 'recognise' the Messiah in this itinerant wonder-worker. 'Jesus must perform the innumerable, these astounding miracles,' writes Bauer, 'because according to the view which the gospels represent, he is the Messiah – and yet no one recognises him as the Messiah!' (ibid., p.149). According to the author, a study of Mark shows that the evangelist was aware of the lack of connection between the Messianic claim and the performance of miracles.

There are many other things in the gospels which would be, historically, inexplicable: the 'betrayal' by Judas, the contradictory accounts of the resurrection, the reference to Jesus' body and blood during the last supper, and so on.

Bauer thinks that the Gospel according to Mark is the most original of the literary attempts to present the figure of the Teacher-Messiah, and he bases most of his observations on his study of Mark who 'loosed us from the theological lie'. He acclaims: 'We should be grateful to the kindly fate which has preserved for us this writing of Mark by which we have been delivered from the web of deceit of this hellish pseudo-science [i.e. theology-AR]' (ibid. p.163).

Till the kingdom come

Other voices were raised which doubted the historicity and good faith of the gospel records. A contemporary of Bauer, David Friedrich Strauss, theologian and radical critic of Christology, caused a furore in Germany with his famous *Life of Jesus*, in 1835. He considers the gospel story as fiction, built around the historical figure, and based largely on the contrived fulfilment of Old Testament prophecy. *The Old Faith and the New*, his second and most important work, contains the following passage; 'Looking at it historically . . . the resurrection of Jesus did not have the slightest foundation. Rarely has an incredible fact been worse attested, or one so ill-attested been more incredible in itself . . . comparing the immense effect of this belief with its absolute baselessness, the story of the resurrection can only be called a worldwide deception. It may be humiliating to human pride, but the fact remains: Jesus might still have taught and embodied in his life all that is good and true, as well as what is onesided and harsh – the latter after all producing the strongest impression on the masses; nevertheless his teaching would have been blown away and scattered like solitary leaves by the wind, had these leaves not been held together and thus preserved, as if with a stout tangible binding, by an illusory belief in his resurrection.' In the same work he quotes a brilliant saying of Diderot who remarked about the wish of the Father to reconcile the world to himself through the sacrificial death of his son: 'Il n'y a point bon père qui voulût ressembler à notre père céleste.'

A similar line of thought can be found in the work of a remarkable Frenchman, a Catholic priest excommunicated by the Church in 1908, Alfred Loisy. He believes that whatever Jesus may have taught and whatever he may have been, his story had been doctored to fit in with the ideas of the Pauline Christian Churches whose scribes re-wrote the accounts of Jesus' life to justify their ritual: they invented the words spoken at the Last Supper, the stories of the burial and the empty tomb, in order to tally with the idea of the Eucharist and the doctrine of the crucified and risen Saviour. Jesus was probably 'a wandering preacher . . . not teaching in the manner of contemporary rabbis but rather as prophet . . . a wonder-working exorcist', except for the Fourth Gospel where 'while the wonders increase in magnitude, the exorcism disappears, as does the story of the temptation'. Jesus avoids large towns, since he finds the atmosphere of villages and small townships more favourable. Loisy is even doubtful whether Jesus visited Jerusalem before the end. His work was concentrated on Capernaum and the surrounding country. Whenever he embarked on longer journeys it was, according to Loisy, in order to escape the hostility of the authorities. The accounts of large crowds and multitudes following him to listen to his words, are 'pious exaggeration'. Jesus' mission covered mainly the area of Galilee and embraced a limited number of religious ideas. 'The Sermon on the Mount', a collection of didactic fragments and sentences originally distinct, was never preached. Jesus' main concern was 'the imminent prospect of the kingdom of God, near the coming of which, with the Messiah in glory, was continuously announced by the first apostles after the death of Jesus'. Loisy is critical of attempts at presenting Jesus as a meek humanitarian or a poetic rebel. 'The dominating thought of Jesus is the concrete, real and realistic conception of the kingdom of God, involving the complete renovation of the human order both inward and outward . . . In sober truth, neither the revelation of divine goodness, not the value of the soul, nor the law of love, nor the dignity of the poor has the eminent place in the primitive Gospel which many in our time would assign to it . . . For the historian, the sum and substance of the Gospel can always be found . . . in the eschatological idea of the kingdom of God, all the rest being subordinate to that.' Jesus may never have seen himself as a king of the Elect, or even as a man playing a leading role in the coming Kingdom. It was as an envoy of God, not as a simple prophet, nor as a sage or moralist, that Jesus presented himself to his contemporaries. He claimed a special and unique mission in regard to the Great Event, but did not define it with precision. Loisy thinks Jesus did not present himself as the Messiah, 'since the Messiah was the Prince of the Great Kingdom and there could be no Messiah till the Kingdom came'. However, shortly before his death he may have thought that the Kingdom was about to materialize, and that he would be called upon to assume the part of the Messiah. This course hastened the end, the description of which is merely christological, and concerned with the association of the Old Testament prophesies with the event surrounding Jesus' death. (A. Loisy, *The Birth of the Christian Religion*, pp. 71/79).

There are authors who consider the story of the gospels and the figure of Jesus as purely fictional. George Brandes, in his *Jesus A Myth*, advances the theory that Jesus never lived, and that the legends concerning him are merely endowing a composite figure with mythical qualities. Another interesting speculation was introduced by a Polish writer, Andrzej Niemojewski, who claimed that Jesus did not exist but was a Syrian sun-god (Joshua), and that the whole religion associated with his name is an astrological cult with sun, moon and zodiac (the twelve apostles) playing important roles. This opinion was shared by some other writers, from the old gnostics to two strange 18th century Frenchmen, Count Constantin de Volney and Charles François Dupuis, who all claimed that Jesus was a solar myth and Christianity a religion of solar mysticism. Niemojewski, however, pushes the theory much further in his lengthy and much-documented study *Gott Jesus*. He attempts to prove that the gospels are not works of chroniclers but of Christian symbolists, highly artistic structures of religious astrology, poetic and philosophical. The geographical proper names used in the New Testament assume astrological significance. Judaea, Galilee and Egypt do not refer to actual locations, but to astrological constellations. The same applies to personal proper names.

Matthew contains a system based on the Ram, Luke on the Twins. The former is fundamentally a sun-myth, the latter a moon-myth.

(Christ is the sun in Matthew, the moon in Luke.) Niemojewski sees in Mark an astral system based on Taurus, and even John is full of astral references. The various events in the New Testament – the Birth, the Disputation in the Temple, the Betrayal by Judas, the episode in Gethsemane, the Denial by Peter, the Passion, Burial and Resurrection – all these must be understood as cosmic events, symbolically disguised. The Virgin and Beth-Lehem are identical astrological symbols. (Bread = Lehem, is a form in which Jesus is represented, especially in Luke.) John the Baptist was not a man but a psychic concept and an astral fish-divinity, the god of the increasing sun. His beheading is symbolic of the shortening days after the summer solstice. The often mentioned fishermen are not real people but followers of the fish-god. Bread and fish have special significance throughout the New Testament. The lamb with the cross is an age-old symbol in astrology. Jesus himself is a psychic figure, not a man. His components are the stone, the vine, the bread, the lamb, the moon, the sun, man. Niemojewski closes his analysis with the words: 'Here, as so often in the history of the world, those events which were the most moving and beautiful, were merely a dream of the impassioned human heart' (III p.488).

George Santayana, the American philosopher, was equally opposed to 19th century historicism. He regards religious ideas as mythical and poetic expressions of a perennial moral truth. In his *Life of Reason* he says about Jesus: 'The figure of Christ was the centre for all eyes. Its lowliness, its simplicity, its humanity were indeed, for a while, obstacles to its acceptance; they did not really lend themselves to the metaphysical interpretation which was required. Yet even Greek fable was not without its Apollo tending flocks and its Demeter mourning for her lost child and serving in disguise the child of another. Feeling was right for a mythology loaded with pathos. The humble life, the homilies, the sufferings of Jesus could be felt in all their incomparable beauty all the more when the tenderness and tragedy of them, otherwise too poignant, were relieved by the story of his miraculous birth, his glorious resurrection and his restored divinity' (quoted from Osborne, *Whom do Men Say that I Am?*, pp.262-2). It was the poetic content of the religion which won the day, and the story of the resurrection not in spite of, but because of its poetic fantasy and lack of realism, became the focal point of Christianity. 'What overcame the world, because it was what the world desired, not moral reform for that was preached by every sect; nor an ascetic regimen for that was practised by heathen gymno-sophists and pagan philosophers; not brotherly love within the Church, for the Jews had and have that in at least equal measure; but what overcame the world was what St. Paul said he would always preach: "Christ and him crucified"' (ibid.p.262).

Santayana's sceptical view of the spread of Christianity still leaves the figure of Jesus unscathed. Another scholar who denies the historical foundation of the gospel stories, was Bertrand Russell, who unlike Santayana was prepared to be highly critical of Jesus himself. 'I do not think,' he writes, 'that Christ was the best and wisest of men, although I grant him a very high degree of moral goodness . . . Having acknowledged the excellence of these maxims . . . I come to certain points in which I do not believe that one can grant either the superlative wisdom or the superlative goodness of Christ as depicted in the gospels, and here I may say that one is not concerned with the historical question. Historically it is quite doubtful whether Christ existed at all . . . and if he did we do no know anything about him . . . I am concerned with Christ as he appears in the gospels, taking the gospel narrative as it stands, and there one does find things that do not seem very wise [Examples of the lack and denigration of foresight follow – AR]. In that respect clearly he was not so wise . . . I cannot myself feel that either in the matter of wisdom or in the matter of virtue Christ stands quite as high as some people known to history. I think I should place Buddha or Socrates above him in those respects' (*Why I am Not a Christian*, pp.7/10).

To the same group belongs J.M. Robertson, the well-known rationalist. His ideas, as expounded in his books, *Christianity and Mythology* and *Pagan Christs*, were influenced by Bauer and Frazer. Without following in Volney's footsteps, he identifies Jesus with figures of folklore and mythical fantasy. His denial of the historical Jesus is not unconditional, but he maintains that history and legend have become so hopelessly intertwined that there is no chance of disentangling them. This is the fate of all great religious teachers: 'The only conclusion open is that the teaching of Jesus of the gospels is wholly a construction of the propagandists of the cult, even as is the wonder-working God' (*Pagan Christs*, p.237).

The most outstanding among the authors denying the existence and historicity of Jesus is Professor G.A. Wells who, in two remarkable books, *The Jesus of the Early Christians* and *Did Jesus Exist?* shows the precipitate retreat of so-called Christology from trying to establish the historicity of Jesus. Modern theologians readily give up dogmatic points concerning Jesus' birth, life, death and resurrection; 'demythologising' him without having the courage to admit that the Churches will not survive if their myths and mystical elements are so hastily abandoned.

Not the wicked, nor the stupid, but the non-men

Another group of writers considers Jesus not as a myth, but as a teacher of remarkable ethical principles, a prophet proclaiming the divine greatness of man. The earliest of these was Franz Volkmar Reinhard who taught that the man Jesus tried to establish the law of love as the supreme synthesis between religion and the moral code: 'Moral instruction was the principal content and the very essence of all his discourses', and Jesus' efforts 'were directed at the establishment of a purely ethical organisation'.

John Stuart Mill, the utilitarian philosopher, wrote in his *Three Essays on Religion*: 'Above all, the most valuable part of the effect on the character which Christianity has produced by holding up in a divine person a standard of excellence and a model for imitation, is available even to the absolute unbeliever and can never more be lost for humanity. For it is Christ, rather than God, whom Christianity has held up to believers as a pattern of perfection for humanity. It is the God incarnate, rather than the God of the Jews or of Nature, who being idealised has taken so great and salutary hold on the modern mind.' There is much truth in this, even if I do not agree with Mill when he ascribes this to an intended benefaction of 'Christianity'.

Ralph Waldo Emerson, the American writer, puts his view very succinctly: 'The belief in Christianity that now prevails is the unbelief of man. They will have Christ for a Lord and not for a Brother. Christ preaches the greatness of man, but we hear only of the greatness of Christ . . . There is nothing in history to parallel the influence of Jesus Christ. The Chinese say of Wan Wang, one of their kings, "From the West, from the East, from the South and from the North, there was not one thought not brought in subjection by him". This can be more truly said of Jesus than any mortal' (quoted from Osborne op.cit., pp. 306).

Ernest Renan was the first who succeeded in writing a 'bestseller' on the life of Jesus. It was published in 1863, and within a few years conquered the world. Since then we have come to see its many faults, the sentimental approach to the figure of the Teacher, and the somewhat precious presentation of the story. Nevertheless, it was pioneer work in an age which still resented modern bible criticism. He speaks of the man Jesus in superlatives: 'In order to make himself adored to this degree, he must have been adorable. Love is not enkindled except by an object worthy of it, and we should know nothing of Jesus if it were not for the passion he inspired in those about him, which compels us still to affirm that he was great and pure . . .

Let us place then, the person of Jesus at the highest summit of human greatness . . . the evangelists themselves, who have bequeathed us the image of Jesus, are so much beneath him of whom they speak that they constantly disfigure him in their inability to attain to his height. Their writings are full of errors and misrepresentations . . . On the whole the character of Jesus, far from having been embellished by his biographers, has been lowered by them . . . This sublime person who each day still presides over the destiny of the world, we may call him divine, not in the sense that Jesus has absorbed all the divine, or has been adequate to it . . . but in the sense that Jesus is the one who has caused his fellow men to make the greatest step towards the divine . . . all the ages will proclaim that among the sons of men there is none born who is greater than Jesus' (*The Life of Jesus*, pp.221/7).

In a similar vein to Renan, the Russian novelist D.S. Mereshkovski gives a poetic eulogy of the divine man. It is difficult to extricate his vision of the man Jesus from the religious tapestry surrounding it. His Jesus is the Teacher presented by the Gospels, the Man who is in God and has God in him, the Man who gives his life as ransom for many, the Man who is glorified and seated at the right hand of God. His suffering is exalted and vicariously relived: 'The more we think of the life of the man Jesus, the more we live it through in thought, the more we get to know that there must have been a minute when he realised – slowly it must have dawned upon him – when suddenly he saw "that he was in the world, and the world was made by him, and the world knew him not", that "he came into his own and his own received him not", and this moment must have pierced his soul as later the nails of the Cross were to pierce his body' (*Jesus Manifest*, pp.152/3).

A mighty spiritual force

Perhaps the most widely known of all bible scholars and critics was Albert Schweitzer whose *Quest of the Historical Jesus* is a landmark of Christological research. His approach is completely eschatological, and while he disagrees with Reimarus, Bauer and Wrede, their ideas have impressed him greatly. Although holding firmly to man's individual vision of Christ, Schweitzer has the courage to say: 'The Jesus of Nazareth who came forward publicly as the Messiah, who preached the ethic of the kingdom of God, who founded the kingdom of Heaven upon Earth, and died to give his work its final consecration, never had any existence. He is a figure designed by rationalism, endowed with life by liberalism, and clothed by modern theology in a historical garb' (p. 396).

That kind of theology which upholds an image of Jesus which is half-historical, half-modern, will have to take into account two centuries of research into the New Testament and its sources, as well as two avenues of approach: (1) that of the skeptics who attack all claims to historicity, and (2) that of the critics like Schweitzer himself who believes Christianity to be an eschatological Messianic conception. This latter group showed the impossibility, and obviated the necessity, of presenting an historical Jesus. A new concept of any 'historical Jesus' will be seen as the realisation of an idea which has taken roots in human history. 'Jesus means something to our world because a mighty spiritual force streams forth from him and flows through our time also. This fact can neither be shaken nor confirmed by any historical discovery' (p. 397). Unfortunately, Schweitzer calls this 'mighty spiritual force' the foundations of Christianity, leaving the question wide open as to whether or not Christianity merely served as a conductor for the ideas associated with Jesus. It cannot be said to have been founded upon them.

However, Schweitzer must have been aware of the problem, otherwise his clear implications could not be explained. Speaking of the theologians of the past, among whom he numbers himself, he says; 'There was a danger of our thrusting ourselves between men and the gospels, and refusing to leave the individual man alone with the sayings of Jesus' (p. 398).

Schweitzer claims that all the research into the actual life and circumstances of Jesus cannot help us to comprehend the enormous spiritual power hidden in his teaching. Basing his view on the words of Paul, 'though we have known Christ after the flesh yet henceforth know we him no more' (*2 Cor.* 5:16) Schweitzer admits that 'we must be prepared to find that the historical knowledge of the personality and life of Jesus will not be a help, but perhaps an offense to religion' (p. 399).

His opinion that Jesus is completely rooted in eschatology convinces him that it is impossible to see Christ historically in a temporal fashion. 'The truth is,' he says, 'it is not Jesus as historically known, but Jesus as spiritually risen within man, who is significant for our time . . . Not the historical Jesus but the spirit which goes forth from Him . . . is that which overcomes the world' (ibid.). Schweitzer calls this spiritual phenomenon 'the historical Jesus' which enables him to state: 'It is a good thing that the true historical Jesus should overthrow the modern Jesus . . . He was not a teacher, not a casuist; He was an imperious ruler . . . The names in which men expressed their recognition of Him as such, Messiah, Son of man, Son of God, have become for us historical parables. We can find no designation which expresses what He is for us' (p.401).

Schweitzer's contemporary, the German Johannes Weiss, one of the most outstanding students of New Testament history, also holds that the eschatological aspect of Jesus' teaching was of supreme importance. According to Weiss, Jesus believed that the kingdom was so near that the Mission of the Twelve became urgent, the Coming was a certainty although the day and the hour were not known. It could have come about without delay had it not been for the hardness and guilt of the people. There were obstacles to be removed before the Coming would occur. Weiss depicts Jesus as a great preacher, modest and restrained, willing to make the supreme sacrifice for what he holds to be true. In Jesus' actions any political aspiration was manifestly absent. 'To hope for the kingdom of God,' says Weiss in his *Die Predigt vom Reiche Gottes*, 'in the transcendental sense which Jesus attaches to it, and to raise a revolution, are two things as different as fire and water.' While it cannot be shown that Jesus thought of himself when he used the expression 'Son of man', he gave these words eschatological and Messianic significance. He may have regarded himself merely as the herald of the 'Son of man', or as the person destined for that role. 'The Messianic Self-consciousness of Jesus, as expressed in the title "Son of man" shares in the transcendental character of Jesus' idea of the kingdom of God and cannot be separated from the idea' (quoted from Schweitzer's op.cit. p.239).

William Bousset, another German professor of theology, opposed the ideas of Johannes Weiss. According to him, valuable ground has been covered by criticism, the sources had been carefully reviewed, the distinction between the synoptic gospels and the Fourth Gospel has been universally recognised, and the theory has gained wide acceptance that the gospel sources are: Mark, primitive versions of the text, and a collection of the words of Jesus. Bousset insists that apart from these sources a number of external influences, notably Persian, have played an important part. A vital personality enters the world of hidebound tradition, and a new concept of the Fatherhood of God and His kingdom is introduced into religious thought. Jesus overcame the stagnant piety of his environment and, conscious of his vital strength and the dynamic power of his message, became convinced that he was the Messiah. His eschatology was not in space and time, but in the spiritual aspirations of the human soul.

Argumentative cunning and penetration

Against these visions of Jesus which endow him with great spiritual strength but deny that any political inspiration is discernible in his work, or even suggest that we deal with an unhistorical entity, many 20th century thinkers have reacted violently. With equally well-reasoned arguments they present a view of Jesus which regards the core of his teaching as a revolutionary and political doctrine. The most outstanding exponent of this approach is Bernard Shaw. He claims that the importance of Jesus lay in his political, economic and moral ideas, and dismisses the rest of the doctrine as psychopathy and superstition. 'There is a man here,' he exclaims, 'who was sane until Peter hailed him as Christ, and who then became a monomaniac . . . his is a very common delusion among the insane and . . . such insanity is quite consistent with the retention of argumentative cunning and penetration which Jesus displayed in Jerusalem after his delusion has taken complete hold of him . . . He was a Communist . . . he regarded much of what we call law and order as machinery for robbing the poor under legal forms . . . he thought domestic ties a snare for the soul . . . he agreed with the proverb "The nearer the Church the farther from God" . . . he saw very plainly that the masters of the community should be its servants and not its oppressors and parasites and . . . though he did not tell us not to fight our enemies, he did tell us to love them, and warned us that they who draw the sword shall perish by the sword' (*Androcles and the Lion*, p.31). Shaw summarises the teaching of Jesus in modern terminology, and very skilfully if the use of such terminology is legitimate: '(1) The kingdom of Heaven is within you. You are the son of God, and God is the son of man. God is spirit, to be worshipped in spirit and truth, and not an elderly gentleman to be bribed and begged from. We are members of one another; so that you cannot injure or help your neighbour without injuring or helping yourself. God is your father, you are here to do God's work, and you and your father are one. (2) Get rid of property by throwing it into the common stock. Dissociate your work entirely from money payments. Get rid of all anxiety about tomorrow's dinner and clothes because you cannot serve God and Mammon. If you let your child starve, you are letting God starve. (3) Get rid of judges and punishment and vengeance. Love your neighbour as yourself. Every mother you meet is as much your mother as the woman who bore you. Every man you meet is as much your brother as the man she bore after you. Don't waste your time at family funerals grieving for your relatives: attend to life not to death: there are as good fish in the sea as ever came out of it, and better. In the kingdom of Heaven which . . . is within you, there is no marriage nor giving in marriage, because you cannot devote your life to two divinities: God and the person you are married to' (ibid.,p.50/1). Apart from the customary flippancy of Shaw's style, there is certainly much of Jesus' teaching in these words.

The vital impetus

Yet another group of thinkers believe that the significance of Jesus lies in the 'vital impetus' his actions and teachings have given to a powerful spiritual event, the birth of Christianity. In this view they come near to Schweitzer who taught that the historical aspect of Jesus is his spirit at work in the Christian Church. The American philosopher Josiah Royce thought that since so little can be known about the person of Christ, it is more important to form a clear view of the Christian community: 'In answer to the challenge, "*either* you must believe that the founder of Christianity was only a man, *or else* you must accept Jesus as the Christ, the divine man"; we must fairly reply . . . by our assertion which is as capable of a reasonable historical confirmation as it is often, at the present moment, neglected. Whatever may be the truth about the person of Christ, and about the supposed supernatural origin of Christianity, the human source of the Christian doctrine of life, and also the human source of all the later Christologies, must be found in the early Christian community itself. The Christian religion in its early form is the work and expression of the Christian Church . . . Meanwhile, since the human founder Jesus gave the stimulus, the signal . . . the vital impetus, without which the Christian community . . . would never have come into existence, we can indeed . . . say that the man Jesus was, in this sense, the founder of Christianity. But we cannot say that, speaking of Jesus as an individual man, we know that he explicitly intended to found the Christian Church' (quoted from Osborne, op.cit., pp.257/8).

Another Christian, Wilhelm Wrede, attributed the decisive influence to the early Christian Church itself. He follows in the footsteps of Bauer, but he does not agree that the Messiahship of Jesus was an invention of the author(s) of the Gospel according to Mark. Wrede thinks that the narrative itself originated from the desire to present the life of Jesus as possessing Messianic portent. Whilst the life of the Teacher did not encourage such speculations, it is nevertheless obvious how, as the gospel story developed, the figure of Jesus became more and more Messianic, until in the fourth and last Gospel the claim is openly made. According to Wrede this was not just an arbitrary act on the part of the evangelist, but it mirrors the significance of the Messianic idea in the early Church. Wrede, alongside with many other critics, says that towards the end Jesus himself avowed faith in his Messianic calling, and repeats Bauer's interesting observation that in the incident at Caesarea Philippi (*Mark* 8:29) 'Jesus does not, as is generally supposed, reveal his Messiahship to Peter, it is Peter who reveals it to Jesus' (quoted from Schweitzer's op.cit., p.339). Wrede also assumes that the evangelists, in recounting the miracles, were influenced by the Messianic expectations surrounding Jesus and his circle: 'The miracles were certainly used by the early Christians as evidence of the nature and significance of Christ . . . I need hardly point to the fact that Mark, not less than Matthew, Luke and John, must have held the opinion that the miracles of Jesus encountered widespread and ardent Messianic expectation' (ibid., p.345).

In our own age, the conviction became widespread that the Christian faith is the repository of the teaching of Jesus, and that it is in practised Christianity we must try to restore the spirit of the teaching to its application to life. An important exponent of this view was Count Hermann Keyserling, founder of the Darmstadt 'School of Wisdom'. He claimed that Jesus was a *practical radical* who is most effectively, though not adequately, represented by the Roman Catholic Church. He thought Jesus went to his death to further his ideas, and surrendered voluntarily to his enemies when he felt that his hour had come. The truth of Jesus' mission is in the fact that he was prepared to bear not only his own guilt but the guilt of all men. At other times, Keyserling was more critical of the Church bearing the name of Christ, as for instance when he said in his *Creative Understanding*: 'Hitherto Christ has had a beneficial influence for the most part in spite of the religion and the Church bearing his name; the great Christ-period can dawn only when the impulse he embodies has been fully understood.' By 'understanding' Keyserling meant, however, a different process from literal comprehension. 'Christ's wisdom seems self-evident to millions who would never be able to understand a modern essayist. And it is self-evident just because it expresses the very deepest, the spiritual core of our being.'

This statement pre-supposes that the millions acknowledging Jesus show a 'real' understanding of him who touched the 'spiritual core' of their being. If that were so how could we explain that the very same millions comprise the 'religion and the Church bearing his name'?

A *dissenting voice*

In his famous book, *The Martyrdom of Man*, Winwood Reade has much to say about the man Jesus. He thinks that Jesus was a complex personality, in whom extreme love was combined with extreme hate. It is in Jesus' strange character that Reade finds the justification and rationalisation of the subsequent intolerance and cruelty displayed by Christians throughout history. 'Believing that it was in his power to condemn his fellow creatures to eternal torture, he did so condemn all the rich and almost all the learned men among the Jews . . . all those who did anything to merit the esteem of their fellowmen. Even those who were happy and enjoyed life – unless it was in his own company – were lost souls . . . He also pronounces eternal punishment on those who refuse to join him' (pp. 223/4). Reade points out that miracle doctors, and some very successful ones, have always existed in the East, and exist there today. He believes that an antagonism between rustic dervishes and learned men is not uncommon, and says: 'At Jerusalem Jesus completely failed and his failure appears to have stung him into bitter abuse of his successful rivals. He called the learned doctors a generation of vipers, white sepulchres and serpents, and declared that they should not escape the damnation of hell. Because they had made the washing of hands before dinner a religious ablution, Jesus, with equal bigotry, would not wash his hands at all, though people eat with the hand in the East, and dip their hand in the same dish' (pp. 226/7).

After so many reverent glowing accounts of Jesus, it is strange to read Reade's summary of Jesus' doctrines: 'A young man named Joshua or Jesus, a carpenter by trade, believed that the world belonged to the devil, and that God would take it shortly from Satan, and that he, the Christ or Anointed, would be appointed by God to judge the souls of men, and reign over them on earth. In politics he was a leveller and communist, in morals he was a monk; he believed that only the poor and the despised would inherit the kingdom of God. All men who had riches or reputations would follow their dethroned master into everlasting pain. Jesus attacked the church-going ever-praying Pharisees, and declared that their piety was worthless if it was praised on earth. It was his belief that earthly happiness was a gift from Satan and should therefore be refused . . . Christ taught that men should sell all that they had and give it to the poor; that they should renounce all family ties; they they should let tomorrow take care of itself; that they should not trouble about clothes . . . the principles of Jesus were not conducive to the welfare of society; he was put to death by the authorities . . . ' (pp. 483/4). When we are to answer the question

'Whom do Men say That I Am'?, we must not forget Reade's picture however unfavourable and, perhaps, unjust.

Was Jesus a Christian?

Finally, I should like to quote a few authors who express a view similar to my own, namely, that Jesus was not responsible for the ideas which, after his death, came to be known as Christianity.

Long before Bruno Bauer whom I mentioned above, H.S. Reimarus, a German professor of Oriental languages and a friend of the great Gotthold Ephraim Lessing, became an exponent of 'enlightenment' in Bible criticism. In his book *The Object of Jesus and His Disciples* he expresses his own aim very succinctly: 'We are justified in drawing an absolute distinction between the teaching of the Apostles in their writings, and what Jesus himself in his own lifetime proclaimed and taught.' Schweitzer, discussing Reimarus, says that according to the latter 'even in His Messianic claims, Jesus remained "within the limits of humanity"' (op.cit., p.17). For Reimarus, Jesus was a man who tried to convince the people of his Messianic claim, and who hoped that with the people's support he would fulfil the biblical prophecy. He promised his supporters material advantages and was, finally, hounded down and put to death by authority.

T.H. Huxley, the famous biologist, wrote in a letter in 1889: 'The pith of my article [which appeared under the title 'Agnosticism in the 19th century'] is the proposition that Christ was not a Christian.' The article itself contained the following passage: 'The sect of the Nazarenes, the brother and the immediate followers of Jesus, commissioned by him as apostles, and those who were taught by them up to the year A.D. 50, were not 'Christians' in the sense in which the term has been understood ever since its asserted origin at Antioch, but Jews – straight orthodox Jews – whose belief in the Messiahship of Jesus never led to their exclusion from the Temple services, nor would have shut them out from the wide embrace of Judaism' (quoted from Osborne op.cit.pp.190/4).

H.G. Wells spoke with more reverence about the person and teaching of Jesus than most other agnostics. It is quite obvious from his writings that he considered Jesus a man whose ideas were undermined by their growth into a 'religion'. He says, 'At the best the story about Jesus' birth and early childhood are events unnecessary to the teaching and rob it of much of its strength and power it possesses when we strip such accompaniments . . . ' (*The Outline of History*, p.498). In the text below it seems that Wells supported views that are developed at length in the present work: 'It is a fact that in the gospels all that body of theological assertion which constitutes Christianity finds very qualified support. There is, as the reader may see for himself, no clear and emphatic assertion in these books of the doctrines which Christian teachers of all denominations find generally necessary to salvation . . . (ibid., p.499). It is difficult to get any words actually ascribed to Jesus in which he explained the doctrine of the Atonement or urged any sacrifices or sacraments upon his followers . . . There is no evidence that the apostles of Jesus entertained the doctrine of the Trinity. Nor does Jesus give his claim to be the 'Christ' or his participation in the Godhead any such prominence as one feels would have been done had he considered it a matter of primary significance. Most astounding is the statement (*Matthew* 16:20) "Then charged he his disciples that they should tell no man that he was Jesus the Christ". It is difficult then to understand this suppression if we suppose he considered this fact was essential to salvation' (ibid.) The important thing, however, is Wells' reference to early Christianity: 'The story of the early beginnings of Christianity is the story of the struggle between the real teachings of Jesus of Nazareth, and the limitations, amplifications and misunderstandings of the very inferior men who had loved and followed him from Galilee, and who were now the bearers and custodians of his message to mankind' (ibid. pp.509/10).

In the 20th century we have witnessed a flood of works: novels, poems, 'biographies', interpretations — all attempting to give us a portrait of Jesus. They all show interest, reverence and an almost moving confidence. The more our disillusionment with our environment deepens, the more grows our admiration for the remarkable man who taught us to aspire to that idea of perfection we have come to call God.

2
The Lord Jesus Christ

The claim

After the death of the man Jesus something strange happened. Slowly but inescapably the Teacher was transformed first into Lord, Messenger and mouthpiece of God, and then into God himself. I am trying to show how this transformation took place, and how, in the process, the teaching was lost to make way for the momentous claims of the Christian religion.

I shall attempt to demonstrate that, while Jesus never called himself God and not even his apostles would have dared to identify him with divinity, certain influences were at work which led to the acceptance of Jesus as Christ, and to the elevation of Christ to godhead.

The claim is based on the following passages:

'I and my Father are one'	*John* 10:30
'No man cometh to the Father but by me'	*John* 14:6
'He that hath seen me, hath seen my father'	*John* 14:9
'And Thomas . . . said unto him, My Lord and my God!'	*John* 20:8
'. . . whose are the fathers and of whom, as concerning the flesh Christ came, who is over all God blessed for ever'	*Rom.* 9:5
'Jesus being in the form of God thought it not robbery to be equal with God'	*Phil.* 2:6
'At the name of Jesus every knee shall bow . . . and every tongue shall confess that Jesus Christ is Lord'	*Phil* 2:10/11
'For in him dwelleth the fullness of the Godhead bodily'	*Col.* 2:9

'God was manifest in the flesh, justified in the Spirit, seen of angels, preached unto the

>   Gentiles'   *1 Tim.* 3:16
> 'But unto the Son he [God] saith, Thy throne,
>   O God is for ever and ever . . . '   *Heb.* 1:8

Each of these passages will be considered below, and I am confident that the reader will see that none of them contains an assertion of Jesus' divinity.

The claim is presented on every level. An example of the lowest level we find in the Roman Catholic *Question Box {henceforth QB}*: Most unbelievers – Harnack, Hegel, Kant, Renan, Spinoza, Strauss, Mill – have acknowledged the surpassing eminence of the character of Christ. He certainly claimed to be God [sic]. If his claim were false, he is not even a good man. As St. John says: 'He that believeth not the Son, maketh him a liar' (*1 John* 5:10). But we know he is the One that is good, God' (*Matt.* 19:17) (p.53). This statement is completely false. Jesus never claimed to be God. The quotation of *Matthew* 19:17 in this form and context shows little regard for the Scriptures.

In attempting to trace the origin of the claim, we should consider a passage from Irenaeus who introduces the subject with great caution and subtlety: 'It has been demonstrated that the Word which exists from the beginning with God, by whom all things were made, who was also present with the race of men at all times, the Word has in these last times, according to the time appointed by the Father, been united to his own workmanship and has been made passible man. Therefore we can set aside the objection of them that say, "If he was born at that time it follows that Christ did not exist before then". For we have shown that the Son of God did not then begin to exist since he existed with the Father always; but when he was incarnate and made man, he summed up in himself the long line of the human race, procuring for us salvation summarily, so that what we had lost in Adam, that is, the being in the image and likeness of God, that we should regain in Christ Jesus' (*Adv. haer.* 3:18).

We find much less clarity in the argument of Athanasius who influenced Christian doctrine more profoundly than any other church father: 'The Word takes on a body capable of death in order that by partaking in the Word that is above all, it might be worthy to die instead of all, and might remain incorruptible through the indwelling Word, and that for the future corruption should cease from all by the grace of his resurrection . . . Hence he did away with death for all who are like him by the offering of a substitute. For it was reasonable that the Word who is above all, in offering his own temple and bodily instrument as a substitute-life for all, fulfilled the liability in his death, and thus the incorruptible Son of God, being associated with all mankind by likeness to them, naturally closed with all the incorruption in the promise concerning the resurrection . . . ' (*De incarn.* IX).

I should like to say here that of the passages quoted on the preceding pages only three recorded words of Jesus, while most of them are from John and Paul, and are missing from the synoptic gospels.

I and my Father are One

John 10:30 is the only passage in the New Testament which could be used to demonstrate that Jesus *did* say he was God. This momentous text is not recorded in any of the synoptic gospels, and has no other similar saying in the Gospel according to John.

The text is preceded by the story of a blind man whom Jesus healed, of how 'the Jews' wondered about the origin of his healing power, of how he compared himself with the loving shepherd who cares for his sheep that hirelings abandon, and how God who knows of the shepherd's love for his charges would restore him to life. After these words 'the Jews' asked him once again whether he was the Christ or not. Jesus answers that God who is greater than all, had put the sheep into his charge and no one would be able to 'pluck them out' of his hand. At this point, quite inconsequentially, are inserted the words: 'I and my Father are one.' Hearing this, 'the Jews' want to stone Jesus for blasphemy, but he quotes Scripture: did not God himself say 'Ye are gods'? (Ye are gods, and all of you are children of the Most High, *Psalm* 82.6). Why would it be blasphemy if he, Jesus, claimed to be a son of God? Jesus cites his works as proof and adds: 'The Father is in me and I in him' (*John* 10:38).

'I am in the Father and the Father is in me' is repeated in *John* 14:10 and again in *John* 14:11. In *John* 17:21 we read: 'Thou, Father, art in me, and I in Thee . . . ' This expression was obviously one of John's stylistic favourites.

The R.C. Professor W. Leonard attaches much significance to *John* 10:30 and shows how the church fathers, notably Cyril, Basil and Chrysostom, used it extensively to combat contemporary heresies. According to Leonard it proves that Jesus revealed his nature as being of the same substance and power as the Father's (*Catholic Commentary on Holy Scripture* [henceforth *CC*, p. 1001). Protestant theologians are not reluctant either to use this passage as conclusive evidence. Professor C.K. Barrett exclaims: 'Say *Jesus* and you have said *God*. This unity between Father and Son is not merely cosmological and metaphysical;

the moral relationship between love and obedience are primary!' [*PC*, p.856].

Most of the apologists' arguments are based on the views of Augustine who, reflecting on this passage, wrote: 'The word *are* delivers you from the heresy of Sabellius, the word *one* delivers you from that of Arius . . . ', and argued that the word *unum* meant *one substance* (*Tract.* 97).

R.H. Lightfoot speaks of Jesus' claim 'to complete union with the Father' (*St. John's Gospel*, p.208) and asserts that 'the union of the Father and the Son is such that the Lord's words and works are indeed the words and works of God' (ibid., p.214). The words of Jesus in *John* 7:16, 'My doctrine is not mine, but his that sent me' and in *John* 5:30, 'I can of mine own self do nothing . . . I seek not mine own will, but the will of the Father which hath sent me. If I bear witness of myself, my witness is not true . . . ', are ignored. Another theologian, Dummelow, even suggests that 'the Greek indicates that the Father and the son are two persons but one God' (*OVBC* p.792).

A point to which many Christians interpreters like to refer is the statement that 'the Jews' who must have understood Jesus, exclaimed 'We stone you . . . because you, being a man, make yourself God' (*John* 10:33). The Christian argument runs: had he not declared himself to be God, his Jewish opponents would not have said so.

The Jewish scholar Joshua Podro remarks: 'Jesus was not empowered to promise everlasting life to his sheep. "I and my Father are one" is Johannite doctrine and even if Jesus had said this – which he could never have done – no attempt would have been made to stone him, instead he would have been examined by the local Sanhedrin . . . *John* 10:30 may be disregarded as a clumsy invention in support of the trinitarian dogma' (*NGR* p.539).

Many scholars have attempted to accept the validity of this passage, yet rescue the reputation of Jesus by explaining away its implications. The bravest attempt of this kind was made in Edmond Fleg's life story of Jesus, ostensibly told by the Wandering Jew in which we read that 'Jesus replied that he and his Father are but one, that the Father is in him and he is in the Father. When the others exclaimed "You blaspheme: you are only a man and you make yourself God!" he could have answered that it is said of the Just Ones of Israel and of the Messiah: they will be named by the name of the Eternal One. But the stones started flying and made it impossible for him to speak . . . ' (*Jésus raconté par le Juif errant*, p.190). Fleg quotes as his authorities *Isaiah* 9:6, *Jeremiah* 23:6 and *Baba Batra* 75b).

As I will attempt to show in a later chapter, modern theologians too have accepted the idea of the literal oneness of Jesus and God. Harnack writes: 'How (Jesus) came to his consciousness of the unique character of his relation to God as a Son; how he came to the consciousness of his power, and to the consciousness of the obligation and the mission which this power carried with it, is his secret, and no psychology will ever fathom it!' (*What is Christianity?* p.98). Karl Barth is even more emphatic: 'Between God and the Word he speaks there is no difference; whereas there is a difference between me and what I say. This Jesus Christ which is the everlasting Word, who is the eternally begotten of God, has been manifested to the world. He is God like his Father . . . ' (*The Faith of the Church*, p.37). Archbishop Temple speaks of a 'stupendous affirmation of union with the Deity . . . He asserts his union with the God to whom the worship of the Church is offered' (*St. John's Gospel*, p.172). Cautiously, Temple adds: ' . . . while the Lord makes it clear that he is not asserting a unique position for himself, neither is he denying it. For the refutation of the charge is enough to show that is was not asserted' (ibid.). Well, was it, or wasn't it?

Brunner expresses himself more carefully: 'He who does not believe that in Jesus God Himself comes to us, does not apprehend the God who reveals Himself to us in the coming of Jesus Christ' (*Our Faith*, p.65). Beautiful circular argument, isn't it? Of course, there are several contemporary theologians who have the courage and wide horizon to go beyond the narrow confines of Christological tradition. It is worth quoting Schillebeeckx's conclusion as a fine example of insight: 'To find a basis for one's own life in the trustworthiness of Jesus, and ultimately of his *Abba* experience (through which Jesus discovers the ground of his own life in God) is of course an act of faith in Jesus which is thus . . . an act attesting faith in God . . . for someone who acknowledges and in faith confesses this trustworthiness of Jesus as grounded in truth and reality, the trustworthiness acquires visible contours in the actual life of Jesus; his faith then perceives Jesus' trustworthiness in the material, the biographical data, which the historian can put before him regarding Jesus of Nazareth. This material at any rate confronts us all with the question: Could this person have been right? Is it in actual fact possible, starting from a deep religious rapport with God . . . really to say something about man, perhaps even the most important things that can be said about human beings? For that was indeed what Jesus claimed. Starting from the religious claim – not in some other way – he says something about man and man's final good' (*Jesus*, p.270). And the great 'demythologizer', Rudolf Bultmann, seems determined to go the whole way: 'Formally, they are quite right: the penalty for blasphemy is stoning and it is blasphemy for a man to set himself up as God. But when "the Jews" [the inverted commas here are Bultmann's own!] talk about God, we can see that they are in no way prepared to hear God when he speaks to them. They cannot grasp that he confronts them in everyday life as a man like themselves. They only know *one* way of "making oneself God" and thus betray their own vanity . . . Yet their unbelief is not merely a rejection and refusal of the revelation, but positive hostility and hatred, a positive onslaught on it. Indeed it could not be otherwise, if the good is understood not as a gift of God, but as the goal of man's efforts in which he realises himself. If the revelation fails to arouse faith then it must arouse hostility' (*John*, p. 388/9).

In my own view the truth about this passage is much simpler than any of these speculations: I had always found it a strange stumbling block – words so unlike the rest of Jesus' sayings – until I hit upon a possible explanation. The Greek text reads as follows:

ἐγὼ καὶ ὁ πατὴρ ἕυ ἐσμευ
I and the father one we are

There are two possible constructions:

to be one	ἕνειναι	to be one	ἐν ἔσμεν
to interpenetrate	ἐνεῖναι	to interpenetrate ~	ἐνὲσμεν

The is a possibility that the word ἀλλήλοις or ἀλλήλως (one another) followed but was suppressed.

The old Greek manuscripts had no gaps between the words, neither did they use much accentuation. The sentence was written thus:

εγοκαιοπατηρενεσμεν

In breaking up this line into its component words, the following would seem to me correct:

ἐγὼ καὶ ὁ πατὴρ ἐνὲσμεν (ἀλλήλως)
I and the father interpenetrate

which is merely a repetition of John's frequently used, favourite passage, 'I am in the Father and the Father is in me'. It may support my argument if I mention that ἔνειμι also means 'to be in' or 'to be within'!

No man cometh to the Father but by me

This phrase of course is not a claim to be God or of a divine nature, merely of being the only mouthpiece through which God has chosen to speak to man. Many religious teachers have made this assertion, or it has been made on their behalf. Essentially it is nothing more than the claim of Moses that he was chosen by God who spoke to him and gave him the Law; or the assertion that 'God is One and Mohammed is His Prophet'. We find the same idea in Paul's Epistle to Timothy: '. . . there is one God, and one mediator between God and man, the man Christ Jesus' (*1 Tim* 2:5).

The context in which this text occurs is the great discourse at the Last Supper, reported in the Fourth Gospel (chapters 13 to 17). Jesus had just answered his apostles that they should discard all doubts and believe in him as implicitly as they believe in God. Thomas, always presented by John as 'the doubter', asks how they, Jesus' friends, should know the way if they do not even know the direction in which he, the Teacher, is moving. Jesus replies: 'I am the way, the truth, and the life: no man cometh unto the Father, but by me' (*John* 14:6). Perhaps, the words he spoke were simply: God is the way, the truth, and the life – that is the direction in which I am moving – and if you want to know the way, follow me. (See sub-chapter 'I am that I am' below.)

If we denude the interpretation by Professor Leonard of its partisan embellishment, we arrive at a meaning not very far from this one. He concludes with the words: 'Coming to the father, is necessarily filial motion through the Son. There is only one Son in whom we are sons, only one Mediator who is our way to the Father . . . " (*CC*, p.1006). In *PC* Professor Barrett is far less explicit, and partisan jargon completely obscures his statement. Yet even he says of Jesus, 'He is the truth and the life, because he is the way to God who is truth and life' (*PC*, p.860). The commentary in Dummelow trivialises the basic idea of Jesus, saying that he presents himself 'as the only mediator between God and man (the Way), the only teacher authorized to reveal things of God (the Truth) and the one author of spiritual and natural life (the Life)' (*Cambridge History of the Bible*, p.799). Of course, these ideas originate from the Church Fathers, notably Augustine: 'Walk . . . in him Who is Man that you may come to Him Who is God' (*Aug. Serm.* 141). Hilary puts the same idea yet more forcefully: 'He who is the Way cannot lead us astray, He who is the Truth cannot deceive, He who is the Life cannot desert us in death' (*De Trin*, 7:9). Considering these comments on the text, we must conclude that it was Jesus himself who expressed its meaning most clearly. But then, Jesus was not a theologian.

Graves and Podro suggest that the whole verse was crudely manipulated and offer important alterations. They believe that Jesus exalted the Law and not himself, not even God. According to them, the passage should read: '. . . whither I go ye know, and the way ye know.

For the Law is the way and the truth and the life. Verily I say unto you: no man cometh to the Father but by the Law!' (*NGR*, p.972).

Be it as it may, it is unlikely that Jesus identified himself with the divine I AM or with the Law but there is no doubt that he believed his way, the direction he had chosen, might serve as a guide to all those who seek to do the will of God.

He that hath seen me, hath seen the Father

John 14:9, following closely upon the preceding saying, is another example of the manner in which the author(s) in the Gospel according to John tried to express Jesus' relationship to God. Unlike Bishop Moule who held that 'a Saviour not quite God is a bridge broken at the farther side', John seems to emphasise that it is the direction of salvation which Jesus can show, even if he does not take the believer by the hand and lead him across the bridge.

Christian commentators often quote this passage as proof of the Incarnation. In the view of Professor Leonard it is a gentle reproach directed at Philip, pointing out that years of being together with Jesus did not suffice to make him realise the Teacher's identity with God (*CC*, p.1006). Lightfoot also states that the passage expresses the fact that Jesus had been in the world and the world did not recognise him (*A Commentary to St. John's Gospel*, p.75). He points out that the intention behind the saying was to make the disciples realise that hitherto they had not known the Father, but now they know Him and have seen Him in the Son (ibid.,p.270). As in the case of the preceding text, the origin of the argument is to be found in the Church Fathers. It was Hilary who first suggested that Jesus' words to Philip were a reproof that after all the miracles he had not recognised that Jesus was God (*De Trin.*, 7). Chrysostom believed that they meant that Philip had not seen Christ aright, as being consubstantial with the Father; in fact, Chrysostom maintained that in this passage Jesus declared and revealed that he was not a creature but God.

Graves and Podro suggest the rewording of this text: 'Philip saith: 'Teach us to see our Father, and it is enough . . . ' Jesus answered: 'Have I been so long with thee, Philip, and yet hast thou not known me? The words that I speak, I speak not of myself, but I deliver the word of God to thee as it is delivered unto me in the Scriptures and in the traditions of the Elders' (*NGR*, p.869).

And yet, there is another possibility. It may be that Jesus did speak those words without claiming identity, co-equality or consubstantiality or any such idea for himself. May he not have meant that the only chance man has to see God is in his fellow men who were created in God's image, just as he himself; and in the spirit which God breathed into his fellow men, just as He did into his own? If that spirit reveals the will of God and the image serves the spirit in its endeavour, the vision of God many be clearer to us in the person who reflects that spirit more than any other thing in creation.

My Lord and my God

His enemies had captured Jesus and the authorities crucified him. No longer did he wander through Galilee, no longer did his words reach the ears and mind of chance audiences. Jesus the man was dead. Christ the Lord appeared among his disciples on a Sunday evening, walking through the walls (the doors were locked for fear of 'the Jews'), as gods usually do; and speaking to them showed his hands and his side. Thomas, who arrived after Jesus had left, refused to believe in the reappearance of the Teacher unless he were permitted to put his finger 'into the print of the nails'. Eight days later Jesus appeared again, walking through the walls, and knowing of Thomas' doubt, told him to put his hands against the wounds. Without doing so, Thomas seems to have been convinced, and believed, saying: 'My Lord and my God!' (*John* 20:27).

This passage is the second of a few in the New Testament which in their present reading are regarded as an assertion that the author believed in the divinity of Jesus. Such 'evidence' extends altogether to two score words in a book containing millions.

Not surprisingly, much is made of Thomas' exclamation by the commentators. In his annotations to the New Testament Bishop Wordsworth claims that this text proves Thomas' belief that Jesus was indeed God. 'He recognises Him as Man, and adores Him as God.' Bishop Wordsworth points out that this saying was regarded by the Church Fathers as conclusive proof of Jesus' divinity. In this context he quotes Cyril, Chrysostom, Athanasius, and especially Augustine who said: 'Thomas beheld Christ as Man, and confessed to Him to be God Whom he did not see or touch' (*The Holy Bible*, I, p.362).

Professor Leonard calls Thomas' confession the most explicit act of faith in the gospels. Yet, he is honest enough to admit that 'the words he spoke do not seem to be either an exclamation or a vocative, but an elliptic proposition: "Thou art my Lord and my God!"' (*CC*, p.1016).

However, he insists on the words being a confession of Christ's divinity. In *PC*, Professor Barrett regards the passage as the final pronouncement and climax of John's Christology, a definite declaration of the identity of Christ with God (*PC*, p.867). Even Lightfoot, an authority on Johannite writings, calls the text 'a complete confession of faith, giving in his last three words the same honour to the Son as to the Father'. Lightfoot refers here to the Introduction of the Fourth Gospel and thinks that with Thomas' confession the Christological doctrine of John has come to full circle (*St. John*, p.334).

Dr. Klausner argues that the appearance of the resurrected Christ to his disciples was regarded as a vision by the early Church which did not differentiate between 'actual occurrence' and 'heavenly vision'. As proof Klausner quotes Paul who describes (*1 Cor.* 15:5-8) the appearance of the Risen Christ, relating his experience on the Road to Damascus (*Acts* 26:19) which he calls a 'heavenly vision' (*JN*, p.359).

Graves and Podro advance a complicated but attractive theory that Jesus was taken down from the cross alive and he recovered from his wounds. It was therefore in the flesh that he appeared to his friends. He warned Mary not to touch him, since, being in his burial shroud, he was ritually 'unclean'. He can allow Thomas to touch him some time later, as he was no longer unclean. It is interesting to note how these students of the New Testament propose to restore the Text: 'When they had dined, he saith unto Thomas reach hither thy finger and touch my hand and my side, and learn whether or no I be a bodiless spirit. And be not faithless but believe in the power of God. Thomas answered: Nay, master, but I have seen, may the Lord forgive me my unbelief! Jesus saith: So be it. But more blessed are they that have not seen and yet have believed!' (*NGR*, pp.781 and 997).

Without any learned proof I am inclined to seek the simplest possible answer. We cannot *know* what actually happened, but I may surmise what the evangelist tried to say when he wrote those lines. They are indeed *not* in the vocative which would have been the case, grammatically, if the words had been addressed to Jesus. Undoubtedly, Thomas invokes the Lord God in some manner to express his surprise and amazement. It was the Christological 'development' which turned his words into an 'elliptical proposition' to serve the Christian argument.

It has been pointed out to me that the word 'God' in an address may occur in the simple nominative instead of the vocative. Indeed, I have found several examples in the Bible to prove the point of my opponent, but I have found not a single example applied to the word 'Lord'.

To be equal with God

The Epistle to the Philippians is a much disputed document and its authenticity cannot be established. Christian authorities are doubtful, but some accept it, pointing out that Marcion and the Muratori fragment (about A.D. 200) name it among the Pauline Epistles. A. Robertson, Macleod Yearsley and many others consider it is likely that at least part of it cannot be attributed to Paul.

If this passage *is* genuine, it is one of the half-dozen texts that *can* be interpreted as saying that Christ is God. The translation is painstakingly correct and reads: 'Jesus being in the form of God thought it not robbery to be equal with God . . . ' (*Phil*, 2:6). The *New English Bible* [*NEB*] translates more freely and, in doing so, interprets the passage: 'For the divine nature was his from the first; yet he did not thing to snatch at equality with God . . . ', which having regard to the Greek syntax seems to me a more likely meaning.

Christian apologists eagerly seized this short passage to demonstrate that Paul believed in the divinity of Jesus. The church fathers showed the way how these words serve as 'evidence'. Chrysostom said: 'Christ did not imagine that his own divine Co-eternity, Co-equality and Consubstantiality with the Father was like a stolen spoil . . . He had not seized it as prey, it was his own . . . The usurper fears to lay aside the purple, for he knows that it is stolen, and does not belong to him. Not so the king; for he is conscious that it is his kingly right. Augustine's argument is similar and ends with the words: 'Jesus was God and being in the form of God, He did not deem *that* existence of equality an usurped thing' (*Serm*. 361). The problem is summarised in the words of Primasius: 'He did not *usurp*, he *had* equality with the Father, which he had by nature and not by seizing it'. The text was widely used in the struggle against 'heretics', and Bishop Bull wrote: 'This one passage, rightly understood, is sufficient for the refutation of all the heresies against the Person of our Lord Jesus Christ' (*Dec.Fid.- Nic*, 2:2:2).

C. Lattey S.J. maintains that the Fathers took the word 'form' to mean the equivalent of 'nature', 'in the rough and ready language of popular philosophy', and he believes that there can be no doubt as to Paul's meaning' (*CC*, p. 1129). The Protestant Dr. Beasley-Murray suggests that 'it is better to interpret the language as relating to the pre-existent Christ in the glory of God, but not viewing it as a privilege that could be forsaken . . . ' (*PC*, 9.987). Once again the conclusion is prior to the premise, and not vice-versa.

I admit that the passage can be interpreted as confirming the divinity of Christ. It is indeed a step in the direction of the man Jesus becoming the God Christ. On the other hand, it is possible to find in the context (*Phil.* 2:5/11) evidence that a clear distinction was made between him who was 'in the form of God' and 'equal with God', and God himself. The fact that the Epistle speaks of equality with God and later mentions that God has exalted Christ and that Christ is Lord to the glory of God, shows that the author(s) did not think of Jesus as God. If we relate the passage to the injunction of the Teacher: 'Be ye . . . perfect as your Father which is in heaven is perfect' (*Matthew* 5:48), and to the words of Paul himself: ' . . . there is one God, the Father . . . and one Lord Jesus Christ' (*1 Cor.*8:6), and ' . . . there is one God, and one mediator between God and men, the man Christ Jesus' (*1 Tim.* 2:5), we can see that a distinction was always made between Jesus and God.

The awkward wording of the passage makes it difficult for me to translate it into a sentence acceptable in the context of Jesus' teaching. Perhaps it could be understood in the sense that God revealed himself to men through Jesus who was not afraid to consider his own words and actions as an expression of God's power and will.

Every knee should bow

The writer(s) of the Epistle went on to say that God had exalted Jesus above all men, and followed this up with the words: '. . . at the name of Jesus every knee should bow . . . and every tongue confess that Jesus is Lord to the glory of God the Father . . . ' (*Phil.* 2:10/11).

Referring to this passage, many Christian commentators say that it also proves the divinity of Jesus, since in the Old Testament God himself says: ' . . . unto me every knee shall bow, every tongue shall swear' (*Isaiah* 45:23). Speaking of God's demand, Paul writes in the Epistle to the Romans: 'For it is written. As I live says the Lord, every knee shall bow to me, and every tongue shall confess to God' (*Rom.* 14:11). It is also interesting to note that the Vulgate translation ends with the words: 'omnis lingua confiteatur quia Dominus Iesus Christus in gloria est Dei Patris' which is perhaps more in harmony with the original and states that 'every tongue should confess the Lord Jesus Christ to the glory of God the Father'. This is also stated in CC by Lattey who admits that the expression *Lord* 'was reserved for God except in the language of Paul who calls Jehovah *Lord* only when quoting scripture'. This excellent argument degenerates when Lattey subsequently says: ' . . . there is ample proof that he [Paul] thought that Christ is God' (*CC*, pp. 1129/30). I shall have more to say about the use of the word 'Lord' in another context. Dummelow shows how the situation can be exploited to provide a *post factum* meaning to an obscure text. He refers to *Isaiah* 45:23 where the prophet foretells that all mankind will acknowledge the God of Israel. 'The glory of the Father,' says Dummelow, 'will be realised in the universal acknowledgement of the Lordship of the Son whom He enthroned' (*OVBC*, pp.973/4). Bishop Wordsworth goes yet further claiming that the text shows that 'the same honour is to be paid to Jesus as to God, because He *is* God' (*The Holy Bible*, II, p.351).

The Greek word ἐξομολογέω means confess, praise, celebrate. The injunction, that at the name of Jesus everyone should bend his knee and praise him, is still offensive to the Jew who is not prepared to bend his knee before anyone but God. The Greek reader of this Epistle may have found nothing objectionable in the demand that he should kneel and praise the God-man Christ Jesus. Even this passage does not prove that Jesus was regarded as God by the biblical author.

Thy throne, O God, is for ever

This passage, almost at the beginning of the Epistle to the Hebrews, is the climax of speculation on the Father's relationship to the Son: 'But unto the Son he [God] saith, Thy throne, O God, is for ever and ever' (*Hebrews* 1:8).

The Epistle to the Hebrews is a second century document and it is generally admitted that it was *not* written by Paul, but probably by a Pauline gnostic who was, unlike Paul, acquainted with the gospel stories. Certain allusions in the Epistle show that he must have read the oldest variants of the gospels, certainly the one according to Mark. Unlike the other epistles ascribed to Paul, it does not commence with the latter's name and salutation. The Muratori Canon does not include it.

The quotation itself originates from the Old Testament where we read: 'Thy throne, O God, is for ever and ever' (*Psalm* 45:6). The Psalm is introduced by the following words: 'To the chief Musician upon Shoshannim, for the sons of Korah, – Maskill, a Song of Love'. It is obvious, therefore, that it is not God speaking but the author. The verse in question in the Jewish Bible translated straight from the Hebrew, shows a marked difference: 'Thy throne, given of God, endureth for ever and ever . . . ' (*Holy Scriptures according to the Masoretic Text*, translated by I. Leeser, p.896). The singer is human, not divine. It seems that it is King David here, whose throne is 'given of God'. The person addressed is the King not Christ! It is this little twist, a hardly noticeable counterfeit, which makes *Hebrews* 1:8 such an important New Testament passage.

The Catholic commentator, Professor Leonard, calls this psalm the nuptial song of a royal prince, from which he concludes, rather inconsequentially, that it must have meant 'the Messiah and most probably the Messiah directly and exclusively' (*CC*, p. 1160). Professor Bruce, in *Peake's*, is also content to tread the beaten track. The Son is addressed as God, in possession of an everlasting throne, and having supremacy over all other rulers. However, Professor Bruce shows a little uneasiness over the translation of the nominative ὁ θεός into the vocative (O God). He comforts himself with the assurance that 'our author certainly understood "God" as vocative, expressing the title of the Son' (*PC*, p. 1009).

Dummelow too claims that the writer 'meant' to assert the unity of the Son with God (*OVBC*, p. 1017). Bishop Wordsworth is another commentator who is troubled by the grammatical discrepancy in the translation, but reassures himself in the same manner as his fellow-Christians. The words ὁ θεός used here by the Septuagint are in his opinion employed as *vocative* and their use in the nominative is, in his view, best illustrated by the words of St. Thomas when he addressed Jesus as God, 'My Lord and my God!' The reader is reminded of the sub-chapter dealing with Thomas' exclamation: Wordsworth accepts one inaccuracy by reference to another, identical, inaccuracy.

Well, the trouble is that the word ὁ θεός just is *not* in the vocative, but in the ordinary nominative. The ὁ is the masculine article of the noun in the nominative: the vocative has no article, or rather changes the noun θεός into θεέ (see *Matthew* 27:46). Only disregard for the 'word of God' can result in such a tendentious mistranslation and its acceptance by 'experts'. The correct rendering (without my pretending to understand the 'meaning') is: 'Thy throne, God, is for ever and ever . . . ' Perhaps the suggestion of the *NEB* that the passage may be read: God is thy throne for ever and ever, i.e. the foundation of Christ's kingdom (p. 373) is not so farfetched after all.

God blessed for ever

Speaking for his kinsmen, the Israelites, Paul says that God singled them out for adoption, for the glory of the Covenant and the Law, and for the promises given to the forbears of Israel 'of whom as concerning the flesh Christ came, who is over all, God blessed for ever' (*Rom*. 9:5).

It was to be expected that the Christian theologians would seize upon this passage which is one of the obvious statements that 'Jesus *was* God blessed for ever'. The Catholic *QB* mentions it among the proofs of Christ's divinity (p.54) and the *CC* contains a lengthy discussion on the subject by Professor Theissen. He claims that the generally accepted reading is correct and that the arguments of those who on grammatical grounds claim that the passage ends with a praise of God and not of Christ (he names Wetstein, Tischendorff, Juelicher and Lietzmann) are farfetched (*CC*, p.1068). Professor Manson in *PC* is more cautious. He too argues that 'the structure of the sentence favours the former view' [i.e. the traditional AV translation], but admits that it is impossible to establish clearly what Paul intended to say (*PC*, p.947). Bishop Wordsworth asserts that here 'the Holy Spirit ascribes to Christ the incommunicable titles of Jehovah and Elohim, in the highest sense of the words . . . declaring that God and Man are one in Christ' (*The Holy Bible*, II, p.247). Wordsworth goes on quoting authorities, ancient and modern, who invoke this passage as proof of Christ's divinity.

It is strange how faith confuses the minds of excellent men who, confronted with Greek syntax, cannot notice what every proficient schoolboy would see. The Greek text is as follows:

. . . ὧν οἱ πατέρες καὶ ἐξ ὧν ὁ Χριστός το κατὰ σάρκα ὁ ὢν ἐπι πάντων Θεὸς εὐλογητός εἰς τοὺς αἰῶνας ἀμήν

The fraudulent translation places a comma between παντῶν and Θεός in an attempt to affect the syntax and mislead the reader.

I have to refer the reader to the translation in the *NEB*, which as far as the intended meaning is concerned is, in my opinion, correct: 'Theirs are the patriarchs, and from them, in natural descent, sprang the Messiah. May God, supreme above all, be blessed for ever. Amen' (p.268).

The fullness of the Godhead

Here I quote two more examples of passages which allegedly support the claim that the authors of the New Testament considered Jesus to be God.

The Epistle to the Colossians 2:9 reads: ' . . . for in him dwelleth all the fullness of the Godhead bodily.' The Greek original, however, says: ὅτι ἐν αὐτῷ κατοικεῖ πᾶν τὸ πλήρωμα τῆς θεότητος σωματικῶς . . . which means 'for in him dwelleth all the fullness of the *divine nature* bodily', a very considerable difference indeed. The word Godhead is just another word for God and would read in Greek Θεός and in the genitive Θεοῦ. The word used is not God, but *divine nature* ἡ θεότης, the genitive of which is της θεότητος. In every man who receives 'the gift of the Holy Ghost', the divine nature is manifest, and fully in Jesus, at least according to Christian teaching. This is just another weighted translation and shows that nowhere in the New Testament is Jesus called God.

Finally, I would like to quote a passage which Christians often use trying to demolish this statement. It occurs in the Epistle to Timothy, one of the so-called Pastoral Letters (*1 Tim.* 3:16). It reads in the Authorised Version: 'God was manifest in the flesh, justified in the Spirit, seen of angels, preached to the Gentiles, believed on in the world, received up in glory.' I find the text in the *NEB* a little more palatable: Speaking about God, the writer says: 'He was manifest in the body, vindicated in the spirit, seen by angels, who was proclaimed among nations, believed in throughout the world, glorified in high heaven' (*NEB*, pp. 358/9).

The commentators try to imply that, since in Jesus God manifested himself in the flesh, the whole passage must refer to Jesus. However, in the same letter, attributed to Paul but written by an unknown author in the 2nd century, we read (*1 Tim.* 3:16) 'there is one mediator between God and man, the man the Messiah Jesus . . . ', which shows that the author regards Christ Jesus as a man. Secondly, if we investigate the grammatical structure, we see that the whole passage is in the Aorist Passive:

Θεὸς ἐφανερώθη ἐν σαρκί, δικαιώθη ἐν Πνεύματι, ὤφθη ἀγγέλοις, ἐκηρύχθη ἐν ἔθνεσιν, ἐπιστεύθη ἐν κόσμῳ, ἀνελήμφθη ἐν δόξῃ

Aor. Pass.	ἐφανερώθη	Root.	φημί	was made manifest
	ἐδικαιώθη		δικαιοώ	was justified
	ὤφθη		ὁπάω	was seen
	ἐκηηρύχθη		κηρύσσω	was preached
	ἐπιστεύθη		πιστεύω	was believed in
	ἀνελήμφθη		ἀναλαμβάω	was received up

The whole passage is *not* a statement saying that Jesus was God. He may have been thought of in the expression that 'God was made manifest' through him, but it is stated that God was justified in the spirit, God was seen by the angels, God was preached to the gentiles, God was believed in and finally, God appeared in glory.

My Father is greater than I

While passages which Christian apologists quote in support of their doctrine are sparse, the New Testament abounds in texts showing that Jesus and his disciples were always anxious to make a clear distinction between God and Jesus. It probably never occurred to them that it was necessary and even imperative to make such a distinction, since no God-fearing Jew would have dreamt of claiming 'to be equal with God'. The disturbing fact remains that even some of the following passages have been turned inside out to serve as witness to Christological speculations.

The following sayings are attributed to Jesus himself:

'Why callest thou me good? There is none good but one, that is God . . .' *Matthew* 19:17
'Why callest thou me good? None is good, save one, that is God . . .' *Luke* 18:19
'Why callest thou me good? There is none good but one, that is God . . .' *Mark* 10:18
'(it) is not mine to give, but it shall be given to them for whom it is prepared by my Father . . .' *Matthew* 20:23
'But of that day and hour knoweth no man, not the angels of heaven, but my Father only . . .' *Matthew* 24:36
'My God, my God, why hast thou forsaken me:' *Matthew 27:46*
'But of that day and that hour knoweth no man, no not the angels which are in heaven, neither the Son, but the Father' *Mark* 13:32
'Ye believe in God, believe also in me . . .' *John* 14:1
'My Father is greater than I . . .' *John* 14:28
'I go to my Father and your Father, and to my God and your God . . . *John* 20:17

The Catholic *QB* ingeniously remarks: 'As John says, ' He that believeth not the Son maketh Him a liar' (*1 John* 5:10). But we know that He is 'the One that is good, God' (p.53). Even in the more sophisticated *CC*, T. Corbishley S.J. on *Matthew* 19:17 (p.886), Professor O'Flynn on *Mark* 10:18 (ibid., p.921), and Professor Ginns on *Luke* 18:19 (p.961) claim that these passages contain no disavowal of Jesus' divinity, and may in fact be interpreted as gentle hints of his real identity. Concerning *Mark* 13:32 O'Flynn suggests that it was no part of Jesus' messianic mission to reveal this information to men. Christ, as a divine Person, knows all the secrets of the Godhead, but it was not the will of the Father that he should make known to men the time of the Last Judgment' (p.927). The author does not hesitate to accuse Jesus of dissimulation rather than admit that the doctrine could be jeopardised by this saying. About the momentous cry in *Matthew* 27:46, which is in fact a quotation from *Psalm* 22, we are reassured: 'The psalm is not a cry of despair but, on the contrary, a hymn of supreme confidence in God, despite profound suffering . . . In our Lord's mouth indeed the words are not even a complaint because his intention is simply to show that the fruitful martyrdom of the innocent psalmist was a shadow of his own . . . ' (p.903).

In *PC*, Professor Stendahl merely remarks about *Matthew* 19:17 that 'poverty rather than altruistic giving is the highest stage of obedience' (*PC*, p.789); speaking on *Mark* 10:18, Dr Wilson quotes from another source that 'Jesus has the natural attitude of every pious and devoted Jew' (ibid., p.810); and dealing with *Luke* 18:19, Professor Lampe remarks only that 'Luke does not tone down the force of this saying, as Matthew does' (p.828). It is to the credit of these commentators that they do not attempt to invert the passages into the opposite of their meaning, as the Catholic interpreters do. When it comes to *Mark* 13:32, however, Dr Wilson is hedging: he does not dare to admit that the passage makes a clear distinction between what the Father alone knows, and what is also known to the Son (p.814). Professor Stendahl is very honest in dealing with *Matthew* 27:46: 'The cry of utter desolation raised grave problems in the later development of Christology, solutions to which are intimated in the variants of some manuscripts and in the Gospel of St. Peter . . . ', although he mentions the possibility that Jesus called upon Elijah to help and his cry was misunderstood for 'Eli' (my God) (p.797). In my view this argument contains still greater dangers for the Christian position, since it suggests that God called upon Elijah to come to his aid, and this after having said that if he [Jesus] wished he could pray to the Father 'and he shall presently give me more than twelve legions of angels' (*Matthew* 26:53).

The Church Fathers made it easy for themselves. Chrysostom and Augustine anticipated all the arguments about Jesus' objection to being called good. However, none went so far as Ambrose who commented on *Matthew* 19:17, that Jesus meant to say 'Quid me dicis bonum, quem negas Deum, Non ergo se bonum negat, sed Deum designat.' The argument runs like this: If Jesus is only 'Master' why call him good? If he is God why call him Master? Only God is good – why not call him God? And concerning the 'cry of utter desolation' Chrysostom says that 'Jesus shows with His last breath that he acknowledges the Old Testament'. Jerome outbids even that: 'Our Lord, with his dying breath, taught us to refer this Psalm to the Messiah; it is therefore impiety *not* to apply it to Him'. Gregory Nazianzus exclaimed: 'This voice is for our sakes; that we may know that Christ was perfect Man, having a human body and a human soul to the last. He spoke in our name.'

Dr. Klausner writes that the passages concerning the goodness of God show how alien the thought would have been to Jesus that he himself was divinity within the Godhead (*JN* pp.364/5). About *Matthew* 20:23 Klausner points out that it was far from Jesus' mind to believe that *all* power was vested in him: 'In the Messianic Age the true redeemer and the final power is God himself: The Messiah is but his most important medium' (ibid.,p.305). *Matthew* 24:36 is also quoted as proof that Jesus never regarded himself as omniscient as God, 'he and the Father are not equal in knowledge'. When Jesus asks the Father to let the cup pass from him and when he cries out on the cross, he addresses himself to God, making the distinction quite clear. Finally, Dr. Klausner draws our attention to the fact that as pharisaic Jew Jesus must have believed in the absolute oneness and unity of God. 'Nor did he regard himself as Son of God in the later, trinitarian sense; for a Jew to believe such a thing is quite inconceivable – it is wholly contradictory to the belief in the absolute unity' (ibid. p.377).

Graves and Podro, too, think that the words concerning goodness are vital, since they 'cut at the root of the Gentile conception of Jesus as God' (*NGR*, p.521). They consider it likely that Jesus' refusal in *Matthew* 20:23 was connected with the Talmudic vision of the Heavenly Jerusalem of which Rabbi Johanan said: 'The Jerusalem of the world to come is not like unto the Jerusalem of this world. Into the Jerusalem of this world all may enter who will, but into the Jerusalem of the world to come only those may enter who are appointed thereto . . . ' (*Baba Batra* 75b). Of *Matthew* 24:6 and *Mark* 13:32 they state that the text is a Midrash on *Isaiah* 63:4. According to the Talmud [*Hagigah* 16a and some other passages] the angels knowledge of God's plan was limited to hints caught while they listened . . . 'from behind the curtain' . . . the precise day and hour of the Son of Man's coming would remain a close secret from them . . . (op.cit., p.634).

It is obvious that the above-quoted passages can be understood only if and when we realise that Jesus did not speak from a position of divinity, but as a man who knew and emphasised that all his power was from the Father. Had he identified himself with the Source of all Power, these texts would be completely meaningless.

On the right hand of God

Not only Jesus himself, but his apostles and disciples, and the evangelists all made it clear that the Almighty might favour his Christ in every respect, but that Christ himself is being distinct from God. Even the expression *made* is misleading, since it had never entered their minds that such an identification was conceivable. Here are a few examples:

'. . . against the Lord and against his Christ . . .' *Acts* 4:26

'. . . God was with him [Christ] . . .' *Rom.* 10:38

'. . . Christ was made of the seed of David according to the flesh, and declared to be the Son of God with power according to the Spirit . . .' *Rom.* 1:3/4

'. . . as Christ was raised up from the dead by the Father . . .' *Rom.* 6:4

'. . . [God] raised up Jesus from the dead . . . he that raised up Christ from the dead . . .' *Rom.* 8:11

'. . . God hath both raised up the Lord and will also raise up us by his own power . . .' *1 Cor.* 6:14

'. . . there is but one God, the Father . . . and one Lord Jesus Christ' *1 Cor.* 8:6

'. . . the head of every man is Christ . . . and the head of Christ is God . . .' *1 Cor.* 11:3

'. . . by man came death, by man also came the resurrection of the dead . . .' [Adam – Jesus] *1 Cor.* 15:21

'. . . he [Christ] shall have delivered up the kingdom to God the Father . . .' *1 Cor.* 15:24

'. . . And when all things shall be subdued unto him [God] then shall the Son also himself be subject unto him, that God may be all in all . . .' *1 Cor* 15:28

'. . . Blessed be God, even the Father of our Lord Jesus Christ, the Father of mercies and the God of all comfort . . .' *2 Cor* 1:3

'. . . For there is one God, and one mediator between God and men, the man Jesus Christ . . .' *1 Tim.* 2:5

Invoking God *and* Jesus, the New Testament always mentions the two names separately:

'Therefore let all the house of Israel know assuredly that God hath made the same Jesus, whom ye have crucified, both Lord and Christ . . .' *Acts* 2:36

'. . . Jesus of Nazareth, a man approved of God among you . . . *Acts 2:22*

'. . . whom [Jesus] God hath raised up . . .' *Acts 2:24*

'. . . and killed the Prince of life [Jesus] whom God hath raised from the dead . . .' *Acts 3:15*
'. . . by the name of Jesus of Nazareth, whom ye crucified, whom God raised from the dead . . .' *Acts 4:10*
'There is: one God and Father of all who is above all . . .' *Acts 4:6*
'The God of our fathers raised up Jesus . . . him hath God exalted with his right hand to be a Prince and a Saviour . . .' *Acts 5:30/1*
'Paul, an apostle of Christ by the will of God . . .' *Col 1:1*
'Paul, unto the Church of the Thessalonians . . . in God and the Father and in the Lord Jesus Christ . . . from God our Father and the Lord Jesus Christ . . .' *1 Tess. 1:1*
'. . . by the commandment of God our Saviour, and the Lord Jesus Christ our hope . . .' *1 Tim. 1:1*
'. . . to God the Judge of all . . . and to Jesus the mediator . . .' *Hebrews 12:23/4*
'. . . the God of peace that brought again from the dead our Lord Jesus . . .' *Hebrews 13:20*
'For Christ is not entered into the holy place . . . now to appear in the presence of God for us . . .' *Hebrews 9:24*
'James, a servant of God, and our Lord Jesus Christ . . .' *James 1:1*
'Blessed be the God and Father of our Lord Jesus Christ . . .' *1 Peter 1:3*
'. . . the knowledge of God, and of Jesus our Lord . . .' *2 Peter 1:2*
'. . . from God the Father, and from the Lord Jesus Christ, the Son of the Father . . .' *2 John 3*
'. . . sanctified by God the Father, and our Lord Jesus Christ . . .' *Jude 1*
'. . . denying the *only* Lord God, and our Lord Jesus Christ' *Jude 4*

On many occasions we find in the Epistles references to both God and Jesus. In a number of these texts the translator played a little trick,

rendering the text	instead of, correctly,
'God and the father of our Lord Jesus Christ'	'the God and Father of our Lord Jesus Christ'
'the mystery of God, and of the Father, and of Christ'	'the mystery of God the father, and of Christ'
'in the sight of God and our Father'	'in the sight of God our Father'
'our Lord Jesus Christ himself and out God even our Father, which have loved us'	' our Lord Jesus Christ himself and out God and Father'

These slight alterations (often punctuations) confuse the reader and make him amenable to the trinitarian approach. Here are some more passages where the distinction between God and Jesus are clear, unlike in the four quoted above: *Rom.* 1:7, *1 Cor.* 1:3, *2 Cor* 11:31, *Gal.* 1:1, *Eph.* 1:1-3 and *17, 5:20 and 6:23, Phil.* 1:2 and 2:9, *Col.* 1:2 and 3, 2:2 and 3:17, *1 Thess.* 1:3, 3:11 and 13, *2 Thess.* 1:1-2, 2:16 and *1 Tim.* 1:2.

On other occasions Christ is described as sitting on the right hand of God, or standing by the throne of the Almighty: *Mark* 16:19, *Acts* 7:55 and 56 *Rom* 8:34, *Col.* 3:1. *Hebrews* 1:3, 10:12, *1 Peter* 3:22, *Rev* 5:7 and 7:10. Jesus himself spoke of the Son of Man sitting on the right hand of God in *Matthew* 26:64, *Mark* 14:62 and *Luke* 22:69, an expression which was probably current in those days. We find it in the Talmud: 'The world to come consists not in eating and drinking, but the righteous sit . . . and enjoy the brightness of the Shekinah . . . ' (*Berachot* 17a, *Kallah Rabb* ii).

In his book on Calvin, Barth says with admiration that in view of the former 'the expression "right hand of God" does not designate a place, but a function, that of "God's lieutenant", the sovereign minister. Christ holds in his hands the power of God. He governs in God's name. Or again: God's power has become his. There is no divine almighty without Jesus Christ. To declare God governs the world amounts to saying: Jesus Christ governs the world.' (*The Faith of the Church*, p.93).

Our Father which art in Heaven

One of the most frequent arguments of the Christians refers to the fact that Jesus used the expression 'Father' in relation to God. He must have been *the* Son of God, if he consistently used the term when speaking of the Almighty.

Professor Stendahl claims that it was 'not unusual for a Jew to call God "Father", but it became distinct *Christian* usage' (*PC*, 9.778). Dummelow argues that the Jews when speaking of God as Father, meant the Father of the nation, while it was Jesus who 'first made the Fatherhood of God the basis of religion' (*OVBC*, p.646). Professor Caird believes he has discovered a momentous difference showing that the Jews would have said 'our Father' (Abinu). but it was Jesus who used the term 'Father' (Abba). He transformed the Fatherhood of God from a theological doctrine into an intense and intimate experience' (*Saint Luke*, p.152). On the other hand Fenton, the commentator of *Matthew*, admits that the phrase and style used in *Matthew* are characteristic of Jewish prayer (*Saint Matthew*, p.100). This may be due to the fact that the Gospel according to *Matthew* is the most Jewish of the four.

It is simply untrue that the Old Testament does not present God as universal Father. Even if God *says*. 'Israel is my firstborn' (*Exod.* 4:22), it merely means that Israel is the first of his children, yet he is the Father of all. In *Deut.* 14:1 we find 'Ye are the children of the Lord your God', and though it may be true that these words refer to the God of Israel: so did the words of Jesus. Talmudic literature is full of examples to the designation of God as Father: 'What shall I do when *my* heavenly Father hath so commanded me?' (*Sifra to Lev.' Qedoshim* 20, 26); 'Since I have done the will of Abba who is in heaven' (*Lev. R.* para 32); followed almost immediately by the phrase 'my Father who is in heaven'. Further examples: 'These buffetings have made me love my heavenly Father' (*Midr. Tehillim* 12:5); 'And God shall call thee Son' (*Ben Sira* 4:10); 'I will exalt the Lord saying, "Thou art *my* Father" (ibid. 51:10); 'Beloved are Israel, for they are called Son of the Highest" (*Aboth* 3:3); and 'even if they are foolish, even if they transgress, even if they are full of blemishes, they are still called Sons' (*Sifra in Deut.*, para. 308).

Dr. Klausner who quotes many of these examples, adds; 'Jesus undoubtedly used the term "Abba, who is in heaven" mainly in the same sense in which it is used in Talmudic literature; God is a merciful Father, good and beneficent to all, from the flowers of the field and the fowls of the air, to the sinful wrongdoer, in whose death God finds no pleasure, but only in his repentance. In this also Jesus is a genuine Jew' (*JN*, p. 378).

We find confirmation of this argument in some of the apocryphal books of the Old Testament:

'. . . he . . . maketh the boast that God is his Father' *Wis.* 2:16
'But thy providence O Father governeth it . . . ' Wis. 14:3
'O Lord, Father and Governor of all my life . . . ' *Eccl.* 23:1
'O Lord, Father and God of my life . . . ' *Eccl.* 23:4

Graves and Podro call the expression 'Our Father which art in heaven' 'One of the three general forms of the address in Jewish liturgy' (*NGR*, p.237).

Let Jesus have the last word against the preposterous argument of many Christian apologists: ' . . . call no man your father upon the earth: for one is your Father, which is in heaven . . . ' (*Matthew* 23:9).

Even if it were true that Jesus made more use of the word 'father' than his contemporaries, it might surprise many readers that he did not always say '*my* Father'. We find the term in various contexts (in the Authorised Version) as follows:

my father	35 times
the father (wrongly translated into '*my* father')	12 times
thy father	3 times
our father	2 times
your father	13 times
the father	63 times
It seems that Jesus used the word 'father' for God	128 times
employing the possessive pronoun '*my*' only	35 times

The Son of God

The nearest Jesus himself came to making the claim that he was the Son of God is recorded in *Mark* 14:61/2, where the High Priest asks him, 'Art thou the Christ, the Son of the Blessed? And Jesus said, "I am ". . .'; and in *Luke* 22:70, 'Then said they all, Art thou then the Son of God? And he said unto them, "Ye say that I am".' As Graves and Podro point out, 'the editor is literally translating an Aramaic or Hebrew idiom, "Amarta" or "Atta amarta", which carried a negative sense, "So you say, but I reserve my opinion"; whereas the corresponding words in Greek and Latin carry a positive sense; "What you say is true"' (*NGR*, p.701). In English both meanings are possible.

A remarkable cleric, J.A.T. Robinson, admits: 'The New Testament says that Jesus was the Word of God; it says that God was in Christ; it says that Jesus is the Son of God, but it does not say that Jesus was God, simply that' (*Honest to God*, p.70). And he continues: 'None of the disciples in the Gospels acknowledged Jesus because he claimed to be God, and the Apostles never went out saying, "This man claims to be God, therefore you must believe in him." Jesus himself said in so many words: "If I claim anything for myself, do not believe me." It is indeed an open question whether Jesus ever claimed to be the Son of God, let alone God' (ibid., p.72).

Not only did the evangelists not claim that Jesus was God but, according to Lietzmann, one of the greatest scholars of Church history, Justin made the following confession before his judges: 'We worship the God of the Christians whom we hold to be the original creator of the whole world, the one God, creator of things visible and invisible; and the Lord Jesus Christ who was predicted by the prophets as the future prophet of salvation for mankind, and as a teacher of noble knowledge' (*The Founding of the Church Universal*, p.109). And even later, about A.D. 200, the presbyters of Noëtos expressed their faith in this statement: 'We also know in truth one God; we know the Christ; we know the Son, suffering as He suffered, dying as He died and risen on the third day, and abiding at the right hand of the Father . . .' (ibid.) Still the distinction between God and Christ is manifest.

Justin's famous baptismal confession, too, declared that God is the Father: 'I believe in God the Father and Lord of all; and in our Saviour Jesus Christ who was crucified under Pontius Pilate; and in the Holy Spirit who prophesied through the prophets' (ibid. p. 110).

In the 19th century Ghillany wrote that Christianity was a branch of gnostic thought, and inasmuch as the disciples believed that Jesus was the Son of God, they understood this in the gnostic sense, believing that the highest of all angels, the 'Son of God' has taken up abode in him' (Schweitzer, *Quest of the Historical Jesus*, p. 167).

Among other recent thinkers, Dr. Drews considered Jesus as having been a pretender to the Jewish throne (developed later in detail by Graves and Podro) who, as king of the Jews, wished to represent the God of Israel before his people. The 'Son of God' meant the ideal king who would free the Jews of the foreign yoke, and re-establish the glory of Israel. In that sense the 'Son of God' was to be acclaimed as a just and righteous ruler, a theocratic king,' thus Conybeare (*The Historical Christ*, p. 11). According to Georges Berguer, people of that epoch believed in divine beings who are subject to human conditions, hence the recurring idea of their relationship in the context of paternity and filiality (*The Life of Jesus*, pp. 52/3). The Muslim scholar, the Khwaja Kamal-ud-Din, thought that in Judaic terminology 'Son of God' meant nearness to God, and nothing else. Kamal points out that in emphasising Jesus' role as Son, the believers soon forgot that the spirit of his teaching attributed much greater importance to his role as our brother, since we are all children of the same Father (Quoted from *Whom Do Men Say that I Am?*, pp. 139/163).

One of the most important Christian theologians of the 20th century, Emil Brunner, waxes poetic: 'The Son of God . . . the first Christians called Him the Word of God . . . who is more than a prophet. One who not only *has* the Word, but *is* the Word! . . . who reveals the mystery of God. No *man* can be that. Man can never be more than a prophet. Above the prophet stands only One who himself equips the prophet, who gives the Word – God . . . Jesus is the Word of God. Jesus is not simply a man like us, but He is God Himself . . . What I can rejoice in every day as a Christian is that God bestows His love upon me in His Son, and that He will give it to all who believe in Him, the Son of God' (*Our Faith*, pp. 64/5).

It seems certain that Jesus *would have thought it robbery to make himself equal to God*. And the very thought of such blasphemy would have been as far from his mind as the thought of robbery itself. Every one of his words shows that his relation to God was based on devotion and worship, and nowhere can we trace the claim made on his behalf for nearly twenty centuries after his death.

The Lord Jesus Christ

A frequent reference to Jesus in the Epistles is 'the Lord Jesus Christ'. How did he, the simple carpenter and itinerant preacher, come by this high-sounding title?

In this connection I am not attempting to present the image of the second person in the trinity, of the everlasting God who is co-equal and co-eternal with the Father, attributes of which the authors of the gospels were no more aware than Jesus himself. I try merely to trace the significance of the title 'Lord' given to Jesus by the devout believers who compiled the gospel stories and the epistles known as works of a number of disciples.

The elevation to this title is stranger still if we realise that 'the Lord' was the name given to Almighty God by the Jews, and to him alone. However, this was the case only where the title was used without the addition of a name. Similarly, in modern English, Spanish, Italian or German, Lord, *Señor, Signore* or *Herr* may refer to God, alternatively these words may be the title or name of a person if it is followed by a proper name. (It is different in French where the term *Seigneur* has disappeared from ordinary usage and always refers to God.) In the same way the Greek κύριος meant master, lord or merely sir, very much of the spirit of the contemporary 'yes, Sir' and 'no, Sir'. The Hebrew words for God were usually *Adonoi* or *Elohim*. When the Seventy translated the Bible (called the Old Testament by the Christians), they rendered *Elohim* by God, and *Adonoi* by Lord, which became interchangeable (with the definite article) as the references to God in modern languages. However, in the New Testament, notably in the Epistles, the meaning of these interchangeable words became more rigid, and the word God was reserved for the Father, while the term Lord preceded the name of Jesus, or Jesus Christ (the Messiah), and sometimes referred to Jesus even if his name did not join it: (*Luke* 7:31 and 10:1) [although some Greek manuscripts omit it], 11:39, 17:5, 18:6 [some manuscripts merely read Jesus], 19:8, 22:31 [some manuscripts omit it].

In the gospel according to Matthew, Jesus is nearly always called

Jesus, and the rare exceptions can be explained easily. On one occasion Jesus calls upon his disciples to collect an ass with her colt, and tells them to reply to anyone trying to intercept them: 'The Lord hath need of them . . . (*Matthew* 21:3). This obviously meant that they were needed for the purposes of God Almighty, not that the Teacher referred to himself as 'the Lord'. Another passage reads: 'Come, see the place where the Lord lay' (*Matthew* 28:6), words spoken by the angel to the woman who came to visit Jesus' tomb. Again, a number of manuscripts omit the word 'Lord' in this instance.

Similarly, in the Gospel according to Mark, we read about the deeds and sayings of Jesus, and not of 'the Lord'. The few occasions where 'the Lord' is referred to: Jesus speaks to the man possessed by devils and cures him, saying 'Go home . . . and tell . . . how great things the Lord hath done for thee' (*Mark* 5:19). The episode with the ass occurs here too, ' . . . if any man say to you, Why do ye this? say ye that the Lord hath need of him' (*Mark* 11:3). In both instances it is obvious that Jesus speaks of God whom the Jews called 'the Lord'. This becomes clearer yet when Jesus himself mentions the Lord: ' . . . the Lord hath shortened those days . . . ' (*Mark* 13:20), and to make the distinction still more obvious, he says in the same speech, ' . . . of that day knoweth no man . . . neither the Son, but the Father.' It is quite evident that speaking of *the Lord* (who shortened those days) he meant the Father. There is one more passage which tells about the farewell scene prior to the ascension of the resurrected Christ: ' . . . after the Lord hath spoken unto them . . . (*Mark* 16:19). This happens to be part of a spurious text probably written by some Pauline scribe to complete the unfinished (or lost part of the) Gospel according to Mark, to complete it. This is the more likely because it finishes with the words, ' . . . and sat on the right hand of God' (ibid.), a Pauline cliché which, incidentally, confirms the distinction between God and Jesus.

Even the Gospel according to John reports about Jesus, and *not* about the Lord. Again in the resurrection story, we encounter the words, 'They have taken the Lord out of the sepulchre . . . ' (*John* 20:2); 'Mary Magdalene . . . told the disciples that she had seen the Lord . . . ' (*John* 20:18); the other disciples said . . . We have seen the Lord' (*John* 21:25); ' . . . that disciple whom Jesus loved saith unto Peter, It is the Lord . . . ' (*John* 21:7; and, ' . . . knowing that it was the Lord . . . ' (*John* 21:12). Apart from *John* 21:7 which in many manuscripts reads 'our Lord', which is very different, the readings of the other passages agree in the manuscripts and shows that Jesus is being referred to as the Lord.

From these facts we may draw diverse conclusions,. Firstly, the expression 'the Lord' had a meaning to the Jewish authors of the gospels, which they were anxious to avoid. Secondly, the few (hardly a dozen) references to Jesus as 'the Lord' are spurious, and possibly later interpolations. The fact that manuscripts differ on this important point shows that later copies were conceivably prepared by men less scrupulous about using this expression. Thirdly, and this is perhaps the most important conclusion: the resurrection stories differ from the gospel texts in a significant manner, since in the former, Jesus is frequently referred to as 'the Lord', just as in the Epistles. The only scholar (to my knowledge) who noticed this difference was the German theologian, Wilhelm Bousset who, I think mistakenly, concluded that the appellation was conferred upon Jesus after his resurrection because it was the resurrection which opened the eyes of the evangelist to his divinity. However, since the gospels themselves were written long after the event, one would think that if it was the resurrection which convinced the authors, they would have called Jesus 'the Lord' throughout! There is another, far weightier possibility. It may be that the early followers of Jesus merely told of his sublime life and tragic death, and that the Pauline doctrine of the resurrected Christ was added to the gospel stories, to each gospel story, at a later date. It is difficult to find another explanation for the discrepancies.

The Pauline Epistles are full of references to the 'Lord Jesus Christ'. This Lord Jesus Christ bears only a vague resemblance to the hero of the gospels. Still, even Paul distinguishes clearly between God and the Lord Jesus Christ as I have shown above, and subsequently did not call God 'the Lord'. It is to this realisation that we owe the interesting rendering of *Phil.* 2:6-7 in the *NEB*: 'For the divine nature was his from the first; yet he did not think to snatch equality with God, but made himself nothing, assuming the nature of a slave' (*NEB*, p. 338).

The statement that Jesus Christ *is* Lord, is based on the Greek text which reads:

πᾶσα γλῶσσα ἐξομολογήσεται ὅτι Κύριος Ἰησοῦς Χριστός εἰς δόξαν Θεοῦ πατρός.

The Authorised Version translates: 'every tongue should confess that Jesus Christ *is* Lord, to the glory of God the Father' (*Phil* 2:11). I suspect that the word ὅτι is an insertion as in so many other texts (see p. 74 of this work). If my assumption is correct and *is* definitely and admittedly an insertion (being printed in italics since it does not appear in the text), we would obtain the much more meaningful statement that 'every tongue should praise the Lord Jesus Christ to the greater glory of God the Father'. Bishop Wordsworth and many other

Christian 'authorities' have arrived at the opposite conclusion and say that this passage shows clearly that Jesus Christ *is* Lord, that is, God. (Wordsworth, *The Holy Bible*, p. 351). I must leave the reader to decide which suggestion seems to him or her more plausible.

The Son of man

Jesus frequently used the expression 'Son of man', for instance, 'The foxes have holes, and the birds have nests, but the Son of man hath no where to lay his head . . .' (*Matthew* 8:20); ' . . . and then shall they see the Son of man coming in the clouds with great power and glory . . .' (*Mark* 13:26) 'The Son of man is come eating and drinking . . .' (*Luke* 7:34); and ' . . . ye shall see the . . . angels of God descending upon the Son of man . . .' (*John* 1:51). As can be seen, the expression is used in every gospel, and altogether 81 times in the four.

There has always been much disagreement as to the meaning of this strange appellation, *bar-nasha*, Son of man. It appears in the Bible where we read ' . . . one like the Son of man came with the clouds of heaven' (*Dan.* 7:13). Speaking to Ezekiel, God uses the expression on many occasions (throughout the Book of Ezekiel). Its use in Daniel and in the Book of Enoch prompted the view that the expression was a Messianic title long before the time of Jesus. This is the opinion of several modern authorities, such as the Protestant Griffith Thomas (*Principles of Theology*, p. 33) and the Jewish Samuel Sandmel (*A Jewish Understanding of the New Testament*, p. 129), although the latter admits that possibly in Aramaic the term could have been used 'in that very pregnant meaning, or else it could have had the simplest of meanings, "I".'

Other scholars assert that the expression denoted 'man' and nothing more. As early as in the 16th century, the Bishop of Aix, Gilbert Génébrard, wrote that 'Son of man' did not refer merely to Jesus but to all men. Later Hugo Grotius, Hans Lietzmann, Heinrich Paulus and many others pointed out that if and when Jesus called himself 'Son of man' he meant 'man'. Klausner believes that Jesus used the term instead of *I* or *man*, in a manner of the English 'one' for the third person singular (in German *man*).

Jesus may have used it to distinguish man from the beasts and the angels. Nevertheless, Klausner feels it necessary to add: 'But even after passing over all the passages where it means "I" or "man", there still remain many instances where Jesus used the expression deliberately: and he used it expressly for the reason that while in Aramaic . . . it had not exceptional meaning in the ears of ordinary people, it had, for the more enlightened hearers, an added significance as in Ezekiel and Daniel. By means of this title he partially divulged his Messiahship but more frequently concealed it . . . And still further, he hinted that he was the Son of man in the sense in which his contemporaries understood the expression in the Book of Daniel . . . the Son of man who was to come "with the clouds in heaven" . . . and who was to possess the kingdom of the King-Messiah, the everlasting kingdom' (*JN*, p.257).

Albert Schweitzer thinks that Jesus comprehended and indeed assumed the part of the Messianic Son of man, which became his 'tragic and triumphant fate' (*QHJ*, pp.368/9).

Many Christian theologians also believe that the term expressed the faith of Jesus in his mission. 'Jesus did not deny His Messianic vocation. In the symbolic words about "the rising after three days", He indicated that His rejection and His death would not be a defeat but rather the necessary steps to His becoming the Christ. He was to be the Christ only as a suffering and dying Christ. Only as such *is* He the Christ, or as He called Himself more mysteriously, the Son of man' (Tillich, *The Shaking of the Foundation*, pp.147/8).

Perhaps the problem is not quite as mysterious as the apologists would have us believe. It is likely that the secret is divulged in the Acts of the Apostles, a writing which speaks of Jesus as a Servant or 'child' of God but, like the gospels, never calls him God. In it Peter tells his listeners about Jesus, the Christ and divine messenger foretold by the prophets: 'Jesus of Nazareth, a man approved by God among you by miracles and wonders and signs, which God did by him in the midst of you . . . ' (*Acts* 2:22). This is how Peter saw his Master, Christ: a man approved by God. This is how Jesus may have seen himself: the Son of man accepted by the Most High.

In the beginning was the word

In the beginning was the word. It was Heraclitus who introduced the *Logos* into philosophy. Of his preserved texts this is one of the most significant:

οὐκ ἐμοῦ, ἀλλὰ τοῦ λόγου ἀκούσαντες ὁμολογέν
σοφόν ἐστιν ἐν πάντα εἶναι (*To Biblion*, p.12).

Freely translated, we may say: 'If you do not hear *me* but understand the Logos (reason, word, meaning, significance) you will comprehend the wisdom of seeing, One in All and All in One.' In another passage he says:

Ψυχῆς ἐστι λόγος ἑαυτός αὐξῶν (ibid., p.22), that is, 'The soul creates the Logos which grows through itself or, more correctly, it is through its creation, the Logos, that the Self grows. This great philosopher elevated the Logos to a creative, unifying principle which, centuries later, inspired Philo, the Alexandrian Jew, to develop his own idea of the Logos.

Philo, a mystical theist, regarded the Logos as the created, externalised 'reason' of God. In the later gnostic interpretation of his philosophy, the Logos appeared as the meeting point between God and man: the point where All meet in One, and where the One can reveal himself to All. The way to freedom lies in meditation upon the Logos (prayer to God). However, Philo would not have dreamt of identifying the Logos (an emanation of God) with the Messiah (a servant of God), or with God himself.

The Alexandrian atmosphere in which Philo flourished was heavy with a quaint symbolism which merged Greek and Judaic concepts, and produced his strange philosophy. The Alexandrian Jews of the first century B.C. believed in a Mediator between God and man, who was sometimes called Sophia (wisdom – fem. noun), and at other times Logos. One of their number wrote the apocryphal scripture known as the *Wisdom of Solomon* which presents Wisdom as a Spirit who is of God and with God, yet a distinct personality – the origin of the Holy Ghost. He (or rather She) is reminiscent of the World Spirit of Heraclitus and even more of the three Spirits with Ahura Mazda, the supreme godhead of the Zoroastrians, one being Vohu Mana, the Archangel of Truth, the other Spenta Manyu, the Holy spirit, and the third Vahista Manu, God's Mind. The Logos plays a similar part in Jewish-Christian gnosticism, into which it enters via the philosophy of the Alexandrian School.

Philo bridged the gulf that yawned between the world of the senses and the infinitely lofty, unknowable, unnameable God by means of 'Powers' which he also calls 'Ideas' and 'Angels', among which he distinguishes six as chief who, like the Six of the Zoroastrian religion, guard the throne of God and act as his ministers in the government of the universe. First among these mediatory Powers stands the Logos who also appears as the essential source of the others and, accordingly, as the 'central mediator of all divine action and revelation'. Philo calls him 'the eldest, the firstborn son of God, the oldest angel, the beginning, the Logos and the name of God, His image and the archetype of mankind' (Pfleiderer, *The Early Christian Conception of Christ*, pp.26/7). Note the reference to Ideas and Angels which show, respectively, Greek and Jewish notions, the merger of which resulted in Philo's doctrine. Note also the role of the Logos, the 'oldest angel' which corresponds entirely to the Vohu Mana of Ahura Mazda.

It is obvious that the ideas of Alexandrian Jews were widespread in the 1st century A.D., when the powerful verses of the Gospel according to John were born:

> 'In the beginning was the Word, and the
> Word was with God and the Word was God.
> The same was in the beginning with God
> All things were made by him; and without
> him not anything that was made
> In him was life; and the life was the
> light of man.
> And the light shineth in the darkness
> and the darkness comprehended it not.' *(John* 1:1-4)

The translation from the Greek opens up many unanswered and, perhaps, unanswerable questions. The passage that carried weighty implications, runs: καὶ Θεὸς ἦν ὁ λόγος and was translated in the Authorised Version: '... and the Word was God'. Many authorities have wondered about the unusual construction, since normally 'God' would be ὁ Θεός, (the God). The omission of the definite article may disguise the corruption of the word θεῖος (divine), which would explain the discrepancy. J.A.T. Robinson suggests that there has been no corruption, but a skilled endeavour to steer between the two possibilities (*Honest to God*, p.71). He commends the *NEB* which, according to Robinson, succeeds in interpreting correctly the author's intention: 'And what God was, the Word was'. This of course presupposes that we accept the claim that Jesus was not the Logos 'made flesh', but that he was the Logos before he was born, and it is by no means certain that the author meant it that way.

Throughout history, Christian scholars have regarded the text as supreme confirmation for their deification of Jesus. Augustine is supported by the authority of many Church Fathers (Chrysostom, Basil, Hilary, Theophil) who regarded the Prologue as evidence for the view that 'the Son' was not circumscribed by any limits of space; and that he was without time, but never without God (Chrysostom, *Hom.* 3).

According to Bishop Barnes it was John's Logos which became 'the highest level of early Christian speculation as to the nature of Jesus' (*The Rise of Christianity*, p.94). The Logos idea which probably originated with Heraclitus was later taken up by Zeno and the stoics. Stoicism was an ethical creed acclaimed by many educated Romans, which explains how certain aspects of its philosophy reached Alexandria and Philo. Bishop Barnes points out that 'after this introduction the term Logos is never used again [in the gospels] but the belief that Jesus *was* the Logos, the Christ, the Son of God, runs through the New Testament. It is perhaps unfortunate that the Bible translates Logos by "the Word", for the term entirely fails to convey to the uninstructed reader the meaning and association which belong to it' (ibid.).

Professor Leonard in the *CC* (p.975) and Professor Barrett in the *PC* both claim that the passage proves conclusively that Jesus was from eternity, was with God, was God. They seem to be quite unaffected by the arguments which have been raging about this obscure text.

'The Word', in the mind of the author(s) of the Fourth Gospel, possibly meant the purpose of God which, potentially present and actually revealed, was with God and one with the unfolding divine principle. When the Word became flesh, that is, when one man in space and time, in human form, gave expression to the divine purpose (the will of God), God and man became one in the sense that two separate roads joined in one common road. This common road is what the Christians call the Incarnation, and 'the Word' is that manifestation in God which gave the Incarnation its divine attribute.

Thou art Christ, the Son of the living God

It happened in Caesarea Philippi that Jesus asked his disciples who people thought that he was. After some suggestions which were not even considered, Simon Peter exclaimed: 'Thou art the Christ, the Son of the living God' (*Matthew* 16:16). The same story is told in Mark, where the exclamation is somewhat shorter: 'Thou art Christ' (8:29, and in *Luke*: 'The Christ of God' (9:20).

These momentous words may well have been the inspiration which started Jesus off on his way to Christhood. Whether he regarded them as a welcome revelation of an old dream, or a sudden flash of lightning which lit up his path – there is no going back once those fateful words were spoken. It is recorded that he did not wish the world to know, but there is no doubt that the idea had taken root in his own mind.

Bernard Shaw believes that this event presented that special challenge which changed an itinerant preacher into an inspired prophet: ' . . . a startling change occurs. One day, after the disciples had discouraged him for a long time by the misunderstanding of his mission, and their speculations as to whether he is one of the old prophets come again, and if so which, his disciple Peter suddenly solves the question by exclaiming, "Thou art the Christ, the Son of the living God". At this Jesus is . . . pleased and excited . . . [and] becomes obsessed with a conviction of his divinity . . . though he forbids his disciples to mention it to others . . . ' (Preface to *Androcles and the Lion*, pp.27/8).

We may not agree with Shaw, but there is no doubt that it would affect the equilibrium of a person if he began to think of himself as the Messiah, the favoured servant of God, who would experience supreme triumph and, possibly, great suffering.

Dr. Klausner also considers this incident as a turning point in the life of Jesus. 'A great event . . . happened then, Jesus was deeply affected to find that . . . his disciples had not despaired and . . . some of them recognised him as the Messiah . . . The three synoptics are, however, unanimous in recording that Jesus forbade his disciples to tell anyone what they had learned' (*JN*, p.300).

The Christian Church has always considered the Incarnation to be the principle theme of the doctrine. Cardinal Newman called it the central truth of the gospels, and the source of all Christian principles. Much is made of the idea that Divinity has taken up human form in space and time – a reassuring thought for men fighting off their fear of insignificance. It *is* a basic tenet of Christianity which makes for both its strength and fragility. The idea of Incarnation is due to the hellenisation of Jewish thought, still without its fatal sequel of a Person in the Godhead who was fully Man, yet fully God. The Word which has become flesh was the Christ, the anointed servant of god, in whom God's purpose held sway because in Christ man had completely abandoned himself to God.

The Greek word Χριστός means Messiah. The addition, 'the Son of the living God', is an ancient Hebrew expression and merely indicates a human being whose contact with the Godhead is direct. As we have seen above, even this expression is not found in the other gospels.

The term 'Christ' later became known as a proper name rather than a religious title which it originally was. A few outstanding examples of its use are the already quoted passages, *Matthew* 16:16, *Mark* 8:29 and *Luke* 9:20. The angel speaking to the shepherds about the birth of Jesus, says: 'For unto you is born this day in the city of David a Saviour which is Christ the Lord' (*Luke* 2:11). The Greek expression used is: Χριστὸς Κύριος which corresponds to the 'Lord Christ' rather than 'Christ the Lord'. As mentioned above, the expression 'the Lord Jesus Christ', is so frequent in the Acts and the Epistles, is very rare in the gospels, and the suspicion that the birth story, too, is a later addition, is not quite unfounded.

While there is little doubt that Jesus regarded himself as the Messiah, at least between Caesarea Philippi and the Crucifixion, the words 'I am the Messiah' were never actually spoken by him. It is also clear that in the Acts and the Epistles, it is not the teacher Jesus but the resurrected Lord Jesus Christ, 'the man approved of God', who is the central figure. However, even the Lord Jesus Christ was only a servant of God, perhaps even the Son of God, but never God himself.

I am that I am

When God appeared to Moses on the Mountain of Horeb, Moses inquired as to the name of God, whereupon the Almighty replied: 'I am that I am . . . Thus shalt thou say unto the children of Israel. I AM hath sent me unto you . . . (*Exo.* 3:14). This Ehyeh (I am) is frequently used in Hebrew scripture to signify God. The Bible (Old Testament) abounds in passages where the first person singular of the word 'to be' is joined to the idea of the Almighty. This is not the usage of the verb in relation to a predicate or an adjective: it is a total, an exclusive, I AM.

Moses and his fellow-Jews referred to the Almighty as *Elohim* which meant God, but his name was a secret not revealed to men. The first verse of the Torah began with the words, *Bereshit bara Elohim* – 'In the beginning created God' (*Gen.* 1:1). 'As "the beginning" means that non-being was charged with time and conscious existence, this sentence may indicate that *God being* was the beginning and that *Elohim* is the object, and not the subject of the sentence . . . Elohim is the name of God, which guarantees the continued existence of creation insofar as it represents the union of the hidden subject *Mi* (Who) and the hidden object *Eleh* (the determinable world). The Hebrew word *Mi* and *Eleh* have the same consonants as the complete word *Elohim* . . . The mystical Nothing which lies before the division of the primary idea into the Knower and the Known . . . this knowledge can be no more than an occasional and intuitive flash which illuminates the human heart, as sunbeams play on the surface of water . . . ' (Scholem, *Major Trends in Jewish Mysticism*, p. 221).

Elohim was merely the word for God, but Moses wanted to know his *name*, since knowledge of the name gave the 'Knower' power over the 'Known', as Adam gained power over the things he named. The revelation which Moses received was incomplete: it was not a name in the proper sense of the word but a statement of the most sublime form of conscious existence: 'I am that I am.' *Ehyeh* equals I am, of which the third person singular is *Jahwe* which equals 'He is'. Now Moses knew how God wished to be referred to, without revealing the magic of a name – and Moses had to be content with the affirmation of a divine *being*. The first person and third person singular of the verb *hayah* or *hawah*, which might be present or future tense, came to be the hidden name of God. It is both the divine Actuality and Potentiality which find expression in this affirmation. The Greek translation reads: ἐγὼ εἰμι ὁ ὤν, the term used by the Seventy.

In writing the Jews use *Yahweh*, but they never read the name. Instead, they read Adonoi (Lord)· or *Elohim* (God). We do not know (apart from the Moses legend) the origin of the name *Yahweh*, but it is likely that it was adopted from the Jews at an early period of their history and not copied from the pantheon of their neighbours. The Masoretic text attached vowels to the original Hebrew *tetragrammaton* YHWH which resulted in the mistaken 'Jehovah', It is likely that the original correct pronunciation *was Yahweh*.

The I, Thou and He manifestations of the Divine played a great part in Jewish mysticism. 'God in the most deeply hidden of His manifestations, when He . . . has decided to launch upon His work of creation, is called He. God in the complete unfolding of His being . . . in which He becomes capable of being perceived by "the reason of the heart" . . . is called Thou. But God in his supreme manifestation, where the fullness of His being finds its final expression in the I . . . is the Shekhina, the presence and immanence of God in the whole creation' (ibid., p.216).

Considering these speculations, the reader may be interested to see how a Jewish translation from Hebrew into English of the momentous story of *Exod.* 3:13-15 deals with the subject: 'And Moses said unto God, Behold if I come unto the children of Israel, and say unto them, the God of your fathers hath sent me unto you; and they say to me. What is his name? what shall I say unto them? And God said unto Moses I WILL BE THAT I WILL BE; and he said, thus shalt thou say unto the children of Israel, I WILL BE hath sent me to you. And God said moreover unto Moses, Thus shalt thou say unto the children of Israel, THE EVERLASTING ONE, the god of Abraham, the God of Isaac, and the God of Jacob, hath sent me unto you: This is my name for ever, and this is my memorial unto all generations' (*A Hebrew Bible* – Masoretic text translated by Isaac Leeser).

It may be farfetched to suggest that many difficult and obscure passages of the New Testament become lucid and acceptable if we assume that Jesus used the ἐγὼ εἰμι (I am) to denote the divine name. We have seen above that this name is never spoken, only written, and many Jews considered it blasphemy to utter the name which could then be mistaken for the ordinary first person singular. This may be the reason why many members of his audience accused Jesus of blasphemy. I have no proof for this assertion and, indeed, sometimes the context seems to give the lie to my interpretation. However, it is possible and even probable that the Greek-speaking authors of the gospels did not understand this peculiarity of Jewish reference to God, and adapted the text to give some meaning to utterances which might otherwise have sounded, to them, meaningless. I submit to the reader a few such passages for his consideration.

Passage	Original	Authorised Version	Suggested changes	Suggested translation
John 4:26	λέγει αὐτῇ ὁ Ἰησοῦς, Ἐγώ εἰμι ὁ λαλῶν σοι.	Jesus saith unto her that I speak unto thee am *he*.	Removes *he* which is an arbitrary insertion.	Jesus saith unto her; God is speaking to you.
John 8:24	ἐάν γὰρ μὴ πιστεύσητε ὅτι ἐγώ εἰμι, ἀποθανεῖσθε ἐν ταῖς ἁμαρτίαις ὑμῶν.	... for if ye believe not that I am *he*, ye shall die in your sins.	*He* is an arbitrary insertion. Ignore 'that', a doubtful conjunctive.	... for if you do not believe (in) God, you die in (your) error.
John 8:28	Ὅταν ὑψώσητε τὸν υἱὸν τοῦ ἀνθρώπου, τότε γνώσεσθε ὅτι ἐγώ εἰμι.	When ye have lifted up the Son of man, then shall ye know that I am *he*.	*He* is an arbitrary insertion. Ignore the doubtful conjunctive.	When you have exalted the Son of man then shall you know God. (Perhaps: When you know God, you will exalt man.)
John 8:58	πρὶν Ἀβραὰμ γενέσθαι, ἐγώ εἰμι.	Before Abraham was, I am.		Before Abraham was God.
John 13:19	ἀπ᾽ ἄρτι λέγω ὑμῖν πρὸ τοῦ γενέσθαι, ἵνα πιστεύητε ὅταν γένηται ὅτι ἐγώ εἰμι.	... when it is come to pass, ye may believe that I am *he*.	Remove *he* which is an arbitrary insertion. Ignore the doubtful conjunctive.	... when this happens you may believe in God.
John 18:6	ὡς οὖν εἶπεν αὐτοῖς ὅτι Ἐγώ εἰμι, ἀπῆλθαν εἰς τὰ ὀπίσω, καὶ ἔπεσαν χαμαί.	As soon then as he had said unto them, I am *he*, they went backward and fell to the ground	Remove *he* which is an arbitrary insertion. Ignore the doubtful conjunctive.	As soon as he uttered the secret name of God, they retreated and prostrated themselves.
Mark 13:6 also Luke 21:8	πολλοὶ γαρ ἐλεύσονται ἐπὶ τῷ ὀνόματί μου, λέγοντες ὅτι ἐγώ εἰμι.	... for many shall come in my name, saying I am *Christ*.	*Christ* is an arbitrary insertion. Ignore the doubtful conjunctive.	... for many shall come in the name of God speaking of God.

Almost all these passages occur in the Gospel according to John, the latest and perhaps least reliable witness of the four. It is strongly influenced by the Pauline version of Jesus as the resurrected Lord Jesus

Christ, and although Godhead is never claimed for Jesus even in this gospel, passages abound which enable Christian apologists to maintain that by implication Jesus was regarded as God. However, 'implication' is always governed by prejudged concepts and *a priori* considerations: the reader who is perhaps not prone to such bias will possibly disagree with statements read into the texts by 'implication'.

I believe that a stricter critical approach will also show that even the Lord Jesus Christ of the New Testament is presented as the supreme mouthpiece of God; the mediator, or if you like, the Prime Angel, the *Metatron* of the Jewish mystics, but never as God who is, to Jews like Jesus and his disciples, One and Indivisible.

3
The God Christ

The new creation

'There is a new creation; the old things are passed away: behold they are become new' (*2 Cor.* 5:17), exclaims Paul. He does not suspect that the new creation – the Christian Church – would before long, become the target of his dread curse uttered in another Epistle: 'But though we, or an angel from heaven, preach any other gospel unto you than that which we have preached to you, let him be accursed' (*Gal* 1:8).

As I have shown in the preceding chapters, there is no text in the New Testament which supports the claim for the Godhead of Jesus, nowhere did *he* call himself God. The curse of Paul therefore would descend upon those who, in contradiction to Scripture, preached another gospel than the one he preached. In fact, his curse is reinforced by the closing words of *Revelation*: 'If any man shall add unto these things, God shall add unto him the plagues that are written in this book: And if any man shall take away from the words of the book of this prophecy, God shall take away his part out of the book of life . . .' (*Rev* 22:18/19).

Calling upon their heads the great curse of the apostles, the apologists of the Christian doctrine have indeed frequently added to the teaching of the New Testament, and also 'taken away' from it where they found it expedient. It is my intention to trace here briefly the tragic story of the Teacher's elevation to Godhead.

Pringle-Pattison writes in his *Studies in the Philosophy of Religion* that the human mind tends to personify abstractions. Theology calls this process hypostatisation and tends to present imagery in the sphere of religion as historical fact. Pringle-Pattison believed that it was for this reason that the Christians found it necessary to endow Jesus with the attributes of divinity, although 'in order to give us authentic tidings of

... God' it would not have been necessary to elevate him to Godhead (*Whom Do Men Say that I Am*, (pp.54/5).

It is a fact, however, that this insidious tendency triumphed and Jesus was required to be God. When the teaching spread among the nations, and eventually broke its links with Judaism, the Christian Church was born or, in the words of I.A. Dorner, 'the awareness of the deity of Christ became free and unrestricted'. Unrestricted is, indeed, the right word: for many pagan concepts, doctrines, sacraments and rites found their way into the 'good tidings'.

As long as the doctrine was spreading among 'the lost sheep of Israel', it was safe from heathen adulteration, since ' . . . to the Jew, God is ONE, and whatever He does is done by Him in the fullness of his Unity-Christianity, because it deified a man, has made concessions to heathenism and idolatry' (C.G. Montefiore, *Jewish Conception of Christianity*). And in his *Ideal Prophet*, Kamal-ud-Din exclaims: 'Ought not we Muslims to resent it, if we find our prophet Jesus divested of the most exalted position a man could claim, Divine Messengership, and given the office of a pagan deity?'

The origins of the myths which 'required' the elevation of Jesus to Godhead, are lost in pre-history. According to Jung, the redeemer-god and the first man are archetypal concepts which can be found in any religion: in the Purusha of Indian philosophy, in the Persian idea of Gayomart, the original man who falls victim to darkness from which he must be freed to redeem the world. From Gayomart through the gnostic redeemer-figures there is a straight road to Christ, the Saviour, who through his life and sacrificial death shows men how, in the place of the world of the Father, lost for ever, can be established the World of the Son. Through the Father 'incarnating' in the son, man discovers the secret of divinity: the original unity of God and Man which is now defined and comprehensible (C.G. Jung, *Psychology and Religion: West and East*, pp.134/5).

More important even than the Vedic and Zoroastrian influences, the Mithras cult had a strong impact on Christianity. Mithras was the son of Ormuzd, and as a god of light himself, he engaged the powers of darkness, Ahriman and his host, in a bitter struggle. Mithras triumphed and cast his adversaries into the nether world. Mithras, too, raised the dead and will find them at the end of time. He, too, will relegate the wicked to hell and establish the millennial kingdom. According to the Mithraic myth, he would undergo a cultic transformation into a bull, or for the benefit of the poorer assemblies, into a ram. He would be killed and his flesh and blood (or wine representing his blood) would be consumed by the faithful. The pictorial and sculpted scenes presenting this sacred meal were the ones which enraged Christian sensitivities, and many smashed-up Mithraeums show the traces of the fury of Christian iconoclasts. Tertullian mentions (*De* praescr., 40) this ritual of the Mithras which was a 'devilish imitation of the Eucharist'. He also mentions that the Mithraists enacted the resurrection.

The adherents of Mithras believed that by eating the bull's flesh and drinking its blood they would be born again, just as life itself has been created anew from the blood of the bull. Participation in this rite would give not only physical strength but lead to the immortality of the soul and to eternal light. Justin also mentioned the similarity between the Mithras ritual and the Eucharist, and there exists a medieval text published by Cumont which contains these words of Zoroaster: 'He who will not eat of my body and drink of my blood, so that he will be made one with me and I with him, the same shall not know salvation . . . ' It is, of course, impossible to establish whether this text, being of a later date, than the New Testament, was inspired by the Christian formula or *vice versa*, but it shows the fundamental affinity between the rite mentioned by Justin and the rite of the Eucharist.

Drews, too, believes that it was the influence of Persian, notably Mithraic, thought which led to the gradual transformation of the human figure of Jesus into a Godhead. Robertson thinks that the rock-tomb resurrection of Jesus is a direct transference of Mithras' rock-birth, and that Jesus also became a sun-god like Mithras, so that they share their birthday at the winter- solstice. Robertson, Niemojewski, Volney and others assert that as son-god Jesus had twelve apostles representing the twelve houses of the zodiac. It may be mentioned here that the Greeks celebrated the birthday of their sun-god Apollo at the winter- solstice. Another important point is the fact that the Christian Church abandoned the Jewish sabbath (contrary to the commandment of their God) in favour of the Mithraic day of the sun.

Conybeare, though he defends the figure of Jesus against the speculations of Drews and Robertson , says emphatically that 'all sorts of Christological cobwebs were within a few generations spun around his [Jesus'] head to the effacement of both the teacher and of what he taught. But in the earliest body of evangelical tradition, as we can reconstruct it from the first three gospels, there is little or nothing that is not essentially Jewish and of the soil of Judaea. The borrowings of Christianity from pagan neighbours began with the flocking of gentile converts into the new Messianic society' (*The Historical Christ*, p.79).

Competition with Mithraism, which had a strong hold on many

parts of the Roman Empire, prompted the Christians of the 2nd and 3rd centuries to transplant into Christianity those aspects of Mithraic mythology which seemed to have mass appeal. Mithras, the god of light, was also the embodiment of Truth, the defender of the righteous, the Mediator (Plutarch, *De Iside*, c.46).

Justin Martyr speaks of the Mithraic initiation rite with 'bread and a cup of water' (*Apol.*, 1:66). Origen mentions Mithraic doctrine, which, according to him, was borrowed from Semitic sources, and which speaks of the soul's return to heaven (*Contra Celsum*, 6:21). The Emperor Julian, a convert to Mithras, tells us that the god was a guide to Everlasting Bliss, the Protector of the Living, a Comforter of departing souls, and a Judge of the Dead (*Convivium*, c.336). Baptism, communion, doctrines of salvation, sin, righteousness and damnation, were all features the two rival religions had in common. For this reason it was important to elevate Jesus to the divine rank Mithras held, in order to enable him to compete with the rock-born god.

However, it was not only Mithras whose mythology bore arresting resemblance to the myths that sprang up among the Christians. Bishop Barnes tells us that the possible etymological origin of the name Dionysus is 'son of god'. This god's frenzied worshippers, playing wild music, sought his incarnation in a bull, ram or goat which they tore to pieces. They devoured the raw flesh and drank the blood in an orgiastic communion. This primitive rite was later replaced by a more sophisticated one, as for instance the mysteries at Eleusis. Another redeemer-figure was Attys, the husband of Cybele, the Great Mother. He rose again from the dead, and his blood was alleged to help man on the road to salvation. The cult of Isis and Osiris is also reminiscent of Christian practices. At the centre of its ceremonies was the passion and resurrection of Osiris, and the veneration of these gods took place in services conducted by tonsured priests in rich linen vestments, who employed public prayer, hymns, litanies, temple choirs and holy water. 'The morning services' showed 'Isis richly attired for adoration – a veritable Egyptian Madonna . . . worshipped as the "mother of sorrows" . . . ' (*The Rise of Christianity*, pp. 55/58).

Berguer also links these religions to the beginning of Christianity. 'Father-gods abound on all sides . . . Zeus pater . . . Earth Mother . . . Mithra, creator of all things and Father . . . Helios (the sun-god) who speaks in the name of the mystic, presents himself to Mithras as "his son begotten today" . . . Cybele, the mother of the gods' (*The Life of Jesus*, pp. 52/3). In another passage Berguer speaks of the 'frequent appearance in ancient religions of father- gods and son-gods (Krishna/Indra, Serapis/Osiris, Osiris/Horus, Ormuzd/Mithras. In the Osiris and Tammuz cults we find accounts of the births at the winter-solstice, of passion, death and resurrection, and festival meals which correspond even in detail to Christian observance' (ibid., p.77).

Believest thou?

At this juncture we arrive at the point of no return. Once the prophet and mouthpiece of God has become the only 'begotten' Son, the supreme mediator between God and His creation, there is only one step from his becoming God, and even a manifestation of the Godhead who shares with him eternity and omnipotence.

The authors of the synoptic gospels carefully avoid this trap. The Pauline and Johannite schools almost go to the brink, but take care not to topple over. Later, Christians went the whole way, and the teacher Jesus, the Lord Jesus Christ of Paul, became Christ the God, co-eternal and co-equal with the Father, God of the same substance 'upholding all things by the word of his power' (*Hebrews* 1:3). In the apocryphal Epistle of Barnabas he is already called 'Lord of the whole world' and Ignatius of Antioch in his seven Epistles speaks of Christ as a man elevated by God to be 'united with the Father . . . at God's right hand before the ages and revealed at the end of them'. Very soon even this fine distinction disappeared. About A.D. 200 Hippolitus of Rome introduced the question to be asked of the candidate for baptism: 'Believest thou in Jesus Christ begotten by the Holy Spirit and the Virgin Mary?' A little later, under the influence of *1 Cor.* 8:6, the Creed came to contain the confession of 'one God, the Father, the Almighty of whom everything is, and . . . one Lord Jesus Christ, the only begotten Son of God, through whom everything is, and the Holy Ghost'.

The trinitarian principle is already apparent. Christ had been elevated to a divine manifestation, almost God – but still: there is a certain reservation. In the third century all caution is thrown to the wind, the principle of the Incarnation translated 'the Lord' into Christ who is 'truly God and truly Man'. Disagreements between the Church Fathers Origen, Eusebius, Methodius and others, as well as the strong influence of Arius, centre around the question of the nature of Christ. The final outcome of the Christological dispute is described with clarity by Harnack: ' . . . in the beginning of the fourth century there appeared a man who saved the Church, seriously threatened by inward strife and outward persecution – Constantine – and at the same time appeared another man who preserved the Church from the complete secularisation of its most fundamental faith – Athanasius – [who] first secured to the Christian religion its own territory upon the preoccupied soil of Greek speculation, and brought everything back to the thought of redemption through God himself, i.e., through the god-man who is of the same essence with God . . . the Divine which appeared in Christ has the nature of the Godhead itself, and only on that account is able to elevate us to a divine life . . . ' (*History of Dogma*, p. 199).

Harnack considers the actions of Constantine and Athanasius praiseworthy and fortunate. Others take a very different view. Friedrich Nietzsche, for instance, writes: 'It is an unprecedented abuse of names to identify such manifestations of decay and such abortions as the "Christian Church", "Christian belief" and "Christian life" with the Holy Name. What did Christ deny? Everything which today is called Christian. The whole of the Christian creed – all Christian truth – is idle falsehood and deception, and is precisely the reverse of that which was at the bottom of the Christian movement . . . ' (*Will to Power*, paras. 158/9). And with yet greater emphasis he exclaims: 'The Church is precisely that against which Jesus inveighed – and against which he taught his disciples to fight' (ibid., para. 168).

Satan introduces confusion

The Athanasian dogma did not become dominant in the Church without a bitter struggle. The ideas of the minority were branded as heresies, and their exponents were cruelly persecuted. Here we can present only a few of these 'heresies'; which, for a short time, rivalled the eventually triumphant doctrines.

Docetism and its various branches held that Christ's human body was merely a phantom, and that his suffering and death were but appearance. If he suffered, he was not God, they argued, if he was God, he did not suffer: a most reasonable conclusion. Then there were the various schools of *gnosticism* which adopted Christianity, or Christians who adopted gnostic ideas. There was a Syrian branch of gnosticism, represented by *Saturninus* in the second century, of whom Irenaeus says. ' . . . Saturninus of Antioch . . . taught that there is one Father, utterly unknown, who made angels, archangels, virtues, powers; and that the world, and all things therein, was made by certain angels. The Saviour was unborn, incorporeal and without form . . . seen as a man in appearance only. The God of the Jews was one of the Angels . . . all the Princes wished to destroy his Father, therefore Christ came to destroy the God of the Jews . . . Two kinds of men were fashioned by the Angels, one bad, the other good . . . the demons aided the worst, the Saviour came to destroy the bad and save the good . . . to marry and to procreate is of Satan . . . ' (*Adv. haer.*, 1:24). Rather far-fetched and irrational prattle, the reader may say. Yet, in the light of reason, perhaps much of the official doctrine is no less irrational, and would appear to be similar prattle, were we not well acquainted with, and accustomed to, its vagaries since early childhood!

The Egyptian variety of Christian gnosticism was represented by *Basilides*, also in the second century. Of his teaching Irenaeus reports: 'The unborn and unnamed Father created the angels, the chief of whom is known as Jehovah, the God of the Jews. This chief angel wished to put all the other nations under the rule of his own people, and for this reason he antagonised the other Princes who resisted him. Then the Father sent his first-begotten Mind who is called Christ to free those on earth who believe in him. The Christ did not suffer in person, but a man called Simon of Cyrenae was made to bear the cross and was crucified in his stead. It was the will of Christ that the people should think that the man crucified was indeed Jesus. Those who still believe that Christ himself died on the cross are still slaves unable to recognise the plan and scheme of the Unknown Father . . . ' (ibid., 24:3/5). We must take into account that these reports were written by Irenaeus, an enemy of the gnostics, and it is not impossible that they are mere caricatures of the true beliefs of Syrian and Egyptian gnostics. The idea described also seems to contain a strong element of Docetism.

Yet another trend among the gnostic Christians was the so-called Judaising type, associated with the name of *Cerinthus*. It is again on Irenaeus that we depend for information: the world was not made by the Supreme Godhead, but by a Virtue separate from God who is above all things. It is even possible that the Creative Virtue did not know the will of God, or even God himself. Jesus was born like any other man, from two honourable parents, Joseph and Mary, but he was superior in wisdom and righteousness to all other men. Because of that the Holy Spirit of God descended upon him and dwelt in him. While the Spirit dwelt in him, he revealed the will of the Unknown Father and performed great deeds of virtue. In the end, however, the Holy spirit departed from him, and left Jesus to suffer and die. After his death, the Spirit willed Jesus to rise, but the Christ can neither rise nor die, being an immortal spirit (ibid., 1:26:1). With little justification, Irenaeus here introduces the *Ebionite* sect which he regards as 'heretics', genuine followers of Jesus and his brother James who withdrew from the rest of the community. Irenaeus said: 'Those who are called Ebionites . . . use only the Gospel according to Matthew: they reject the Apostle Paul, calling him an apostate from the Law. They strive to expound

... the prophetic writings; they are circumcised and persevere in the custom of the Law and in the Jewish mode of life, even to the extent of worshipping Jerusalem as if it were the abode of God ... ' (ibid., 1:26:2). In a word, they were true followers of Jesus' doctrine and example, and if they did *worship* Jerusalem as if it were the abode of God — so it was, harbouring the one and only Temple!

Other heresies, which sprang up in the Church were *Monarchianism* which emphasised the unity of God; *Patripassianism* which totally identified the Son with the Father; and *Sabellianism* which taught one God in three contemporaneous manifestations. The most 'dangerous' heresy for the course which the Church seems to have set for itself was *Arianism* that the Son had a beginning while God was without beginning — thus denying the Trinity in a most effective manner. Another influential 'heresy' was *Adoptionism*, associated with Theodotus of Byzantium who revived the Ebionite doctrine that the Son was a mere man adopted by God, that is, endowed with divine power.

There are some contemporary documents which shed light on the teachings of the 'heresies'. I can quote here only a few passages. Elsewhere the reader will find an interesting text on Sabellianism by Epiphanius, bishop of Salamis. A spark of humour, intentional or not, can be discerned in the account concerning 'Patripassian' Monarchianism written by the otherwise humourless Tertullian: 'The devil has fought against the truth in many ways. Sometimes he sought to destroy it by defending it. He advocated the unity of God, the all-powerful creator, only to turn the advocasy of that unity into a heresy. He says "the Father Himself descended into a Virgin, was Himself born of her, Himself suffered: in fact that He Himself was Jesus Christ ...". It was Praxeas who brought this Asian perversity to Rome ... he put the Paraclete to flight and crucified the Father' (*Adv. Praxeam*, 1).

The Arian 'heresy' can be presented to the reader by quoting extracts from a famous letter written by Arius to Eusebius, bishop of Nicomedia, A.D. 321: '... the bishop [of Alexandria] persecutes us ... because we do not concur with him when he preaches "God always, the Son always; at the same time the Father, at the same time the Son; the Son co-exists with the Father, unbegotten; he is ever-begotten, he is not-born-by- begetting; neither by thought, nor by any moment of time does God precede the Son; what *we* say and think [is] ... that the Son is not unbegotten, nor part of the unbegotten in any way, nor is he derived from any substance; but that by his own will and counsel he existed before time and ages, fully God, only-begotten, unchangeable. And before he was begotten or created or appointed or established, he did not exist for he was not unbegotten". We are persecuted because we say that the Son has a beginning, but God is without beginning' (Quoted from *Documents of the Christian Church*, pp.55/6). The Church Father Socrates preserved the much discussed Arian syllogism which says: 'If the Father begat the Son, he that was begotten had a beginning of existence: hence it is clear that there was a time when the Son was not. It follows then of necessity that he had his existence from the non-existent' (ibid., p.57). And I am afraid, here we must let the matter rest.

The Light prevails

The Christological argument was fought in the 4th and 5th centuries, since when the Church has accepted the trinitarian principle and the idea that Christ is the Second Person of the Trinity.

The Reformation not only refrained from 'shaking these foundations', but confirmed the dogma of the Incarnation and all its attendant aspects. 'We lay under God's wrath and displeasure.' writes Luther, 'doomed to eternal damnation, as we had deserved. There was no counsel, no help, no comfort for us until this only and eternal Son of God, in his unfathomable goodness, had mercy on our misery and came from heaven to help us' (*The Large Catechism*, p.58). With somewhat more sophistication, he speculates: 'Light does not shine in darkness unless it is reflected by an object. One can see this if one holds a candle outside a door which has a hole in it. The light can only be seen if it hits a solid object. Thus the middle region of space, where the devils are, is wrapt in darkness. No sun shines there but the sun shines upon the earth where its rays are reflected. And this is the idea of the Incarnation of the Son of God. He is the ray of the Father, He can only shine by coming down to a world that reflects him . . . ' (*Luther im Tischgespräch*, V. 5968).

An aspect of the Christological tradition, always a thorn in the flesh of Christian apologists, is the term 'begotten'. This is also reflected in the metaphor used by Tertullian, and later by Luther, 'the ray of the Father'. This expression relegates the Son to the second place after the Father – a fact which greatly disturbs those who elevated Christ to divinity and then found that Jesus had to be satisfied with the second place, after the indisputable First Person of the Godhead, the Father.

Theologians try to overcome this difficulty by saying that Christ was 'begotten from everlasting of the Father'. By this clumsy trick it is attempted to present the argument that the Son's co-existence with the Father is eternal. In that case the use of the terminology of a Father/Son relationship is misleading and unjustified. As discussed in another chapter, it was insisted upon that the Son is not *merely like* the Father, but identical with him. However, the final deification of Christ only became possible with the defeat of the Arian 'heresy' of which Griffith Thomas says, 'the Arians were ready to place our Lord at any point above manhood as long as he was kept lower than Deity . . . ' (*The Principles of Theology*, p. 36).

Christ the God prevailed, and how complete his victory was can be seen in the wording of Article II of the Church of England.

Filius qui est Verbum Patris,	The son which is the Word of the Father,
ab eterno a Patre genitus	begotten from everlasting of the Father,
versus et aeternus Deus,	the very and everlasting God,
ac Patri consubstantialis,	and of one substance with the Father,
in utero Virginis ex illius	took man's nature in the womb of the
substantia naturam humanum assumpsit:	Blessed Virgin of her substance:
ita ut duae naturae, divina et humana,	So that two whole and perfect natures, that is to say the Godhead and Manhood,
integre atque perfecte in unitate personae,	Were joined together in one Person,
fuerint inseparabiliter conjunctae:	never to be divided:
ex quibus est unus Christus, verus Deus et verus homo: qui vere	whereof is one Christ, very God and very Man, who truly
passus est, crucifixus, mortuus, et sepultus,	suffered, was crucified, dead and buried,
ut Patrem nobis reconciliaret	to reconcile our Father to us,
essetque hostia non tantum pro culpa originis,	and to be a sacrifice, not only for original sin,
verum etiam pro omnius actualibus hominum peccatis.	but also for all actual sins of men.

Almost every word can be seen to fulfil a task in eliminating certain possible objections and criticisms. The words have found their way in the Statement of the Creed by being needed to meet the assault of the so-called heresies. The question which the learned theologians would find most uncomfortable is whether these sophisticated speculations, these pseudo-subtleties, ever formed part of the teaching of Jesus? Being fairly well acquainted with the whole range of reported sayings, I can safely state that Jesus is completely innocent of these theological absurdities.

God humanised

Alan Watts made the acute observation that Christianity is 'God humanised instead of Jesus rendered transcendent' (quoted from *Philosophers Speak of God*, p.325). This humanisation of God has become the main preoccupation of the Christian religion and, indeed, the extravagant claims made for Jesus must sound blasphemous in the ears of any confirmed believer in a 'One and Indivisible God'.

The deification of Jesus is the pattern of all Christian writings from the self-confident Roman Catholic to the ranting preachers. In the Catholic *QB* we read of Christ who 'as God knows the innermost thoughts of men', who is 'identical with the Jehovah of the Jews', and is 'the Creator of the Universe' (pp.52-56). The *QB* claims that 'St. Paul often teaches that Christ is God and Man at the same time' (p.47).

The following is written specially for children in a book that is widely used in Catholic schools: 'Jesus Christ is God the Son, made man for us. Jesus Christ is truly God, Jesus Christ is truly God because he has one and the same nature with God the Father. Jesus Christ was always God, born of the Father in all eternity. Jesus Christ is truly man. Jesus Christ is truly man because he has the nature of man, having a body and a soul like ours. Jesus Christ was not always a man. He has been man only from the time of His Incarnation. I mean by Incarnation that God the Son took to Himself the nature of man: "The Word was made flesh." These are two natures in Jesus Christ, the nature of God and the nature of man. There is only one Person in Jesus Christ, which is the Person of God the Son. God the Son was made man to redeem us from sin and hell, and to teach us the way to heaven. As God, Jesus Christ is everywhere. As God made man, He is in Heaven, and in the Blessed Sacrament of the altar . . . ' (*A Catechism of Christian Doctrine*, pp.7/8). And to the question: 'After your night prayers what should you do?' the hapless child is given this advice: 'After night prayers I should observe due modesty in going to bed, occupy myself with the thoughts of death; and endeavour to compose myself to rest at the foot of the Cross, and give my last thought to my crucified Saviour' (ibid., p.64).

For grown-up children the Catholic Enquiry Centre provides a pamphlet entitled *Jesus Christ* which contains these sentences: 'He demands to be accepted as God-made-man, the Saviour of mankind', and 'Faith is a supernatural gift from God which enables us to accept Jesus as God the Saviour'.

For the educated adolescent the same doctrine is formulated with more sophistication: 'We must believe and confess that our Lord Jesus

Christ is the Son of God, true God and true Man. He is God before all eternity, begotten from the essence of the Father; He is Man in time born of the substance of his Mother. Perfect God, perfect Man, comprised of Spirit-soul and human body. In Godhead equal to the Father, in Manhood less than the Father. Although God and Man, there are no two Christs, but only one Christ . . . ' (*Kleine Glaubenslehre*, p. 12).

But for the really 'adult' mind is reserved this kind of sophistry: '. . . when a man, led on by these motives [in his acceptance of the divinity of Christ], makes the act of faith, then it can still be said that not by the virtue of any of them does he believe, neither on account of the evidence of reason, nor through the witness of the Law, nor as moved by what has come to him through preaching, but solely on account of the Truth itself – *propter ipsam veritatem tantum* (Thomas Aquinas, *Comm. on John* Cap. IV Lect. 5:2).

A God who condescends

Are the Protestant Christians any different? I have reason to think they are not. Dummelow takes *John* 10:30 as proof that the Father and the Son are two Persons but one God (*OVBC*, p. 792). Lightfoot claims that the close union between Father and Son is sufficient evidence to show that the words and works of Christ should be regarded as the words and works of God (*St. John's Gospel*, p. 214). Speaking of *John* 14:1, Walsham How says that Christ demanded faith in the Father *and* in himself as Son of God and One with the Father.

In one of the more remarkable textbooks of Protestant theology, Griffith Thomas argues that without the idea of Incarnation man could not recognise the union between God and man in Christ, and have no knowledge of God in relation to human life. He emphasises that the more important aspect of the Incarnation is God's becoming Man, not Man becoming God. But for this divine act there would be no redemption, since there would be no direct contact between God and the sinner. Salvation is a miracle which can only be performed by a divine Saviour (*Principles of Theology*, pp. 37-39). And the whole psychological need is laid bare in a quotation from Mead's *Irenic Theology*: 'The Incarnation may be inexplicable as a psychological and ontological problem, but it satisfies [sic] the yearnings of those who seek after God and his righteousness' (ibid., p. 38).

Professor Altizer states that, while in Hegel the appearance of Christ is the historical manifestation of man's unity with God, and the spirit of God becomes manifest in Christ to set man free in the consciousness of his divine attributes, in Kierkegaard the approach is reversed. The Incarnation presents 'the absolute paradox of an eternal and infinite God becoming temporal and finite man. Jesus Christ is the Eternal made "Paradox" whose historical garb is accidental'. It is only "the leap of faith" which can help us become aware of the "Incarnate Moment" which is a suspension of history, a branch between the being of God as absolute, and his being as function. In his omnipotence God can triumph even in the garb of weakness' (*Handbook of Christian Theology*, p. 190).

Karl Barth's approach is similar. This devout follower of the doctrines of Calvin says that 'in Christ the eternal God comes down into human existence, bears sin, pain and death. It is a sign of his omnipotence that he can triumph through the Cross, the symbol of shame and humiliation. In Christ, God who is free over all, reveals his love, his self-chosen bond. In Christ, God the Judge, exercises mercy' (*The Faith of the Church*, p. 37/8).

The whole chorus of Protestant theologians joins in this argument, Glover says that Christ brought a new form of existence into the world, enabling the world to turn to God as it finds him in Christ (*The Influence of Christ*, p. 121). 'Jesus is more than a prophet,' exclaims Brunner 'Jesus is the Word of God.' Brunner continues saying that Jesus is not simply a man like us, but He is God himself. 'That is the inconceivable doctrine, and precisely in that subsists the Christian faith. Non-Christians have everything but this, they have the commandments of God, even the commandment to love one's neighbour, the omnipotence and wisdom of God. But this they do not have – God, Who Himself comes to us and shows Himself to us as God-man, longs for fellowship with us, and shows that He – in spite of all – is not ashamed of us, but loves us and desires to bring us to glory. This God who condescends to man and comes so near the human kind as though He were one of them – this God the heathens do not have. This self-condescension, this God we have in Jesus Christ' (*Our Faith*, p. 65). 'All that is to be found in God,' asserts Bonhoeffer, 'can be discerned in Jesus Christ' (*Letters from Prison*, p. 130). Bishop Gore even admits that Jesus did not intend to startle and shock his disciples by proclaiming himself as God: 'But he had done something which in the long run would make any other estimate of Him hardly possible,' he adds ingenuously (*Reconstruction of Belief*, p. 364).

Then of course there are the gospellers of various sects, 'freelance theologians' who join the choir singing hymns to Christ as to God'. Gordon Powell believes that 'the logic of the universe prompts us to accept an incarnation, the appearance of God in human form . . .'.

With disarming naiveté he remarks that no one in his senses would deny that Jesus Christ lived on this earth. He must have had a wonderful power to start such a movement as Christianity and exercise such a remarkable influence in the world. This seems to Gordon Powell adequate proof that God was in Him (*The Blessing of Belief*, pp. 39/44). Crossley bases his belief that Jesus was *God* on the New Testament, *John* 1:3 tells him that Jesus was Creator: *John* 1:4 and *Col.* 1:16/17 that he gave life to man; *John* 5:22, *2 Cor.* 5:10 and *2 Tim.* 4:1 that he is the Judge of the World; *Phil.* 2:10/1 and *Rev.* 5:13/4 that he is the object of the worship of all Creation; and *Col.* 2:9 that in him dwells the fullness of the Deity (*The Holy Trinity*, pp. 11/13).

There is no doubt that most Christians insist on the Incarnation as the central tenet of their faith. If Scripture contains but scanty references to support their doctrine, and if the words of Jesus often contradict it, the believers are not disturbed. They believe in the Incarnation, because 'it is *the* Truth'.

Conclusion

I have called the three opening chapters of this book, dealing with the transformation of the itinerant Jewish preacher Jesus, son of Joseph, of Nazareth, into God, Creator and Lord of All: *The Man Jesus, The Lord Jesus Christ* and *The God Christ*, attempting to show three significant phases of the development of Christian doctrine. Firstly, I have presented Jesus, the remarkable man of truth. Secondly, I have tried to show, how, in the first few generations after his death, he was misunderstood and translated into the Lord Jesus Christ, a religious figure, 'standing at the right hand of God' and reconciling the Almighty to His erring creation. Finally, I have described his fatal apotheosis into Deity: the Second Person of the Trinity, true God and true Man who has lost all similarity to the simple carpenter who had set out to recover 'the lost sheep of Israel.'

It cannot be said strongly enough that Jesus is only responsible for the abuse of his teaching to the extent that we are each to blame if we are misunderstood. Somewhat more responsibility is borne by the pseudo-gnostic schools associated with the names of Paul and John, although even they never expressed views that would justify Christian theology. If blame be attached we have only ourselves to blame, modern thinkers, Christians and non-Christians, who have allowed the figure of Jesus to be obscured by unworthy speculations which make up the body of Christian doctrine.

Yet, in spite of the power of his detractors, in spite of the great gap in time which separates him from us, and even in spite of his modern 'liberal' apologists who, in their enmity to the Church, present him as a meek and humble reflection of their own selves, Jesus remains a living figure reminding us of our humanity – the kingdom of Heaven which is within us. This vital appeal of his spirit makes it even more important that we should try to free it from the doctrinal encumbrance which blurs our vision.

4
The Holy Spirit

Introduction

Jesus and his disciples did *not* teach that the Holy spirit is a Person. The claim that the Holy Spirit is, in fact, the Third Person of the Trinity is founded upon a few New Testament passages:

Go ye therefore, and teach all nations baptising them in the name of the Father, and of the Son, and of the Holy Ghost.   *Matthew 28:19*
For there are three that bear record in heaven, the Father, the Word, and the Holy Ghost: and these three are one   *1 John* 5:7
The Holy Ghost shall come upon thee, and the power of the Highest overshadow thee . . .   *Luke* 1:35
And I will pray the Father, and he shall give you another Comforter that he may abide with you forever; *even* the spirit of truth; whom the world cannot receive, because it sees him not, neither knoweth him: but ye shall know him, for he dwelleth with you, and shall be in you. *John* 14:16/7
But the Comforter *which is* the Holy Ghost, whom the Father will send in my name, he shall teach you all things, and bring all things to your remembrance, whatsoever I have said unto you.   *John* 14:26
But when the Comforter is come, whom I will send unto you from the Father, *even* the Spirit of truth, which proceedeth from the Father, he shall testify of me . . .   *John* 15:26

The words from the passage in *Matthew* do not refer to a 'person'. The passage from *1 John* 5:7 is an unscrupulous interpolation, referred to as the Johannite Comma (see next chapter on 'The Blessed Trinity), not to be found in any original Greek text prior to the 15th century. It is now being omitted from all modern Bibles, including the Roman Catholic ones. Luke's words are beautiful symbolism, degraded to an indelicate literalness if associated with a 'Person'. There remain the three passages from John's Gospel, which are considered below.

What *is* the Holy Ghost? It is my intention throughout to interpret as little as possible, and to find answers in the Scriptures themselves. I suggest, therefore, that the explanation may be found in these passages:

'. . . the Comforter . . . the Spirit of truth . . . . *John* 14:16.7
'. . . when he, the Spirit of truth is come, he will guide you into all truth . . .' *John 16:13*
'. . . the Spirit is truth . . .' *1 John* 5:6

The only clue to the nature of the Holy Spirit given in the New Testament is a concept of the Spirit of truth emanating from God, and received as a gift by man. It is in this light that the grave words of Jesus can be understood: 'All manner of sin and blasphemy shall be forgiven unto men, but the blasphemy against the Holy Ghost shall not be forgiven . . .' (*Matthew* 12:31, *Mark* 3:29, and *Luke* 12:10).

The word βλασφημία means injury, offense, reviling, treating with contempt. It is an offense against truth which cannot be 'forgiven', because in itself it denies man access to God who, in the mind of Jesus, is Perfection and the Source of Truth.

The Shadow

Not a ripple disturbs the surface of the lake, and the small white clouds on the vault of an immense sky chase across the surface of the water like ghostly shadows, dispersing and reforming in endless variations.

Perhaps it was such a commonplace experience which inspired the Hebrew poet when he wrote the tremendous words: 'And the Spirit of God moved upon the face of the waters.' For the Hebrew mind the presence of God was like an unfathomable Shadow, and at the same time the reflection of blinding light. The Hebrew language called it *Shekinah*, an untranslatable word which may only be rendered by 'divine presence'.

We encounter it when Moses, following the call of the Lord, goes up Mount Sinai. 'There had been a thick cloud upon the mount', heralding the Presence. It persisted for six days, and 'the sight of the glory of the Lord' overawed the people 'like devouring fire' (*Exod.* 19:16, 24:16/7). This idea of God who, being himself consuming light, appears in a thick cloud, is a recurrent theme in the Bible. The cloud and the Presence it hides are manifest to men's eyes, and yet it spares them the blinding impact of radiance. God himself says to

Moses: 'I come unto thee in a thick cloud . . . ' (*Exod.* 19:9), and indeed appears in that form upon the mountain (*Exod.* 19:16). Yet, we are told, he 'descended upon it in fire' (*Exod* 19:18) and the cloud was but the smoke of that conflagration.

While Aaron spoke to the children of Israel, 'they looked towards the wilderness, and behold, the glory of the Lord appeared in the cloud' (*Exod.* 16:10). The Spirit of the Lord leading Israel through the wilderness goes before them 'by day in a pillar of cloud . . . and by night in a pillar of fire' (*Exod.* 13:21), revealing both aspects of the *Shekinah*. With mighty words Moses enjoins his people to worship only One God, reminding Israel that 'upon earth he shewed them only his great fire: and thou heardest his words out of the midst of the fire' (*Deut.* 4:36). God, who is spirit, becomes manifest to men in the form of fire which is the bearer of the word. Similarly, the closing passages of Exodus presents the deity in its two aspects: 'The cloud of the Lord was upon the tabernacle by day, and fire was on it by night, in the sight of all the house of Israel, throughout all their journeys' (*Exod.* 40:38).

The presence of God, the *Shekinah*, accompanies Israel throughout the ages. It is felt always, everywhere, both in individual and collective destinies. This ever-present, protective Shadow, this ever-invoked guiding radiance is the holy spirit of God. The psalmist exclaims: 'Whither shall I go from the spirit? or whither shall I flee from thy presence?' (*Psalm* 139:7). The spirit of God is the dispenser of prophesy: 'The Spirit of the Lord will come upon thee, and thou shalt prophesy . . . and shalt be turned into another man' (*1 Sam.* 10:6). When Samuel, the prophet, anoints David, he anoints him with the Holy Ghost: 'The Spirit of the Lord came upon David from that day forward . . . ' (*1 Sam.* 16:13).

The Holy Spirit is not only God's guiding emanation, it is also his creative power, omnipresent as is his sunlike radiance. In their greatest collection of religious poetry, the Psalms, the Hebrews present us with this aspect of the *Shekinah*: 'Thou hidest thy face, they [men] are troubled: thou takest away their breath, they die, and return to their dust. Thou sendest forth thy spirit, they are created, and thou renewest the face of the earth' (*Psalm* 104:29/30). And Job employs almost the same eloquence in the praise of his God: 'He divideth the sea with his power, and by his understanding he smiteth through the proud. By his spirit he hath garnished the heavens' (*Job* 26:12/3). Job is fully aware of the Presence filling his consciousness: 'All the while my breath is in me, and the spirit of God is in my nostrils' (*Job* 27:3).

Finally, there is the aspect of God as Redeemer, the *only* Redeemer of Israel. 'The Lord Almighty is God alone, and beside him there is no other Saviour'. . . (*Eccles.* 24:24). He sends the prophets to deliver his message, to exhort, to warn, to cajole, to frighten, and it is in this power of the divine spirit that the Christian apologists think they can discover the distinct personality of the Holy Ghost. 'And now the Lord God,' says Isaiah, 'and his spirit hath sent me' (*Isaiah* 48:16).

The English text 'the Lord God, and his Spirit, hath sent me' suggests that the Lord and the Holy Spirit, two distinct Persons, sent the prophet. The Jewish translation of the Hebrew Bible still allows a certain ambiguity: 'And now the Lord Eternal hath sent me, and his spirit.' The French translation comes nearer to the meaning of the passage: 'Et maintenant, le Seigneur, l'Eternel m'a envoyé avec son esprit.' We cannot blame the Septuagint for the confusion, since the Greek text is quite clear: καὶ νῦν κύριος κύριος ἀπεστελε με, καὶ τὸ πνεῦμα αὐτοῦ, rather like the French, but less ambiguous in Greek. The only translation (in a language I understand) that is unequivocal is the Swedish one which reads: 'Och nu har Herren, Herren sänt mig och sänt sin Ande', which means that now the Lord sent me and sent his spirit. I see no reason to doubt that the intended meaning of the phrase was the prophet's claim that he has been sent by God imbued with the spirit of God.

'But they rebelled,' say another passage in Isaiah, 'and vexed his holy spirit . . . ' (*Isaiah* 63:10), which is quoted by the apologists as another example of personification. The French translation is once again helpful: 'Mais ils ont été rebellés, ils ont attristé son esprit saint . . . '. The translation in the Septuagint: Αὐτοι δὲ ἠπείθησαν, καὶ παρώζυναν τὸ πνεῦμα τὸ ἅγιον αὐτοῦ makes it clear that there is no question of a separate personality: the passage suggests that man's rebellion grieves the holy spirit of God.

In his *Principles of Theology* Griffith Thomas says that in the Old Testament the Holy Spirit appears to be a Divine Agent rather than a distinct Personality. He regards as significant the fact that apocryphal literature between Malachi and Matthew contributes nothing to the doctrine of the Spirit as Person. However, he invalidates this sound argument with the dubious statement that 'the real implications of the old Testament' are more clearly understood by Christians 'in the fuller light and richer experience of the days of Christ' (*The Principles of Theology*, p.91).

Does Jewish Scripture anticipate the Holy Ghost?

There are a number of words in the Old Testament which may be rendered in English as 'spirit'. One meaning may imply the self's awareness of itself. Another the soul God breathed into man. The most common word signifies breath or the breath of God, and that is the divine aspect which Christians claim is a distinct, separate manifestation of the deity: God the Holy Ghost.

It is this meaning they attribute to the Old Testament and to passages such as 'Cast me not away from thy presence, and take not thy holy spirit from me . . .' (*Psalm* 51:11); 'The spirit of God hath made me, and the breath of the Almighty hath given me life . . .' (*Job* 33:4); 'I will put my spirit within you . . .' (*Ezek.* 36:27) and ' . . . truly I am full of power by the spirit of the Lord . . .' (*Micah* 3:8).

The most sophisticated and daring attempt to introduce the Spirit of God as God the Holy Ghost into Old Testament Scripture was made by a remarkable Catholic theologian, Jean Daniélou S.J. whose *Théologie du Judéo-Christianisme* was published in 1957. He attempts to prove that God the Son is represented in the Old Testament by the Archangel Michael, and God the Holy Ghost by the Archangel Gabriel.

Daniélou bases his argument on an apocryphal Jewish scripture, the *Ascension of Isaiah* translated into French by Cardinal Tisserant. This writing, which dates from the first century, shows Christian influences yet retains its Judaic approach. Just as in other scriptures Daniélou discovers traits of the Archangel Michael which shows his identity with the Word, so in this apocryphal book Daniélou finds traits of Gabriel's affinity with the 'Angel of the Spirit', i.e. none other than the Holy Ghost. Tisserant remarks that reading the 'Ascension' makes one wonder whether the description of Gabriel is that of the Archangel or of the Holy Ghost. We find Gabriel standing by the left hand of God, just as elsewhere Michael is said to be standing by His right hand. Daniélou admits that there is, as yet, no mention of co-equality; in fact, both archangels praise and worship God. Yet he does find passages in the 'Ascension' which convince him that Gabriel is shown in roles generally reserved for the Holy Spirit: he is a Comforter, he is sent 'to convict many' and, in 11:4, he appears to Joseph and Mary, surprisingly introduced as an agent of divine intervention (pp. 177/180).

This speculation appears far less contrived if we consider that the New Testament associates Gabriel with the Annunciation when Mary is over-shadowed by the Holy Ghost, and even puts these words into the mouth of the archangel: 'I am Gabriel, that stand in the presence of God . . .' (*Luke* 1:19), that is, who is part of the *Shekinah*.

However, whether the doctrine of the Holy Spirit was foreshadowed in the Old Testament or not, there is no doubt that the monumental poetry of Isaiah anticipated the Beatitudes: 'The spirit of the Lord God is upon me, because the Lord hath anointed me to preach good tidings unto the meek; he hath sent me to console the broken-hearted, to proclaim liberty to the captives, and release to the prisoners; to proclaim the year of favour of the Lord . . . to comfort all that mourn . . .' (*Isaiah* 61:1/2). When 'the Spirit' is at work in Isaiah or in Jesus, the fruits seem to be similar.

The power of the Highest shall overshadow thee . . .

The archangel Gabriel appears to Mary, the wife of the carpenter Joseph, in the small township of Nazareth in Galilee. Like every Jewish woman she looks forward anxiously to the moment when she will give birth. She hopes desperately that it will be a male child to continue his father's lineage. All this Gabriel promises her and adds: 'He shall be great, and shall be called the son of the Highest, and the Lord God shall give unto him the throne of his father David; and he shall reign over the house of Jacob for ever; and of his kingdom there shall be no end . . . The Holy Ghost shall come upon thee, and the power of the Highest shall overshadow thee . . . ' (*Luke* 1:32, 33 and 35).

The power of God which overshadows his creature: that is the Shekinah, the divine Presence, the Holy Spirit. The explanation of the miracle is given by the angel: ' . . . with God nothing shall be impossible' (*Luke* 1:37). The early believers, acquainted with stories of gods who come down to mortal women to sire demi- gods and heroes, unhesitatingly accepted the story of the Annunciation with a literalness as moving as it is primitive. The result was the belief that Jesus was in some physical sense the son of God, that the Holy Spirit had provided the power of fertility which enabled Mary to bear the child, and that the relationship between God and Jesus was that between a human father and son.

The Catholic Professor Ginns mentions that a frequent criticism against this passage in Luke is 'that the idea and terminology are completely un-Hebraic, since Spirit in Hebrew is feminine and therefore could not have been used to express the active principle in conception'. He counters this criticism by saying that 'Luke is writing in Greek, not Hebrew' (*CC*, pp.940/1). However, the Greek text reads as follows: Πνεῦμα Ἁγιον ἐπελευσεται ἐπι σὲ'. The operative word ἐπιλεύσσω means to look towards, to see before one, and the correct translation would be 'The Holy Spirit shall look upon thee', rather than 'come upon thee'; and we may assume that it comes much nearer to the original meaning that the latter translation with its possible physical and indelicate undertones.

This strange discrepancy seems striking to some more sensitive Christian commentators. Dummelow admits that 'Mary would doubtless understand "the Holy Ghost" impersonally, as the creative power of God, but Luke's readers would understand it personally' (*OVBC*, p.739). Professor Caird misses this fine point, and merely tells us that 'Jesus entered upon this status of sonship at his birth and by a new creative act of that same Holy Spirit which at the beginning brooded over the waters of chaos' (*The Gospel of St. Luke*, p.53). This is a typical example of word-spinning which disregards the weighty implications of the passage.

Once again it is an anti-Christian, Alfred Loisy, who frees the gospel account from crude associations: 'The culminating point of the mythical legend is the miraculous conception by the action of the Holy Spirit. Jesus is the Son of God because, physiologically speaking, God is the operative cause of his generation. This is not offered in the grossly primitive sense of the old mythologies, the Greek, for example, which describes the amours of Zeus and other gods, with metamorphoses appropriate to the different circumstances. Even among the pagans of that time, a few pious and enlightened men were taking the matter more seriously, Plutarch holding the opinion of the Egyptians to be plausible that a woman might conceive by the approach of the spirit of God. But this idea was not reached at a single bound from the starting point. In the ancient literature of Christianity we catch glimpses of the successive stages or, one might well say, the gropings by which the apotheosis of Jesus was realised in the faith of believers and in their catechisms' (*The Birth of the Christian Religion*, pp.279/280).

He shall baptise you with the Holy Ghost

Many centuries before the advent of Jesus, the dove was regarded as a symbol of purity and, consequently, of holiness. We read of the great regard in which it was held by the peoples of Syria, and of the Roman custom of sacrificing it to Venus, the goddess of love (*Propertius* 4:5, 62). At a much earlier period, the Phoenicians saw in the dove a companion and symbol of Astarte, their love-goddess in whose rites this bird played an important role (Aelian, *De natura animalium* 4:2). In the Jewish purification rites it was a prescribed sacrifice, while Roman matrons often used the services of Syrian soothsayers who, from the entrails of the bird, foretold the future.

The ritualistic quality of the dove, as well as its association with purity, holiness, foreknowledge and love, may account for the baptismal scene in the New Testament where the Holy Ghost descends upon Jesus in the form of a dove. It is, of course, not symbolic of a distinct divine personality but of the holy and merciful spirit of God.

It is this event to which Paul refers when he says, speaking of Jesus, that he was 'made of the seed of David according to the flesh; and *declared* to be the Son of God with power, according to the spirit of holiness' (*Rom.* 1:3/4). It was in the baptismal scene that Jesus, a mere *man* of the seed of David, was declared by the Spirit of God to be the Son with power. The voice and the dove (both coming down from the opened heavens) represent the *Shekinah*, and meet Jesus, the man, 'coming up straightway out of the water', that is, ascending in purity, to announce God's fatherhood and pleasure. (See chapter on the Blessed Trinity.)

In the preceding scene John the Baptist had spoken of the difference between the ritual he was performing, that is, baptising with water, and the rite to be performed by him whose shoes he was not worthy to bear. 'He,' John exclaims 'shall baptise you with the Holy Ghost and with fire' (*Matthew* 3:11). The baptismal scene in *Mark* 1:7/11; *Luke* 3:16 and 21/22 and *John* 1:26/34 contains the promise that Jesus will 'baptise with the Holy Ghost'.

Baptism is an old Syrian, and possibly universal, rite of purification, known to and practised by the Qumran community which was conceivably the spiritual influence behind the Baptist's doctrine. The Baptist, himself a historical figure, is mentioned by Josephus: 'Now, some of the Jews thought that the destruction of Herod's army came from God, and that very justly as a punishment of what he did against John, that was called the Baptist; for Herod slew him, who was a good man and commanded the Jews to exercise virtue, both as to righteousness towards one another and piety towards God, and so come to baptism, for that the washing with water would be acceptable to Him, if they made use of it; not in order to the putting away of some sins only, but for the purification of the body; supposing still that the soul was thoroughly purified beforehand by righteousness. Now, when others came in crowds about him, for they were greatly moved by hearing his words, Herod, who feared lest the great influence John had over the people might put it into his power and inclination to raise rebellion (for they seemed to do anything he should advise), thought it best by putting him to death, to prevent any mischief he might cause, and not bring himself [Herod] into difficulties by sparing a man who might make him repent of it when it should be too late. Accordingly, he was sent a prisoner . . . to Macherus . . . and was there put to death' (*Antiquities* 18:5:2).

Jesus himself is not reported to have baptised anybody, with or without the Holy Spirit. It seems to me that the expression 'Holy Spirit' was used meaning an emanation of God and not a distinct 'name'. There are noteworthy differences on this issue between the various gospels. Matthew speaks of 'your Father which is in heaven' (*Matthew* 7:11), while, in the same context Luke records: ' . . . your heavenly Father shall give the Holy Spirit to them that ask him' (*Luke* 9:13).

Bishop Barnes has an interesting comment on the question of baptism: 'How then did the idea arise? Plainly, when the Christian movement began to gain strength, there was need of some rite of admission to the society of believers. Remembering the association of Jesus with the Baptist's movement, and their Master's own baptism, the early missionaries, with the Galilean apostles as their nucleus, began to baptise the converts' (*The Rise of Christianity*, p.274).

In this context it ought to be mentioned that *Acts* 11:16 reads: 'Then remembered I the word of the Lord how that he said, John indeed baptised with water; but ye shall be baptised with the Holy Spirit'. This refers to the Baptist's saying in *Matthew* 3:11, *Mark* 1:8, *Luke* 3:16 and *John* 1:26 and 33; but there is no record in the gospels of Jesus himself ever having spoken those words which are here attributed to him. We find a similar mistaken allegation in *Acts* 1:5.

The Jewish scholar David Daube points out that when the Baptist says he is 'not worthy to bear the shoes of Jesus' (*Matthew* 3:11), he means he is not worthy to be a slave of Jesus. Rabbi Joshua ben Levi taught that the disciple should do anything for the teacher a slave would do – except take off his shoes. (*Bab. Ket.* 96a).

There is much ritual symbolism in baptism, apart from the idea of purification. The baptism in the Jordan indicates a new entry into the Promised Land, the 'coming up' is symbolic of the rising from the grave. Baptism was the way in which certain Jewish sects received a new convert, and according to the sacred writings 'a convert has the status of a new-born child' (*Bab. Yeb.* 48b). Hence the often quoted expression 'lest ye be born again'. The rite also indicated 'entry in the Kingdom'. It is likely that baptism alone was considered sufficient by the end of the first century for a person to be accepted as a Jew, and women converts were admitted even earlier to become members of Israel through baptism.

The Qumran documents show that baptism was practised among the members of the brotherhood. Passages such as ' . . . He cannot be cleared by mere ceremonies of atonement, not cleansed by any waters of ablution, nor sanctified by immersion in lakes and rivers, nor purified by any bath . . . Only through the holy spirit can he achieve union with God's truth and be purged . . . Only thus can his flesh be sprinkled with waters of ablution. Only thus can it be sanctified by waters of purification . . .' show where the Baptist learnt the rites he performed, unless they were much more widespread among the Jews than we know today.

A sin against the Holy Ghost

A mysterious saying is reported by the three synoptics, concerning the blasphemy against the Holy Ghost. In its simplest form we find it in the Gospel according to Mark: 'Verily I say unto you, All sins shall be forgiven unto the sons of men, and blasphemies wherewith soever they shall blaspheme. But he that shall blaspheme against the Holy Ghost hath never forgiveness, but is in danger of eternal damnation' (*Mark* 3:28/29). Matthew is more explicit and solemn: 'All manner of sin and blasphemy shall be forgiven unto men but the blasphemy against the Holy Ghost shall not be forgiven unto men. And whosoever speaketh a word against the Son of man, it shall be forgiven him, but whosoever speaketh against the Holy Ghost, it shall not be forgiven him, neither in this world, neither in the world to come' (*Matthew* 12:31/32). Likewise in Luke: 'And whosoever speaketh a word against the Son of man, it shall be forgiven him, but unto him that blasphemeth against the Holy Ghost it shall not be forgiven' (*Luke* 12:10).

This solemn warning has puzzled theologians throughout the ages, and because of its context they have concluded that 'the sin against the Holy Ghost is the view that Jesus' miracles are inspired not by God but by the devil.'

Walsham How, for instance, exclaims: '. . . no one who reads our Lord's terrible words can help anxiously asking, What is this unpardonable sin? To this question different answers have been given. Observe, it is not merely sin against the Holy Ghost, it is "blasphemy". All resistance to the Holy Spirit's influence is sin against him. But that may find forgiveness. This cannot. Again observe, it is a sin which the Pharisees were in great danger of committing. They stood on the brink of the precipice, if they had not yet fallen over. Now they had wilfully ascribed to Satan the work of the Spirit of God. May we not then conclude that the unpardonable sin here spoken of is such a wilful and obstinate resistance to the Holy Spirit' work as openly and deliberately to ascribe that work to the devil? . . . The sin they dread is unpardonable, not because God is unable to forgive, but because man has barred his heart against the entrance of faith and repentance.'

Dummelow comes to a similar conclusion: 'What this sin was is not really doubtful. St. Matthew intimates that the Pharisees had come very near to committing it. St. Mark states exactly what their sin was. It lay in the malignant slander that Jesus was possessed by an unclean spirit. They regarded the spirit of holiness which showed itself in the acts of miracles of Jesus, as diabolical . . . The sin is not a sin against the Holy Spirit as a divine Person, but against the Spirit as manifested in the perfect life of Christ, whose acts so evidently reflect God's own benevolence and holiness that to ascribe them to the devil, was a sin of the most deadly character. This, and not blasphemy against Christ in general, or denial of his claims, or active opposition to him, is the unpardonable sin.' (*OVBC*, p.668).

Professor Stendahl, in *PC*, concurs: 'There is a distinction between the blasphemy against the Son of man, which can be forgiven, and the blasphemy against the Holy Spirit which cannot: that is, during the ministry of Jesus it was permissible and understandable not to recognise Jesus as the Messiah, but after Pentecost there was no excuse' [sic] (p.785). Discussing the passage in Mark, R.M. Wilson writes: 'A solemn warning, uttered with great emphasis. The Q version occurs in a different context and contrasts the words spoken against the son of man (or a son of man, any man?) with speaking against the Holy Spirit. The sin against the Spirit is the wilful blindness of those who refuse to see, who persist in putting the worst construction on the acts of others, who as here ascribe a work of healing manifestly wrought by the Spirit of God to the agency of Beelzebub' (ibid., p.803).

This view seems to be the orthodox interpretation of all Christian theologians, since even the Catholic Professor Jones expresses the same opinion: '. . . what precisely is the sin in question? The context . . . is decisive. The sin referred to is the one of which an example has just been furnished by the Pharisees. They have perversely attributed to Satan what is clearly the work of God . . . ' (*CC*, p.874). He then quotes St. Thomas Aquinas on this question, who wrote: 'It is called unforgivable because of its very nature it precludes those things which induce forgiveness. However, we cannot exclude the power and mercy of God, which can find ways of forgiveness . . . by which, as it were miraculously, he heals such sinners . . . ' (S.T. ii:2:14a 3). But, remarks Jones, even if the quasi-miraculous grace requires acceptance on the part of the sinner, that is, his readiness to repent the blasphemy against the Holy Ghost. Professor Jones concludes: 'Our Lord's statement is therefore literally true: it shall never be forgiven, because it refuses to be forgiven'.

The anthology given here proves that the Christian apologists, treading in the path of St. Thomas Aquinas, do not take the trouble to go more deeply into the question of the 'unforgivable sin'. They believe that the saying is merely a retort to perverse criticism concerning Jesus' miraculous deeds: this despite his previous generous concession that the sin against the Son can be forgiven.

To understand this profound saying of Jesus we must anticipate the question: What *is* the Holy Ghost? The Gospel according to John provides the answer: it is the Spirit of Truth. This spirit of God is the awareness of truth in man, an emanation, a breath of the divine principle in man's soul. The central point of the doctrine is, therefore, that *truth matters*. On one occasion at least, Jesus clearly identified God with the truth, when he said: 'I am [in my reading 'God is'] the way, the truth and the life' (*John* 14:6). There is some validity in the view expressed by some Christian theologians that the rejection of the Holy Spirit is self-defeating: if anyone rejects truth and refuses to consider it, then indeed there can be no 'forgiveness' for him, because his attitude itself is complete negation. If we refuse to be concerned with truth (the Holy Spirit), the truth will escape us forever.

A man who repudiates the consideration of what is true and right will inevitably assume the nihilist position which is indeed self-defeating, since anything that such a man may say has no relevance to whatever is true or right. It is an inescapable conclusion that in his actions and words he will be '*néant*', negation of himself, non-existent as an ethical being.

In the context of the gospel-event this argument may seem far-fetched, yet no other explanation of Jesus' words seem meaningful to me. Temporal and spatial accuracy and consistent 'context' were certainly not one of the characteristics of the evangelists. Unfortunately, the disciples, who did not grasp the implications of the saying, succumbed to the temptation of presenting it in a manner that accorded with their limited comprehension.

The Paraclete

Many Christians claim that it is the Gospel according to John rather than the synoptic gospels which provides evidence for the distinct personality of the Holy Spirit. They quote the words of Jesus concerning the Paraclete, the Comforter, to show that he spoke of a Person with distinct attributes and functions:

THE HOLY SPIRIT

καὶ ἐγώ ἐρωτήσω τὸν πατέρα, καὶ ἄλλον παράκλητον δώσει ὑμῖν ἵνα μένῃ μεθ' ὑμῶν εἰς τὸν αἰῶνα, τὸ πνεῦμα τῆς ἀληθείας, ὃ ὁ κόσμος οὐ δύναται λαβεῖν, ὅτι οὐ θεωρεῖ αὐτό, οὐδὲ γινώσκει αὐτό. ὑμεῖς δε γινώσκετε αὐτό, ὅτι παρ' ὑμῖν μένει, καὶ ἐν ὑμῖν ἔσται.

And I will pray the Father, and he shall give you another Comforter, that he may abide with you for ever; the Spirit of truth; whom the world cannot receive, because it sees him not, neither knoweth him; but ye know him; for he dwelleth with you, and shall be in you. (*John* 14:16)

ὁ δὲ παράκλητος, τὸ Πνεῦμα τὸ Ἅγιον ὅ πέμψει ὁ πατήρ ἐν τῷ ὀνόματι μου, ἐκεῖνος ὑμᾶς διδάξει πάντα, καὶ ὑπομνησει ὑμᾶς πάντα ἃ εἶπον ὑμιν.

But the Comforter, the Holy Ghost, whom the Father will send in my name he shall teach you all things, and bring all things to your remembrance, whatsoever I have said unto you. (*John* 14:26)

Ὅταν δε ἔλθῃ ὁ παράκλητος, ὃν ἐγὼ πέμψω ὑμῖν παρά τοῦ πατρός, τὸ Πνεῦμα τῆς ἀλ · ηθείας ὁ παρὰ τοῦ πατρὸς ἐκπορεύεται ἐκεῖνος μαρτυρήσει περὶ ἐμοῦ.

But when the Comforter is come, whom I will send unto you from the Father, the Spirit of truth, which proceedeth from the Father, he shall testify of me. (*John* 15:26)

. . . συμφέρει ὑμῖν
ἵνα ἐγώ ἀπέλθω.
ἐὰν γὰρ μὴ ἀπέλθω
ὁ παράκλητος
οὐκ ἐλεύσεται πρὸς
ὑμᾶς, ἐὰν δὲ
πορευθῶ, πέμψω
αὐτὸν πρὸς ὑμᾶς.

It is expedient for you that I go away: for if I go not away, the Comforter will not come unto you, but if I depart, I will send him unto you. (*John* 16:7)

ὅταν δὲ ἔλθῃ
ἐκεῖνος, τὸ Πνεῦμα
τῆς ἀληθείας,
ὁδηγήσει ὑμᾶς εἰς
πᾶσαν τὴν
ἀλήθειαν, οὐ γὰρ
λαλήσει ἀφ᾽ ἑαυτοῦ,
ἀλλ ὅσα ἄν ἀκούσῃ
λαλήσει, καὶ τὰ
ἐρχόμενα ἀναγγελεῖ
ὑμῖν. ἐκεῖνος ἐμέ
δοξάσει, ὅτι ἐκ τοῦ
ἐμοῦ λήμψεται, καὶ
ἀναγγελεῖ ὑμῖν.

When he, the Spirit of truth is come, he will guide you into all truth: for he shall not speak of himself; but whatsoever he shall hear, shall he speak; and he will shew you things to come. (*John* 16:13)

Comparison with the Greek original shows that wherever Jesus speaks of the 'Comforter', he uses the masculine pronoun, but where he speaks of the 'Spirit', he correctly uses the neuter pronoun 'it', since the word τό πνεῦμα – spirit, is neuter. In *John* 16:13 ἑαυτοῦ may be either masculine or neuter, while ἐκεῖνος which is correctly translated as 'he', may be made by the (fraudulent?) addition of an 's' (ἐκεῖνο would be neuter).

I believe that the transformation of the neuter 'spirit' (the Spirit of God – it) into the masculine spirit (the Holy Ghost – he) took place when the Greek text was translated into Latin and τό πνεῦμα became *animus* or *spiritus*.

The metamorphosis resulted in the following texts:

John 14:16
Et ego rogabo Patrem, et alium Paraclitum dabit vobis, ut maneat

vobiscum in aeternum. Spiritum veritatis, quem mundus non potest accipere, quia non videt eum, nec scit eum; vos autem cognoscetis eum, quia apud vos manebit, et in vobis erit.
John 14:26
Paraclitus autem Spiritus Sanctus, quem mittet Pater in nomine meo, ille vos docebit omnia, et suggeret vobis omnia, quaecumque dixero vobis.
John 15:26
Cum autem venerit Paraclitus, quem ego mittam vobis a Patre, Spiritum veritatis, qui a Padre procedit, ille testimonium perhibebit de me.
John 16:7
. . . expedit vobis ut ego vadam, si enim non abiero, Paraclitus non veniet ad vos; si autem abiero, mittam eum ad vos.
John 16:13/4
Cum autem venerit ille Spiritus veritatis, docebit vos omnem veritatem. Non enim loquetur a semetipso sed quaecunque audiet loquetur, et quae ventura sunt annuntiabit vobis. Ille me clarificabit, quia de meo accipiet, et annuntiabit vobis.

As can be seen it was easy for the Latin reader to accept that the Spirit, 'he', was a Person. When the doctrine concerning the Holy Ghost developed, the reading of the Latin translation guided those who eventually incorporated the Holy Ghost as the Third Person of the Trinity into Church dogma.

Can we discern the teaching of Jesus about the Holy Spirit of God in that welter of verbiage? It becomes simple if we set aside Church doctrine and confine ourselves to Jesus' words. The Holy Spirit of God, the πνεῦμα τῆς ἀληθείας, the spiritus veritatis, comes in the form of truth as a gift from the Father to man, as a fruit of man's love and inquiry.

While Jesus was with his disciples they could expect the truth from him. When he departed, God's holy spirit would guide them when they sought the truth. The spirit of truth is not self-seeking, but surmounts all self-interest, it wants truth for its own sake whether it is soothing and encouraging, or stern and forbidding. The world does not know truth yet, but when the divine spirit is its guide, it will find its way to truth that sets men free. And when these things come true, Jesus will be vindicated, he will be clarified (glorified) and his teaching will be comprehended (seen) by all to have been *truth*. The words of Jesus, now overlaid with verbiage that accumulated during the centuries, are among the most moving human documents, the testament of a man who loved both truth and his fellow men.

The Holy Spirit in the New Testament

Nowhere in the New Testament does the Holy Spirit appear as a distinctive person, neither in the words of Jesus nor in the account of his disciples. Let us peruse the Scripture for evidence of the *Shekinah* and see how the authors of the New Testament presented this 'evidence'.

We are told that the Baptist 'shall be filled with the Holy Ghost' (*Luke* 1:15). His father, Zacharias, too 'was filled with the Holy Ghost' (*Luke* 1:67). After his baptism, 'Jesus, being full of the Holy Ghost, returned from the Jordan' (*Luke* 4:1). Simeon, the old man who was present in the Temple when Jesus was brought for circumcision, rejoiced and 'the Holy Ghost was upon him' (*Luke* 2:25). The apostle, Peter, spoke 'filled with the Holy Ghost' as recorded in *Acts* 4:8. We learn of Stephen, the first martyr, that he was 'a man full of faith and of the Holy Ghost' (*Acts* 6:3/5). The apostles call upon their disciples to elect 'seven men of honest report, full of the Holy Ghost' (*Acts* 6:3), and in the same book we read that 'the disciples were filled with joy, and with the Holy Ghost' (*Acts* 13:52). One of the disciples, Barnabas, who was sent on an errand by the apostles, is described as 'a good man, and full of the Holy Ghost' (*Acts* 11:24). In all these passages the Holy Ghost is presented as the divine spirit which by the grace of God enters into human beings who do his will.

There are some texts where it is evident that the Holy Spirit was regarded as a gift of God. Jesus himself is reported to have said: 'If ye know how to give good gifts to your children, how much more shall your heavenly Father give the Holy Spirit to them that ask him' (*Luke* 11:13). The New Testament abounds in saying which bear witness to the gift-like nature of the Holy Spirit. 'Ye shall receive the gift of the Holy Ghost' (*Acts* 2:38), which means that you will receive the Holy Ghost as a gift. If anyone doubts this interpretation let him consider the words of Peter: ' . . . the Holy Ghost whom God hath given to them that obey him . . . ' (*Acts* 5:32). The Greek original, of course, does not say 'whom' but 'which' (ὅ in the accusative) – the Holy Ghost not being a person. We read that 'on the Gentiles also was poured out the gift of the Holy Ghost' (*Acts* 10:45). Here again, the gift was not given *by* the Holy Ghost, but the Holy Ghost was the gift given by God. This is further confirmed by the passage which reads: ' . . . God giving them [the Gentiles] the Holy Ghost, even as he did unto us' (*Acts* 15:8).

The apostles and disciples had the power to invoke the help of God through proffering the gift of the Holy Ghost upon their converts. 'Through laying on of the Apostles' hands the Holy Ghost was given . . .' (*Acts* 8:17 to 19); '. . . while Peter yet spake these words, the Holy Ghost fell on all which heard the word . . .' (*Acts* 10:44); and 'When Paul laid his hands upon them, the Holy Ghost came on them . . .' (*Acts* 19:6).

As shown in the words of Jesus in *Luke* 11:13, the most important aspect of God's gift is that it sets apart the children of God who have established their relationship with the Father through obedience (see note on *Acts* 5:32 above). The Holy Spirit enters the individual and guides him to the truth and into the Presence.

'Your body is a temple of the Holy Spirit', we read in *1 Cor* 6:19. Another Epistle speaks of the Holy Ghost which dwelleth in us . . .' (*2 Tim.* 1:14). Even the kingdom of God which is within us, is redefined: 'The kingdom of God is . . . Righteousness, and Peace, and Joy in the Holy Spirit' (*Rom* 14:17). But the *summa theologica* is given in these words: 'For as many as are led by the Spirit of God, they are sons of God' (*Rom* 8:14). This passage many sound strange to the ears of many Christians, yet it contains the teaching and message of Jesus in a clearer and more concise form than most church doctrines. The Holy Spirit is the realisation of God's will in the mind of men.

The Holy Spirit becomes a Person

It is likely that early Christianity did not think of the Holy Ghost as a Person. Even the great experience of Pentecost was not the manifestation of a distinct Personality but rather the adoption of the 'ecclesia' by God who poured out his spirit upon the congregation. Peter even says to the assembled Jews that God promised that he would 'pour out his spirit upon all flesh . . . and . . . whosoever shall call the name of the Lord shall be saved' (*Acts* 2:17 and 21). However, the growing Church soon doubted the simple Jewish concept of the spirit as an emanation and gift of the deity. Speculation concerning the divinity of Jesus and the Blessed Trinity soon necessitated the re-thinking of this concept. Yet, had the early 'heresies' not shaken the Church in its very foundations, it is possible that the doctrinal definition of the Holy Ghost would not have been undertaken. The Presence, the *Shekinah*, or the Holy Ghost were taken for granted, and their attributes were not questioned as long as they were implicit in the teaching.

The dispute became more acute when the Arian 'heresy' was conquered and the divinity of Jesus within the Blessed Trinity firmly established. This process was complete when the Nicaean Creed, which closes with the affirmation of belief in the divinity of Christ 'and in the Holy Spirit', was generally accepted in the fourth century.

When it was acknowledged that Jesus the Christ was God the Son, the authors of the doctrine felt the need to extend the manifestations of the Godhead through the function of God the Holy Spirit. There was, of course, general reluctance to consider the Holy Ghost as a separate divine Person since no explicit statement could be found in the New Testament to justify such a belief. The trinitarians (see chapter on the Blessed Trinity) and Athanasius, their leading advocate, called their opponents 'enemies of the Spirit'. The routing of the *pneumatomachi* (those who 'battle against the Spirit') and their leader, Bishop Macedonius of Constantinople, was final in the Second General Council which, held in 381 in Constantinople, extended the Creed by adding the words 'the Lord, the Life-Giver, that proceeds from the Father, that with Father and Son, is together worshipped and together glorified'. The form of the Creed was confirmed in 451 by the Council of Chalcedon. The Holy Ghost had become a distinct divine Person, just as the Son had done at Nicaea just a century earlier.

However, the battle did not end there. The nature of the relationship between the Father and the Son on the one hand, and the Holy Ghost on the other provided material for many centuries of controversy. Slowly the pattern emerged which has remained with us to this day: the Western Churches believe that the Holy Ghost proceeds from the Father *and* the Son (filioque), while the East European churches adhere to the old form of the Creed without this addition. This is at the core of the schism between Eastern and Western Christianity, which has persisted for nearly fifteen hundred years.

Hundreds of thousands if not millions of lives were lost because of a slight difference in the dogma (probably due to difficulties of translating Greek into Latin) and the inability of theologians to agree as to whether a mythical Holy Ghost proceeds from a mythical Father alone, or from a mythical Father *and* a mythical Son.

Exactly how mythical the Holy Ghost is, we realise when we observe the difficulties theologians face in their endeavour to explain this distinct aspect of the Godhead to the satisfaction of their less sophisticated believers.

Griffith Thomas makes a brave attempt: 'The Holy Spirit is at once the personal life of God and "the Executive of the Godhead" in relation to man . . . ' (*The Principles of Theology*, p.96). 'It is the Spirit,' says

S.R. Hooper, 'which comes to man and delivers him from sin, death and the law, and opens the way to freedom and all the fruits of the Spirit – faith, righteousness, joy and peace. The work of Christ makes possible the renewal of the Spirit within us. The Spirit becomes the mode whereby the Christ becomes the in-dwelling and dynamic principle of productive power within us . . . As such the Spirit become almost [sic] a metaphysical principle, and Spirit and truth are identified' (*Handbook of Christian Theology*, p.174). The Roman Catholic M. Bévenot and R. Russell emphasise a point which modern theology is fond of making, namely, that the Holy Spirit is the love between Father and Son: 'The mutual knowledge of the Father and the Son is not separable from the love whereby the Father loves the Son and is loved by him. Therefore men can share it only in the unity of the love of the Holy Spirit, who pours the love of God into their hearts. As later theology recognised, he is the bond of love in the Trinity . . . as the Spirit of Love he assimilates us to the union of the Son and the Father . . . he assures our spirit that we are sons of God and intercedes for us with groans beyond all utterance' (*CC*, p.793). The wheel has turned full circle and the dove is once more the symbol of love, as it was in the case of Astarte and Venus.

T.A. Lacey speaks of the Holy Ghost as 'witness'. 'A synthesis will be found in the thought that believers in the external witness of the Gospel pass on to the witness of the Spirit, which confirms and renders them independent of further corroboration . . . a twofold witness to the Gospel: the witness of men, which is for us the tradition of the Christian Church, and the witness of the Spirit, dwelling in the hearts of the believers . . . a movement of the Spirit is to be judged in conformity to the tradition of the Church' (*Essays in Positive Theology*. pp.23/30). A sophisticated argument which disarms doubt and criticism by skilfully turning the conclusion into a premise.

Harnack views the doctrine in its 'historical context'. The scientific theology of the apologists did, in general, not know what to do with the belief in the Holy Spirit, and even in the third century the majority viewed the Holy Spirit as a Power. However, already Tertullian and Irenaeus tried to honour it as a divine Power within the Deity. Tertullian admitted it as 'God' and 'Person' into his descending but consubstantial Trinity. Origen, in accordance with and following the Bible, took the Holy Ghost into his theology as the third constant Being; to be sure as a creature subordinate to the Son, governing the smallest sphere, the circle of the sanctified. The manner of disposing of the doctrine of the Holy Spirit by Tertullian and Origen . . . shows that in general there did not exist a specific Christian interest in this point of the doctrine (*History of Dogma*, pp.266/7).

But of course, the Reformation changed all that, Pauline doctrine came to the fore once again. Paul's 'justification through faith' could not be had without vigorous help from the Holy Ghost. Luther who revived Pauline Christianity, was emphatic about the believers' need for the help and power of the Holy Spirit.

Luther and the Holy Spirit

'Recently some green youth,' Luther was told, 'came to this conclusion: 'The Holy Spirit is not active in those who resist Him, therefore he is active in those who want Him, therefore the will is *causa efficiens* [effective cause] of our faith.' 'Not so,' said the Doctor, the will *does* nothing, but is the *causa materialis* [material precondition] in which the Holy Ghost is active; even in those who resist Him, as Paul did. And after He had been effective in the will of the resister, it was He who created a will which consents' (Luther's *Table Talk*, V 5189:2,55).

These words of Luther deny man his freedom of choice and elevate the grace of God (the Holy Ghost) to the sole agent who can bring about man's spiritual emancipation. 'The truth will set you free' means in effect that the truth of dogma is the emancipating factor, and freedom is – unfreedom! And this 400 years before Orwell's Newspeak!

Luther continues: 'However, we have to distinguish carefully between the various offices of the Holy Spirit. Sometimes we receive the word from outside, with the Holy Spirit being involved. At other times He moves the hearts from inside and "bloweth where it listeth" (*John* 3:8), but not even in this case without the participation of the Word. Because God has ordained that none should come to faith without the participation of the Word, just as no one can defend himself unless within the State, and none can produce children unless in marriage; and yet not all married partners have children, neither can peace be always maintained in the State, nor will the Holy Spirit always be present in the word preached.'

And he concludes: 'Thus the activity of the Holy Spirit is twofold (1) in public teaching – where He is not always present – see the example of marriage; (2) in the human heart, here He does not attempt to have an effect without the Word, but he has an effect when it so pleases God.' Some of Luther's audience object that the conversion of St. Paul is a special case, since his conversion can give no clue to the conversion of others. The Doctor answers: 'Others will be converted in the same way as Paul was. We all resist the Word. Therefore the Holy Spirit will affect us through the Word when it is His will. It is for this reason that we should highly value the spoken word (verbum vocale) since those who despised it soon turned renegades. And the Pope has very little esteem for this role of the Word.' (ibid.)

If we reduce this diatribe to its essential we find Luther suggesting that Faith acts as an interpreter of the Holy Spirit only where the word is an expression of God's chosen mouthpiece — therefore Luther who values the Word, *is* chosen, while the Pope who does *not* esteem it, is condemned. Of course, Luther carefully hides behind the saying of Jesus who is regarded as 'the Word': 'No man cometh unto the Father, but by me' (*John* 14:6).

In his *Catechism* Luther devotes much time to the elucidation of the concept of the Holy Spirit. He explains that the trinitarian dogma enables us to see in the Father the Creator, in the Son the Redeemer, and in the Holy Ghost the 'Sanctifier, the One who makes holy'. The means whereby the Spirit achieves this end are 'the communion of saints or the Christian Church, the forgiveness of sins, the resurrection of the body, and the life everlasting'. It is the Holy Spirit who leads us into His community, the Church; it is He who helps us comprehend the salvation by Christ, and who maintains us in this state of blessedness. Luther compares the Church of the Holy Ghost to a mother who bears and teaches her children through the Word. Again the papacy is singled out for the accusation that 'through it faith was entirely shoved under the bench and no one recognised Jesus Christ as the Lord and the Holy Spirit as the Sanctifier'. Christ is not being preached and thus the Holy Spirit is not able to 'create, call and gather' the community of the faithful.

In Luther's theology the Holy Spirit is an emanation of the Father through the office of the Word. This is trinitarian doctrine and not a return to the original idea which presented it as a gift of God to help man in his quest for truth.

Twentieth-century theology and the Holy Ghost

Contemporary theologians seem to attribute more significance to the Holy Ghost than their predecessors did.

Tillich, for instance, says that words like 'spirit; and 'flesh' and 'death', in their various combinations appear to us as 'philosophical abstractions' rather than as concrete descriptions of Christian experience . . . To be a Christian means to have the Spirit, and any description of Christianity must be a description of the manifestations of the Spirit . . . Man's body, according to Paul, can become a Temple of the Spirit . . . 'Flesh' is the distortion of human nature [sic], the abuse of its creativity . . . in the service of its unlimited desire and its unlimited will to power. The desire of which we know something through recent psychology, and this will to power, of which we have learnt much from modern sociology, are rooted in our individual existence . . . And finally, Spirit is life. "To be carnally minded is death." There is a man in our time who discovered the truth of this profound statement. Siegmund Freud recognised that at the root of our infinite desire lies the will to death . . . Not only must we die, we also want to die, for "to be carnally minded is death"' (*The Shaking of the Foundations*, pp. 133/142).

Tillich's outstanding disciple, J.A.T. Robinson, brings into play his favourite cliché: 'The deepest ground for our being', which is the Holy Spirit, analysing the words of Paul very much in the same way as Tillich. Robinson does not fall far behind his master in woolliness: 'The deepest groans of suffering of which the apostle had been speaking, so far from separating us from the source of our being in the love of God, are in fact pointers to it, inarticulate sighs too deep for words, which the Spirit can take up and translate into prayer, because "the Spirit" represents the link between the depth of our individual being (however shallow) and the unfathomable abyss of all being in God. God is not outside us, yet he is profoundly transcendent (*Honest to God*, pp.59/60). This 'yet'-philosophy is a typical example of a mannerism which has been called, perhaps unfairly, 'German metaphysical fog'.

Many contemporary theologians are forced to admit that New Testament evidence for the personal nature of the Holy Ghost is, to say the least, indistinct. Professor Jackson concedes that New Testament witness of the Holy Spirit is scanty and concludes: 'Our traditional religious phraseology has fixed so firmly in the popular mind the threefold distinction of Persons within the Godhead that many readers often fail to note how much less definite is the language of the Scripture . . . often wavering and indistinct, so indistinct that the conceptions of Son and Spirit often fade unconsciously one into the other . . . ' (*What do we mean by the Holy Spirit?* Hibbert Journal, April 1926). Emil Brunner cautiously defines the Holy Ghost, to which he continually refers as the Holy Spirit of God, as the effective power of God's salvation reaching us through the word of his Son. I regret to say that orthodoxy prompts him to add to this quite meaningful definition the words 'three in one', thus once again enveloping us in 'metaphysical fog' (*Our Faith*. pp.73/6). Describing the approach of the primitive

Church to the Holy Spirit, Bultmann also refrains from personalising the concept: the early Christians regarded the Holy Spirit as a divine gift which the convert received in baptism. It revealed to him a new idea of freedom, a new power of life, of experience. The popular concept of prophesy merely meant a new openness to the future: the idea of glossolalia (gift of tongues) meant ability to transcend the confines of national and racial limitations; the experience of ecstasy meant a growing intensity of response to external stimuli; and miracles were the boundless confidence in the power of spirit over matter. Of course, the popular mind gave all these concepts a literal, objective interpretation which merely reflects the narrow bounds within which the minds of the new converts moved (*Das Urchristentum*, pp. 190/1). Dr. Matthews also admits that 'New Testament evidence for the personal conception of the Holy Spirit is mixed' (*God in Christian Thought and Experience*, p.195). Slowly, but surely the view gains ground that the 'distinct personality' is not so deeply rooted in doctrine as had been believed for centuries.

According to Karl Barth, 'the Holy Spirit is nothing other than the relationship between Christ and us' (*The Faith of the Church*, p.105). It is our means of gaining knowledge, of becoming conscious of our salvation through the Son and the heritage of divine benefits showered upon us: 'Whatever gifts are offered us in Christ, we receive them by virtue of the Spirit' (ibid.) Here, too, we encounter the 'metaphysical fog': 'The Holy Spirit is God giving us the freedom we were seeking in vain without ourselves: freedom for Him' (ibid. p.106). After this introduction, however, he makes a most important statement: 'Calvin, in conformity with Scripture, does not conceive of the Holy Spirit independently of Jesus Christ. The Holy Spirit *is* the Spirit of Jesus Christ' (ibid.). Barth goes on to interpret Calvin by saying that it is wrong for the Christian to look for anything beyond Christ. He accuses Catholicism of doing exactly that, of wanting to add to the Person of Christ. The same accusation is made against Protestant modernism which also 'fancies that Christ is not enough and tries to complete him with all sorts of religious, humanitarian, scientific experiences presented under the vocable of the Spirit' (ibid. 109). Barth believes that there is an absolute [!] identity between the Holy Spirit and the Person and work of Christ. Yet, after all these statements Barth, orthodox Protestant that he is, wags a finger in the direction of those who dare to draw conclusions from his own admissions. 'According to the New Testament,' he declares, 'the Holy Spirit is one of the object of faith. The Creed too says in conformity with the New Testament; "I believe in the Holy Ghost." The Holy Spirit, an object of faith, is also an object of prayer. We must not only pray that we may receive the Holy Spirit. We must pray *to* him. "Veni creator spiritus". A Christian prayer will always be directed to the Holy Spirit also' (ibid., p. 110). It seems that even this thoughtful theologian would react with wrath and disapproval if we were to take his findings too literally. And what are the feelings of the attentive Christian reader, when having read on page 105 that 'the Holy Spirit is nothing other than the relationship between Christ and us', he encounters on page 111 the theological platitude that 'the Holy Spirit is . . . the bond between the Father and the Son . . . the means and the expression of love . . . '?

The gnostic Holy spirit

Many centuries before gnosticism was born, a Hebrew poet wrote these magnificent words: 'And the Lord God formed man of the dust of the ground, and breathed into his nostrils the breath of life, and man became a living soul' (*Gen.* 2/7). This admirable gnostic image haunted the authors of the Bible: 'The spirit of God hath made me, and the breath of the Almighty hath given me life' (*Job* 33:4). 'All the while my breath is in me, and the spirit of God is in my nostrils' (*Job* 27:3). 'Cease ye from man whose breath is in his nostrils' (*Isaiah* 2:22).

We see that the spirit has always been associated with the divine breath which hath made a creature of the dust into a god (' . . . ye are gods . . . , *Psalm* 82:6). This image also affects The New Testament: 'He breathed on them, and saith unto them: Receive ye the Holy Ghost' (*John* 20:22). The word pneuma means air in motion, breathe, wind, spirit, soul. This identification of the pneuma with the divine breath is significant if we consider that God's prerogative to 'breathe' upon man is exercised by Jesus in John whose gospel is nearest to the time of Jesus' deification.

We can trace the idea of the Holy Spirit to the Egyptian concept of *Ka* (the most appropriate translation would be 'soul'). It is that aspect of the personality which is rooted in the divine, and indeed the Egyptian belief in immortality concerned the immortality of the *Ka*. It is identical with the person and yet separate, capable of communicating, parting and reuniting with it. It dwells in man, guides him and evokes in him an 'inner light'. Great men have more *Kas* than average men, and the kings of Egypt boasted of a great number. It is recorded of Ramses II that he had no less than twenty-three *Kas*. In pictorial form the *Ka* of a king is presented as walking behind him or standing by him.

According to Jung, 'The *Ka* is the life-spirit, the animating principle of men and gods, and therefore can be legitimately interpreted as the soul or spiritual double . . . *Ka-mutef* (the begetter) is a hypostatisation of procreative power. In the same way the Holy Ghost is hypostatised procreative power and life-force (*Psychology and Religion: West and East*, pp. 131/2).

If the view, also expressed by Freud in his *Moses and Monotheism*, that the Jewish religion had its origin in Egypt, is correct, we may notice the link between the *Ka*-concept and the Hebrew idea of the soul breathed into man by god. This breath, the *pneuma*, God's gift to man, elevates man above creation in that he possesses a spiritual consciousness of the divine. Such consciousness may be at the root of the dichotomy of body and soul: the body being that which man has in common with all animate nature, and soul that which only he possesses by virtue of his unparalleled realisation of life and death, of good and evil, of creation and destruction – in brief, his awareness. As Jung puts it, 'God becomes manifest in the human act of reflection' (ibid. p. 162).

This interpretation coincides with the Hebrew poet's passage and permeates the gnostic and early Christian ideas of the Spirit. Being a human state of consciousness, the Spirit bears not only the divine attributes with which man had invested it, but also the attributes of human comprehension. The religious mind first associates the Spirit with the principles of fertility, creativeness and abundance – all attributes of female character. Animus becomes anima, a feminine gendered concept in most languages.

The Old Testament word for Spirit is *ruach* or breath. *Ruach-Adonai* or *Ruach-El* (the origin of the name Rachel) signifies the spirit of God; a 'feminine' emanation of the 'masculine' siring principle, the circle of the creative and procreative process isolated from its material consequence. The consequence, however, cannot be completely ousted: 'the Word became flesh', and out of the self-fertilisation of the Divine springs the Son: man as the child of God.

Jung expresses this tribute of the Holy Ghost with deep insight: 'The Mother quality was originally an attribute of the Holy Ghost, and the latter was known as Sophia-Sapientia by certain early Christians. The feminine quality was not entirely eradicated; it still adheres to the symbol of the Holy Ghost, the *columba spiritus sancti.*'

The transformation of animus into anima is always accompanied by the parallel process, the soul becomes spirit, and it is the divine mediator who acts as catalyst. The Gospel of Thomas reports the following dialogue: 'Simon Peter said to them; Let Miriam go away from us, for women are not worthy of Life. But Jesus said: I will draw her so that I will make her a man and she too may become a living spirit which is like you men, for every women who makes herself a man will enter into the kingdom of heaven' (99:18/26).

Jung who tried to trace the relation between gnosticism and early Christianity writes: 'The doctrine that the Paraclete was expressly left behind for man raises an enormous problem . . . Why in the name of all that's wonderful wasn't it "Father, Mother and Son"? . . . That would be far more "reasonable" and "natural" than "Father, Son and Holy Ghost" . . . It is significant that early Christian gnosticism tried to get round this difficulty by interpreting the Holy Ghost as the Mother ("Come, O communion of the male; come she that knoweth the mysteries of him that is chosen . . . Come, holy dove that beareth the twin young: Come hidden Mother")' (*Acts of Thomas*, translated by James, p.388). On the other hand, the mother-interpretation would reduce the specific meaning of the Holy Ghost to a primitive image and destroy the most essential qualities attributed to him: not only is he the life common to Father and Son, he is also the Paraclete whom the Son left behind him, to procreate in man and bring forth works of divine parentage . . . Out of the tension duality (Father and Son) life always produces the "third" that seems somehow incommensurable and paradoxical. Hence, as the "third", the Holy Ghost is bound to be incommensurable and paradoxical, too. He is a function, but that function is the third Person of the Godhead' (ibid. 158/9). To me, this final conclusion seems a *non-sequitur*, but logical consistency cannot be demanded from religious mysticism.

From Jung's interpretation of early Christian gnosticism it emerges that originally the Holy Ghost was probably a feminine concept (*ruach* – anima) which lost its second place in the mystic triad and moved into a masculine form to the third place. The complementing feminine element was an addition to the trinitarian idea, hence the cult of the Mother of God. As Jung puts it, Holy Ghost and Logos merge in the gnostic idea of *Sophia*, and again in the *Sapientia* of the medieval natural philosophers, who said of her: '*In gremio matris sedet sapientia patris.*' These psychological relationships do something to explain why the Holy Ghost was interpreted as the Mother, but they add nothing to our understanding of the Holy Ghost as such, because it is impossible to see how the Mother could come third, when her natural place would be second' (ibid., p.162). The Paraclete, sharing the breath of the Father and the Son, becomes the provider of the life-breath common to God and man, and thus a common bond between masculine elements. The feminine *ruach* and the neuter πνεῦμα are replaced, inevitably by *him*, the Holy Ghost.

5
The Blessed Trinity

Even before you left the wilderness

In the four thousand year old epic of Gilgamesh we are told about the dream of the hero in which he witnesses the encounter between a soothsayer and a strange 'noble savage', Enkidu. Enkidu is told by the sybil to go forth in search of Gilgamesh who will become his beloved friend. 'Shamash, the glorious Sun, has given his favour to Gilgamesh, and *Anu of the heavens and Enlil, and Ea the Wise* has given him deep understanding. Even before you have left the wilderness . . .'

Even before man left the wilderness of a semi-savage existence, he dreamed of the Trinity of Heaven, and Earth, and the fruit of their union, Man. Heaven is the male principle, Earth the female, and Man is their child. In a later stage another Trinity appears. The giver of life from whose rib is torn the sustainer of life, becomes father to the child, the fruit of their restored unity. Man becomes aware of the mystery of the encounter between male and female, and the issue of that encounter: the concept of the triune oneness, of the Trinity, is born.

This magic symbol is one of the oldest religious formulae. In the Gilgamesh epic, inscribed on tablets by Semitic Accadians and later adopted by Assyrian and Babylonian scribes, we gain a glimpse into one of the most ancient trinitarian revelations. Ana or Anu is Heaven, the father of the great gods, creator and supreme divinity. Ea or Aa was originally the female principle of the Earth, later turned masculine, 'the lord of the earth'. He was also called the 'king of the abyss' and 'lord of wisdom;. Finally, there was Enlil or Enlilla or Bel [Bel or Baal meant 'god']. He was referred to as the 'lord of the mist', the spirit-god. A masculine Trinity appeared: Anu the Father, Ea god of the Son (God made man) and Enlil, god the Holy Ghost. 'Prayer to these three was as good as invoking all the gods of the universe' (Pinches, *Religion of Babylon and Assyria*, p.54).

In the later Assyrian and Babylonian period Shamash became the supreme divinity, and in Egypt Ra. Both were none other than the Sun, itself not a deity but the reflection of the glory and light of the supreme god. It can be seen by man but he is unable to rest his eyes upon it without being blinded. The spouse of Shamash, although not playing a special part in the later Babylonian pantheon was Aa, inherited from an earlier period and restored to her original femininity, probably as symbol of the earth. She had, however, ceded her place of importance to two other major godheads, the spouses Tammuz and Ishtar. As early as 3500 B.C. tablets mention the god Tammuz whom they call 'the shepherd'. His Sumerian name was Dumu-zi or Dumu-zida, meaning true or faithful son. He was probably understood as the embodiment of Truth. His wife was Ishtar, the goddess of beauty and love. Again we see the ancient endeavour to unite the most revered gods into a trinity: Shamash the Father, was described as 'the light of things above and things below', 'the supreme judge of heaven and earth', and the 'lord of living creatures'. Tammuz may be compared to God the Son: the divine principle of Truth, the 'shepherd' who descends to the underworld, the 'truthful son'. The third divine principle, Love, in the form of the goddess Ishtar, corresponds to the Holy Ghost (himself originally a female principle). We should not forget either that according to many theologians the Holy Ghost is indicative of the love between the Father and the Son, or the love between God and Man (see chapter on The Holy Ghost).

In Egypt too, after a long period of the unquestioned supremacy of Ra, the supreme gods were Osiris, Isis and Horus: father, mother and son. Osiris was the life-giving principle, symbolised by the river Nile, which after dispensing its life-giving flood to man, is 'killed' and 'buried'. However, the love of his wife, Isis, the counterpart of Ishtar, brings Osiris back to life and to his life-giving power. Horus, the son of Osiris and Isis, is a sage and miracle-worker, and according to some traditions, is greatly skilled in the art of healing.

In the four-thousand-year-old Hindu religions we also find a concept not dissimilar to the triune Godhead: the complementary divinities Brahma, Vishnu and Shiva, intertwined in their origin and in their cosmic functions. Brahma is the creative principle, Vishnu the sustainer and Shiva the destroyer. Vedic philosophy often sees them as the emanation of a fundamental concept, Devas, God, of which they present three different aspects. This trinity, too, is masculine, but their mother is Bhawani, the divine Primaeval Force, from which everything originates. As we see, we have here the idea of three complementary godheads in association with the Mother of gods.

When the teaching of Lao-Tzu, Taoism, became corrupt, the taoist religion embraced the trinitarian idea. The parts of the godhead were P'an-ku, the source of creation (corresponding to the concept of the Father), the teacher Lao-tzu himself (corresponding to the Son) and the 'Ruler of the Universe' (corresponding to the Holy Spirit). The 'Ruler' is probably the monotheistic God-idea which had been prevalent in China for many centuries. The triune idea of the Divine was called San-tsing and flourished in the third or fourth century B.C.

Mithraism had its roots in the Vedic hymns in which Mitra, the sungod, was always joined to Varuna (Uranos), the skygod (the god of heaven). The two together were the creators of heaven and earth, they together brought light, life and fertility. Eventually Mitra became the god of truth and the source of power vested in the righteous ruler. In the Zoroastrian interpretation of the Vedic cosmogony Ahura-Mazda (Ormuzd) was the god-creator, the source of light, and the father of all. Anahita, the goddess of love, and Mithra (Mithras), possibly their son, were first minor deities joined with Ahura-Mazda in triunity. There were of course other 'powers' or demi-gods who shared in the being of Ahura-Mazda. Of these I should mention Spenta Manyu, the holy spirit of the god, because he is fully hypostatised and bears almost all the attributes of the Holy Ghost of Christianity. This was the religious thought prevalent at the time of the Persian king Artaxerxes II Mnemon, a mythology easily assimilated to the more ancient Babylonian deities: Ahura to Bel, Anahita to Ishtar, and Mithra to Shamash, a slight change of roles but retaining the threefold pattern.

In the name of the Father, and of the Son, and of the Holy Ghost

Since the fourth century all Christians (with the notable exception of the unitarians and with some reservations by other sects) have accepted that in God there are three Persons in one Divine Essence. This doctrine is described as a mystery revealed to, though not comprehended by, man. It also claimed that the trinitarian idea is completely original. Although the doctrine is an essential part of Christianity, it is certainly *not* contained in the teaching of Jesus, nor in that of his apostles.

In support of the trinitarian doctrine Christians quote the following passages:

'Go thee therefore and teach all nations, baptising them in the name of the Father, and of the Son, and of the Holy Ghost' *Matthew* 28:19
'And Jesus when he was baptised, went up straightway out of the

water: and lo the heavens were opened unto him, and he saw the Spirit of God descending like a dove, and lighting upon him: And lo a voice from heaven saying, This is my beloved Son, in whom I am well pleased' *Matthew* 3:16/7

'And straightway coming out of the water, he saw the heavens opened, and the Spirit like a dove descending upon him and there came a voice from heaven, saying, Thou art my beloved Son, in whom I am well pleased' *Mark* 1: 10/1

'Jesus also being baptised, and praying, the heaven was opened, and the Holy Ghost descended in a bodily shape like a dove upon him, and a voice came from heaven which said, Thou art my beloved Son, in thee I am well pleased' *Luke 3:21/2*

'And John bare record, saying, I saw the Spirit, descending from heaven like a dove, and it abode upon him . . . the same is he which baptizeth with the Holy Ghost. And I saw and bear record that this is the Son of God' *John 1:32 to 34*

'And I will pray the Father, and he shall give you another Comforter, that he may abide with you for ever . . . ' *John* 14:16

'The grace of the Lord Jesus Christ, and the love of God, and the communion of the Holy Ghost . . . ' *2 Cor* 13:14

'For through him [Christ] we both have access by one Spirit unto the Father' *Eph.* 2:18

'Elect according to the foreknowledge of God the Father, through sanctification of the spirit, unto obedience and sprinkling of the blood of Jesus Christ' *1 Peter* 1:2

'That I should be the minister of Jesus Christ to the Gentiles, ministering the the gospel of God, that the offering up of the Gentiles might be acceptable, being sanctified by the Holy Ghost . . . ' *Rom.* 15:16

'God hath from the beginning chosen you to salvation through sanctification of the Spirit and belief in the truth: Whereunto he called you by our gospel, to the obtaining of the glory of our Lord Jesus Christ . . . ' *2 Tess.* 2:13/4

'For there are three in heaven that bear record, the Father, the Word and the Holy Ghost. And these three are one.' *1 John* 5:7

Apart from *1 John* 5:7. of which later, the doctrine of the Trinity is *nowhere* stated. The Christian argument that it is implied, depends entirely on interpretation and must, therefore, be considered as valid and relevant in the same way as the interpretation which claims that it is not implied anywhere.

THE BLESSED TRINITY

Let us make man in our image, after our likeness

Christian apologists like to argue that even the Old Testament shows that God revealed his triune nature on many occasions. The following passages are quoted:

'In the beginning God (Elohim) created the heaven and earth . . .
Gen. 1:1
'And the Lord God said, Behold, the man is become as one of us to know good and evil'. *Gen.* 1:26
'The Lord bless thee, and keep thee: The Lord make his face shine upon thee, and be gracious unto thee: the Lord lift up his countenance upon thee, and give thee peace.' *Num.* 6:24-26
'The voice of the Lord is upon the waters: the Lord of glory thundereth: the Lord is upon many waters.
The voice of the Lord is powerful: the voice of the Lord is full of majesty.
The voice of the Lord breaketh the cedars: yea, the Lord breaketh the cedars of Lebanon.' *Psalm* 29:3-5

As regards the passages in Genesis, the Jews have never dreamt of the possibility of a trinitarian polytheistic interpretation. When in the third century the Christians began to exploit the Bible (Old Testament) for their own purposes, we find the Hebrews protesting against the suggestion that the seeming plural 'Elohim' may indicate discourse within the godhead. Rabbi Isaac was the first to explain that the seemingly plural word 'Elohim' is used with the singular form of the verb – *God creates, not create (Gen. Rabba* on 1:1) and Rabbi Pappias pointed out that God's words 'man is become as one of us' likened man to the angels. Rabbi Akiba rejected this interpretation and asserted that it meant 'Man is become as one of himself' since the Hebrew *mimmenu* may mean either 'of us' or 'of himself'. According to Akiba 'of us' is a mistranslation (Daube, *The New Testament and Rabbinic Judaism*, pp.61 and 218). My own opinion is that the plural Elohim possibly remained God's name after the many semitic Palestinian godheads had become One in the religion of the Jews. The personal pronoun in the first person plural is perhaps an indication of God's majesty, nothing more.

Centuries passed before Jewish philosophy was ready and able to deal with the propositions of Christian theology which laid claim to the very foundations of Hebrew religious thought. The first important voice raised in the mediaeval period was that of Saadiyah Gaon, the author of *Emunot ve-Deot*, 'Faith and Knowledge'. In the tenth century Jewish thought was greatly influenced by the Karaite 'heresy' and by Islamic ideas. Saadiyah attempted to counter this trend with the armoury of traditional Judaism. He admitted that Islam moved in the direction of Jewish thought, with its emphasis on strict monotheism and the doctrine of free will. The character of his work was a confrontation between reason and revelation, between knowledge and the truth of faith. He was hostile to the then current ideas of relative and multiple truth which allowed every religion to have its share in the Truth of God. According to him, the Jewish revelation is the only safe anchor of reason, supplying a firm foundation which obviates any doubt. Revelation is uncorrupted reason, while Christianity and Islam are but human creations falsely claiming divine origin. At the centre of his criticism of Christianity was the analysis of the trinitarian idea in the light of the traditional Jewish doctrine. Saadiyah attacked Christian attempts to read trinitarian ideas into Jewish Scripture, but he attacked the Christians patiently and rationally (*Faith and Knowledge*, 2:18/22).

The decisive factors in the Jewish concept of God are Life and Wisdom, without which creative power cannot be sustained. Saadiyah claimed that the Christians tried to abstract these from God himself, and to attribute them to separate Persons in God; Jesus as God representing the life principle and the Holy Ghost the principle of divine wisdom. Christian theology rendered God as a composite Being whose three aspects are existence, life and wisdom. However, everything that is capable of differentiation, division and separation is corporeal. All things corporeal are created things: the Creator himself cannot be created. Life and wisdom, in their divine aspects, are emanations of God's power, not separate agents. According to Saadiyah, the trinitarian doctrine goes contrary to the first principle of belief in God: that God is necessary existence. Claiming that the Son is begotten, the Christian assert that God is begotten. If that is the case, he is created and caused. 'Whatever begets is the cause of the existence of the begotten.' Anything created is not necessary existence, and thus God would not be necessary existence. Saadiyah also refuted the Christian endeavour to hypostatise the various attributes of divine activity (2:2), and engaged in a polemic against the Christological Logos idea (2:25).

A number of mediaeval Jewish thinkers continued the argument against Christian theology on the grounds of Saadiyah's criticism. The most outstanding of these were Moses ben Salomo and Jehuda ha-Levi. In the 16th century a powerful critic arose in the person of Isaac Troki who compiled an interesting catalogue of unfulfilled Old Testament prophesies. The great Jewish philosopher, Moses Mendelssohn, a friend of Frederick the Great, was optimistic about certain trends in Christendom which seemed successful in those days, such as Deism and Unitarianism. He believed that they would eventually expurgate from theology its irrational elements, the doctrines of Trinity, original sin, incarnation and ascension. He hoped that due to the work of these thinkers 'who have the best intentions towards truth and the Christian religion, all these beliefs which seem to be repugnant to sound reason will be explained as human additions' (Quoted from Schoeps, *The Jewish-Christian Argument*, p.105).

As we know now these hopes were unjustified and the beliefs 'which are repugnant to sound reason' are the very strength of a religion that can maintain itself in the 'age of ideology' just because ideologies are irrational and Christianity *is* an ideology.

In the meantime, modern theologians continue to assert that the word Elohim suggests a triune divinity, that the word 'us' and 'our' denote 'self-converse of God', that the frequent mention of the spirit of God is an 'obvious' reference to the Holy Ghost, and that the Logos of *John* 1 and the Wisdom of *1 Cor.* 1 are concepts derived from Old Testament Scripture.

The most ingenious argument we encounter, however, is that which asserts that the Old Testament contains 'hints' as regards the threefoldness of divine names and actions. In this context *Numbers* 6:24/6 and *Psalm* 29:3/5 (see above) are quoted. So is Isaiah 6:1/3: 'In the year that King Uzziah died I saw also the Lord sitting upon a throne, high and lifted up, and his train filled the Temple. Above it stood the seraphim: each one had six wings; with twain he covered his face, and with twain he covered his feet, and with twain he did fly. And one cried unto another, and said, Holy, holy, holy is the Lord of hosts: and the whole earth is full of his glory.' Try as we may, we cannot discover any 'hint' of the Trinity in this text. Yet a responsible theologian, Griffith Thomas, says about these clumsy examples: 'While they may not be pressed, they cannot be overlooked' (*Principles of Theology*, p.26).

Unless we assume too much and *want* to be convinced, we shall not be able to find many things in the over 1200 pages of the Bible (called Old Testament by the Christians), that could be construed as a 'hint' of anticipated trinitarian doctrine.

The words of farewell

After the resurrection Jesus commanded his disciples to meet him on the mountains in Galilee where he spoke the last words recorded in the Gospel according to Matthew.

'All power is given unto me in heaven and in earth. Go ye therefore and teach all nations, baptizing them in the name of the Father and of the Son, and of the Holy Ghost: Teaching them to observe all things whatsoever I have commanded you and, lo, I am with you alway, even unto the end of the world. Amen' (*Matthew* 28:18/20).

There is a disturbing mistranslation even in this short passage. The word Ἐξουσία used by the evangelist does not mean power but authority. Power and authority differ in that authority is vested in somebody by someone else. It is God who vests authority in his Christ. The *NEB* corrects this mistake.

The 'mission charge' is to be found both in Mark's Gospel: 'Go ye into all the world, and preach the gospel to every creature' (*Mark* 16:15) and in Luke's: '. . . repentance and remission of sins should be preached in his name among all nations' . . . ' (*Luke* 24:47). However, place and event differ greatly in the various gospels. Matthew speaks of a mountain in Galilee, Mark also of Galilee and Luke of Bethany outside Jerusalem, while John mentions the shore of the Lake Tiberius as the place where Jesus bade farewell prior to leaving the earth. The words used differ completely in Matthew, Mark and John, and in Luke only the fact is recorded that Jesus blessed his disciples. The ascension is mentioned in Mark and Luke only, the miraculous event is missing in Matthew and John. It should not be forgotten here that the Gospel according to Mark is a mutilated substitute version which was provided with a doubtful ending.

From a thorough reading of the New Testament the reader may ascertain that *Matthew* 28:18/20 is, apart from the so-called 'Johannite Comma' which I shall discuss later, the *only* passage in which the Holy Trinity (not the *doctrine* but the *Persons*) is named. It is significant that the words do not occur in any other version of the Farewell.

The text itself is considered an interpolation by several critics. It is indeed a strange reversal of the attitude of Jesus as revealed in other parts of the New Testament, including the Gospel according to Matthew itself. Firstly, it contains the command of a mission to 'the nations' which was an expression used by the Greek Jews in reference to non-Jews, or as we say 'Gentiles'. In fact, every time the Greek original of the New Testament mentions Gentiles, the word ἔθνοι is so translated. Thus the text could be regarded as revoking *Matthew* 10:5/6

(. . . Go not into the way of the Gentiles, and into any city of the Samaritans enter ye not, but go rather to the lost sheep of the house of Israel . . .), changing it by omission to the extent of excluding the Jews from salvation! Secondly, while Jesus did not himself baptise (*John* 4:2), he is recorded as having encouraged his disciples to do so. And if he commanded them to baptise in the name of the Father, and of the Son, and of the Holy Ghost, why is it recorded that they have consistently baptised 'in the name of Jesus Christ'? (*Acts* 2:38, 8:16, 10:48, 19:5, Rom. 6:3, *Gal*. 3:27) It is also implied in *1 Cor* 1:13 that baptism was practised in the name of Christ. From all the records of Jesus' utterances it seems most unlikely that he would have arraigned in such strange verbal manner the three Persons who play a part in the drama of salvation. He would certainly never have placed the Son (if by that expression he meant himself) between God the Father and the Holy Spirit.

Yet most Christian commentators gloss over these difficulties and state categorically that the passage is 'one of the leading dogmatic texts in the New Testament' (*OVBC*, p.721). The *CC* ingeniously remarks: 'It is possible . . . that our Lord is not prescribing the exact formula to be used, but describing the effects of the rite – consecration to the Blessed Trinity' (p.904). *PC* admits that 'the mission is described in the language of the Church and most commentators doubt that the trinitarian formula was original at this point in Matthew's Gospel, since the New Testament elsewhere does not know of such a formula. However, the practice of the Church (with or without the trinitarian formula) is well in keeping with this epiphany which pictures the situation in all its other details' (p.798). It is strange to note that the commentator, Professor Stendahl, realises the weakness of the only trinitarian text in the New Testament, yet sees it proper to gloss over this discrepancy. Professor Fenton merely mentions that this is the only explicit command of Jesus to baptise, and adds that the first disciples baptised in the name of Jesus, and not in the threefold name (*Saint Matthew*, p.453). With great honesty, he admits the improbability of the text in view of the early disciple's reluctance to preach to the Gentiles (*Acts* 11:1f. and 11:19).

We cannot avoid mentioning here another aspect of the 'mission charge' which no Christian commentator could possibly put on record. Jesus asked his disciples 'to observe all things whatsoever I have commanded you'. The church can hardly claim to be the bearer of the 'mission charge' unless it can be shown that for twenty centuries it has observed all those things! If the church had done so, this book would not be necessary.

By way of interpretation which is, of course, always open to doubt, I suggest that in his lifetime Jesus may have said these words: 'I have authority from the Almighty, blessed be his name, to send you out in the name of the Father full of his Holy Spirit, and in the name of the Son, to teach the people and free them from their errors.'

But then, the resurrected Christ spoke otherwise. and the words which have come down to us certainly suit 'his church'.

The baptism story

The story of Jesus began with his baptism in the river Jordan, the story which is told by the evangelist with moving simplicity:

'And Jesus when he was baptised, went up straightway out of the water: and lo the heavens were opened unto him, and he saw the Spirit of God descending like a dove, and lighting upon him: And lo a voice from heaven, saying, This is my beloved Son, in whom I am well pleased'. *Matthew* 3:21/2)

The version in the Gospels according to Mark (*Mark* 1:10/1) and Luke (*Luke* 3:21/2) are almost identical with that of Matthew, whilst the Fourth Gospel contains a slight theological aside:

'And John bare record saying, I saw the Spirit descending from heaven like a dove, and it abode upon him. And I knew him not: but he that sent me to baptise with water, the same said unto me, Upon whom thou shalt see the Spirit descending, the same is he which baptiseth with the Holy Ghost. And I saw, and bare record that this is the Son of God.' *John* 1:32/4)

More credulous and simple-minded Christians often quote these passages which, according to them, present the three Divine Persons, so to speak, in one tableau. The voice in heaven of the Father, the Son Christ in the river, and the descending dove: the Holy Ghost. I doubt whether the presentation of such a tableau was in the minds of the evangelists; it is more likely that the scene was considered as depicting the moment when God revealed his choice of the man Jesus to be his Christ; when, in the words of Paul, Jesus was declared to be the Son of God with power . . . (*Rom* 1:4). The choice was visibly sealed with God's spirit descending as a dove, the Jewish symbol of purity and holiness. We also encounter it as a symbol of peace (*Gen* 8:11), and of love (Song of Songs 1:15 and 5:2). Philo even claimed that the dove represents wisdom, *Nous* and the *Logos*. More generally it was regarded as one of the symbols of the House of Israel.

The story contains many echoes from the Old Testament: 'Though ye have lien among the pots, yet shall ye be as the wings of a dove covered with silver and her feathers with yellow gold' (*Psalm* 68:13). Elsewhere I shall deal with the similarity between the conceptions of Samuel by Hannah and that of John the Baptist by Elizabeth. The similarities with Samuel pervade the baptism story too. Samuel recognises Saul (God's elect) one day after God announced his coming (*1 Sam* 9:15). In the same way, John the Baptist recognises Jesus one day after he announced the coming of one 'who is preferred before him' (*John* 1:19). When Samuel perceived Saul, God speaks to him: 'Behold the man I spake to thee of, this same shall reign over my people' (*1 Sam* 9:17). Seeing Jesus, the Baptist exclaims: 'Behold the Lamb of God which takes away the sin of the world. This is him of whom I said . . .' (*John* 1 29/30). Saul is proclaimed king after Samuel had seen a miraculous sign; the Baptist proclaims Jesus Son of God after seeing a miraculous sign. When Saul was about to be acclaimed as king, he tried to hide himself, and had to be brought to Samuel (*1 Sam* 10:21). We read in the Fourth Gospel that Jesus when the people would 'come and take him by force that they make him king, he departed again into a mountain himself alone' (*John* 6:15). The examples are taken from Daube (*The New Testament and Rabbinic Judaism*, pp. 17/19). The strange coincidences seem to be due to the fact that the Baptist was styled after the image of Samuel, since he was to be regarded as the prophet giving sanction to the election of Jesus as king of the Jews. Later this aspect was glossed over and forgotten, but the obvious parallel points to the origin of the relevant verses.

Daube's work contains other interesting observations concerning the baptism story. Baptism was not unusual among the Jews, and apart from the symbol of purification it also signified, especially if it was performed in the river Jordan, a new entry into the Promised Land. Before baptism, man is in the wilderness, in the grave, impure and full of error (sin). Baptism is therefore not only entry into the Promised Land and an end to the wandering in the wilderness, but it is also like being born from the dead. 'A convert . . . had the status of a new-born child' (*Bab. Yeb.* 48b); and 'when he has undergone baptism and *come up* he is like an Israelite in all respects' (*Bab. Yeb.* 47b), we read in the Talmud. It is no accident that two evangelists talk about 'coming up' since coming up is like rising from the grave. 'Jesus when he was baptised went up straightway out of the water' (*Matthew* 3:16), and 'straightway coming out of the water'. Daube concludes: 'As for Christian baptism, since, in a way, the kingdom has arrived, the rite symbolised entry into the kingdom' (op. cit. p.119).

The Voice from heaven is quoting Jewish scripture: 'Thou art my son, this day I have begotten thee' (*Psalm* 2:7). Graves and Podro believe this text to represent the declaration of kingship, since they regard the Second Psalm to be the Hebrew Coronation Psalm. The latter half of the divine utterance ' . . . in whom I am well pleased' does not continue the text of the Psalm, but is taken from the Testament of Levy (17:2/14) which is probably but a variation of Isaiah's . . . in whom my soul delighteth . . . ' (*Isaiah* 42:1), while the substitution 'beloved Son' is taken from *Gen.* 22:2.

However, not only the simple-minded consider this text as a trinitarian revelation. In Dummelow's *OVBC* it is called 'one of the leading Trinitarian passages . . . the voice of the Father is heard proclaiming the essential divinity of the Son, as he rises from the baptismal waters: the Holy Ghost, the living bond and unity in the Godhead, descends . . . ' (p.632).

In his commentary on *The Gospel of St. Matthew*, William Barclay points to the improbability that before Jesus, children of Israel underwent baptism which was reserved for 'sin-stained, polluted proselytes' (pp. 52/3). Following up this argument, one tends to give more weight to the hypothesis of Graves and Podro who consider the Baptism story a garbled version of the report on the Coronation of Jesus. According to them this ceremony established Jesus as king of the Jews in the place of the usurper Herod: his political crime for which he had to suffer the death penalty. The hypothesis is not unattractive if we bear in mind that, not unlike a coronation, the ceremony was performed by a 'prophet', the Coronation Psalm was quoted and 'Jesus was declared the Son of God with power . . . '.

Commentators admit that the Voice spoke to 'those present' in Matthew, to Jesus in Mark, to the Baptist in John.

Furthermore, I should like to present the reader with some more accounts of the baptism story in apocryphal scripture. In the Gospel of the Hebrews we read: 'And it came to pass when the Lord was coming up out of the water, the whole fount of the Holy Spirit descended and rested upon him, and said unto him: My son, in all the prophets was I waiting for thee that thou shouldst come, and I might rest in thee. For thou art my rest, thou art my first begotten son, that reignest for ever . . . Behold the mother of the Lord and his brethren said unto him: John baptiseth unto the remission of sins, let us go and be baptised by him. But he said unto them: What have I sinned that I should go and be baptised by him? unless peradventure this very thing that I have said is a sin of ignorance . . . ' (*The Apocryphal New Testament*, pp. 5/6). Although this writing is obviously of later origin than the canonical gospels, the author still seems to know nothing about the Trinity, and 'the Voice' itself is called 'the fount of the Holy Spirit'.

Another story in the Gospel of the Ebionites, tells us that 'After people were baptised, Jesus also came and was baptised by John; and as he came up from the water, the heavens were opened, and he saw the Holy Ghost in the likeness of a dove that descended and entered into him, and a voice from heaven saying: 'thou art my beloved Son, in thee I am well pleased: and again: This day I have begotten thee'. And straightway there shone about the place a great light. Which when John saw he saith unto him: Who art thou, Lord? And again there was a voice from heaven saying unto him: This is my beloved son in whom I am well pleased . . . (ibid., p.9). As we see, here the Voice reveals itself both to Jesus and to the Baptist, resolving the contradiction which exists in the canonical writings.

A very strange account is given in the Book of John the Evangelist: ' . . . Satan the prince of the world perceived that I was come to save them that were lost, and sent his angels even Elijah the prophet, baptising with water: who is called John the Baptist. And Elijah, who is the prince of the world? How can I know him? Then the Lord said: On whomsoever thou shalt see the spirit descending like a dove and resting upon him, he it is that baptiseth unto forgiveness of sins: thou wilt be able to destroy him . . .' (ibid., p.191).

I do not propose to deal here with the problem of trinitarian implications alleged to exist in the sayings concerning the Holy Ghost as Comforter.

I dealt with this subject exhaustively in the chapter on the Holy Spirit. Suffice it to say that the trinitarian doctrine is by no means explicit in those passages. Even if the Christian apologists could show that Jesus did speak of the spirit as distinct from God the Father, it would still remain to be proven that he spoke of the Spirit as a separate Person.

Grace, love and communion

The frequently quoted passage in 2 Cor. is very slender evidence that there is trinitarian thought in the New Testament: 'The grace of the Lord Jesus Christ, and the love of God, and the communion of the Holy Ghost . . . ' *(2 Cor.* 13:13/4). It is the conclusion of the Epistle and finishes with the words ' . . . be with you all. Amen'. It is an epistolary benediction, a kind of 'with best wishes and kind regards, Your sincerely'. Commentators regard it is as an affirmation of the

Trinity, because the alleged 'three Persons' are mentioned in one phrase.

Another passage for which trinitarian significance is claimed is: 'That I should be the minister of Jesus Christ to the Gentiles, ministering the gospel of God, that the offering up of the Gentiles might be acceptable, being sanctified by the Holy Ghost' (*Rom.* 15:16). Firstly, it is clear that in the language of Paul 'God' is not the Trinity, but the Father. In fact, the text seems to bring out the distinction rather than the oneness of Christ and the Holy Ghost with the Father, i.e. 'God'. There are passages in Paul's Epistles where he makes that distinction clear ' . . . to us there is but one God, the Father . . . and one Lord Jesus Christ . . . ' (*1 Cor* 8:6); ' . . . the head of every man is Christ, and the head of every woman is the man, and the head of Christ is God' (*1 Cor.* 11:3); and 'For there is one God, and one mediator between God and man, the man Christ Jesus' (*1 Tim.* 2:5). Even the spurious Epistle to the Hebrew contains passages making that distinction: 'How much more shall the blood of Christ who through the Eternal Spirit offered himself without spot to God' (9:14); ' . . . this man after he hath offered one sacrifice for sins for ever, sat down on the right hand of God . . . whereof the Holy Ghost also is a witness to us . . . ' (10:12/15).

The frequent accusation that the Jewish faith does not enjoin kindness towards strangers, is completely untrue. ' . . . And thou shalt not oppress a stranger . . . seeing ye were strangers in the land of Egypt' (*Exod.* 23:9); 'Love ye therefore the stranger: for ye were strangers in the land of Egypt' (*Deut.* 10:19); and, 'Should anyone turn aside at the sight of a stranger, it is as though he turned aside at the sight of the Most High God' (*Hagigah 5a*). Rabbinic literature speaks of two kinds of proselytes: those who accepted circumcision and the full weight of the Law, and those who, living in the country, accepted the Jewish Law as binding upon them. Proselytes were always made welcome and conversion was encouraged: some teachers even regarded it as a work of great merit. Rabbi Simon ben Eleazar asserted: 'The Holy One, blessed be He, gave Israel over into dispersion among the nations that they might attract to themselves proselytes.' From the third century onwards the desire to proselytise declined and eventually vanished. However, at all times, Jews were conscious of being 'the chosen people' and regarded admission into their ranks as a great honour. They were proud even of their suffering: 'We glory in tribulations.' The Tannaites demanded that a new convert, in presenting himself for baptism, should be told about the persecution and suffering of Israel he would have to share, and was expected to answer: 'I know, and I am not worthy.'

During his ministry Jesus does not appear to have encouraged proselytising outside Israel. Many of his sayings show that he was concerned only with 'the lost sheep of Israel'. In this respect only the two mission-passages differ. It is Paul who was the great proselytiser, and it seems that the Apostles did not share his zeal for the conversion of the Gentiles.

The expression, 'Sanctified by the Holy Ghost', may mean the efficacy of the divine spirit aiding the words and deeds of Paul in his arduous effort of bringing the gospel to the Gentiles. It is by no means implicit that a 'Person' is alluded to who, separately from the Father and Jesus Christ, forms with them in a Trinity, worshipped by Paul. The *CC* has the honesty to say about this passage: 'To bring the Gentile world as a worthy sacrifice to the altar of God is probably all that Paul meant to say' (p.1079). I can only express my profound agreement.

We both by one Spirit

After speaking of the great honour his Gentile listeners or readers were accorded when they were admitted into Israel and the knowledge of God, Paul says: 'For through him [Christ] we both have access to one Spirit unto the Father' (*Eph*. 2:18). This passage too, has been exploited by the trinitarians to show Paul's awareness of the Trinity: he mentions the Father, the Son, and the Holy Ghost in one single sentence. It is obvious that many apologists find it necessary to search through the New Testament for texts which, however remotely, can be arrayed in support of the trinitarian argument.

In Dummelow's *OVBC* we find this attitude clearly demonstrated: 'Quite incidentally, the recognition of Son, Spirit and Father, comes to the surface. The Apostle habitually [sic] thinks of the Godhead as threefold' (p.962). Professor Lacey says: 'By his [Christ's] merits and propitiatory sacrifice we are both (Jews and Gentiles) introduced into the presence of the Father in One Holy Spirit. The bond of love and peace which joins the Father to the Son is also the bond of union for the members of the Church' (*CC*, p.1123). In *PC* Professor Chadwick puts it even more simply: 'The unity is derived wholly from Christ of whose indivisible body both Jews and Gentiles are members' (p.983). The passage is mentioned as proof of God's triune nature in Crossley's *The Holy Trinity* (p.24), and in many other books dealing with the subject.

Once again I suggest a paraphrasing of *Eph*. 2:18 which may appeal to those who, like myself, believe that the Epistles were written in simple language to simple men and women: 'It is through the teaching and example of Jesus Christ that we acquire the spirit which leads us both, Jews and Gentiles, to the Father.'

The sprinkling of blood

The Apostle Peter, or whoever wrote the Epistle in his name, opens the letter with a greeting to the scattered people of God who live in Asia Minor: 'Elect according to the foreknowledge of God the Father, through sanctification of the Spirit, unto obedience and sprinkling of the blood of Jesus Christ, Grace unto you and peace . . .' (*1 Peter 1:2*). This rigmarole is simplified in the *NEB* to read 'Chosen of old in the purpose of God the Father, hallowed to his service by the Spirit, and consecrated with the sprinkled blood of Jesus Christ'. This rendering makes more sense, even if the first version is considerably nearer to the wording of the Greek original. This is another text used by the trinitarians to justify their doctrine.

It is indeed considered a 'weighty' passage by many apologists (Griffith Thomas *Principles of Theology*, p.23; *PC*, p.1027; Dummelow's *OVBC*, p.1041 etc). But the crown goes to Bishop Wordsworth, a renowned 19th century theologian who, in his commentary on *1 Peter* 1:2, writes: 'These blessings which flow from the love of God the Father, through the mediation of God the Son, are applied personally to each believer by the sanctification of the Spirit – God the Holy Ghost. Thus . . . each of the three Persons of the ever-Blessed Trinity is here presented to us by the Apostle, as co-operating in the work of our salvation,' II, p.47).

Professor Willmering in the *CC* is more cautious. All he says about this passage is that Christians 'are called to the faith according to the foreknowledge of God the Father, who decreed to give them all the means of salvation and sanctification through the Holy Spirit, which goal is achieved by obedience to Jesus Christ' (p.1178), although on the same page there is a careful reminder of the different parts played in the work of salvation by the three Persons, according to Peter's Epistle.

Once more I should like to paraphrase the salutation: 'God in his omniscience has chosen you to be moved by the divine spirit to heed the teaching of Jesus Christ who gave his blood for you.' Freed from its archaic trappings the text can be used as a powerful argument not for, but against, the trinitarian doctrine.

The Johannite Comma

One, and only one passage in the whole New Testament and its million words appears to confirm the doctrine of the Holy Trinity. It is the famous text in the First Epistle of John, referred to as the 'Johannite Comma': 'For there are three in heaven that bear record, the Father, The Word and the Holy Ghost. And these three are one' (*1 John* 5:7).

Unfortunately for the trinitarian apologists, this passage is a fraudulent insertion. Any New Testament in the English language since (and including) the Revised Version, and even the new Roman Catholic editions omit it. No self-respecting theologian would today claim that the text is genuine.

It is missing from Greek manuscripts prior to the 5th century and from good copies of Eastern language New Testaments. It was not quoted by the Early Fathers, not even during the great Arian/Trinitarian controversy where it would have been a most valuable piece of the trinitarian armoury. It was first used by Priscillian at the end of the 4th century, who probably included it from some marginal gloss. It may be that he himself saw a manuscript which incorporated the marginal note from an earlier copy. From Spain the passage spread, especially after the trinitarian victory in the 4th century had made it 'respectable'. Later African writers, such as Vigilius and Fulgentius made use of it, and eventually it found its way into the early extant versions of the Vulgate. At the end of the 5th century, the Bishop of Carthage, Eugenius, presented a 'Profession of Faith' to the Vandal King Hunneric, which contained this passage. Some critics argue that Tertullian knew it, although this cannot be proved by any conclusive evidence. It seems likely, however, that Cyprian was aware of it and that it circulated (though not necessarily as part of Scripture— as early as the end of the 3rd century.

Thus the Comma Jahanneum or the 'Three Heavenly Witnesses', as the passage came to be known, was generally accepted in the Latin Church, but found its way only into very few Greek manuscripts. When Erasmus edited the New Testament for its printed publication in Greek, he omitted the phrase in the first and second editions, only to include it in the third (1522) since the omission was fiercely attacked by many powerful critics of his time.

We have it on the authority of an important student of the New Testament, F.H. Scrivener, that 'the authenticity of the words . . . will, perhaps, no longer be maintained by anyone whose judgment ought to have weight' (*Introduction to the Criticism of the New Testament*, p. 560). This was written over a hundred years ago. Yet most laymen, guided by the Authorised Version, still quote the text and believe that explicit scriptural evidence exists for the trinitarian doctrine. This is not surprising when we consider that at about the same time Scrivener disowned the passage, Bishop Worsdsworth, while also disowning the words of the Johannite Comma, wrote: 'No one need be disturbed by their non-appearance in the text. It is certain . . . that the Anti-Nicene and Nicene Fathers confuted Arianism without the aid of this passage, to which they never refer, because it was not in their copies of this Epistle; and the doctrine of the Trinity had been clearly established by other Scriptures, and by the consentient voice and concurrent practice of the Church' (*The New Testament*, II, p. 123).

It seems that no amount of proof and evidence will ever prevail against the consentient voice and concurrent practice of the Church!

The birth of the Trinity

In other chapters I try to show how Jesus came to be regarded as God among the Christians. A strange statement by a 19th century theologian, W. Sanday, seems to sum up the thought processes involved in the evolution of the trinitarian doctrine: 'If the Son of God was really there, and if there was nevertheless a Godhead in heaven, then in the language of men we must needs say that there were two Persons in the Godhead; and if two, then it was a comparatively easy step to say that there were three. The doctrine of the Trinity is only one of the necessary sequels of the doctrine of Incarnation.' Well said, and I do not think that any satire on trinitarian Christianity could have put it better. We may even go further and say: not only was it possible to state that there are three, but it was necessary to do so. First of all, there was a trinitarian tradition in various heathen religions; secondly, the elevation of the God-Man to God was easier if he was not joined to the stern father-figure of Jewish monotheism, but to a wider concept of a triune Godhead in which he was but one of three equal Persons.

The trinitarian idea must have had currency as early as the middle of the second century, but its first great exponent was the remarkable Tertullian. He was one of the first Christian authors who wrote in Latin rather than Greek, and became the originator of Latin Christian terminology. His work had enormous influence on the later Church Fathers, and his *Against Praxeas* contained passages of an explicit trinitarian approach: 'All are of one, by unity of substance; while the mystery of the dispensation is still guarded which distributes the unity into a Trinity, placing in their order the three, the Father, the Son, and the Holy Spirit; three, however . . . not in substance, but in form; not in power, but in appearance, for they are of one substance and one essence and one power, inasmuch as He is one God from whom these degrees and forms and aspects are reckoned under the name of the Father, and of the Son, and of the Holy Spirit' (*Praxeas*, 2).

This remarkable passage was written more than a century before Athanasius and Nicaea. In the same work Tertullian claims that these aspects of the Godhead are Persons, but meaning by the word not our usage in the sense of personalities, but objective modes of being' (Quoted from Walker, *History of the Christian Church*, p.66). Yet Tertullian would have been a heretic from the point of view of Nicaea because he claimed that since 'both Son and Spirit are derived from the Father by emanation, both are subordinate to him' (ibid.). A revealing remark by Tertullian deserves to be quoted here in full: 'The simple – I will not call them unwise or unlearned – who always constitute the majority of believers, are startled at the dispensation of the three in one, on the ground that their very rule of faith withdraws them from the world's plurality of gods to the one only true God' (*Praxeas* 3).

The simple ones were of course the overwhelming majority of 3rd-century believers: they were on the whole 'adoptionists' (God adopted Christ as His Son) and unitarian. Within the wider context there were many variations of which I shall mention only one of the most influential doctrines, the so-called Sabellian 'heresy'. As I have mentioned in an earlier chapter, Sabellius (early 3rd century) taught that 'Father, Son and Holy Ghost are all one and the same. They are three names of the one God who manifests himself in different ways. As Father he is the lawgiver of the Old Testament, as Son he is incarnate, as Spirit he is the inspirer of the Apostles' (Walker, *History of the Christian Church*, pp.69/70). Although Sabellius was much abused by most of his contemporaries and eventually excommunicated by the Church, his influence was widespread and the later official trinitarian doctrine is, in fact, a compromise between Tertullian's teaching of 'Three Persons' and the ideas of Sabellius establishing the identical status of the three aspects of God.

We owe our knowledge of Sabellius largely to Epiphanius, a Church Father who wrote more than a century later. Calling the idea of Sabellius a folly, he nevertheless attempts to explain it by introducing the analogies of body, soul and spirit which correspond to the Father, the Son and the Holy Ghost. He mentions another analogy – the sun has three manifestations: light, heat and the orb itself. The heat may be compared to the Spirit, the light to the Son, while the Father is the actual substance (*Adv. haer.*, 63:1). His explanation sounds almost as if Epiphanius, officially rejecting the 'heresy' were in secret sympathy with it.

Novatian's *Trinity*, written in Latin about A.D. 250 was the first treatise devoted entirely to the doctrine of God's triune nature. He taught that Father and Son have a 'complete union of substance' (*Trinity*, 31). Concerning *John* 10:30 he says that Jesus meant 'one thing' (unum): let the heretics understand that he did not say One Person. For 'one' used in the neuter intimates the social concord, not the personal unity (ibid., 27). Novatian was also the first to emphasise that Christ was fully God and fully Man.

We owe another interesting document concerning the same debate to Athanasius. It is an extract from a letter written by Dionysus, bishop of Rome, to Dionysus, bishop of Alexandria. The first named criticises the latter's teaching and suggests that certain doctrines reduce the One God to three powers and, indeed, to three deities, 'dividing the sacred Monad into three substances' while really 'the Divine Triad is gathered into a unity'. Dionysus of Rome already performs the intellectual somersault of the later trinitarians: *We must believe in God the Father all sovereign, and in Jesus Christ his Son, and in the Holy Spirit, and hold that the Word is united to the God of the Universe. For "I" says he, "and the Father are one", thus both the Holy Triad and the holy preaching of the Monarchy will be preserved*' (*Athanasius, De decretis*, 26).

Herein we can recognise the source of Athanasius' inspiration. The letter also contains the condemnation of Sabellius by means of the usual dialectical trick of putting something in the mouth of our opponent, and then proceeding to belittle a statement that was never made.

The heirs of salvation

Arius, presbyter of Baucalis, was a subordinate of Alexander, the influential bishop of Alexandria, It was about A.D. 320 that he turned against his superior whose trinitarian and 'Romanist' trends he deplored. We owe it to Theodoret, bishop of Cyrrhus, that the text written by Arius to Eusebius, bishop of Nicomedia, has been preserved. I quote some of its text, to show the perverse and obtuse nature of the arguments that paved the way for the official doctrines of the Christian faith which have endured into our own time: ' . . . Alexander drives us from the city as atheists because we do not concur with him when he publicly preaches "God always, the Son always; at the same time the Father, at the same time the Son; the Son co-exists with God, unbegotten; he is ever begotten, he is not born by begetting;

neither by thought nor by any moment of time does God precede the Son; God always, the Son exists from God himself' . . . bishops of the East have been condemned for saying that God existed without beginning, before the Son . . . the heretics threaten us with a thousand deaths. But what we say and think . . . that the Son is not unbegotten, nor part of the unbegotten in any way, nor is he derived from any substance' but that by his own will and counsel he existed before time and ages – fully God, only begotten, unchangeable. And before he was begotten or created or appointed or established, he did not exist; for he was not unbegotten. We are persecuted because we say that the Son has a beginning, but God is without beginning . . . he is neither part of God nor derived of any substance . . . ' (Bettenson, *Documents of the Christian Church*, p.55). This letter, probably written in A.D. 321, states the Arian case: God is one and self-contained; Christ is a created being who has a beginning. He is the only-begotten and first-born Son of God, but not of the same substance. In fact, Christ is neither God nor Man, he is the Lord Jesus Christ. A faithful echo of Paul's teaching.

Bishop Alexander was greatly vexed and called a synod in Alexandria which promptly condemned Arius and his followers. Eventually Arius had to flee to Eusebius who gave him refuge and protection. It happened about the same time that Constantine, Emperor of Rome, defeated his rival Licinius and become sole ruler of East and West.

A sinner saved by grace

For twenty years (285-305) the Roman Empire was ruled by a wise and circumspect man, Diocletian, the last of the great 'pagan' emperors. One of the manifestations of his wisdom was his abdication when he thought he had accomplished the aim of his rule. Years later some of his admirers expressed their wish that in view of the turmoil in which the realm found itself, he should return to the throne. He wrote to them 'Could you but see the vegetable garden which I have planted with my own hands, you would not advise me to take such a course of action.' Another sign of his wisdom was that, seeing the extent of his dominion, he elevated his most trusted general to the rank of fellow-emperor. At the same time he made two more of his generals viceroys, bestowing on them the title 'Caesar'. Under his powerful leadership the system worked, but after his abdication the haggling for power began, and soon the Empire was saddled with seven rulers, each claiming the title of Emperor. Among these there was an ambitious young man, Constantine. He was the son of Constantius Chlorus, one of Diocletian's Caesars. His mother, Helena, whom the Church later canonized, was Constantius Chlorus's wife by his first marriage. In order to strengthen his hand, the young Constantine married Fausta, the daughter of one, and sister of another, of his fellow-'emperors'. Luck was on his side: his father, Constantius Chlorus died in 306, his colleague Severus was killed in a campaign against another 'emperor', to be replaced by Licinius. Diocletian's fellow-emperor, Maximian, Constantine's father-in-law, fell out with his son Maxentius (another emperor) and fled to Constantine whose protection he invoked. Constantine had him strangled (311). Yet another 'emperor', Galerius, died in the same year. Finally, Constantine engaged Maxentius, his brother-in-law, in battle. Maxentius lost his life in this encounter (312), leaving Constantine and Licinius as sole claimants to supreme power.

By that time Constantine has discovered his deep interest in the Christian faith. Legend has it that in his battle against Maxentius a large cross appeared on the sky with the inscription 'In this sign conquer!'. Some historians believe that his partiality for Christianity was due to the fact that many of his best generals and soldiers were Christians, and that their service was the more devoted and fanatical the more lip-service he paid to their faith. It is significant that Constantine himself did not submit to baptism until shortly before his death.

From 312 onward it seemed that the ambitious Constantine was quite prepared to share power with Licinius – he even gave his sister in marriage to his fellow-emperor. Together the two issued the famous Edict of Toleration (311) which 'gives Christians the right to exist and set up their places of worship, provided always that they do not offend against public order'. The Edict also contained this intriguing provision: 'In return for this our indulgence it will be the duty of Christians to pray to God for our recovery [meaning the recovery of the mortally sick Galerius], for the public weal and their own; that the State may be preserved from danger on every side . . . '. The Edict of Toleration was followed by the Edict of Milan (313) which gave Christians full right of worship, and restored to them any place they had previously purchased for that purpose. It provided for the restitution of all church property and for considerable grants to be paid to the clergy, exempting clergymen from all public taxes and duties. Constantine gave rulings in ecclesiastical disputes (Case of Caecilian, 316), decreed the suppression of 'soothsayers' (i.e. priests of the old religion), and gave State recognition to the Christian Sunday.

A few years later Constantine turned against his fellow- emperor

THE BLESSED TRINITY

Licinius whom he defeated in a long drawn-out campaign. After a period of banishment the hapless Licinius was strangled (324), allegedly on the instigation of Constantine. Not satisfied with the removal of his rival, he ordered the execution of his own nephew, the eleven-year-old son of Licinius, who might have served as focus for an opposition to Constantine's autocracy.

After the death of Licinius, the ruthless murderer was sole ruler of the whole Roman Empire. Grateful for his pro-Christian legislation, Christian historians call him Constantine the Great, the main merit of this monster having been the expedient favour shown by him towards the Church. Eusebius, the Church historian, goes as far as to call him 'the most holy Emperor Constantine'.

A little lesson in Greek

I am afraid that at this point I must devote myself to some fine points of etymology and translation which have played an important role in the disagreements of the early Church and have confronted seventeen subsequent centuries of theological thinking. Very few people study Greek today, yet most have strong opinions on the subject of the trinitarian doctrine. Their statements are invariably based on the translation in which they have studied the subject.

Ὅμοιος, -α, -ον means similar, like, resembling, common, mutual, equal. In the English usage words like homeopathy, homonym, homosexual, homogeneous, still preserve the original meaning of the word. ἡ οὐσία means that which it one's own, one's property, one's nature, essence, substance, state, condition, being. κατα may mean a multitude of things, often depending on the preposition or context, for our purposes it is sufficient if we remember that in the New Testament its meaning is often 'according to'. κατ' οὐσίαν means similar in nature or similar in essence. A contraction of the words resulted in ὁμῶσίος, a term we frequently encounter. It is used to denote the doctrine that the Persons in the Trinity are of the same substance.

Another word with which we have difficulties is ὑπόστασις from ὕπο meaning mainly under, below, beneath, and στάσις, again a word which has many meanings: standing, position, station, party. The English words apostasy, state, static and stand, are of the same origin. At the first word ὑποστάσις meant sediment, support, subject-matter: it came to mean foundation, substance, reality, and in theology: nature, substance, essence. Eventually it became the Greek word corresponding to the Latin 'persona' for the Persons in the Trinity.

This terminology presented considerable difficulties, ὑπόστασις should translate 'substantia', a word with which it is etymologically identical (substantial). The term 'substantia', however, was already reserved for the Greek οὐσία. Centuries of fatal conflicts and murderous controversies were caused by the difficulty in finding the exact Latin counterparts for Greek concepts and vice-versa.

The Council of Nicaea

The bitter quarrel between Arius and Alexander split the Church into two warring factions. The Emperor Constantine who, for political reasons of his own, wished to utilise his influence over the clergy, was irked by its disunity. Intending to put an end to the quarrel which seemed unimportant to him, he sent his counsellor Hosius, bishop of Cordoba, to Alexander. He demanded that the dispute over such an 'unprofitable question' should be shelved. When this attempt failed, the Emperor convened a Church Council. 325 saw the constitution of the First General Council of the Christian Church in Nicaea.

The Council rejected almost immediately the Creed presented by the Arians. Eventually it adopted a Creed which was an amendment of the text proposed by Eusebius of Caesarea, and which came to be known as the Creed of Nicaea. This is not the same as the famous Nicene Creed which probably dates from 381. and was adopted in Constantinople: it is more correctly called the Niceno-Constantinopolitan Creed. The Creed of Nicaea reads: 'We believe in one God the Father All-sovereign, maker of all things visible and invisible. And in one Lord Jesus Christ, the Son of God, begotten of the Father, only begotten, that is, of the substance of the Father, God of God, Light of Light, true God of true God, begotten not made, of one substance with the Father, through whom all things were made, things in heaven and things on earth; who for us men and for our salvation came down and was made flesh, and became man, suffered and rose on the third day, ascended into the heavens, is coming to judge living and dead. And in the Holy Spirit. And those that say "There was when he was not", and "Before he was begotten he was not", and "He came into being from what-is-not", or those who allege that the Son of God is "of another substance or essence" or "created" or "changeable" or "alterable", these the Catholics and Apostolic Church anathematises.'

As can be seen, the Creed of Nicaea was drawn up to deal with the Arian 'heresy'. Many theologians believe that Hosius, the Emperor's favourite, played a dominant part in formulating this document. At the Council the Emperor demanded the universal adoption of the Creed with its trinitarian undertone, and only two of the bishops present had the courage to reject it. They, and Arius, were of course banished and declared heretics. Even Arius' friend, Eusebius of Nicomedia, signed the Creed, although the victors did not trust him, and before long he had to follow Arius into exile. It is noteworthy that Constantia, the Emperor's sister, used her influence to have Eusebius reinstated, and for a short period he became the Emperor's trusted adviser. However, Constantine soon died (337) and thus the decisive victory of the anti-Arians could not be reversed.

Like Father, like Son

The sorry tale of Rome's decline continued after Constantine's death. His three sons, Constantine II, Constantius II, and Constans, were supposed to share the Empire as co-emperors. Soon they fell out with each other, and in the ensuing struggle both Constantine and Constans lost their lives. Constantius II, now sole emperor, was a fanatical supporter of the Arian doctrine and a persecutor of the trinitarians. He caused the synod at Milan to be convened (355) at which he declared: 'Let my will be deemed a canon among you, as it is among the Syrian [Arian] bishops.' His wrath led to the exile of Athanasius (356) and to the Council at Sirmium (357) which accepted the Arian attitude without demur. It stated: '. . . two Gods must not be spoken of, since the Lord himself says, "I go to my Father and your Father, and to my God and your God . . ." (*John* 20:17), that there are two persons of the Father and the Son; and that the Father is greater, the Son subject together with all things that the Father has subjected to Himself. The Father has not a beginning . . . the Son has been born from the Father . . .' (Socrates, *H.E.* 1:9). [This Socrates is, of course, not identical with the great Greek philosopher, and lived about 440 A.D.] Once more Eastern Christianity, which always leaned toward the Arian view, and the Western Church were united. The aged Hosius and Athanasius were in banishment and their opponents seemed firmly established. The concept of the οὐσία and of any of its combinations were forbidden, 'heretical' and unscriptural. The Sirmian declaration, a complete reversal of the Creed of Nicaea, was signed even by Hosius before he went into exile, and the whole Church accepted the new teaching which is often referred to as the doctrine of ὁμοιούσιον. The enemies of Christianity were greatly amused at the amount of hatred and persecution occasioned by the difference of an iota (homoousion and homoiousion).

Constantius was not less ambitious and ruthless than his father, and among his many misdeeds the most fateful was the murder of his cousin Gallus (354). The son of Gallus, Julianus, spared because he was considered too insignificant, later became the leader of a successful rebellion against the emperor, and Constantius died of a fever in 361 during a campaign to quell the rebellion. Julianus, a notable and talented youth, became emperor. Christian historians hated his memory and added the word 'Apostate' to his name, because he made an abortive attempt to stem the rise and spread of Christianity in the realm. He made some forceful literary attacks upon the new religion and liked to be entertained by enforced public discussions between Greek philosophers and Christian theologians.

The return of Athanasius

In 362 Julianus permitted the return of all the banished bishops and 'heretics'. Thus we find Athanasius once again in Alexandria where one of his first acts was to pronounce anathema upon 'the Arian heresy' and demand a return to the Creed of Nicaea. He insisted upon the full content of a trinitarian definition: the Godhead in one essence (substance) and three hypostases.

On the death of the young Julianus, who lost his life on the battlefield, a Christian ascended the throne once more. It was Jovianus who interfered little in Church affairs. The same applies to his son and successor Valentinian. Athanasius, who remained in Alexandria until his death in 373, now became the dominant influence in Western Christianity. His intellectual heritage was taken over by a new Nicene party, led by three men of exceptional vigour and ability, referred to as the Cappadocians. They were Basil of Caesarea, his friend Gregory Nazianzus, and Basil's younger brother, Gregory of Nyssa. They continued the work of Athanasius, although their trinitarian ideas were more emphatic about the unity of the Godhead than the Trinity of Persons. In his *History of the Christian Church*, Walker claims that the Cappadocians did not present God as three personalities in our sense of the word but rather as 'three modes of being', of an identical essence. One personal God exists in three interpenetrating modes and not in three-fold individual separation (p. 117).

As we have noted, imperial interference had brought about first the triumph of the trinitarian view, and then its temporary eclipse. Once again it was a powerful emperor who settled the dispute once and for

THE BLESSED TRINITY

all in favour of the New Nicene trend. Theodosius (378-395), sole emperor from 392, was the last Augustus to rule the united imperial realm. He too is called 'the Great', in recognition of the support he gave to the emerging powerful Church. Among his more saintly deeds I may mention the way he revenged the assassination of a few imperial officials in Thessalonia. He invited the population of the city to a free circus show and, when the crowd assembled, they were attacked and massacred by the Emperor's soldiery. More than seven thousand people, men, women and children perished on the occasion. Even the Church raised its voice against this dastardly action, but Theodosius was eventually forgiven by a grateful clergy. His advisers were followers of the Nicene doctrine and it is not surprising that he himself became an ardent supporter of that faction.

In 380 he issued an edict, an extract of which is quoted here, since it is relevant to our theme. 'It is our desire that all the various nations which are subject to our Clemency and Moderation, should continue in the profession of that religion which was delivered to the Romans by the divine Apostle Peter, as it has been preserved faithful tradition, and which is now professed by the Pontiff Damasus . . . According to the apostolic teaching and doctrine of the Gospel, let us believe that one deity of the Father, the Son, and the Holy Spirit, in equal majesty and in a holy Trinity. We authorise the followers of this law to assume the title of Catholic Christians; but as for the others, since in our judgment they are foolish madmen, we decree that they shall be branded with the ignominius name of heretics, and shall not presume to give their conventicles the name of churches. They will suffer in the first place the chastisement of divine condemnation, and in the second the punishment which our authority, in accordance with the will of Heaven, shall decide to inflict' (Bettenson, op.cit., p.31). Here we see the origin of Roman papal power, religious intolerance, and sixteen centuries of trinitarian dogmatism in one imperial document.

A year later Theodosius issued an even more ruthless decree against 'the heretics': 'Let them be entirely excluded even from the threshold of churches, since we permit no heretics to hold their unlawful assemblies in the towns. If they attempt any disturbance, we decree that their fury shall be suppressed and that they shall be expelled outside the walls of the cities, so that the Catholic churches throughout the world may be restored to the orthodox bishops who hold the faith of Nicaea' (ibid.,pp.31/2).

In the same year (381) Theodosius convened an Eastern Synod in Constantinople where the so-called Nicene Creed was adopted, a slight modification of the Creed of Nicaea. The need to combat Arianism had disappeared which explains certain omissions, and the additions too can be explained by the sense of security now felt by the New Nicene faction. This creed was again adopted in 451 in Chalcedon, but possibly the text of 381 was not substantially altered.

The Nicene Creed reads as follows: 'We believe in one God the Father All-sovereign, maker of heaven and earth, and of all things visible and invisible; And in one Lord Jesus Christ, the only-begotten Son of God, Begotten of the Father before all the ages, Light of Light, true God of true God, begotten not made, one of substance with the Father, through whom all things were made; who for us men and for our salvation came down from the heavens, and was made of flesh of the Holy Spirit and the Virgin Mary, and became man, and was crucified for us under Pontius Pilate, and suffered and was buried, and rose again on the third day according to the Scriptures, and ascended into the heavens, and sitteth on the right hand of the Father, and cometh again with glory to judge living and dead, of whose kingdom there shall be no end: And in the Holy Spirit, the Lord and Life-giver, that proceedeth from the Father, who with the Father and Son is worshipped together and glorified together, who spake through the prophets: In one holy and Apostolic Church: We acknowledge one baptism unto remission of sins. We look for a resurrection of the dead, and the life of the age to come' (ibid.,pp.36/7).

From that time onward there was only one religion and one creed in the whole Empire. Any form which denied the one divine essence in three hypostases, or in Western terms, the one substance in three Persons, was subject to savage persecution. Theodosius also forbade 'heathen' worship, under severe penalties, such as were meted out only for the most heinous crimes.

A short resumé

For better understanding I shall attempt once more to summarise the relevant points of the debate. The doctrine of the Trinity states that God the Father, creator of heaven and earth, and God the Son, the redeemer of man, and God the Holy Ghost, the Comforter and link between God and man, are three separate and distinct manifestations (Person) of the One God. The three Persons are of the same essence – homoousion. The idea that they are of similar essence (homoiousion) is rejected. The three manifestations (hypostases) are separate in spite of their essential identity. That separateness is indicated by the word 'persona' which is not what is meant by 'person' in common language. 'Persona' is an individual but distinct way of being of the same entity.

As Claude Welsh puts it, 'the doctrine of the Trinity is intended to affirm, not deny, the oneness of God' (*Handbook of Christian Theology*, p. 370). How the three separate Persons can be one 'Thou' is, even for Christian theologians, a divine 'mystery' which human comprehension cannot fathom. Thus its validity should depend, for the follower of Jesus, on the answer to the question whether it is contained, or at least *clearly* implied, in scriptural revelation or not.

Augustine of Hippo

One of the most outstanding leaders of Western (Latin) Christianity was Augustine, born in 354 in Tagaste, Numidia (now Algeria). His father embraced Christianity only towards the end of his life, but his mother was a zealous believer and, it seems, exerted some influence on her son. Yet it was many years later, in 386, that he was fully converted to the Christian faith. After his baptism in 387 he returned to his native country and in 395 became bishop of Hippo. There he spent the rest of his life, studying and writing, founding a monastery and a school for the clergy. He died in 430 while the Vandal king Gelimer besieged his beloved Hippo.

His teachings are the last important writings relevant to the trinitarian doctrine. *On the Trinity* has become a textbook of the Church and has determined the Christian approach to the problem ever since. 'Father, Son and Holy Ghost, one God, alone, great, omnipotent, good, just, merciful, creator of all things visible and invisible.' 'Father, Son and Holy Spirit, of one and the same substance, God the Creator, the omnipotent Trinity, works invisibly.' 'Neither three Gods, nor three gods, but one God, good, omnipotent, the Trinity itself.' 'There is so great an equality in that Trinity that not only is the Father not greater than the Son [sic] but neither are the Father and the Son together greater than the Holy Spirit.' 'When it is asked what are the three? human language labours under great poverty of speech. Yet we say, three 'Persons', not in order to express it, but in order not to be silent.' These quotations show that Augustine was an unconditional follower of the Nicene Creed, merely elaborating its various points.

Augustine also attempted to provide illustrations for the Trinity by comparing it with Memory, Understanding and Will; or, Lover, Beloved and Love. 'Which of us comprehendeth the Almighty Trinity?' he exclaims, 'and yet which speaketh not of It, if indeed it be It? . . . Now the three I spake of are, To Be, To Know, and To Will. For I am, and know, and will; and I am knowing and willing: and I will to be and to know. In these three then, let him discern that can, how inseparable a life there is, yea, one life, one mind and one essence, yea, lastly, how inseparable a distinction there is, and yet a distinction' (*Confessions,* pp. 317/8). Fascinating sophistry indeed, yet – sophistry.

One of Augustine's more profound statements was, 'It is easier to say what God is not than to say what God is.' He was weary of the word *substantia*, yet he used it; also of the word *persona*, yet he used it. He considered that it was better to say anything than to remain silent.

Struggling with these difficulties, Augustine came to the not surprising conclusion that no verbal formula can adequately express something so remote from human experience as the innermost nature of the Godhead . . . it must be left unresolved, as we have it in *Quicunque vult*, the first part of which is . . . a summary of the conclusions of Augustine's treatise. We had better stick to it, undeterred by Herbert Spencer's cumbersome jest about 'three incomprehensibles which are one incomprehensible,' quotes Lacey in his *Essays in Positive Theology* (pp. 185/6). The 'cumbersome jest' is, I am afraid, about all that can be expected when reflecting on these cumbersome speculations.

Scholasticism

Throughout the Middle Ages lively discussion prevailed in the schools of Christian theology and, although nothing very original or new came to light, there was a universal endeavour to submit the abstruse doctrines of the Church to scrutiny. This trend, called scholasticism, begun with Boëthius, who translated Aristotle and Porphyry into Latin. It reached its height in the 11th century with the greatest scholastics: Anselm, Abelard and Hugo St. Victor. None of these thinkers contributed anything of importance to the trinitarian debate. The first mentioned, Anselm, was Archbishop of Canterbury from 1093 to 1109 and theology owes him the basic law of the Trinity: 'In God all is one except for the opposition of relations.' Whatever that means.

The mediaeval development of the trinitarian doctrine was, on the whole, an ossification of earlier dogma. Adolf Harnack points out that mediaeval theologians tried to reconcile Augustine's doctrine of the Trinity with revelation *and* reason, in order to maintain the basic monotheism of the Christian faith. Nevertheless, when contemplating these ideas, they had to have recourse to the Athanasian dictum: 'He who will be saved must believe them.' The Athanasian Creed transforms the doctrine into an ecclesiastical law 'upon the observance of which salvation depends'. For the scholastics the trinitarian speculations became a question of submission and obedience (*History of Dogma*, p. 273).

Even the later development of the scholastic trend, the so-called High Scholasticism and its outstanding representatives, Albertus Magnus, Thomas Aquinas, Duns Scotus and William of Occam (13th and 14th centuries) did not contribute anything substantial to the Nicene Creed.

The Reformation

For all his scriptural zeal Martin Luther did not, or dared not, discover that Scripture does not contain the trinitarian teaching. As a result of this omission the reform movement, in which Luther played a leading part, paid little attention to the problems raised by belief in the Trinity, problems which caused so much agitation in the 3rd and 4th centuries. Without hesitation the leaders of the reformation agreed to the doctrine of the Godhead which is a trinity, 'the former being the necessary foundation and pre-supposition of the latter'. This idea was incorporated in Article 1 of the Confession of Augsburg (1530 and Article 13 of the Concordat of 1538 with Pope Paul III).

The record of Luther's *Table Talk* contains this entry for Whitsun 1540: 'If we rely on reason it cannot confirm our articles of faith. The Turks hold their subjects more through religion than through force of arms, because they believe that God is the almighty Creator of heaven and earth, that Christ was a prophet, that we may gain heaven through well-performed citizens' duties. But I have learnt in the Scriptures and through many personal vicissitudes that Christ *is* God who has been made flesh and blood, and about those articles of the Trinity and now I do not believe but *know* from experience that these articles are true . . . And so we shall stand by these articles, if necessary against our reason. They have remained with us and shall continue to do so' (IV/4915).

Similar trinitarian loyalties can be shown in the attitudes of other outstanding figures of the reformation, Zwingli, Melanchton, Hutten and Calvin.

It was in 1531 that a Spanish physician and philosopher, Miguel Servetus, incurred the wrath of the Roman Church by the publication of his *De Trinitatis Erroribus*, an attack on the Nicene Doctrine. He regarded this dogma as one of the most dangerous errors of the Christian Church. In 1543 he entered into correspondence with Calvin whom he admired at first, only to be completely disenchanted in the course of their exchange of letters. In 1553 he published another book bearing the title *Restitution of Christianity*. For his heretical views this remarkable man, philosopher, theologian and physician of universal fame was imprisoned in Vienne (France) and condemned to be burned at the stake. He escaped and trusting, it seems, Calvin's magnanimity, sought refuge in Geneva which was, at that time, under Calvin's rule. On arrival in Geneva, he was arrested (August 1553), tried and condemned to death by fire. Calvin's treacherous act was hailed as a victory of Christian steadfastness, and Melanchton applauded the course Calvin had taken.

Yet the reformation produced a small but tenacious movement, the Unitarian Church which, after many vicissitudes and much persecution, has survived into our own age. Its beginnings may be traced to the activities of Fausto Socinus (1539-1604), a son of the distinguished Sozzini family of Siena. Influenced by the writings of Servetus, he devoted himself to the spreading of a unitarian faith based on Scripture. His success was, however, confined to Transylvania and Poland where he spent the last decades of his life. Shortly after his death his followers published the Racovian Catechism which became one of the fundamental documents of the Unitarian movement. The creed later spread to the Netherlands, to England and to the United States. Ralph Waldo Emerson was a distinguished representative of unitarian Christianity.

Without body, parts or passions

Article 1 of the Thirty-Nine Articles of the Church of England reads:

Unus est vivus et verus Deus,	There is but one living and true God,
aeternus, incorporaeus,	everlasting, without body,
impartibilis, impassibilis,	parts or passions,
immensae potentiae, sapientiae,	of infinite power, wisdom,
ac bonitatis	and goodness,
Creator et Conservator omnium,	The Maker and Preserver of all things,
tum visibilium, tum invisibilium.	both visible and invisible.
Et in unitate hujus divinae	And in the unity of this divine
naturae,	nature,
tres sunt Personae,	There be three Persons,
ejusdem essentiae,	of one substance,
potentiae, ac aeternitatis;	power and eternity;
Pater, Filius et	the Father, the Son, and
Spiritus Sanctus.	the Holy Ghost.

Concerning this Article, the commentator remarks: 'It was essential to put this subject in the forefront to show the fundamental beliefs of the Reformers as against Rome, and also against extremists on the Protestants' side, some of whom had gone so far [sic] as to deny the Doctrine of the Trinity' (Griffith Thomas, *Principles of Theology, p.3*).

Christians, including Protestant Christians, have always been anxious to remain loyal to this 'specific view of God', and to the idea of the Trinity which for them meant a trinity with all its mystical ramifications. Most Christian theologians agree that the Jews were 'rigid' monotheists, and that the New Testament does not contain any explicit statement of the dogma. However, they argue, even the apostles confirmed the divine nature of Christ, and for fuller instruction added 'the personal knowledge and experience of the Holy Spirit'. According to them, the teaching of the Godhead contained and revealed in Christ, and of the Holy Spirit at work in the Church, is clearly implied in the Scriptures.

In his lengthy commentary on Article 1, Griffith Thomas asserts that the apostles stated unmistakably that Jesus was God, and that the triune God is more 'real' than any unitarian God idea which makes God a deistic transcendent concept (Islam) or a pantheistic immanent concept (Buddhism), while the Christian view of God is both transcendent and immanent. The argument which follows after these sophistries is worthy of verbatim quotation:

'In the Puritan age and in the Deistic period which arose after it, the Semitic conception dominated thought. Then came the pantheistic tendency of the Aryan [sic] rebellion against the Semitic conception, and this tendency has been found in the philosophical thought of German writers and in devout circles in Mysticism . . . that the modern Jew has a higher conception of God is amply disproved by the spiritual sterility that has overtaken the race [sic], a sterility which is true of every unitarian conception. There are men, both Jews and Gentiles, who have shown remarkable prowess in art, in music, in science, in finance, and in other natural abilities, whose mental powers are of the highest, and yet in moral force they are decidedly lower and their conception of God has been tried and found wanting. The one thing lacking in their vision of God is that reality which is so characteristic of the Christian conception' (ibid., pp.23/28). If we accepted this strange pseudo-argument, it would follow that Jesus of Nazareth, a strictly monotheistic semite, lacked moral force and a clear conception of God! Indeed, he must have been without that 'vision of

God which is so characteristic of the *Christian* conception'. And with this last view one can only concur.

The curious number three

'It is curious how the number three starts up to meet us unsought and unsuspected,' said a devout Christian, H.R. Mackintosh, in his *Ut supra*. Indeed, in all folklore, religious or secular, we encounter the number three. Divine figures are joined in threes as I have shown at the beginning of this chapter. The Scriptures are full of the threefold: the angels appearing to Abraham or to Saul are three; Noah has three sons, to be the ancestors of mankind. Before Jesus started his ministry he was tempted three times; later he cursed three cities; in the scene of the transfiguration Peter offered him to build three tabernacles; there were three days between crucifixion and resurrection; Jesus asks Peter three times if he loved him. The curious number three does seem to appear 'unexpected' in almost every period and every part of the world. The unseeking and unsuspecting Mackintosh may well be surprised.

In Greek and Roman mythology, too, the number three is omnipresent. Hellen, the ancestor of all Greeks, has three sons, Aeolos, Doros and Xythos. The Gorgons, the Graces, the Harpies, the Furies (who guard the three phases of human fate – birth, life and death), the original Hesperides, the servants of Nemesis: they are all three in number. In Germanic mythology all German tribes are descendants of the three sons of Mannus: Istio, Ignio and Hermino. In Shintoism deities are threefold, appertaining to individuals, groups or qualities. The supreme godheads of Hindu religions are three, Brahma, Vishnu and Shiva.

Indeed, the curious number three appears again and again, and the reader may wish to consider a few more ingenuous statements of Christian apologists in recent times, in which they are trying to explain 'the mystery of the Godhead which human minds just cannot fathom'.

'No one who studied the biblical evidence impartially can possibly doubt the full deity of Christ and of the Holy Trinity,' writes R.S. Crossley, 'we must conclude . . . there are three Persons but one God. This may seem impossible, but it is quietly accepted and assumed throughout the New Testament. It was not initially a matter of doctrine but . . . of experience. The New Testament shows us the first Christians ransacking their vocabulary to find words to express the tremendous truths which had been shown to them . . . '. This is a convenient explanation of why the doctrine is not mentioned in the

Scriptures. Crossley even admits that 'the word Trinity does not occur in the New Testament, but the doctrine could hardly be more plain . . . The writers of the New Testament did not speculate on the matter. They knew God their Father, they knew Jesus Christ their Lord and Saviour, and they knew the Person of the Holy Spirit dwelling within them and giving them power. Yet the idea that there could be more than one God never arose in their minds' (*The Holy Trinity*, pp. 20/24).

A similar idea is expressed by W. R. Matthews: 'The doctrine itself is no part of the original gospel. The Athanasian Creed and even the Nicene Creed would have been strange to the ears of St Paul and St John. Nevertheless, the experience to preserve that which the dogmas of the Incarnation and the Trinity formulated, is clearly expressed in the New Testament . . . ' (*God in Christian Thought and Experience*, pp. 85/6).

In Cooper's anthology *Religion and the Modern Mind*, we find the peremptory statement: 'Every Church which has departed from this [trinitarian] faith has *ipso facto* signed its own death-warrant. It is beyond question that those Churches which, in the 18th century, let go the doctrine of the Trinity, faded away and disappeared' (p. 145).

'They', that is the Christians, says Illingworth, 'did not accommodate the Christian religion to their philosophy, but philosophy to their Christian religion. It appeals first to the elemental humanity in the hearts of the unsophisticated men: far removed from Alexandria or Athens, yet the very words in which it does so turn out upon analysis to involve a view of the personality which the word had not attained but which, once stated, is seen profoundly, philosophically, true' (*Personality Human and Divine*, p. 212).

Christian philosophers hasten to confirm this. Berdyaev assures us: 'Personality exists in the relation of love and sacrifice. It is impossible to conceive of a personal God in an abstract monotheistic way. A person cannot exist as a self-contained and self-sufficient absolute. Personalistic metaphysics and ethics are based upon the Christian doctrine of the Holy Trinity. The moral life of every individual must be interpreted after the image of the divine Tri-unity, reversed and reflected in the world' (*The Destiny of Man*, p. 74).

Baron von Huegel supports the same view: 'Real personality ultimately involves systems of emotions which organise feelings. We claim that God is personalistic – consists of Persons.' [Gone is the reluctance to use the concept of Person where the Church Fathers meant manifestations.] 'But where is such a system in God if God is joy alone? There are other emotions in God besides joy: there is also love, the primary emotion, and delectation, and these emotions are evoked in Him – from the mutual love of the Three Persons in the Godhead for each other . . . these add to the articulation of the whole emotional life of God' (*Essays on the Philosophy of Religion*, p.199).

This insight into the innermost life of the Deity is, of course, not confined to von Huegel. E.S. Brightman writes: 'The Christian doctrines of the Trinity and the Atonement have been attempts to express the complex and even tragic nature of the inner life of God. They convey the expression not only of variety but also of definite limitations within the Divine Being. They present a God who struggles and suffers for the world's salvation. Whatever one may think of the traditional formulations of these doctrines, they certainly are closer to the facts of moral experience, and to the experienced tragedy of life than is the notion of a blankly [sic] unitary God who has no genuine diversity to deal with' (*The Problem of God*, p.96).

Today this evaluation of the Trinity has become general. F.J. Ripley, a Roman Catholic, states it with emphasis: ' . . . The Blessed Trinity might truly be paraphrased as the "inner life of God"'.

The gnostic Trinity

If we wish to understand the significance of the Trinity in human thought, we may have to abandon the search for an underlying logical idea and accept Jung's invitation to consider it as a 'psychological reality'. To do this we must, according to Jung, seek the archetype behind the concept which contains its full justification.

Jung believes that the earliest expression of the archetype is to be found in the Egyptian *Ka-mutef*, the principle of the unity of the Supreme Ruler, the begetter (the Father), and his begotten one (the Son). The *Ka* itself, the emanation of every personality, the spiritual double of every being, corresponds to the Spirit of God (the Holy Ghost). 'The *Ka-mutef* is a hypostatization of procreative power', says Jung in whose view it brings together the principle of the creator and the created in unity' (*Psychology of Religion: West and East*, p.132). The important issue is not that no trinitarian reference can be found in the New Testament but we find in it three figures in relationship to one another, the Father, the Spirit of the Father, and the Son begotten through the Spirit, 'clear indications of an active archetype operating beneath the surface' (ibid. p.139). 'Without realising it, the Church Fathers of Nicaea restored the *homoousia* of the ancient Egyptian model. The amplifications, so far as they were naive and unprejudiced, are direct proof that what the New Testament is alluding to, is in fact the

'Trinity' (ibid., p.140). Thus Jung, though for reasons of his own, holds with the Church that the New Testament contains a fulfilment of ancient archetypal aspirations. As a consequence the trinitarian idea had established itself long before the Creeds gave it form and expression. Jung quotes Origen who wrote in his *First Principles* that there is not one passage in the New Testament which would justify that the Holy Spirit is to be considered as made or created. When the word *homoousios* found its way into theology, it had already played an important part in gnostic thought which held that Aeons were descended from the Logos. The Logos itself proceeds from the Nous, which in turn is the direct emanation of Bythos, the Creator of All.

Jung mentions a work which attempts a psychological interpretation of the Trinity: it was widely read in the Middle Ages. Its title is *Liber de Spiritu et Animu*, and it was attributed to St. Augustine, but it is more likely that an unknown Christian gnostic wrote it. 'The intellect sees how wisdom (sapientia) proceeds from it and how it loves this wisdom. But from intellect and wisdom, there proceeds love, and thus all three, intellect, wisdom and love, appear in one. The origin of all wisdom, however, is God. Therefore intellect (nous) corresponds to the Father, the wisdom it begets, corresponds to the Son (logos) and love corresponds to the Spirit (pneuma) breathed forth between them. The wisdom of God was often identified with the cosmogonic Logos and hence with Christ. The mediaeval mind finds it natural to derive the structure of the psyche from the Trinity, whereas the modern mind reverses the procedure' (ibid., pp. 146/7).

Pre-Christian religions are full of triads of gods, says Jung, even though these triads were separate godheads in family relationships. All the same, he thinks that these triadic patterns were at the root of the Christian trinitarian idea. He is confirmed in this view by the role of goddesses in quaternitarian systems – the similarity to the theotokos (god-bearer) is inescapable. He also mentions the emphasis Egyptian religious thought placed on the relationship between father and son, and on the hypostatisation of the bond between the divine elements. In this context he quotes Karl Barth: 'When the Bible speaks of the Holy Ghost, it is speaking of God as the combination of Father and Son, of the vinculum caritatis (the bond of love). 'Jung elaborates: 'The divine procreation of Pharao takes place through *Ka-mutef*, in the human mother of the king. But like Mary, she remains outside the Trinity' (ibid., p.116). It is noteworthy that the early Christians in Egypt found it easy to transfer their traditional ideas about *Ka* to the Holy Ghost, and that the Coptic version of the '*Pistis Sophia*' simply presents the Holy Ghost as the '*Ka*', the double of Jesus.

Jung does not accept the widespread view that the Christian religion owes little or nothing to Egypt and Babylonia. Through Plato and Plutarch, ideas passed from Egypt into Hellenic thought, and thence into Christianity. At the same time strong Babylonian influences entered it through the agency of Jewish thinkers. Pythagorean number-speculations also made a strong impact through the gnostic inspiration discernible in the Fourth Gospel and in *Revelation*.

Another idea which greatly influenced gnosticism and through gnosticism Christianity, originated from Plato's *Timaeus*, a work frequently quoted by Jung.

We shall only cite a short passage in Jowitt's translation: 'God in the beginning made the body of the universe consist of fire and earth. But two things cannot be held together without a third, they must have some bond of union. And the fairest bond is that which most completely fuses and is fused into the things that are bound; and proportion is best adapted to any other power, there is a mean, and the mean is to the first term as the last term is to the mean . . . all things will of necessity come to be the same, and being the same with one another will all be one . . . ' (*Plato's Works*, II p. 526). We can see how the trinitarian idea of the Christians arose from the gnostic understanding of this passage.

Jung's conclusion as regards the ritualistic and psychological value of the trinitarian idea is as difficult to accept as it is to refute: ' . . . the three Persons are personifications of three phases of a regular instinctive psychic occurrence that always tends to express itself in the form of mythologems and ritualistic customs (i.e., initiations at puberty, and the various rites for birth, marriage, sickness, war and death). As the medical lore of the ancient Egyptians, myths as well as rites have a psychotherapeutic value, and they still have today' (op. cit., pp. 193/4).

In the terms of a philosophical phenomenon Jung suggests that Christ should be regarded as a symbol for the Self. The entry or 'descent' of the Holy Spirit can be understood as the self-actualisation of man. The Self, representing something of the substance of the Father, cannot provide empirical proof that its own symbol and that of its 'begetter' are distinct. Yet, psychologically, they are experienced as distinct entities. For this reason, suggests Jung, it is not surprising that the *homoousia* should have triumphed over the *homoiousia*, since 'through the descent of the Holy Ghost, the Self of man enters into a relationship of unity with the substance of God' (ibid., pp. 194/5). This view which explains the strength and durability of the doctrine, must necessarily presuppose a concept of the Holy Ghost that establishes 'the relationship of unity'. No wonder, says Jung, 'that the Church did not insist on any further elaboration of the Holy Ghost'.

Jung's understanding of the Holy Ghost brings us full circle to the original teaching of Jesus: the Holy Spirit as the spirit of truth, a gift of God to man, which enables creation to raise itself to full oneness with the Creator, and to bring about a unity with God, through which even the threat of death would lose its sting.

6
The Virgin Birth

How it all began

Before him, on the rough table, lay clay and needle, and he wondered if the words he was searching for, would come to his mind. He wished to comfort the king whose tablet, demanding urgent attention, lay before him. Ahaz, the king of Judah, was in great distress. He had intelligence that Pekah, the king of Israel, and Rezin, the Syrian king, were plotting to conquer his country, and take the Holy City by force. The letter read: 'To my beloved servant Isaiah, the son of Amoz – from Ahaz, the son of Jotham, king of Judah. For many years hast thou served my father and myself, and hast always counselled us faithfully and well. Betrayed by Israel and harassed by Syria, I am sore afraid. The Holy City is so near the border, and the number of the enemy is beyond counting. I want thy counsel . . . wilt thou meet me at the end of the conduit of the upper pool in the highway of the fuller's field? Keep secret our meeting and bring with thee none but thy son. I too shall come alone with only two of my counsellors on horseback.' Isaiah read the tablet again and again. It flattered him that the son of David should ask for his advice, but his sick and weary body shrank from the command to be in person at the encounter. Finally he seized his needle and engraved his reply on the dampened tablet: 'To Ahaz, the son of Jotham, King of Judah, from the servant of God and the King, from Isaiah, the son of Amoz. I shall be there at the appointed time, with Shear-jashub, my son. Fear not, O King, for the Most High, blessed be His name, is with thee. I know thou wilt not ask Him for a sign, as thou wouldst not wary the Lord, but He in his mercy commanded me to give thee a sign: *"Behold a young woman shall conceive and bear a son* and he will walk with God. Butter and honey shall he eat so that he may learn to reject evil and choose the good. But even before he groweth to understand the choice between good and evil, thine enemies will loose their power. I counsel thee not to seek the aid of the king of Assyria.

Put thy trust in the Lord, and not in Tiglat-pileser. He is a mighty king, and his aid would be costly. But trust the Lord, and Damascus will be razed and Ephraim will depart from Samaria. All these things I shall tell thee in person, although my body is weary and sick, but my spirit is anxious to serve the Lord and His Anointed.'

Isaiah himself described these events which took place in the 8th century B.C. In the Old Testament we find his account in Isaiah 7:1ff.

A fateful gathering

Many centuries had passed. The conquest of Egypt by Alexander the Great left the Ptolemy dynasty in control. The ambition of its founder, Ptolemy I, created the world's biggest and best-stocked library in Alexandria, the new metropolis which became his capital city. His son and successor, Ptolemy II, continued his father's work including the enrichment of the great library. With this object in mind, he summoned its director, Demetrius of Phalerum. Explaining that he had learned about the remarkable book of law of the Jews, he expressed his wish that this valuable scripture should be translated into Greek. The king himself wanted to read it and, at the same time, make it available to educated Greeks and even Jews who did not understand Hebrew or Aramaic.

Demetrius went to work at once. Setting his reed to papyros, he wrote a letter to the High Priest in Jerusalem explaining the king's desire. The letter was accompanied by valuable gifts and an offer to repatriate several thousand Jews who had been forcibly removed from Palestine to Egypt.

The High Priest complied at once. Six scholars from every tribe were called to Jerusalem. They were tested to see whether their knowledge of Greek was adequate for the delicate task of translating the Law of Moses and the writings of the prophets. The seventy-two started off on their arduous journey to Alexandria where they were received with great hospitality and immediately put to work. Each was given a separate cell, and the whole of the Pentateuch to translate. After seventy-two days when the work was done and they emerged from their cells, a comparison showed that the translations were miraculously alike. The seventy-two humbly refused credit for the excellence of their work, and pointed out that only divine inspiration could have brought about so great an achievement.

This is the legend, as recorded in one of the Old Testament epigrapha, the *Letter of Aristeas*, written between 200 and 150 B.C. It describes the origin of the Greek text of the Old Testament, the version later known as the *Septuagint* (LXX) or 'the Seventy'. This version which first included the Pentateuch only, was later extended to embrace the whole of the Old Testament (the Jewish Bible). Initially it was accepted by the hellenised Jews who rejected it only when it became the 'authentic' Old Testament of the Christian Church. The final version is believed to have emerged about 100 B.C., including also the prophetic and hagiographic writings. A study of the *Septuagint* reveals that the translators were more versed in Hebrew than in Greek, and that more than one translator worked on each book. Some of the translations are literal, others free, again others paraphrase or make use of classical poetry. The Pentateuch is deemed to be the most accurate, followed by the Proverbs, while the Psalms and other books are poorly translated. That of Daniel was so clumsy that it was discarded altogether by the early Church.

The Alexandrian Canon, as the books contained in the LXX were known, was drawn up in the vernacular idiom of Alexandria which we encounter in many contemporary papyri. Josephus, the historian, was familiar with it but he, like most Jewish scholars, preferred the so-called Hebrew Canon. Both canons were based on manuscripts originating from the fifth and fourth centuries B.C.

The best known copy of the LXX is the famous Codex Vaticanus which dates from the fourth century A.D. By then the Christian Church had adopted this version of Jewish scripture. The synods of Hippo and Carthage decreed the acceptance of the Alexandrian Canon by the Church.

The legendary gathering at Alexandria had come across the text of Isaiah referred to above. The word 'alma' (young woman, maiden) was translated παρϑένος (virgin), with disastrous consequences. Παρϑένος may in fact mean young woman or maiden, but in the earliest days of Christianity its primary meaning seems to have been 'virgin'.

It has taken nearly two thousand years for the mistake to be acknowledged and corrected. In the new edition of the Roman Catholic Bible *Isaiah* 7:14 reads: 'Behold, a young woman shall conceive and bear a son . . . '

Throughout the centuries countless thousands of dissenters were burnt at the stake for saying less.

Virgin birth a universal fashion

Virgin birth was not an unfamiliar idea to the men of antiquity. Great kings, religious leaders and teachers were born of divinity by a human

THE VIRGIN BIRTH

mothers whom no man had touched before. Elsewhere we may hear about gods descending to mortal women, the fruit of their union being the admired hero. Here we must confine ourselves to examples of birth due to divine intervention.

The only way to explain a leader's or teacher's perspicacity, wisdom and power seemed to be through the acceptance of the view that he was born miraculously and from divine ancestry. 'Such tales of virgin mothers,' writes Sir James Frazer, 'are relics of an age of childish ignorance, when men had not yet recognised the intercourse of the sexes as the true cause of offspring. That ignorance, still shared by the lowest of existing savages, the aboriginal tribes of Australia, was doubtless at one time universal among mankind' (*Adonis, Attis, Osiris,* II, p.220).

In this manner every mythology produced its distinctive legends. There is said to be an Egyptian parallel to the Annunciation in the sculpture of the temple of Luxor. This work, dating probably from the 13th century B.C., presents the ibis-headed god Toth, who announces the forthcoming birth of a son to the virgin-queen Mautmes. The next illustration depicts the queen in the company of the goddess of Love, Hathor and the goddess of Birth, Nechbet. They hold her hand and make her bring her lips to the *crux ansata*, the symbol of life. The following carving shows the birth of the infant Pharao and his adoration by the gods. The inscription, the sun-god's address to the infant, reads: 'I am thy Father, I have begotten thee upon thy revered mother.' (J.M. Robinson, *Christianity & Mythology*, p.305).

In the Parsee mythology, Saoshyas or Saoshyant, the future saviour of mankind and conqueror of death, will be miraculously conceived by his virgin-mother from the seed of Zarathustra (J.M. Robinson, *Pagan Christs*, p.322). There is a legend concerning Zarathustra himself, according to which he was born of a fifteen-year-old virgin, Dughdova or Dogduyah, who had been visited by a shaft of light. Just as Jesus' lineage is traced through his father Joseph to Adam, and not through the Virgin Mary, so Zarathustra's line is linked to Gayomart, the Iranian Adam, through his father Pourushaspa, and not through the virgin Dughdova.

The name Moses, that is, the Hebrew equivalent Moshe, is believed to originate from the Hebrew verb 'masha', i.e., to draw out (of the water). Others argue that it is derived from the Egyptian 'mes' or 'mose', meaning 'son' or 'child'. It is even possible that it comes from the Egyptian 'mashah', i.e., deliverer or or saviour (Potter, *The Story of Religion*, p.47). Flinders-Petrie, the Egyptologist, suggests that the

Egyptian word 'Moses' means 'unfathered son of an (unmarried) princess, i.e., the royal son of a virgin.

The god who died and rose again, the royal child of a virgin, who saved the world, was the theme of many Oriental myths, to mention only Horus, Attis and Mithras, A.C. Bouquet comments on this strange phenomenon:

'If we are to posit a primitive divine object for human devotion, it seems much more likely that this was ... the Great Mother, symbolizing the fecund creative force of nature ... the tendency of the Mediterranean peoples to prefer what is called the Catholic form of Christianity with its exaggerated emphasis upon the Virgin Mother, and the Northern European preference for Protestantism with its male Saviour, who teaches people to say the Lord's Prayer rather than the Angelus, is obviously so extraordinary ... that it cannot be accounted for by saying that two sets of theologians argued out the matter differently.' (See p.153).

Indian mythology too produces a wealth of examples. Krishna was believed to have been born from the rib of a virgin of the royal line of Devaci (R. Taylor, *Diegesis*, p.169), and some myths concerning the birth of the Buddha relate that he was born through divine intervention, not in the way of ordinary humans.

Even a civilisation which was completely isolated from the Western European world has its virgin birth stories. We are told that the Mexican god-hero Quetzalcoatl was virgin-born. He opposed war and insisted on worship without human or animal sacrifices. Similarly, the Mexican sun-gods Huitzipochtli and Texcatlipoca were sons of the virgin-goddess Coatlicue (J.M. Robertson, *Pagan Christs*, pp.359 and 372).

Germanic mythology tells of Odherir, the magic cauldron, which was guarded by the giant Suutungr and Gunnlodh, his beautiful daughter. The cauldron held a potion conferring wisdom and the power of poetic expression. Odin, who wanted to drink of this potion, disguised himself as a snake and made his way to the cauldron through the forbidding rocks surrounding it. When he reached his destination, he saw there the beautiful Gunnlodh with her flaxen hair. She gave him a drink, and lay with him for three days and three nights. Before he left, he drained the cauldron, and, transforming himself into an eagle, flew away. The fruit of this divine indiscretion was the hero-god Bragi, the god of eloquence and poetry (H. Jens, *Mythologisches Lexicon*, p.133).

Mithra or Mithras, the Persian divinity, was carried by Roman legions into every corner of the Empire. They worshipped him as the Son of God, born from a rock or a virgin mother: in either case by intervention of his divine father, Ahura Mazda. For centuries Mithras contested the triumph of Christ, and only by adopting many of his (Mithras') attributes, did the Church succeed in presenting an image of the 'Christ' which would eventually prevail.

More than a hundred years before the Christian era, the Gauls in the area of Chartres celebrated an annual festival in honour of *Virgo Paritura* (the virgin who will bring forth). Other Celtic mother-goddesses, usually three in number, were later adopted by the Christians and interpreted as the three Maries in the New Testament. In this disguise ancient fertility goddesses were worshipped by Christians in Metz well into the eighteenth century.

Virgin birth in Greek-Roman antiquity

Greek mythology abounds in stories of gods embracing mortal virgins, and of the heroes born of such unions. Perseus was the son of Zeus by Danae, virgin daughter of the king Akrisios. The Cretan king, Minos, was born from the union of Zeus and Europa, virgin daughter of Agenor, king of Phoenicia. Another son of Zeus was the ancestor of Achilles and Ajax, born out of the embrace of their mother Aigina with the father of the gods.

Plato himself was believed by many Athenians to have been conceived by his mother, Perictione, of the god Apollo, before her marriage. Diogenes Laertius, writing about A.D. 200, also mentions the fable that Perictione received a visit from Apollo, although he adds that he himself does not believe this story nor does he think that any of Plato's disciples believed it.

In the Eleusian mysteries, suppressed by the Christians, torch-bearers dressed as shepherds displayed the infant Dionysus in a harvest basket. He was supposed to be the child of Brimo, a virgin fertility goddess. A newly-reaped sheaf of corn dressed up as a child was presented and the high-priest chanted in a loud voice: 'Holy Brimo has given birth to a child! Holy is the spiritual, heavenly, most high generation, and holy is he who is so conceived!' The resemblance to the story of the virgin birth in Bethlehem (bethlechem, the house of bread) is, to say the least, striking.

Alexander the Great was thought by many to be the son of Zeus who had visited Queen Olympias, in the form of a serpent, before her marriage to King Philip of Macedonia was consummated. The reader may be interested to note the significance of serpents in ancient myths

(Pfleiderer, *Early Christian Conceptions of Christ*, p. 34). Apollonius, a disciple of Pythagoras, a teacher and miracle worker, was regarded by the people of Tyana as a son of Zeus and himself more than human (ibid.).

Scipio Africanus was believed to be a son of Apollo, and so was the Emperor Augustus. Suetonius wrote about A.D. 120: 'I find in the theological books of Asclepiades . . . that Atia (the mother of Augustus), upon attending a midnight service in honour of Apollo, when the rest of the matrons had returned home, fell asleep on her couch in the temple. A serpent [sic] crept to her, and soon after withdrew. Awakened by this she purified herself, as usual after the embraces of her husband . . . Augustus, it was added, was born in the tenth month after, and for that reason was thought to be the son of Apollo' (*Caesar Augustus,* chapter XCIV).

The virgin birth of Jesus

'Now the birth of Jesus was on this wise: When as his mother Mary was espoused to Joseph, before they came together, she was found with child of the Holy Ghost. Then Joseph her husband, being a just man, and not willing to make her a public example, was minded to put her away privily. But while he thought on these things, behold, the angel of the Lord appeared unto him in a dream, saying, Joseph, thou son of David, fear not to take unto thee Mary, thy wife: for that which is conceived in her is of the Holy Ghost. And she shall bring forth a son, and thou shalt call his name Jesus: for he shall save his people from their sins. Now all this was done, that it might be fulfilled which was spoken of the Lord by the prophet, saying, Behold a virgin shall be with child, and shall bring forth a son, and they shall call his name Emmanuel, which being interpreted is, God with us. Then Joseph being raised from sleep did as the angel of the Lord had bidden him, and took unto him his wife: And knew her not till she had brought forth her first-born son: and called his name Jesus' (*Matthew* 1:18/25).

In movingly simple language, the author of this gospel tells the story of a poor Jewish couple in the city of Bethlehem who find themselves in a human situation many other couples experienced before them: the husband finds his bride with child before the consummation of their marriage. The rigid Jewish Law has a severe stricture for the unfortunate woman: when a man hath taken a wife, and married her, and it come to pass . . . that he hath found some uncleanness in her: then let him write her a bill of divorcement . . . and send her out of his house! (*Deut.* 24:1). However, Joseph was a just

THE VIRGIN BIRTH

man, and a man of kind heart who did not intend to resort to this harsh law, preferring to part with her in a quiet manner, without the usual scandal attached to a divorce. And this he would have done, had not an angel appeared to him in a dream saying that the child his wife would bear was of the holy spirit of God, and should be named Jesus which means 'God saves'. Deeply moved by his dream, Joseph decided to stand by his wife, and to look forward to the birth of her firstborn with pious hope and confidence.

The author of the gospel according to Luke, tells a more intricate story, being a poet of much greater vision and delicacy: 'The Angel Gabriel was sent from God unto a city of Galilee, named Nazareth, To a virgin espoused to a man whose name was Joseph: and the virgin's name *was* Mary. And the Angel came in unto her, and said, Hail *thou that art* highly favoured, the Lord is with thee: blessed *art* thou among women. And when she saw *him*, she was troubled at his saying, and cast in her mind what manner of salutation this should be. And the Angel said unto her, Fear not, Mary: for thou hast found favour with God. And beyond, thou shalt conceive in thy womb, and bring forth a son, and shalt call his name Jesus. He shall be great, and shall be called the son of the Highest: and the Lord God shall give unto him the throne of his father David: and he shall reign over the house of Jacob for ever; and of his kingdom there shall be no end. Then said Mary unto the Angel, how shall this be, seeing that I know not a man? And the Angel answered and said unto her, the Holy Ghost shall come upon thee, and the power of the Highest shall overshadow thee: therefore also that holy thing which shall be born of thee shall be called the son of God . . . with God nothing is impossible. And Mary said, Behold the handmaid of the Lord; be it unto me according to thy word. And the Angel departed from her' (*Luke* 1:26/38).

There are some important differences in the two accounts. In Matthew's story the couple was in Bethlehem in Judaea. In Luke's Gospel they were in Nazareth in Galilee. The angel spoke to Joseph in the first, to Mary in the second account. That Mary 'knew no man' we hear from her own lips, not from the narrator. Finally, Joseph seemed to be completely unaware of the 'supernatural' conception of his son in the account of Luke – the first gospel seems to have been written for Jews with a strict idea of what was lawful, while Luke's gospel is a poetic story meant to move the heart of the listener.

The poet continues: 'And Mary arose . . . and went into the hill country with haste into the city of Juda; and entered into the house of Zacharias, and saluted Elizabeth . . . [who] spake out with a loud voice and said, 'Blessed art thou among women and blessed is the fruit of thy womb' (*Luke* 1:45/55).

In conjunction with the above-quoted passage we have here the beautiful prayer of the Roman Catholics, conjuring up many a line of the exquisite poetry in which the ancient prayers to the Earth Mother, to Isis, to Vesta, abounded.

The poet rises to still greater heights: 'And Mary said, My soul doth magnify the Lord, and my spirit hath rejoiced in God my Saviour. For he hath regarded the low estate of his handmaiden: for, behold, from henceforth all generations shall call me blessed. For he that is mighty hath done to me great things; and holy *is* his name. And his mercy *is* on them that fear him from generation to generation. He hath shewed strength with his arm; he hath scattered the proud in the imagination of their hearts. He hath filled the hungry with good things, and the rich he hath sent empty away. He hath holpen his servant Israel, in remembrance of *his* mercy; as he spake to our fathers, to Abraham, and to his seed for ever' (*Luke* 1:46/55).

Our admiration for the poet is slightly less when we discover the source of his inspiration:

Magnificat (Luke 1:46/55)	*Hannah's Song of Praise* (1 Samuel 1:18 and 2:1/10)
My soul doth magnify the Lord and my spirit hath rejoiced in God my Saviour	My heart rejoiceth in the Lord because I rejoice in thy salvation
For he hath regarded the low estate of his handmaiden from henceforth all generations shall call me blessed	Let thy handmaiden find grace in thy sight (*Mal.* 3.12) And all nations shall call you blessed
For he that is mighty hath done to me great things and holy is his name.	For the pillars of the earth are the Lord's There is none holy as the Lord.
And his mercy is on them that fear him from generation to generation.	(*Ps.* 103:17) The mercy of the Lord is from everlasting to everlasting upon them that fear him.
He hath shewed strength with his arm	He shall give strength unto His king
He hath scattered the proud in the imagination of their hearts	Talk no more so exceeding proudly
He hath put down the mighty from their seats	The bows of the mighty are broken

THE VIRGIN BIRTH

and exalted them of low degree. He hath filled the hungry with good things and the rich he hath sent empty away, He hath holpen his servant Israel	He raises up the poor out of the dust they that were hungry ceased They that were full hired out themselves for bread He will keep the feet of his saints (or *Ps.* 98:3) He hath remembered
in remembrance of his mercy	his mercy and his truth toward the house of Israel
As he spoke to our fathers, to Abraham, and to his seed for ever.	Neither is there any rock like our God. (or *Gen* 17:19) God saying to Abraham, I will establish my everlasting covenant, and with his seed after him.

Then the narrator tells us that the Emperor ordered a census to be taken in all his realm, and that everyone had to return to his place of origin, to be counted. For this reason Joseph, a scion of King David's family, had to go to Bethlehem, the city of David and, naturally, took with him Mary, his espoused wife being great with child. And so it was that, while they were there, the days were accomplished that she should be delivered. And she brought forth her firstborn son, and wrapped him in swaddling clothes, and laid him in a manger; because there was no room for them in the inn' (*Luke* 2:5/7).

Apart from the passages at the beginning of the Gospels according to Matthew and Luke, there is no mention of the virgin birth in the whole New Testament, Matthew and Luke never speak of it again throughout their narratives. Mark, John, and even Paul seem to have been unaware of the story. Jesus himself never mentioned it.

What do we know about the Virgin?

The New Testament reveals nothing about the origin and the family of Mary. Since the statement concerning Jesus' Davidic descent is much emphasised, many attempts were made to prove that Mary herself is a descendant of David, especially since the more elaborate genealogies (see chapter on Genealogies) proving Joseph's origin can be dismissed if Joseph was not the father of Jesus. The arguments are usually based on tenuous circumstantial evidence. The most frequent claim made is that the difference between the two genealogies (in Matthew and Luke respectively) is due to the fact that Matthew gives the genealogy of Joseph, while Luke's genealogy is really that of Mary. If this were true,

Matthew would be guilty of inserting a completely irrelevant genealogy in his gospel, and Luke could be accused of forgetting to mention that Joseph was not the son but the son-in-law of Heli.

Another frequent argument refers to the relationship between Mary and Elizabeth, indicated by the words 'thy cousin Elizabeth' (*Luke* 1:36). The New Testament deals with the origin of Elizabeth only to the extent that she is said to be 'of the daughters of Aaron' (*Luke* 1:5) which means that she was *not* of Davidic origin. Aaron lived long before David, and was a son of the tribe of Levi, while David belonged to the tribe of Judah. Elizabeth's husband, Zacharias, was 'of the course of Abia' (ibid) which would make him a descendant of David according to Matthew's genealogy (*Matthew* 1:7) but not according to the relevant genealogy supplied by Luke.

A third argument is based on apocryphal writings such as the *Protevangelium*, or 'Book of James', which is largely an account of the life of the Virgin. It is first mentioned by Origen, and modern research regards it as a hotch-potch of so-called 'infancy gospels' current in the early centuries of our era. In this narrative Mary is presented as the daughter of an 'exceeding rich' Jew, Ioacim, and his wife Anna. Like Sarah, Hannah and Elizabeth, Anna conceives miraculously at an advanced age, after being told by an angel that her child 'shall be spoken of in the whole world' (4:1). The angel does not fail to inform Ioacim, too, of the great news and the usual shepherds are invoked. In her third year Mary is 'given' to the temple of the Lord where she remains 'as a dove that is nurtured: and she received food from the hand of an angel' (8:1). When she reaches her twelfth year, the 'high priest' Zacharias sends out messengers to all the tribes of Israel saying that the maiden will be given in marriage to the man who comes with a rod [sic] 'and to whomsoever the Lord shall show a sign, his wife shall she be' (8:3). Among the suitors is Joseph and when he presents his rod, a 'dove came forth of the rod and flew upon the head of Joseph' (9:1). The priest awards Mary to Joseph, but the latter protests that he is an old man with sons, who cannot take away a virgin girl. But the high priest insists that he should take Mary in his custody. In the next part of the narrative it is mentioned that the child Mary 'was of the tribe of David and undefiled before God' (10:1). This story seems to have had currency in the early Church, since even St. Leo, the bishop of Rome, spoke of the 'Electa Virgo de semine Abrahae, et radice Jesse' (Sermon 29).

The Book of James continues Mary's story with the Annunciation narrative, Mary's visit to Elizabeth, and Joseph's dream, which shows that the author knew both Matthew's and Luke's version of the birth story. The rest of the Protevangelium is not important except that again and again Mary's virginity is emphasised as well as Joseph's awareness that the child is not his. A later variant is the Gospel of Pseudo-Matthew which draws most of its information from the Book of James. Here Joachim 'of the tribe of Judah' and Anna, daughter of Isachar 'of the tribe of Judah' are Mary's parents. The angel appears to both and promises that their long childless marriage will be blessed by a girl-child. A deviation from the Protevangelium is the story that the priest Abiathar offers valuable gifts to Mary if she would marry his son. She refuses since 'she hath vowed perpetual virginity' (vii). She leaves the temple, accompanied by five virgins as ladies-in-waiting, to join Joseph. For the rest this gospel follows the Book of James, except that it deals in greater detail with the childhood of Jesus. Here, too, it is made clear that the brothers mentioned in the New Testament were the sons of Joseph and not Mary's! The so-called Armenian infancy-gospel is another text which depends for information on the Protevangelium. Opinions vary as to whether it originated as early as the 6th, or as late as the 12 century. It is quite unoriginal and probably a mere copy of other contemporary texts.

Other apocryphal stories

Believed to be a fourth-century document, the writing known as the 'Death of Joseph' contains some interesting and unusual passages. It is of Egyptian origin, written in Egyptian dialects and later in Arabic. It glorifies Joseph, the father of Jesus, and contains meditations upon death as well as stories about the death of the parents of Jesus. It is noteworthy that it refers to Joseph as 'the carpenter, the father of Jesus according to the flesh' (Proem to the Book). It names the sons, Judas, Joses, James and Simon, and uniquely among the apocryphal texts, the daughters also: Lysia and Lydia. In common with the other manuscripts of the early Church it claims, however, that these were Joseph's children from his first wife who died while James was still small. Further interesting details: Joseph lived to be 111 years of age, and was Mary's husband for two years before Jesus was born. At that time Joseph was 91 years of age. Jesus was present at Joseph's death, and afterwards he prayed to God saying, 'I prayed to my Father with heavenly prayers which I wrote with my own fingers before I took flesh in the holy Virgin Mary' (xxv). This is indeed in strange contradiction to the Proem where Joseph is called Jesus' father 'according to the flesh'.

There are, of course, completely fanciful accounts of the Virgin's further life and of her death in the apocryphal writings. The Coptic texts describe how she lived with the apostles and her fellow-virgins till the day when Jesus came to earth again to call for his mother. Jesus speaks to Death: "Come, appear to my virgin mother but not in a fearful shape." He appeared and when she saw him, her soul leapt into the bosom of her son . . . Jesus shrouded the body in heavenly garments . . . and . . . ascended with Mary's soul in the chariot of the Cherubim (*Evodius Hom.*, xii to xv). Another account is in the *Twentieth Discourse* of Cyril of Jerusalem. According to this text John and Mary lived together in Jerusalem when Jesus appeared and bade her to surmount her fear of death. When Mary saw Death coming for her, her soul leapt into the bosom of her son and 'he wrapped her into a garment of light'. Evodius speaks of bodily assumption while Cyril does not, otherwise the two record show much agreement. In another Coptic fragment there is even an account of Mary's bodily resurrection and ascension.

The Greek versions also contain stories of the Virgin's death, similar to the Coptic accounts: Jesus appears to carry his mother away and the apostles take her body to the sepulchre whence she is 'translated' into paradise. Latin narratives (Pseudo-Melitus, Joseph of Arimathea, etc.) present like stories. All these writings originated probably in the fifth and sixth centuries.

The mother of Jesus in the New Testament

In the New Testament itself there is little information about the mother, after the poetic and beautiful birth-legend is told. And what there is makes us wonder if Jesus did, in fact, hold his mother in high regard. There is the story about the wedding in Cana: 'The mother of Jesus was there. And both Jesus was called and his disciples to the marriage. And when they wanted wine, the mother of Jesus saith unto him, They have no wine. Jesus saith unto her: Woman, what have I to do with thee? Mine hour is not yet come' (*John* 2:4). Even if we take the sting out of the expression τί ἐμοὶ καὶ σοί, γύναι and translate it, as I would, 'Woman, leave me alone!' it is still a disrespectful way of addressing one's mother.

Another strange event is recorded in three out of the four gospels. It occurs during Jesus' visit to Nazareth and it seems to indicate that he had broken his family ties – even the bond uniting him with his nearest relatives. 'While he yet talked to the people, behold, his mother and his brethren [correctly brothers] stood without, desiring to speak to him. But he answered and said unto him that told him, Who is my mother and who are my brethren [correctly – brothers]? And he stretched forth his hand toward his disciples and said, Behold my mother and my brethren [correctly – brothers]. For whosoever shall do the will of my Father, which is in heaven, the same is my brother, and sister, and mother' (*Matthew* 12:46/50), (*Luke* 8:19/21).

Mary is mentioned by the people of Nazareth who exclaim: 'Is not this the carpenter's son? Is not his mother called Mary? . . . ' (*Matthew* 13:55); 'Is not this the carpenter, the son of Mary (*Mark* 6:3); and 'Is not this Jesus, the son of Joseph, whose father and mother we know . . . ?' (*John* 6:42). Later in this chapter I shall have occasion to return to these passages.

Mary's presence at Golgotha is recorded by Matthew, Mark and John. 'And many women were there beholding afar off, which followed Jesus from Galilee, ministering unto him: Among which was Mary Magdalene, and Mary the mother of James and Joses, and the mother of Zebedee's children' (*Matthew* 27:56). It may be seen that this Mary is not called the mother of Jesus, although she may have been his mother if we accept the witness of the New Testament that she was also the mother of James and Joses. 'There were also women looking from afar off: among whom was Mary Magdalene, and Mary the mother of James the less and of Joses and Salome (who also when he was in Galilee followed him and ministered unto him), and many other women who came up with him unto Jerusalem . . . ' (*Mark* 15:40/1). Again the strange omission, Mary is not called the mother of Jesus. The only gospel which identifies Mary, the mother of Jesus, as one of the bystanders, is the Gospel according to John. 'Now there stood by the cross of Jesus his mother, and his mother's sister, Mary the wife of Cleophas, and Mary Magdalene. When Jesus therefore saw his mother and the disciple standing by whom he loved, he saith unto his mother, Woman behold thy son! Then saith he to the disciple, Behold thy mother! And from that hour that disciple took her unto his own home' (*John* 19:25/27). Apart from a very short mention, the final appearance in the New Testament is to be found in the Acts of the Apostles: 'These all [the apostles] continued with one accord in prayer and supplication, with the women, and Mary, the mother of Jesus, and with his brethren' (*Acts* 1:14). These few passages comprise all there is to be found about Mary, the mother of Jesus, to justify the extraordinary reverence in which she has been held throughout centuries of Christianity.

Try as we may no consistent portrait of Mary can be evolved from any or all of these writings. Even the apostles show some qualities or failings which make them appear comprehensible, and in character with certain types of human behaviour. None of this applies to Mary, and her distant, mythological personality is in keeping with the Mother Goddess of early history.

Mary, his espoused wife

The genealogy in the Gospel according to Luke is introduced by the words 'And Jesus himself began to be about thirty years of age, being (as was supposed) the son of Joseph . . . (*Luke* 3:24). The Greek ὡς ἐνομίζετο, i.e., 'as was supposed', which is bracketed in English, is an integral part of the text. Yet this parenthesis, or the idea behind it, deprived an honest, hard-working Jewish carpenter of his legitimate fatherhood, and the Christian world of its ability to think clearly and dispassionately about the birth of Jesus. It may even be argued that the verb does not necessarily mean 'to suppose', but may signify 'to hold to be' or 'recognise as'. Indeed, Luther translates more accurately, without brackets, 'ward gehalten für einen Sohn Josephs'. The Vulgate 'which is probably the source of this special slant' translates explicitly 'ut putabatur', without doubt the equivalent of 'as was supposed'. The parenthetical words may be an interpolation by some believers: if they were not, the two genealogies are quite irrelevant. In any case they have caused disagreement and confusion among Christians for many centuries.

Two short passages in the Gospel according to *Matthew* (1:16/25) and *Luke* (1:28/35), are the foundation upon which one of the central doctrines of Christianity, the Virgin Birth, was built. We may add to these passages the parenthetical 'as was supposed'. Only one document was discovered, a Syriac manuscript, where the text of *Matthew* 1:16 does not contain the ambiguous 'And Jacob begat Joseph the husband of Mary, of whom was born Jesus, who is called Christ', but reads quite unequivocally: 'Joseph to whom was espoused the virgin Mary, *begat* Jesus who is called the Messiah'. Perhaps this *was* the original text which would not effect the relevance of the genealogy.

In all probability Jesus was, as Klausner rightly remarks, 'as legitimate as any other Jewish child in Galilee' (*JN*, p.232), and the stories intending to prove that he was both the Messiah as the son of David's descendant Joseph, and the Son of God in the physical sense as the child of a virgin, were possibly interpolated at a later date. There was fierce competition among the deities of the Near East, and 'Son of God' was the humblest title the Christians could bestow upon their legendary saviour. In the process a colourless Jewish woman, Mary, became a 'Holy Virgin', and the honourable Jewish carpenter, Joseph, a cuckold.

There has been much controversy about the term 'espoused'. The Greek μνηστεύω (-ειν) means 'to 'betroth', and like its English counterpart may mean the status both before and after marriage; just as the words μνηστήρ, νύμφιος, may mean the fiancé as well as the husband. It is more than unlikely that the strict morality of the Jews would have allowed a virgin maiden to live and travel with her bridegroom prior to their marriage; and there would have been no reason why she should have been 'taxed' in Bethlehem had she not been his spouse in the sense the English language uses the word to indicate the status of a young wife.

There are many passages in Scripture which show that the marriage between Joseph and Mary had been contracted in its final, irrevocable form. The child was taken to be circumcised which implies that, according to Jewish ritual, Joseph had to confirm that he was the lawful father. (Lawful meant bodily father.) Of course there were certain exceptions but this special case was not provided for. Luke tells the story of the child Jesus being found discussing the Law with the doctors in the Temple. His mother reproaches him: 'Son, why hast thou thus dealt with us? behold, thy father and I sought thee sorrowing' (*Luke* 2:48), which shows that she referred to Joseph as the father of Jesus. In the same gospel the evangelist talks about the *parents* of Jesus. The expression in *Luke* 2:27 and 2:41 'Joseph and his mother' is a tendentious change of the text which reads in most Greek versions ὁ πατὴρ αὐτοῦ καὶ η μήτηρ or ὁι γονεῖς αὐτοῦ (his father and mother or his parents).

The question of Jesus' brothers and sisters is also relevant here, but it will be considered in detail below. Suffice it to say now that the neighbours did not know, or even suspect, any peculiarity about the marriage of Joseph and Mary, and their words show that the parents and family of Jesus were ordinary people. The neighbours grumble because they think it presumptuous that one who grew up in their midst should be regarded as a great teacher, perhaps the Messiah himself.

It may be interesting to quote a few Christian commentators who try to prove that Mary was not really the wife of Joseph by resorting to speculations which cannot be substantiated. A typical example is Professor Barclay: 'To our Western way of thinking the relationship is very bewildering. First Joseph is said to be betrothed to Mary; then he is said to be planning quietly to divorce her; then she is called his wife. The relationship represents normal Jewish marriage procedure. In

Jewish marriage there were three steps. First, engagement – often made when the couple were only children . . . Second betrothal . . . ratification of the engagement into which the couple had previously entered . . . once the betrothal was entered it was absolutely binding. It lasted for one year. During that year the couple were known as man and wife . . . It was at this stage Joseph and Mary were . . . Third . . . the marriage proper which took place at the end of the year of betrothal' (*The Gospel of St. Matthew*, I, p.9). Professor Fenton, a more reliable commentator, also indulges in fanciful speculation. He points to *Deut.* 22:23ff. as a proof for the difference between the betrothed and fully married state. 'If a damsel that is a virgin be betrothed unto an husband, and a man find her in the city, and lie with her; Then ye shall bring them both out unto the gate of that city, and ye shall stone them with stones that they die; the damsel, because she cried not, *being* in the city; and the man, because he has humbled his neighbour's wife: so thou shalt put away evil from among you.' The Catholic Bible puts it also emphatically, calling the woman concerned [the culprit's] the neighbour's wife: so Professor Fenton has quoted a passage which invalidates *his* own argument and demonstrates that a betrothed woman was the cuckolded man's *wife*. After quoting the Bible passage, Fenton continues: ' . . . to the Jews betrothal was a more important step than engagement is with us, compare *Matthew* 1:20, where Mary is called 'your wife', although they are not yet married' (*The Gospel of St. Matthew*, p.42). [This is untrue, see *Matthew* 1:18 which reads 'Mary was espoused to Joseph . . . '.] And to clarify the nonsense that is confusing the readers of the New Testament I would like to quote here a passage relating to the journey to Bethlehem: 'Joseph went up to Bethlehem . . . To be taxed with Mary his espoused wife . . . ' (*Luke* 2:5). This example is one of the many instances where Christian theologians argue from their conclusion to the premise because it does not suit their argument that Joseph and Mary were man and wife. They take their conclusion for granted and impose it upon the text without any justification.

Dummelow merely remarks that 'betrothal was almost equivalent to marriage, and could not be broken off without a formal divorce' (*OVBC*, p.625), although he later admits that 'they were probably married, because it was contrary to Jewish custom for betrothed persons to live together' (ibid., p.741). It was indeed!

Against these speculations we have the word of a near-contemporary, Paul, who is his Epistle to the Galatians, wrote: 'God sent forth his Son, born of a woman, born under the Law' (*Gal.* 4:4), which suggests that Mary was the lawful wife of the carpenter Joseph, and that her first-born son was 'born under the Law'.

Presentation and purification

'When eight days were accomplished for the circumcision of the child, his name was called Jesus, which was so named of the angel, before he was conceived in the womb. And when the days of her purification according to the Law of Moses were accomplished, they brought him to Jerusalem, to present him to the Lord; (as is written in the Law of the Lord, Every male that openeth the womb shall be called holy to the Lord;) and to offer a sacrifice according to that which is said in the Law of the Lord, a pair of turtle-doves or two young pigeons' (*Luke* 2:21/4).

What was this Law of the Lord which had to be satisfied? 'He that is eight days old shall be circumcised among you, every man child in your generations . . . ' (*Gen.* 17:12). 'Sanctify unto me all the firstborn, whatsoever openeth the womb among the children of Israel, both of men and of beast: it is mine' (*Exod.* 13:2); 'Thou shalt not delay to offer the first of thy ripe fruits, and of thy liquors, the firstborn of thy sons shalt thou give unto me' (*Exod.* 22:29); 'If a woman have conceived seed, and born a man child: then she shall be unclean seven days; according to the day of the separation for her infirmity shall she be unclean. And in the eighth day the flesh of his foreskin shall be circumcised . . . And when the days of her purification are fulfilled . . . she shall bring a lamb . . . for a burnt offering, and a young pigeon or turtledove, for a sin offering, unto the door of the tabernacle of the congregation, unto the priest . . . And if she shall not be able to bring a lamb, then she shall bring two turtles, or two young pigeons: the one for the burnt offering, and the other for a sin offering; and the priest shall make an atonement for her, and she shall be clean' (*Lev.* 12:2); 'because all the firstborn are mine: for on the day that I smote the firstborn in the land of Egypt I hallowed unto me all the firstborn in Israel, both man and beast: on the day I smote every firstborn in the land of Egypt I sanctified them for myself' (*Num.* 3:13 and 8:17). Jesus, firstborn child of Joseph and Mary, had to be presented to the Lord and circumcised, and Mary had to be purified by offering *two* pigeons. One pigeon cleansed her from blood, and the other from sin!

It is generally believed that Jesus was circumcised in the synagogue but possibly he was not. In his days circumcision took place in the father's house. It was performed by a mohel or qualified surgeon, but not before centuries later did it become customary to circumcise in the synagogue (Graves/Podro, The *NGR*, p.71). The historian Josephus gives an account of the performance of such an operation on Izates, king of Adiabene (*Ant.* 20:2:4).

Christian commentators find the episode embarrassing and try to gloss over it. Even the most outspoken among them find it impossible to face its implications. Professor Lampe, for example, explains that the episode 'is seen as a presentation of the child rather than a purification of the mother, and speaks of *their*, and not *her* purification, which some manuscripts have tried to correct' (*PC*, p.826). In fact, the Revised Version does speak of *their* purification, as if it made the slightest difference whether the expression refers to the 'pure' Virgin alone, or to her holy child as well. Dummelow's commentary ingeniously asserts: 'Strictly speaking . . . only the mother (not the child) was ceremonially unclean' (*OVBC*, p.743). No explanation is given as to why these divine persons should have to be cleansed from sin.

The Catholic apologist is equally embarrassed. Professor Ginns says that 'Mary seeks no exemption from the Law although, as Catholic tradition teaches, there was no cause for Levitical purification in *her* case' (*CC*, p.943).

The presentation in the Temple introduces Simeon, the first of Israel to recognise the Saviour in the child Jesus. 'There was a man in Jerusalem, just and devout, and the Holy Ghost was upon him. And it was revealed unto him by the Holy Ghost, that he should not see death, before he hath seen the Lord's Christ. And he came by the Spirit into the Temple: and when the parents [sic] brought in the child Jesus, to do for him after the custom of the Law, he took him up in his arms, and blessed God, and said: Lord, now lettest thou Thy servant depart according to Thy word, in peace: For mine eyes have seen Thy salvation, which Thou hast prepared before the face of all people; a light to lighten the Gentiles, And the glory of Thy people Israel.' And his father and mother marvelled at those things which were spoken of him. And Simeon blessed them, and said unto Mary his mother: Behold this child is set for the fall and rising again of many in Israel; and for a sign which shall be spoken gainst; (Yea, a sword shall pierce through thine own soul also), that the thoughts of many hearts may be revealed' (*Luke* 2:25/35).

The words of Simeon known as *Nunc Dimittis* (from the Latin text of Luke 2:29 – Nunc dimittis servum tuum, Domine . . .) are an example of how the skilful editor of the Gospel succeeded in assembling a number of outstanding passages of the Old Testament into a moving document of great poetic beauty:

Gen. 46:30   'Now let me die, since I have seen thy face . . .'
Psalm 42:10   'With a sword in my bones, mine enemies reproach me . . .'
Isaiah 9:2   'The people that walked in the darkness have seen a great light . . .'
Isaiah 42:6   'I . . . will . . . give thee for a covenant of the people, for a light of the Gentiles . . .'
Isaiah 49:6   'To restore the preserved of Israel: I will so give thee for a light to the Gentiles . . .'
Isaiah 60:2/3   'The Lord shall arise upon thee, and his glory shall be seen upon thee. And the Gentiles shall come to thy light . . .'
Isaiah 8:13   'For a gin and for a snare to the inhabitants of Jerusalem. And many of them shall . . . fall . . .'

In this context I would like to say a few words about the name of the child. Had the prophecy of Isaiah referred to him, his name would have been Emmanuel. However, we learn in the New Testament of the command of the Angel of God to name the child 'Jesus'. (*Matthew* 1:21 and *Luke* 1:31). Much is made by reference to this name which means 'God saves' or 'God is the Saviour'. It is really Yoshua or Yeshua which means 'Jehovah is salvation'. Using the word 'God' as part of a per name is as old as mankind. In fact, names like Johanan (John), Hannibal, Theophil, Amadeus, Gottlieb and Bogumil all mean the same thing, namely, the 'Love of God'. Whenever the 'J' or 'El' or 'Y' appears in Hebrew names, they contain a reference to God: Elijah means my God is Jehovah; Israel means soldier of God. Johanan means Jehova is gracious or Jehova is love, Jonathan means whom Jehovah gave, and so on. More on this subject is to be found in the first chapter 'The Man Jesus'.

His brothers James, Joses, Judah and Simon

Twice we come across this statement in the New Testament: 'Is not this the carpenter's son? Is not his mother called Mary? and his brothers [translated brethren in the Authorised and Revised Versions, and 'brothers' in the *NEB*] James, and Joses, and Simon and Judas, and his sisters, are they not all with us?' (*Matthew* 13:55/6); and, 'Is not this the carpenter, the son of Mary, the brother of James, and Joses, and of Judah, and Simon? and are not his sisters here with us? and they were offended in him' (*Mark* 6:3).

There is nothing strange in the correspondence of these passages, since in most essentials Matthew followed the older narrative of Mark, and we can take it for granted that the older chronicler was convinced that Jesus had four brothers and several sisters. However, when Jesus the teacher was forgotten and replaced by Christ the God, his mother became a Holy Virgin who did not know her husband even after the birth of the god-child. Do the gospels give us any information on this point? Indeed, they do: 'Then Joseph being raised from sleep did as the Angel of the Lord had bidden him, and took unto him his wife: And he knew her not *till* she had brought forth her firstborn son: and he called his name Jesus' (*Matthew* 1:24/25). This fatal little word 'till' ἕως has caused much heartsearching and led to many 'heretics' being burnt at the stake. The new edition of the Roman Catholic Bible, an otherwise reasonably honest re-rendering of the text, has this to say about its 'until': This means only that Joseph had nothing to do with the conception of Jesus. It implies nothing as to what happened afterwards.' (p.239).

The Catholic *QB* is not quite so modest. It poses the question: 'Do not the words 'before they came together' and 'till she brought forth her firstborn son' prove that the marriage of Mary and Joseph was really consummated later on? and the *QB* provides the answer to its own question: 'They prove nothing of the sort. These texts were adduced against the Virgin Birth by Helvidius in the fourth century, ably answered by St. Jerome. In reply he cited many passages from the Scriptures to prove that the words '*before*' and '*till*' did not imply the subsequent occurrence of the things in question' (p.356).

The *QB* continues: 'Do not the words 'She brought forth her firstborn son,' imply that Mary had at least two children? Not at all; the Mosaic Law of the firstborn held as soon as the mother had given birth to a son, whether he was the only one, or whether he was succeeded by other children. The Jews frequently spoke of a mother dying, when bringing forth her firstborn son' (ibid.).

From the Scriptures it emerges, however, that four men and several women were held to be the brothers and sisters of Jesus. The early Christians were fascinated by this 'problem' and supplied several explanations. The 'Hieronymian View' associated with St. Jerome, held that they were cousins of Jesus, sons of Clophas and the Virgin's sister Mary, mentioned in *John* 19:25. Some supporters of this view contended that the men called the 'brothers' of Jesus were, in fact, apostles.

Several adherents of this idea believed that the words 'brother' and 'sister' had to do with a relationship described today as 'cousin'. Against this *Luke* 1:36 may be quoted where Elisabeth is described as a cousin (συγγένης), a relative of Mary. Of course, the word might also signify 'cousin', although the Greek word for cousin is ὁ ἀνεψιός, ἡ ἀνεψία. Furthermore, the text of *John* 19:25 probably does not call Mary's sister Mary. It reads: ἡ μήτηρ αὐτοῦ, καὶ ἡ ἀδελφή τῆς μήτρος αὐτοῦ, Μαρία ἡ τοῦ Κλωπᾶ καί Μαρία η Μαγδαληνή, which I would translate: His mother and her sister, Mary the wife of Clophas, and Mary Magdalene. It is unlikely that two sisters would have received the name Mary.

A second theory, the Epiphanian View, is attributed to St. Epiphanius. It states that the brothers and sisters mentioned in the gospels are Joseph's children from his first marriage. As we have seen, this view appears in some apocryphal writings which are of very doubtful authenticity. Yet, it is widely held in the Eastern Church, and was also advanced by Bishop Lightfoot. Its advocates claim that it represents a very old tradition, and quote as circumstantial evidence the view that had Mary been the mother of several children, her sons would have held high positions in the early Church, and thus the idea of her perpetual virginity would not have taken root. Furthermore, they refer to Jesus' words on the cross: 'Behold thy mother', addressed to John and 'Woman, behold thy son', addressed to his mother (*John* 19:26/27). They consider this unlikely if she had been the mother of other grown-up sons.

St. Jerome and St. Augustine condemned the view that the children mentioned were of a former marriage of Joseph. They claimed that Joseph, like the virgin herself, was 'inviolate' to the end of his days. Augustine's contemporary, St. Ambrose, exclaimed: 'There have been some who denied that the Blessed Virgin persevered in maintaining her virginity. Hitherto we have preferred to remain silent in dealing with so great a sacrilege: but because the matter has been brought forward . . . by reason of the fact that even a bishop had been found guilty of this lapse into heresy, we do not consider that it ought to be left uncondemned' (*De Inst. Virg.*, 5:35). He also denies the impious assertion that 'another birth came forth from that same virginal womb from which Christ was born according to the flesh' (*Ep.* 79).

Finally, there was the 'Helvidian View', advanced by the 'heretic' Helvidius, who maintained that the children in question were born of Joseph and Mary who indeed 'came together' after the birth of Jesus. It accepted the Scriptural mention of Jesus' brothers and sisters, and insisted that *Matthew* 1:18/25 indicates that it was at least probable that Joseph and Mary lived an ordinary married life after Jesus was born. It also claimed that the unqualified term 'brother' does not refer to cousins, half-brothers or step-brothers, and that the subterfuges of the other 'views' were due to the wishful thinking of those who did not like to contemplate that the mother of Jesus could have been the mother of other children.

Not only Catholics but many Protestant writers shrink from this conclusion. For example, Professor Fenton thinks that the expression 'knew her not until she had brought forth her firstborn son' may not imply that Joseph did know her afterwards. Fenton admits, however, that the Scriptural references to Jesus' brothers and sisters suggest that Joseph did (*Saint Matthew* p.44). He also confirms that Matthew's statement could be taken to mean that the brothers and sisters were the younger children of Joseph and Mary (ibid., p.206).

There is another episode involving the relatives of Jesus, and perhaps even his mother and brothers. 'And when his friends (οἱ παρ αὐτοῦ) [i.e. those with him, his relations] heard of it, they went out to lay hold of him: for they said, he is beside himself' (*Mark* 3:21). This story is followed by an account of the abortive attempt of his mother and brothers to see him (*Mark* 3:31ff). It is likely that Jesus' family were concerned about his mental state, and where the Authorised Version speaks about 'his friends', the Greek text uses the above-mentioned words and the *NEB* translated 'his family'. It is also recorded that his deeply concerned family wished to speak to him calling at one of his meetings, probably with the intention of persuading him to leave with them. He refused to meet them which shows, incidentally, how little family ties meant to Jesus.

This story has always fascinated scholars. 'Dr. Schmiedel . . . draws attention to the narrative of how Jesus, at the beginning of his ministry, was declared by his own household to be out of his senses, and how, in consequence, his mother and brothers followed him to put him under restraint. The story offended the first and third evangelists, and they partly omit it, partly obscure its drift. The fourth evangelist limits the disbelief to the brothers of Jesus. The whole narrative is in flagrant contradiction to the Birth stories in the early chapters of Matthew and Luke, and to the whole subsequent drift of Church tradition. Being gifted with commonsense, Schmiedel argues that it must be true, because it could never have been invented' (Conybeare, *The Historical Christ*, p.175).

Schoeps regards the insistence on Mary's virginity both before and after Jesus' birth as a false midrashic interpretation of *Isaiah* 66:7: 'Before she travailed, she brought forth: before her pain came, she was delivered of a man child'. According to Luke, Schoeps says, the birth of Jesus had been proclaimed to Mary by an angel, and yet it is stated that his mother and brothers did not believe in him. This contradiction is made even more blatant when his brother James is numbered among his disciples (*The Jewish Christian Argument*, pp.76/7).

Lietzmann quotes Helvidius who says that Mary lived in a state of marriage with Joseph and had several children by him. 'And why not,' exclaims Helvidius, 'indeed? Are virgins in any way superior to Abraham, Isaac and Jacob, who were married men.' This attack on the monkish idea of celibacy induced Jerome to counter-attack, summoning his most vitriolic language to defend the virginity of the 'Mother of God' (*The Era of the Church Fathers*, p.180). Another scribe, Jovinian, adopted the Helvidian view, and claimed that after the birth of Jesus, Mary was no longer a virgin. For this heinous heresy he was banished to a Dalmatian island (398) where he died a few years later. Jerome, the arch-enemy of the Helvidian view, succeeded in having Jovinian's supporters arrested and thus broke the back of this 'heretic' movement. He even wrote two books to refute Jovinian, which, according to Lietzmann, were so full of perverse distortions and exaggerations so outrageous that even Jerome's keenest supporters felt ashamed. He was called upon to revoke some of his statements, but eventually his hostile attitude prevailed. Lietzmann makes this acute observation: 'Asceticism had been the only thing to give him a purchase on morality, he could only evaluate marriage in the light of the brothels he had known in his youth, and out of the salacious images drawn from them, which only too often flickered in and out among the elements that constituted his religious life' (ibid., p.182).

These words apply not only to St. Jerome, but to many advocates of the belief in Mary's 'perpetual virginity', and perhaps even to the idea of the Virgin Birth itself.

Jewish reaction to the myth

Jewish reaction was not immediate, but as Christianity spread, they had to consider the claim that the illegitimate child of a Galilean woman was the Messiah spoken of by the prophets. The middle of the second century, several generations after Jesus' death, brought about this reaction in the form of stories circulating among the Jews which cast doubt on the chastity of Mary. Origen preserves one of these in his *Against Celsus*. It tells us how Mary, as a result of her adulterous association with a Roman soldier, Panthera, brought forth a male child, Yeshua. Origen indignantly rejects this slight on the honourable parents of the Saviour. He argues that the 'unhallowed intercourse' with a Roman soldier would have sired 'a fool doing injury to mankind' and not 'a teacher of temperance and righteousness' (1:19 and 133).

It is, of course, not to be expected that a Christian author should show understanding for the Jewish reaction to the doctrine of the Virgin Birth. After all, more than seventeen-hundred years later, a Church of England commentator can state: 'In Jewish thought the Holy Spirit had certain definite functions. We cannot bring to this passage the Christian idea of the Holy Spirit in all its fullness, because Joseph would know nothing about that. We must interpret it in the light of the Jewish idea of the Holy Spirit, for it is that idea that Joseph would bring to this message, for that was all he knew. According to the Jewish idea of the Holy Spirit was the person [sic] who brought God's truth to men. It was the Holy Spirit who taught the prophets what to say; he taught men of God what to do, it was the Holy Spirit who, throughout the ages . . . brought God's truth to men' (Barclay, *The Gospel of St. Matthew*, I, p. 11). This was written by a professor of theology of our own age and, unfortunately, has the authority of the remarkable Roman Catholic apologist, Jean Daniélou, to back it up in its preposterous and wholly unfounded claim.

Dummelow's *OVBC* is more to the point: 'That Mary fully understood who her child was to be, cannot be supposed. The thought of such a condescension of the Author of nature as is implied in the words of the Creed 'conceived by the Holy Ghost, born of the Virgin Mary' is overwhelming even to us; to Mary it would have been so appalling that she could not have performed her duty of a mother. Hence the angel was only permitted to reveal to her that her son would be the Messiah, and the Son of God in some specifically exalted yet human sense. The whole narrative moves within the circle of Jewish Old Testament ideas' (p. 738). This is very true, and had it been otherwise it would have been unacceptable to the early Christians who were, after all, practising Jews. James himself, who is referred to as 'the brother of the Lord' (*Acts* 12:17, 21:18, *Gal.* 1:19 and 12) and 'James the Righteous' (Eusebius, *H.E.* 2:1) was to end his life as a pious Jew who observed all the ceremonial laws.

Klausner, who studied the Jewish reaction to the Christian story throughout the ages in great detail, writes: 'The accounts in Matthew and Luke about the birth of Jesus by the Holy Ghost are lacking in Mark; they stand on the same footing as the stories of Celsus' Jew and of the Toldoth Yeshu; and the Talmud which regards Jesus as illegitimate and the son of Pandera or Panthera, and both alike came into existence only after the Christian dogma had determined that not only was Jesus the Messiah, but also the Son of God. So long as Jesus was regarded as the Messiah it was necessary to show that his father Joseph was of the stock of Jesse, but as the Son of God it was not possible for him to have a human father: therefore he was born of the Holy Spirit by whom his mother conceived in a fashion incomprehensible to mortal beings. This became a matter of dispute among the earliest Christian sects. And the Jews who also lacked the critical faculty and the historic sense (but remained strictly monotheistic), confirmed the view that Jesus had no legitimate father, but, instead of the Holy Spirit, introduced into their legends the notion of an illicit union' (*JN*, pp.232/3).

Another Jewish scholar, Joshua Podro, also mentions the deep roots the Panthera calumny has taken: 'Celsus, writing about A.D. 175, describes Jesus as the fruit of his mother's seduction by a Roman soldier named Pantherus: and it is recorded in the Talmud (*San.* 43a) that he was related to the Government ... Though the talmudic authority for this, Ulla, a fourth century scholar, has here confused Jesus with a Messianic pretender from Lydda, who appears in the time of Hadrian, states that 40 days had elapsed between his apprehension and death, a more plausible version of the libel appears in the third century talmudic record (*Shabb.* 104a). Moreover, the Jews could disprove the legitimacy of Jesus' birth merely from the account given in *Matthew* 1:18 and the Protevangelium 17. Their [the Jews'] God did not father sons on mortal maidens in the style of Zeus, and if Mary had already been contracted in marriage to Joseph before he found her pregnant, this would in Jewish Law (*Deut.* 22:13/21) have bastardised her child even if the marriage had not been consummated' (Graves/Podro *NGR*, p.49).

Bishop Barnes introduces an interesting slant into the Panthera story: 'The artificial nature of the calumny recorded by Celsus is apparent from the name Panthera. Those familiar with the way in which ... the ancients took pleasure in playing with words, will recognise in 'Panthera' a transformation of παρϑένος, the Greek word for 'virgin'. The malice of the story is singularly childish' (*The Rise of Christianity*, p.89).

The Virgin cult begins

As the memory of the man dwindled, as Jesus, the son of Joseph, became a distant myth, so the glory of the Christ-Mithras moved more and more to the foreground. When the gospels were written down by Greek-speaking Jewish Christians on the basis of various verbal traditions, the confusion between the legend of the divine man and the human god was already apparent. The figure of the emergent God Christ was accompanied by a female addition to the Christian pantheon: Miriam the simple, careworn, ageing Galilean woman was elevated to the Mother of God, the 'theotokos'. Imperceptibly, she merged with the 'Great Goddess', with Mother Earth, with Isis, with Astarte. In the context of the Old Testament, she became the 'Second Eve' who, due to the part she played in the drama of Salvation redeemed the share the First Eve had in the Fall.

An early exponent of the new creed, himself a figure of near-legend, St Ignatius of Antioch, is reported as having been the first to acclaim the Virgin. Speaking of Christ, he said: 'He is truly of the race of David according to the flesh, but the Son of God by the Divine Will and Power, truly born of a Virgin . . . '. This view is completely in line with Paul's Epistle to the Romans 1:3/4, but it already contains the mention of the Virgin. Two years later Ignatius is said to have written that Jesus was 'God in man . . . both of Mary and of God' (*Ad Eph.*, 7:2).

The Apology of Aristides, written about twenty years later, contains these words; 'Having been born of the Holy Virgin . . . He took flesh and appeared unto men . . . '. Aristides cautiously begins the sentence with the words, 'It is said . . . '.

It is in St. Justin that we find for the first time the alluring parallel between Eve and the Mother of Man, and Mary the Mother of God, which has appealed greatly to centuries of Christian apologists. 'For Eve, being a virgin and undefiled, conceiving the word which was from the Serpent [sic], brought forth disobedience and death; but the Virgin Mary, through faith and joy . . . answered. "Be it unto me according to thy word . . . "', (*Tryph.*, C:100). St. Irenaeus, develops this theme yet further: 'With a fitness Mary the Virgin is found obedient, saying: "Behold thy handmaid, O Lord, be it to me according to thy word . . . ". But Eve is found disobedient; since she obeyed not while still a virgin. Through being disobedient, she became the cause of death, both to herself and to the whole human race; whereas Mary, having a husband fore-appointed, and yet a virgin, became the cause of salvation, both to herself and the whole human race' (*Cont. Haer.*, 3:22). And he coins the expression which found its way into the Creed, the expression confessing belief 'in one God . . . and the Birth from the Virgin . . . ' (ibid. 10:1). It is from Irenaeus that St. Clement of Alexandria took his ' . . . the Son of God, Who made all things, took flesh and was conceived in the womb of the Virgin . . . ' (*Stromateis*, 6:25:127).

The great Tertullian of Carthage, the creator of Church Latin, was contemporary of St. Clement. He did not qualify for canonisation since towards the end of his life he became a 'heretic'. He advanced the theme of Mary as 'second Eve' with consummate skill: 'Into Eve, as yet a virgin, had crept the word which was the framer of death. Equally into a virgin was to be introduced the Word of God which was the builder up of life; that which by that sex had gone into perdition, by the same sex might be brought back to salvation. Eve had believed the serpent, Mary believed Gabriel: the fault which the one had committed by believing, the other by believing has blotted out' (*De Carh. Chr*, c.17). He attacks the Patripassian 'heresy' which identifies the Son with the Father: 'The devil says that the Father Himself descended into the Virgin, was Himself born of her; in fact that He Himself was Jesus Christ' (*Adv. Prax.*). Tertullian speaks of 'God's Son brought down . . . into the Virgin Mary, made flesh in her womb, and was born of her' (*De Prae. Haer.*, c.13), and of 'The ray of God [which] glided down into a virgin, in her womb was fashioned as flesh, is born as man mixed with God' (*Apol.* 21).

Origen, another great Church Father who did not make the grade of becoming a Saint, (he is said to have castrated himself to become a 'eunuch for heaven's sake') wrote about A.D. 220; 'The body of Jesus was born of a virgin and of the Holy Spirit' (*De princ.*, 1, 1, 1:4). And in his famous *Contra Celsum* he exclaims: 'Who has not heard of the Virgin Birth of Jesus?' (1:7). St. Cyprian who died a martyr's death in 258 quoted the above-mentioned mistranslation of *Isaiah* 7:14, and said: 'That this should be the sign of his nativity that he should be born of a Virgin' (*Test. contr. Iud.*, ii, cc.8/9). When Athanasius arrived on the scene, it was already common currency that 'For us He took flesh in the Virgin Mary, Mother of God' (Or. iii c.14). Of course, Athanasius does not say Mother of God, but theotokos (God-bearer) which is the origin of the Catholic Church's expression; 'Mother of God'.

Athanasius's contemporary, St. Cyril of Jerusalem, repeats the old adage, which probably had universal application in the early Church: 'Since through Eve, a virgin, came death, it behoved that through a Virgin should life appear; that as the Serpent had deceived the one, so to the other Gabriel might bring good tidings' (*Cat.*, 12:15). As we have noted above this was said much more effectively and dramatically by Tertullian, nearly two hundred years earlier. Cyril also took it upon himself to defend Mary's title theotokos which had been rejected by Nestorius and his followers: 'If anyone does not acknowledge that Emmanuel is in truth God, and that the Holy Virgin is, in consequence, theotokos, for she brought forth, after the flesh, the Word of God who has become flesh, let him be anathema!' (*Ep.* xvii). Another contemporary, St. Ambrose, calls Mary a Virgin 'by grace, entirely free from every stain of sin' (*Serm.* 22:30). 'This is the Virgin,' says Ambrose, 'who conceived in the womb, and as a virgin, bore a son. For so it is written, "Behold, the Virgin shall conceive in her womb and shall bring forth a son". For the Prophet said not only she should conceive as a virgin, but that as a Virgin she should bring forth' (*Ad. Siric.*, ep. vii). The most succinct formulation of the Eve-Mary complex comes from St. Jerome: 'Mors per Evam, vita per Mariam' – Death through Eve, through Mary Life' (*Ep. 22 ad Eust*, 21).

Without a doubt the greatest figure among the Church Fathers was St. Augustine. By giving his sanction to the fast developing mariolatry (Cult of Mary) he added the figure of the Mother of God to the threefold divinity of the Christians. Thus he enabled the worshippers to address themselves to the Mother-Goddess, a course denied them by the patriarchal approach to the kingdom of Heaven, which was a Jewish heritage to Christianity.

Augustine says, 'All have sinned except the Holy Virgin Mary, concerning whom, for the honour of our Lord, I wish no question at all raised when we speak of sin' (*De Nat. et Grat.*, c.36). The Latin text is almost untranslatable, making it difficult to show the degree of arrogant intolerance displayed by one of the greatest exponents of Christian doctrine, while advancing a completely unsubstantiated statement. The old theme of death through Eve and Life through Mary also finds expression: 'It is a great mystery that by woman came death to us, so to us was born through woman Life' (*De Agone Chr.*, c.24). It must be admitted that with a fine turn of phrase he succeeded in surpassing Tertullian's linguistic elegance.

The closed door

Augustine also revived the image of 'the closed door', first used by Jerome, after whom it played a great part in the doctrine of the Virgin Birth. 'The closed door formed no obstacle to the substance of that Body in which Godhead was; for He at whose birth the virginity of His Mother remained inviolate, could enter it when it was not opened' (*Super Ioann.*, tr. 121). 'Ye shall therefore have no doubt that the Virgin could bring forth without taking away her virginity' (*De Fide Rer.*, 5). Christ was 'born of a Mother who, although she had conceived without being defiled and ever had remained undefiled – a Virgin in conceiving, a Virgin in her bringing forth, and a Virgin until her death – was yet married to a workman' (*De Cat. Rud.*, 40). In fairness to Augustine he did not use the expression 'defiled', which shows the state of mind of the translator. The word used was 'virgo intacta', nevertheless we can see how the idea of the Mother of God was made respectable through its adoption by one of the greatest minds of the fourth-and fifth-century Church.

Little wonder that his contemporary, St. Chrysostom goes the whole length of the new argument beginning to speak of the Virgin's intercession on behalf of sinful man: 'We have the Holy Virgin and Mother of God interceding for us . . . Let us beseach Mary, the holy and glorious Virgin and Mother of God' (*De uno legisl.*).

St. Jerome, St. Ambrose and St. Augustine regard the image of 'the closed door' as the fulfilment of Old Testament prophesy. I quote the passage in order to present the reader with an example of the incredible somersaults the Christian mind performs to prove the unprovable: 'This gate shall be shut, it shall not be opened, and no man shall enter by it, because the Lord, the God of Israel, hath entered in by it, therefore it shall be shut' (*Ezek.*, 44:2). This happens to be *not* a prophesy at all, but a matter of fact description of the Temple, and of the reason why the Eastern Gate of the Temple, through which the Ark had been carried, should be permanently shut. Even in the Houses of Parliament in London there is a gate which is opened only once a year when the sovereign passes through it. An interesting example of the misuse of Ezekiel's text may be found in the writings of the apologist Rufinus of Aquilea. He fraudulently alters the text and his Latin reads as though Ezekiel had said that ('Dominus Deus Israel transibit per eam' – whilst the Latin text reads: ' . . . vir non transibit per eam, quoniam Dominus Deus Israel ingressus est per eam'). And this is what Rufinus has to say as a commentary to the Old Testament passage: 'Just as in the sanctification of the Holy Ghost no thought of frailty is to be admitted, so in the Virgin Birth no defilement [and Rufinus *does* say defilement – corruptio] is to be imagined . . . The prophet Ezekiel . . . had predicted the miraculous manner of that Birth, calling Mary figuratively 'the Gate of the Lord' . . . What could be said with more evident reference to the inviolate preservation of the Virgin's condition? That Gate of Virginity was closed: through it the Lord of Israel entered, through it He came forth from the Virgin's womb into the world; and the Virgin's state being preserved inviolate, the gate of the Virgin remained closed for ever' (*Symb. Ap.*, c.9).

This commentary and this 'interpretation' have received the general consent of the Church and have been common Catholic currency ever since.

The Virgin becomes part of the doctrine

In the writings of St. Epiphanius there is mention of an earlier Creed, or statement of doctrine, to which he refers as the 'Creed of Marcellus', now known as the 'Old Roman Creed'. Article 3 of this reads: 'I believe in Christ Jesus . . . who was born of the Spirit and the Virgin Mary . . . ' (*Apo. Epi.* 1:8). The Church made an attempt to state a universally accepted doctrine at Nicaea in 325. The first draft, probably submitted by Eusebius of Caesarea, was in fact the Creed of the Caesarean Church (*Epi Eus. apud Socr.*, U.E. 1:8). It was an entirely orthodox statement but was believed to be inadequate in its condemnation of the Arian position. That 'heresy' denied the equality and consubstantiality of the three Persons of the Trinity, and admitted only a doctrine of 'like' nature whilst claiming that the Father was supreme. The Caesarean Creed was widened to help the Church in its struggle against Arianism, and thus the Creed of Nicaea was born. Neither the Caesarean nor the Nicaean Creed contains any mention of the Holy Virgin. However, the statement now known as 'Nicene Creed' had its origin in the Catechetical Lectures of St. Cyril of Jerusalem, and seem to be a merger of the Creeds of Nicaea and Jerusalem. It first appears in the *Ancoratus of St. Epiphanius* and was probably written in 374. The statement which was read and accepted at the Council of Chalcedon in 451 contains the words: 'Was made flesh of the Holy Spirit and the Virgin Mary'.

By that time the adulation of the Virgin was universally accepted in the Church. Even the great Pope St. Leo I, during whose reign Chalcedon took place, says with emphasis: 'He was conceived by the Holy Ghost within the womb of His Virgin Mother, who brought him forth with her virginity preserved even as she had conceived him with her virginity preserved' (*St. Leon P.l and Flav. Ep.*, Ep.2). In 449 Leo wrote to Flavian: 'He was conceived of the Holy Spirit, in the womb of his Virgin Mother, whose virginity remained entire in His birth as in His conception . . . it is true that the Holy Spirit gave fruitfulness to the Virgin, but the reality of His body was received from her body' (ibid., Ep.28).

The Council of Chalcedon confirmed the Virgin's title 'theotokos', which had been a matter of dispute for over a century. In 482 the Christian East Roman Emperor Zeno wrote: 'We confess that He, having come down and made incarnate of the Holy Spirit and the Virgin Mary, the Godbearer . . . ' (*Zeno Apud Evagrius*, H.E. iii/14).

Despite his eagerness to bring about agreement, Zeno's *Henotikon* (Edict of Reunion) was condemned by Pope Simplicius because of its implied criticism of the Council of Chalcedon. This led to a schism between State and Church which was only overcome by the agreement with Emperor Justinian I, who reaffirmed the statement of Chalcedon.

From then onward every Council included a reverent mention of the Virgin. The Second Council of Constantinople (553) hastened to add an article to its Canons: 'If anyone applies the title 'God-bearer', to the glorious and ever-virgin Mary in an unreal and not in a true sense, as if a mere man was born and not God the Word made flesh and born of her . . . Let him be anathema' (*Mansi* 9, 375:D). Similarly, the Second Council of Nicaea (787) speaks in its *Definition* of 'our undefiled Lady, the holy God-bearer', a language already familiar to our ears. In a letter addressed to the Empress Irene, the Council calls Jesus' mother 'the Immaculate Mother of God and Ever-Virgin Mary'.

The status of the Virgin did not change considerably during the Middle Ages: if anything, her cult increased the more monolithic the Church became. The 'Doctor' of mediaeval Christendom, St. Thomas Aquinas, speaking of *Exod.* 13:2, wrote: 'Christ went forth from the closed womb of the Virgin and opened it not, and therefore he ought not have been presented in the Temple in accordance with the Law' (*Summa*, iii/Q37:A:3). On the same subject he adds: 'Christ, although not liable under the Law, nevertheless willed to undergo circumcision and the other burdens of the Law to set an example of humility and obedience; for the same reason He willed it that His mother should fulfil the observance of the Law, although she was not liable to it . . . for as far as she was personally concerned, she needed no purgation' (ibid., A.4). Aquinas repeats the words of St. Ambrose almost literally: 'It must be asserted without any doubt that the Mother of Christ was a virgin even in the act of bringing forth; for the prophet does not only say, "Behold a virgin shall conceive", but he also adds, "and she shall bear a son" (ibid., Q38:A.2).

Another mediaeval philosopher, John Duns Scotus, the Scholastic, joins the chorus with a cautious: 'It seems probable that everything that is excellent should be assigned to Mary' (*Sent.*, III/3/1), and he thought it right that she should be regarded as immune from Original Sin. Towards the end of the Middle Ages the Council of Basle (1439) declared that the 'glorious Virgin Mary, Mother of God, by the anticipating and operating special grace of Divine Power, was never actually subject to original sin, but was always immune from all original and actual sin and undefiled' (*Sess.* XXXVI).

The Virgin in England

While the Reformation deprived Mary of her astrological titles, her role as mediatrix, and her immunity from original sin, it did not question her position as 'theotokos'. Even Luther and Calvin acknowledged the divine motherhood and accorded full honour to Mary as the Mother of Christ. Luther wrote: 'There is no honour, no beatitude capable of approaching an elevation which consists of being, among all humans, the sole person – superior to all others – in the privilege of having one Son in common with the Heavenly Father' (*Deutsche Schriften*, 14:25). And Calvin states; 'We cannot acknowledge the blessings brought us by Jesus without acknowledging at the same time how highly honoured and enriched was Mary in being chosen for the Mother of God' (*Comm. sur l'Harm. Evang.*, 20).

In the Thirty Nine Articles of the Church of England, too, the Virgin makes an appearance: 'In utero virginis ex illius substantia naturam humanam assumpsit', i.e., 'he took human nature in the womb of the Virgin, of her substance' (Art. II).

Bishop Lancelot Andrewes, who deplored the exaggerated veneration of the Virgin, himself spoke of the 'sanctissimae, intemeratae, super caeteros benedictae, Deiparae et semper Virginis Mariae' 'the Most Holy, Immaculate, pre-eminently Blessed God-bearer and Ever-Virgin Mary' (*Preces. Priv.*, p.141). He also said: 'The light cometh through the glass, yet the glass is not perished. No more did the God of heaven, by His passage, violate in any whit the virginity of His Mother' (Sermons, p.74).

At the beginning of the seventeenth century, Bishop Hall of Norwich said: 'Jesus that meant to take man's nature without man's corruption, would be the seed of woman without man; and among all women of a pure virgin . . . How justly do we bless her whom the Angel pronounced Blessèd! How worthily is honoured of men, whom the Angel proclaimed beloved of God! O Blessed Mary, he cannot bless thee, he cannot honour thee, that deifies thee not' (*Hall's Contemplations*, 3:23/4).

Dr. Mark Frank, a Cambridge divine of the seventeenth century, wrote: 'She was an immaculate and unspotted Virgin – to such a Virgin, one so highly favoured as to be made the Mother of God, what messenger could come less than an Angel . . . Gabriel, too . . . ' (*Sermons on Festivals*, II, pp.38/9). His contemporary, Archbishop Bramhall, made it clear that 'We admit the perpetual virginity of the mother of God' (*Complete Works*, I, p.53). Bishop Pearson went even further: 'We believe the Mother of our Lord to have been, not only before and after his Nativity, but forever, the Most Immaculate and Blessed Virgin . . . She is to be acknowledged the Ever-Virgin Mary. As if the Gate of the Sanctuary in the Prophet Ezekiel were to be understood of her . . . (*On the Creed,* I, p.272). At least Pearson was conscientious enough to say 'as if' before quoting the passage in Ezekiel, and even to quote the text correctly.

In Dummelow's *OVBC* it is claimed that the abandoning of the doctrine of Virgin Birth would only increase most believers' difficulties (p.626). Langmead-Casserley exclaims reprovingly that 'those who deny the Virgin Birth usually end towards some kind of adoptionism or Nestorianism in Christology – what is often called "reduced Christology" – and towards some kind of naturalism in philosophy'. He adds the ingenuous remark: 'The New Testament evidence is not so strong in the case of the Virgin Birth as it is in that of the Resurrection. There is, however, no evidence at all for any other alternative' (*A Handbook of Christian Theology,* p.372). Even Bishop Lightfoot defends the 'Ever-Virginity' of St. Epiphanius, in his *Commentary on the Galatians.*

In conclusion let me quote here one of the *Ecclesiastical Sonnets* of the poet, William Wordsworth, an Anglican:

Mother! whose virgin bosom was uncrost
with the least shade of thought to sin allied!
Woman! above all women glorified;
Purer than foam on central ocean tost,
Brighter than Eastern skies at daybreak strewn
With fancied roses, than the unblemished moon
Before her wane begins on Heaven's blue coast;
Thy image falls on earth.

It is not a good poem but it shows clearly the adulation rendered to Mary even in the Protestant world.

Mary, the Mother of God

We have seen how Mary, the wife of a craftsman in a small Galilean township and mother of many children, became the immaculate, ever-virgin Mother of God. Although in the the New Testament Jesus had hardly any kind, and a few rather unkind words for her, man's desire to elevate a woman into heaven has overcome the strictly patriarchal theism of the Jews, and added the Virgin Mother to the addressees of prayer and worship.

A modern American thinker, Alan W. Watts, presents a convincing motivation for Mariolatry which has reached new heights in the Roman Catholic Church of today. 'Whatever they may have meant to the theologians, there can be no doubt as to the popular significance of such terms as Mother of God, Queen of Heaven, Mistress of the Angels, or of the hymnody which praised her as the "glorious Lady throne in rest amidst the starry host above", and as "she that riseth up in the morning, fair as the moon, clear as the sun." Mary rather than Jesus, was the image where mediaeval man (as well as the simple Catholic of today) understood the love and beauty of God, the fertility and power of divine nature. To her the most depraved sinner could pour out his heart in the certainty that he would be accepted in a loving embrace as infinite and all-inclusive as the sky that was symbolized by her star-decked robe of blue . . . In Mary, the Queen of Heaven, this tenderness is entirely beautiful, but thus far our attempts to mix it in with the image of the King of kings have been quite disastrous . . . When we try to combine righteousness and love in one symbol, the result is often that the most unedifying tyrant who enforces his tyranny by constant harping on how much his children's misbehaviour "wounds his love" for them; and administers judgment with "this hurts me more than it's going to hurt you" line. We allow in God what we deplore in parents and teachers' (*Behold the Spirit*, pp. 170/1).

It was to meet this growing need of men to worship a woman, a Mother, with a clear heart and conscience, that prompted the Catholic Church under Pope Pius IX to assign superhuman status to the Virgin. in his 'Ineffabilis Deus', given on the 8th December 1854, Pius proclaimed the dogma of the 'Immaculate Conception' which declares that Mary was born without the stigma of Original Sin. The actual words were: 'Beatissimam Virginem Mariam in primo instanti suae conceptionis fuisse singulari omnipotentis Dei gratia et privilegio, intuitu meritorum Christi Jesu Salvatoris humani generis, ab omni originalis culpae praeservatan immunem.'

The dogma is not without theological pitfalls. It thus assumes that Christ, born of the Holy Ghost and the Immaculate Virgin, did not share the sinful nature of our humanity. Elevated above man, the God Christ lost the last bond that related man to the Man Jesus and his human nature. How could he have been 'fully man'?!

The Mother-worship of the Roman Catholic Church received its crowning confirmation through the dogma of Mary's bodily Ascension into heaven which was defined by Pope Pius XII in November 1950 in the Apostolic Constitution and in an Encyclical Letter of 11th October 1954 'Ad Caeli Reginam'. The same Pope instituted a feast to be observed yearly in honour of Mary's 'regalis dignitas' as Queen of

Heaven and Earth. As Jung says, 'the Assumptio Mariae paves the way not only for the divinity of the theotokos [i.e. her ultimate recognition as a goddess] but also for the quaternity' (*Psychology and Religion: West and East*, p. 171).

Of course, Roman Catholics are adamant that Mary is not being worshipped, and that she is merely implored to act as intercessor between God and sinful humanity. 'The International Marian Congress in Fribourg declared in 1902: 'This assembly . . . lifts its voice . . . to protest solemnly against the calumny . . . that Catholics make the august Mother of God an object of adoration . . . This lie and calumny . . . should at length cease. It calls attention to the irrefutable truth that the Catholic Church knows of no other adoration but that of the Triune God and of Jesus Christ our Lord; and that all love and confidence in the Blessed Virgin is . . . limited to such love and veneration as, according to the words of the Archangel Gabriel, the eulogy of St. Elizabeth, and the requirements of reason itself, is owing to a creature who was elevated to the position of Mother of Jesus Christ, and to whom even an Apostle was committed from the cross as a child to its mother.'

She is, as is made clear in this declaration, merely considered an advocate, a mediator. 'Her office is that of perpetual intercession for the Church Militant' (A.T. Wirgman, *The Blessed Virgin*, p. 103).

In a book which discusses the problem of the Virgin Birth throughout its 214 pages, we find this statement: 'The Virgin Conception of our Lord is a miracle which transcends all human power of explanation' (ibid., p. 109), words, though honest, make the value of that hefty volume rather questionable.

The theologian perturbed

In defending Article 2 of the Articles of the Church of England, Griffith Thomas makes a point which is worth repeating here: 'We may say: Mary was the Mother of Lord. Our Lord was God. Therefore Mary was the Mother of God. Our premises are absolutely correct; our logic perfectly flawless; and yet we know that the conclusion is strictly untrue, since there is another thought implied (our Lord's humanity) which finds no place in the syllogism' (*The Principles of Theology*, pp. 35/6). A few pages later the same theologian argues that every effect must have an adequate cause, and that is only through the Virgin Birth that we can account for the uniqueness of Christ. The miraculous entry suitably matches the miraculus exit, i.e. the Resurrection. To save man, the son of Adam, from sin, a new start had to be made: hence the

Virgin Birth. Once we have accepted the much greater miracle of the Resurrection, we should find no difficulty in accepting the mystery of the Virgin Birth. Finally, like so many Christian thinkers, Griffith Thomas falls into the trap of making his own conclusion the premise. 'How,' he exclaims, 'could the narratives have obtained such appearance of trustworthiness unless they were historical?' (ibid., pp.47/49).

It may be said, on the whole (Griffith Thomas and Wirgman are exceptions), Protestant theologians avoid the delicate subject. It is Roman Catholicism which, not content with having established the dogma of the Immaculate Conception, hastened to introduce the final apotheosis, the dogma of the Bodily Assumption of the Virgin.

The heated discussions about the Virgin Birth and the status of Mary took place in the distant past, and it was more than twelve hundred years ago that an anonymous Christian wrote this prayer which reflects the Christian attitude even in our days: 'Blesséd art thou, O Virgin Mary, who has carried the Lord, the Maker of the world. Thou hast born Him who created thee, and thou abidest a virgin forever.'

The psychologist speaks

Psychologists have always been fascinated by the figure and role of the Virgin in the Christian religion.

For the most profound interpretation of the need of the religious mind to worship the Virgin Goddess, we are indebted to C.G. Jung. He approaches the problem 'objectively', inasmuch as he does not consider whether the problem is true of false, but whether it satisfies a social need. He claims that 'the idea is shared by society – by a *consensus gentium.*' (op. cit., p.6).

The Virgin Goddess, one of the most significant archetypes of humanity, was easily transferred to the simple, elderly Jewess, Mary, the wife of Joseph, a Galilean carpenter: 'In 421, at the Council of Ephesus, whose streets had once rung with hymns of praise to many-breasted Diana, the Virgin Mary was declared the *Theotokos*, the Mother of God. As we know from Epiphanius, there was even a sect, the Collyridians, who worshipped Mary after the manner of an antique goddess. Her . . . most enthusiastic devotees being women . . . their provocation moved Epiphanius to the rebuke that "the whole female sex is slippery and prone to error, with a mind that is very petty and narrow" . . . priestesses on certain feastdays decorated a wagon . . . on which they placed offerings of bakemeats "in the name of Mary", afterwards partaking in the sacrificial meal. This plainly amounted to a

Eucharistic feast in honour of Mary, at which wheaten bread was eaten. The orthodox standpoint of the time is aptly expressed in the words of Epiphanius: "Let Mary be held in honour, and the Father and the Son and the Holy Ghost be adored, but let no one adore Mary . . . " (ibid., pp. 129/130).

Jung also gives examples of the fairy tale notion that the stern godhead (the beast) could only be moved to love by the intervention of a pure virgin (the beauty). 'Even as late as the 17th century the learned Jesuit, Nicolas Caussin, declared that . . . the God of the Old Testament . . . in his wrath . . . reduced the world to confusion . . . until, overcome by the love of a pure virgin, he was changed in her womb into a God of Love.' Jung also quotes Philippus Picinelli who wrote: 'Of a truth God, terrible beyond measure, appeared before the world peaceful and wholly tamed after dwelling in the womb of the Most Blessed Virgin.' St. Bonaventura said that Christ was tamed and pacified by the most kindly Mary, so that he could not punish the sinner with eternal death (ibid., p. 270).

Jung believes that Protestantism resembles Mithraism in its reluctance to admit woman to metaphysical representation. He shows how Mithraism suffered for this one-sidedness, and eventually lost the battle against Christianity which, in the form of the Virgin, could boast of a female element in its mythology. The fear of the Protestants that the cult of the Virgin might lead to a decline of the adulation of Christ, is justified. However, the rejection of the archetype which personified the yearning in the 'collective unconscious' of the masses can only lead to a decline of Protestant influence (ibid., p. 465).

The Mary cult which made her into a 'sinless vessel', immaculately conceived and ever-virgin, restored in her person the human condition prior to the Fall. From this follows, however, an argument which reveals a great flaw in the Plan of Redemption. 'By having these special measures applied to her, Mary is elevated to the status of a goddess, and consequently loses some of her humanity: she will not conceive her child in sin, like all other mothers, and therefore he also will never be a human being, but a god. To my knowledge at least, no one has ever perceived that this queers the pitch for a genuine incarnation of God, or rather that the Incarnation was only partially consummated. Both, mother and son, are not real human beings at all, but gods.' (ibid., pp. 397/9).

Jung's argument is weighty indeed. If Jesus did not inherit full humanity from either parent, then the idea of incarnation is not fulfilled. Similarly, the claim to Christhood on the basis of the Old Testament must fail, since Jesus is not of the seed of David – if we accept the Virgin Birth. The Christian claims are unconvincing, because the significance of the Christ-idea is the divine incarnation in human form.

By making him a god, the *grava superstitio* deprived us of Jesus the man.

7
Power And Authority

Hebrew Scripture

Ancient Hebrew Scripture shows that many of its authors admired power and authority. The Old Testament glorifies God as Lord and King, but there are also many earthly kings who are praised and endowed with near-divine qualities. At the centre of this cult is King David, 'a man according to God's heart', who was a merciless robber and killer (*1 Sam.* 20:2, 27/9 and *2 Sam.* 8:2), an adulterer (*2 Sam.* 11:2 to 5), a traitor (*2 Sam.* 11:14/5), and a hater unto death (*1 Kings.* 2:6 to 9).

Even the earliest writers, the authors of the Pentateuch, attempted to impress upon their readers the need for obedience to authority. 'Thou shalt not revile thy Judges, nor curse the rulers of thy people' (*Exod.* 22:28). In the history of the house of Israel there were periods of great power, during which the rulers 'showed a mighty hand and a great terror' (*Deut.* 34:12). Here the Bible speaks of Moses, but the words could equally apply to a number of kings, the greatest of whom was said to be David. The Psalms are full of eulogies heaped upon him, although they have been regarded until recently his own hymns to the Almighty. In fact, these remarkable poems were written by the scribes at his court. One of them foreshadows the Temptation Story: 'Ask of me and I shall give thee the heathens [correct translation: 'the nations'] for thine inheritance, and the uttermost parts of the earth for thy possession' (*Psalm* 2:8).

There were, however, long periods of subjection: to Egypt, Assyria, Babylon, Persia, Macedonia and, finally, Rome. These periods were regarded by pious Jews as a punishment imposed upon them by their only *real* ruler, their Almighty God. As a consequence, they often had to obey two sets of laws: that of the foreign ruler as well as the Law of their own God. The latter always took precedence over the former and thus many injunctions were obeyed which conflicted with the foreigners' demands. The most important of these was the total prohibition of graven images (*Exod.* 20:4, *Lev.* 26:1 and *Deut.* 4:16), which frequently brought them into conflict with their conquerors. Even the introduction of Roman coinage into Palestine, with the Emperor's head and superscription 'High Pontiff and son of the Divine Augustus' was a transgression against the Law of God. According to Graves and Podro, 'Jews who paid tribute in this coinage were technically worshipping the God Augustus' (*NGR*, p.586), an important point to which I shall revert later.

Another law often ignored by authority was Moses' prohibition of any census (*Exod.* 30:12) which was ordered by the rulers on several occasions. When a native sovereign committed this breach of the Law, retribution was immediate, as in the case of King David whom God punished by taking the lives of seventy thousand of David's subjects (*1 Chr.* 21:1, 11 to 15 and *2 Sam.* 24:1 to 15). But when the Roman Procurator of Syria, Quirinus, intending to impose a poll-tax ordered the counting of the population; the Jewish leaders agreed to this, permitting even the inclusion of the Levites whom God had quite especially exempted (*Num.* 1:49).

On the whole it seems that the Jewish rulers showed a readiness to abide by the wishes of foreign conquerors. In Jeremiah God says, 'And now I have given all these lands into the hands of Nebuchadnezzer, the king of Babylon, my servant: and the beasts of the field have I given him also to serve him. And all nations shall serve him, and his son, and his son's son, until the very time of his land come: and then many nations and great kings shall serve themselves of him. And it shall come to pass that the nation and kingdom which will not serve the same Nebuchadnezzer the king of Babylon, and that will not put their neck under the yoke of the king of Babylon, that nation will I punish saith the Lord, with the sword, and with famine, and with pestilence, until I have consumed them by his hand. Therefore hearken ye not to your prophets, nor to your diviners, nor to your dreamers, nor to your enchanters, nor to your sorcerers which speak unto you saying, Ye shall not serve the king of Babylon' (*Jer.* 27:6/9). The whole 28th chapter of Jeremiah is a tirade against those who advocate resistance to Babylon. Throughout its length it preaches unconditional surrender.

In the same book we read: 'Thus saith the Lord of hosts, the God of Israel: Behold, I will send and take Nebuchadnezzer the king of Babylon my servant, and will set his throne upon these stones that I have hid . . . And when he cometh, he shall smite the land of Egypt, and deliver such as are for death to death; and such as are for captivity to captivity; and such as are for the sword to the sword. And I will kindle the fire in the houses of the gods of the Egyptians; and he shall burn them, and carry them away captive . . . He shall break also the images of Bethshemesh, that is in the land of Egypt; and the houses of the gods of the Egyptians shall he burn with fire . . . ' (*Jer.* 43:10/13). The apocryphal Book of Baruch calls upon the faithful to pray 'for the life of Nebuchadnezzer, and for the life of Balthasar, his son, that their days may be upon earth as the days of heaven' (*Baruch* 1:11). Speaking to Nebuchadnezzer, the prophet Daniel exclaims 'It is thou, O king, that art grown and become strong: for thy greatness is grown, and reacheth unto heaven, and thy dominion to the end of the earth . . . ' (*Dan.* 4:22), and 'Thou, O king, art a king of kings: for the God of heaven hath given thee a kingdom, power and strength, and glory' (*Dan.* 2:37).

The fortunes of war changed. When victorious, the Persian kings received the same extravagant praise from the scribes of the subject Jewish people. Ezra reports: 'Thus saith Cyrus king of Persia. The Lord God of Heaven hath given me all the kingdoms of the earth; and he hath charged me to build him an house at Jerusalem which is in Judah' (*Ezra* 1:2). Nine years after the death of Cyrus, Darius became king and called upon the Jews 'to pray for the life of the king, and of his sons' (*Ezra* 6:10). His grandson Artaxerxes, expressed the view of the majority of his Jewish subjects (otherwise why would his words be recorded?) when he said: 'Whatsoever is commanded by the God in Heaven, let it be diligently done for the house of the God of heaven: for why should there by wrath against the realm of the king and his sons?' (*Ezra* 7:23).

It is understandable that the Jewish leaders sought the means of peaceful co-existence with their mighty conquerors. After all, God himself had declared: 'By me kings reign, and princes decree justice. By me princes rule and nobles, even all the judges of the earth' (*Prov.* 8:5/6). And did not the great lawgiver admonish his people: 'Thou shalt not . . . curse the rulers of thy people'. The same sentiment is echoed in Ecclesiastes, although with a slightly ironical undertone: 'Curse not the king, no not in thy thought: and curse not the rich in thy bedchamber: for a bird of the air shall carry the voice, and that which hath wings shall tell the matter' (*Eccles.* 10:20).

In the apocryphal Books of Maccabees we read of 'burnt sacrifice that was offered for the king' (*1 Macc.* 7:33), and of God's permission to mint coins: 'I give thee leave also to coin money for thy country with thine own stamps' (*1 Macc.* 15:6) which promptly enabled Judas Maccabeus to produce his own coinage.

Compromise was difficult with the Roman rulers when their ordinance clashed with the Mosaic Law. We have seen how the question of the census troubled the minds of many law-abiding Jews, and the most vexing problem was the paying of tax in coinage that bore the image of the Roman Emperor. However, the desire to accommodate the Romans was strong. The legitimacy and authority of Roman rule was generally acknowledged, while subversion of it was discouraged and treated with emphatic disapproval. There is every reason to believe that in the days of the Roman Procurators (Coponius A.D. 6 to 9; Marcus Ambibulus 9 to 12; Annius Rufus 12 to 15, Valerius Gratus 15 to 26 and Pontius Pilate 26 to 36) the high priests bought their office by bribing the procurators (*Yoma* 8b).

There were, of course, voices which cried out against the corruption and cowardice which beset the rulers of the Jewish lands. Speaking of these, Ezekiel said: 'her princes . . . are like wolves ravening the prey, to shed blood and to destroy souls, to get dishonest gain' (*Ezek.* 22:27), and in Zephaniah we read: 'Her princes within her are roaring lions, her Judges are evening wolves; they gnaw the bones till morning. Her prophets are light and treacherous' (*Zeph.* 3:3/4).

This was the background against which must be seen Jesus' spirited opposition to Mammon. Clashes between the authorities and the Jewish people were frequent, but they usually ended with the victory of the mighty. The events connected with Jesus and his followers can only be understood if we realise that the rulers (Roman *and* Jewish) wished to forestall any possible action against their power, and acted with their usual disregard for life and law.

The Temptation story

The story of the temptation of the saint, the Teacher, the Son of God, by the Evil Spirit, can be found in almost every religious scripture, in every 'Bible' of the world. One of the most beautiful temptation stories is told about the Buddha who was assailed by Mara, 'the enemy of liberation'. But Gautama was not to be shaken. 'He who, when he beholds the world drowned in the great flood of existence and unable to reach the further shore, tries to bring them safely across – would any right-minded soul offer him wrong? The tree of knowledge whose roots go deep in firmness, and whose fibres are patience, whose flowers are moral actions, and whose branches are memory and thought . . . surely when it is growing it should not be cut down' (The Life of Buddha, *The Bible of the World,* pp. 208/9). Similarly, Zarathustra is tempted by the deadly Angra Mainyu, the king of demons: 'Renounce the good religion of the worshippers of Mazda, and though shalt gain such a boon as Vadhaghna gained, the ruler of the nations'. Three times addressed by the demon, thrice Zarathustra fights off the assault with words of godly wisdom. These passages of the *Zendavesta* (ibid., pp.586/7) precede the New Testament by centuries.

In the New Testament we find two dignified and beautiful versions of this eternal theme. The passage concerning the promise of authority is quite explicit: 'The devil taketh him up into an exceeding high mountain and showeth him all the kingdoms of the world and the glory of them; And saith unto him, All these things will I give thee, if thou wilt fall down and worship me. Then saith Jesus unto him, Get thee hence, Satan: for it is written, Thou shalt worship the Lord thy God, and him only shalt thou serve' (*Matthew* 4:8/10). The same story is told in Luke: 'And the devil, taking him up into a high mountain, showed unto him all the kingdoms of the world in a moment of time. And the devil said unto him, All this power will I give thee, and the glory of them: for that is delivered unto me; and whom ever I will give it. If thou therefore wilt worship me, all shall be thine. And Jesus answered and said unto him, Get thee behind me Satan: for it is written, Thou shalt worship the Lord thy God and him only shalt thou serve' (*Luke* 4:5/8).

The answer given by Jesus is a paraphrase of an Old Testament passage: 'Thou shalt fear the Lord thy God, and serve him' (*Deut.* 6:13 and 10:20), and this is probably how he, matured still further in years and experience, conceives his own role as king and servant of Israel.

Among the many interpretations of this momentous event, the attempt to deflect Jesus from his chosen path, the most arresting one was advanced by Dostojevski in his great novel, *The Brothers Karamazov*. In a story entitled 'The Grand Inquisitor' he shows how the desire of the compassionate to give man bread rather than responsibility, security rather than choice, something to worship rather than independence, was the first temptation. The second was to replace truth by fantasy, reason by mystery. The third and greatest temptation, however, was the offer of Caesar's crown, the offer to bear the burden of responsibility himself and thus save man from the dire consequences of individual freedom. Jesus rejects all three and by so doing condemns man to become a forlorn and insecure creature. Or we can reverse the judgment and say: he makes it impossible for man to abandon his humanity and the obligations arising from his humanity. 'We have corrected thy work' exclaims jubilantly, yet with bitterness the Grand Inquisitor, 'and have founded it upon miracle, mystery and authority. And men rejoiced that they were again led like sheep, and that the terrible gift [freedom] that had brought them such suffering was, at last, lifted from their hearts' (Everyman edition, pp.254/269). The shattering story of the encounter between Jesus and the Grand Inquisitor is one of the most profound literary confrontations between the Teacher and Christianity.

Christian apologists have laboured hard to trivialise the significance of this gospel story. With its usual sophistry the *QB* points out that Christ, the Divine Person, could not be subject to temptation, but as True Man he could have been, and was, tempted. The Epistle to the Hebrew is quoted: 'For in that He Himself hath suffered, and been tempted, he is able to help those who are tempted' (*Hebrews* 2:18), and 'We have . . . one who in every respect has been tempted as we are, without sinning' (*Hebrews* 4:15). The *QB* insists that, as no one was present, and yet the accounts of Matthew and Luke agree, 'a fair-minded reader cannot deny the truth of the narrative which must have come from our Lord Himself' (p.59). Fairminded or not, the *QB* does not refrain from quoting the more realistic account of Bishop Camus of La Rochelle: 'It would be simpler, perhaps, to concede that the Gospel Story relates to us, in metaphors, the threefold interior combat which Jesus sustained against Satan, and from which he came forth completely victorious . . . All these details plainly cause this story to hover between the material and external reality which is rather difficult to admit, and the psychological internal reality which explains the important moral message of Jesus. It was in imagination that Satan placed Christ on the pinnacle of the Temple and on the mountain, and it was before His mind only that He called up the kingdoms of the earth. No more was needed to try Jesus. Physical reality would add nothing to the temptation' (p.60). I am not sure how the fairminded reader feels about this interpretation – being not so fairminded myself, I tend to agree with his Grace.

The approach of Protestant theologians does not differ greatly. Both attitudes may be found among their representatives. 'The narrative which can only have come from our Lord's own lips, describes an actual historical fact' (Dummelow, *OVBC*, p.632). One despairs of the words 'historical' and 'fact'. But even so, the author admits that 'our Lord records his experience in symbolical language' (ibid.). The argument continues by stating that the devil is justified by Scripture in saying that the wealth and power he offers are his to give away. 'The devil often tempts men most severely by making them rich and great.' Yet this privilege is dependent on the permission and overruling providence of God. And this flight of fancy is topped by the assertion that 'since the Ascension of our Blessed Lord, the devil's power over the kingdoms of the earth, at least in Christian lands [sic] has been greatly reduced' (p.633).

Walsham How subscribes to the view that the threefold temptation corresponds to the threefold description of sin given by St. John: 'The lust of the flesh, and the lust of the eyes, and the pride of life, is not of the Father, but is of the world' (*1 John* 2:16). William Barclay regards Jesus' rejection of power as an injunction to Christians to reject compromise which would enable them to adjust themselves to the world by becoming like the world' (*The Gospel of St. Matthew*, p.63). Admittedly, power requires its holder to compromise continually, yet this interpretation renders the episode trivial. The act of Jesus is clearly a repudiation of dominion offered to him by the spirit who can claim that power was 'delivered to him'.

It is interesting to note that the Jewish scholar, Dr Klausner, has a completely different story to tell. He believes the power temptation signifies Jesus' understanding that even if he is the Anointed One of God, he must not try to overcome the Gentiles by force, and rule over Israel and the nations as a wordly king. The second temptation meant that Jesus originally saw himself as a supreme teacher of the Law and an advocate of its renewal. However, he realised the overbearing pride inherent in this attitude, and accepted the humbler role of the bearer of good news, a servant of God. Finally, he was tempted to bring the world material welfare, the Bread of the millennium, to fulfilment of the promised 'world without want'. This temptation, too, he conquered saying that 'man shall not live by bread alone' (*Matthew* 4:4, *Luke* 4:4 – a quotation from *Deut*. 8:3).

The Christian attempts to divert attention from the condemnation of power and dominion implicit in these verses can only strengthen our resolve to understand the teaching contained in the Temptation Story. Jesus, having spent a long time (40 days, years etc, mean in scriptural language a long period) in meditation and prayer, confronts the final decision he must make. Should he, or should he not, concern himself mainly with the alleviation of physical suffering of hunger, misery and want? His answer is: Man shall not live by bread alone. Should he, or should he not, use power as the lever of his ideas, as a means to realise the aim of his mission? He decided that one cannot serve God *and* Mammon – he will serve God. Should he, or should he not, risk his life for the success of his endeavour? To do so would mean tempting God, is the reply of Jesus.

We can only understand the greatness of this story and its hero, if we assume the humanity of the Teacher. God cannot be tempted with things he can do or possess or know anyhow in his omnipotence and omniscience. Only man can be subject to temptation. If the man in question knew of his identity with God it would not be an impressive gesture to reject a ludicrous offer. And if he *did not know* of that identity what are we to make of the Christian's claim that Jesus revealed his identity with the Father? One of the two arguments must go by default!

Whoever will be chief let him be servant

We know nothing of Jesus' 'formative years', and of his relation to power and violence during that period. The symbolic tale of the temptation may give us a clue to his early life. Some of his followers may have prompted him to strive for national leadership and make himself Lord over kings through victory over Rome, as promised by the prophets. By the time he started on his ministry, Jesus had probably arrived at the wisdom of Hillel and 'hated lordship', except the lordship of God. When he walked through Judaea teaching the kingdom of God, he was possibly no young man. He may even have been near his fiftieth birthday: 'Then said the Jews unto him, Thou art not yet fifty years old, and hast thou seen Abraham?' (*John* 8:57). We do know however that he was unequivocal on the subject of power. 'Ye know,' he said, 'that the princes of the Gentiles exercise dominion over them, and they that are great exercise authority upon them. But it shall not be so among you: but whosoever will be great among you, shall be your minister: and whosoever will be chief among you, let him be your servant. Even as the son of Man came not to be ministered unto, but to minister' (*Matthew* 20:25 to 28, compare *Mark* 10:42 and *Luke* 22:25/6). We see him performing the symbolic act of washing the feet of his disciples, an act of humility and service (*John* 13:4ff.).

What do Christian commentators make of these words? Dummelow simply ignores the three passages. William Barclay has not much to say on the matter, and what he does say is trite: 'Out in the world, says Jesus, it is true that the great man is the man who controls others; the man who is the master, to whose words of command others must leap; the man who with the wave of his hand can command service, and have his slightest need supplied. Out in the world there was the Roman governor with his retinue; the Eastern potentate with his slaves; the man of affairs with his staff of attendant slaves. The world counts them great. But in the Christian assessment service alone is the badge of greatness' (op. cit., p.256).

Fenton merely remarks that 'among the Gentiles greatness is demonstrated by power and authority. In the Church it will not be so:

those who hope for a place of authority in the kingdom must be servants of the community' (op. cit., p.325). Professor Nineham regards the Marcan passage as a reference to Jesus' approaching passion (*St. Mark*, p.280). In *PC* we find little on the subject, and its Roman Catholic counterpart, *CC*, contains the strange remark: 'It is a commonplace of political kingdoms that rulers are heavy-handed and their ministers officious. There *will* be rank in our Lord's kingdom [sic], but it must not be used for selfish ends. Let all know who would seek that rank that it is the rank of servant, even of slave' (*CC* p.887). The interpretation of Mark's words is similar: 'The apostles will have authority in the Church, but in the exercise of that authority they are not to imitate rulers and high officials who rule tyrannically and arbitrarily in their own interest. Rather they should make the service of those entrusted to them the ideal of their office (ibid. 922). The Lukan passage is not considered in detail.

I should like to contrast these passages with an interpretation which endows the saying with the significance it no doubt possesses: the latest entrant, the weakest novice, the least of the assembly, should be its ruler. One of the services he should perform is the onerous task of 'governing his fellows', of taking practical decisions on their behalf so that their minds may remain devoted to more important issues. He should 'rule' the community and exercise this odious task until a new entrant is admitted, and the position of the 'least' filled by another. This daring vision which presents power as a hateful burden, is the only alternative to its present destructive role. It is the only way to surmount power before power destroys us.

The tribute money

One of the most important episodes regarding the Teacher's attitude to power is the famous incident when his adversaries attempted to induce him into making a compromising statement which would condemn him in the eyes of the Roman authorities, or, alternatively, lessen the esteem in which he was held by his Jewish followers. Let me tell the story in the words of the evangelist: 'Then went the Pharisees, and took counsel how they might entangle him in his talk. And they sent out to him their disciples with the Herodians, saying, Master, we know that thou art true, and teachest the way of God in truth: for thou regardest not the person of man . Tell us therefore, What thinkest thou? Is it lawful to give tribute unto Caesar or not? But Jesus perceived their wickedness and said: "Why tempt ye me, ye hypocrites, shew me the tribute money." And they brought unto him a penny. And he saith unto them. "Whose is this image and superscription?" They say unto him, "Caesar's". Then saith he unto them, "Render therefore unto Caesar the things which are Caesar's, and unto God the things that are God's". When they heard these words, they marvelled and left him and went their way' (*Matthew* 22:15/22, also *Mark* 12:13/17 and *Luke* 20:20/26).

From this narrative it emerges clearly that Jesus was opposed to the things the coin represented, namely, power and wealth; that he spoke in a way his enemies believed would incriminate him if the Herodians [the quislings] heard it; that Jesus saw through their scheme and made abundantly clear his realisation of the trap; that with sublime skill he gave a truthful answer yet one that could not be used against him; and that his adversaries seeing that he had evaded the trap left him with grudging admiration. As to the answer itself: in the context of his whole teaching the meaning is plain. Leave money and power to the rich and mighty (in whose image the coin was minted) and give yourselves and that which is within you to God (in whose image you were created). He never suggested that there are two orders of things in which man ought to divide his loyalties: the demands of the worldly authorities in which we should obey *them*, and the other order, that of God, in which we should obey *him*. This completely unjustifiable creed which implies a denial of God's claim on man's moral attitude was advanced much later, for reasons of expediency, by power organisations 'representing' Jesus. They could summon a good authority, that of Paul, for their anti-Jesus attitude. Unfortunately, all concordates with the devil, from Constantine to Adolf Hitler, have been justified on such grounds. His adversaries were outwitted by Jesus, but they prevailed in the end.

What is God's and what is Caesar's? The Old Testament is quite unequivocal. Addressing God, David says: ' . . . all that is in heaven and in the earth is thine . . . all things come of thee, and of thine own have we given thee . . . ' (*1 Chr.* 29:11/14). And in the Talmud, similarly, we read: 'Give unto God of his own: for thou and all thou ownest belong to him' (*Abo.* 3:7).

The argument as to what Jesus *meant* turns largely around words used in the Gospel. All three evangelists use the word διδόναι (Vulgate: *dare*) to give, when Jesus is asked about the lawfulness to pay (give) tribute to Caesar. However, in his answer ἀποδίδοναι (Vulgate: *reddere*) to give back, render, restore, deliver up, appears. It is of course impossible to assess what the author(s) of Q (the source of Matthew and Luke) and Mark meant exactly when they used these words, or indeed whether the use of the terms is not due to later interference, as Robert Graves suggests.

The French translation contrasts *payer* and *rendre*, Luther's German uses *geben* in both instances, in Italian the contrasting words are *pagare* and *rendere*. It is fascinating to observe that in the Spanish translation based on the Vulgate, the words corresponding to the French and Italian translations, *pagar* and *dar* are used, while the Protestant version unscrupulously reverses the terms *dar* and *pagar*, thus making it appear as if Jesus had commanded the paying of tax. The *NEB*, another Protestant product, uses the word *pay* in both instances. These facts are important when we consider the official Christian arguments with regard to this saying.

Apart from the linguistic aspects it may be important to know some of the historical implications of the story. Probably the family of Jesus, his teachers, and indeed most people around him who wished for 'peaceful coexistence' with the all-powerful conqueror, willingly paid the tribute. The Alexandrian Philo, a remarkable Jewish philosopher-mystic, wrote with fine irony that the Emperor is like a shepherd, and the tax-paying cities like sheep – year after year they laid down patiently to be relieved of their thick coat of wool (*Op. Mundi*, 28:85f.). The Emperor Tiberius, a man not without a sense of humour, remarked: 'It is the part of a good shepherd to shear, not flay his sheep' (Suetonius, *Tiberius*, 32:2).

However, there were also many sympathisers of Judas, the Galilean, another would-be Messiah, who 'prevailed with his countrymen to revolt; and said they were cowards if they would endure to pay a tax to the Romans: and would after God, submit to mortal men as their lords' (Josephus, *Wars* 2:8:1). Many leading Jews may have seen in Jesus the Galilean a similar rebel with similar aims. This explains why his adversaries, probably Sadducee officials and members of the priestly cast, taunted him to give a clear answer to the problem which presented both political and religious difficulties.

The religious difficulties arose from the fact that the 'new denarius' bore the image of the Emperor and the inscription TI CAESAR DIVI AVG F AVGVSTVS, an abbreviation of 'Tiberius Caesar, the venerable Son of the Divine Augustus'. Since the Jews could not tolerate 'graven images' of any kind, and found the words even more insulting, they were deeply offended by the ritual character of the coin. The Emperor himself seems to have regarded the use of his image and legend as a kind of religious homage, since it is reported that 'it became a capital offence for a man . . . to have his own head stamped upon a coin . . .' (Suetonius, *Tiberius*, 58).

Refusal to pay tribute or criticism of the imperial image would have meant an act of rebellion. Combined with his recent triumphal entry into Jerusalem, Jesus' subversion would have brought upon him the most severe retribution from the authorities. Eventually, as we know, he did not escape the fate of a rebel, but his answer in our story shows that he was aware of the trap and refused to walk into it.

It is instructive to examine the Christian commentators' reaction to this saying. The earliest response can be observed in the Epistles of Paul, Peter and Jude who blissfully reversed the meaning, and made it the foundation of their servile approach to the State. In the early Church we find Origen suggesting that according to the teaching of Jesus the paying of tribute to Caesar means merely returning to Caesar what is lawfully his. An embarrassed Church gratefully grasped for this explanation which remained henceforth its official interpretation. Justin Martyr claimed that God alone can demand our worship, but Caesar can demand our service. And he asserted: '. . . everywhere we, more readily than most men, endeavour to pay to those appointed by you the taxes, both ordinary and extraordinary . . .' (*Apo.* 11 and 17). Hilary, bishop of Pictavium in A.D. 350, also said with emphasis: 'Quibus sit: Caesari reddibenda esse, quae Caesari sunt, Deo autem reddenda esse, quae Dei sunt.' In all later arguments much is made of the term $\grave{\alpha}\pi o\delta \acute{\iota}\delta o\nu\alpha\iota$ in the sense of paying back, restoring.

The *CC* adds little to the usual arguments. Incorrectly, it states that the Pharisees arrived at a temporary truth with the Herodians 'in their interim policy of subservience to Rome.' It argues that the coin which demonstrably came from Caesar should be returned to him, which is true as far as it goes. But the author adds: 'These civil transactions are on one plane, God's rights on the other. There is no inevitable clash, provided . . . the civil demands did not encroach upon the duties of man to God.' And the argument finishes with a reference to 'the due delimitation of spheres' (p.891). In another part the unjustified accusation against the Pharisees is repeated: 'It was known to all that neither Pharisees nor Herodians offered opposition to Roman domination . . . the former having even asked for incorporation into the Empire on the death of Herod the Great' (Josephus, *Ant.* 17:11:2). This is a double mistake, since, firstly, the Jewish emissaries mentioned in *Ant.* 17 are not stated to have been Pharisees and, secondly, they did not ask for 'incorporation' but merely that they should be subject to the Governor of Syria [the *Roman* governor] rather than to a puppet ruler of Judaea.

The Protestant counterpart of this huge tome, *PC*, states quite correctly that Jesus' statement coincided with the view of the Pharisees, who, while resenting the Romans, considered insurrection a 'lack of faith in God's power to set Israel free . . . ' (p. 79). Concerning the Marcan passage, we read another valid point: 'the coin had to be fetched: neither Jesus nor his opponents possessed any silver money, or refused to use the pagan coinage' (p. 812). This would, after all, show their obedience to the Law (*Exod.* 20:4) which forbids any form of graven image. A little later, however, we read the sorry conclusion reached by the Church in the wake of the Teacher's argument: 'The final answer is not an evasion, nor is it a complete solution of the problems of Church and State, but it does lay down a fundamental principle: Jesus held that the claims of God are all-embracing, but he does recognise that obligations due to the State are within a divine order. Loyalty to the Emperor need not be inconsistent with loyalty to God . . .'

O sancta simplicitas! It is most unlikely that the problem 'Church versus State' ever occurred to Jesus. Israel was a theocracy, and no temporary human ruler was acknowledged unless anointed by a prophet of God. Israel could not be conceived of as a society in which there was a polarity between 'Church' and 'State'. Caesar was the 'State' in the external sense only, an intruder into the life of the Jewish people, a barrier between God and men. This barrier would only come down if the pillar sustaining it, man's love for Mammon, crumbled. To speak of Jesus' loyalty to the Emperor is not merely ludicrous, but in the context of the alleged faith in him, it is downright blasphemy.

Misrepresentation becomes more offensive where the Lucan passage is discussed. 'Jesus asserts that Caesar has a right to obedience within the scope of man's all-embracing obligation to God' (p. 839). Similar conclusions are reached by other Protestant commentators. Dummelow calls the saying 'a pregnant utterance . . . defining the relation between Church and State for all time . . . Christ showed (1) His sympathy with imperialism [sic] as . . . opposed to national and racial particularism, intending Himself to found a universal Church. He openly showed His sympathy with the great and benevolent empire which broke down the barriers of national hatred and prejudice . . . (2) that submission and loyalty to civil power is a duty binding on the conscience. Christ says not only *give* but *render*, signifying that submission is due; (3) that nevertheless there are limits to the obedience due to the civil power. When Caesar asks for worship as actually happened at this time, he is to be resisted . . . (4) that Church and State are not one thing, but two, each with its own particular powers given by God . . . ' (Dummelow, *OVBC*, p. 697).

The episode as reported by Matthew is discussed at great length in

Barclay's *The Gospel of St. Matthew*. To quote some passages: 'Here Christ lays down a very great and important principle. Every Christian has a dual citizenship. He is a citizen of the country . . . in which he happens to live. To that country he owes many things. He owes the safety against lawless men which only settled government can give, he owes all public services to the State . . . In a welfare State the citizen owes still more to the State . . . education, medical services, provision for unemployment and old age [I have always thought that we pay heavily for these bounties – in taxes and contributions]. This places him under an obligatory debt. Because the Christian is a man of honour, he must be a responsible citizen; and failure in good citizenship is also a failure in Christian duty. Untold troubles can descend upon a country or an industry when Christians refuse to take part in the administration of the country, and leave that administration to selfish, self- seeking, partisan and unchristian men. The Christian has a duty to Caesar in return for the privileges which the rule of Caesar brings to him . . . Where the boundaries between the two duties lie, Jesus does not say. That is for man's own consciousness to test. But a real Christian – and this is a permanent truth which Jesus here lays down – is at one and the same time a good citizen of his country, and a good citizen of the kingdom of Heaven. He will fail in his duty neither to God nor to man. He will, as Peter said, 'fear God and honour the King' (*1 Peter* 2:17 pp.II, 302/3).

Even Ethelbert Stauffer comes to the sorry conclusion: 'It [the saying] is a political Yes to the question of the imperial power of a foreign conquering nation ruled by a polytheistic Emperor. The imperial tax paid by the Jews is the due contribution of God's people towards the maintenance of the imperial realm, not only in the financial but also in the historical sense' (*Die Botschaft Jesu,* p.107). And he quotes Lagrange who wrote: 'Jésus a donné plus qu'une permission, il a tracé la règle á suivre.'

It is refreshing to encounter a Christian commentator who avoids the pitfalls into which so many of his co-religionists have fallen. D.E. Nineham, in his *Gospel of St. Mark* writes: ' . . . But does not civil obedience, attested by the payment of tax, conflict with the obedience due to God? To understand Jesus' words here, we must keep in mind his conviction that the future of the world, and of the Roman Empire within it, would be short; very soon the kingdom of Heaven would arrive and the rule of Rome would disappear, not through man's agency but through God'. Essentially, therefore, Jesus is not enunciating any principle bearing on the problem of 'Church and State', he is saying simply that men's duty to Caesar does not contradict their duty to God; it is insignificant in comparison with it . . . Men should perform the first without attaching to it greater importance than it really possesses, but they should concentrate above all to their relationship to God whose coming is now so imminent . . . Subsequently, when the immediate pressure of eschatology was removed, the Church rightly sought a more positive doctrine in the relation between Church and State, and far more has been read into the saying than it originally meant, no doubt . . . because it was interpreted along the lines of St. Paul's teaching in e.g. *Rom.* 13:1ff. that the saying was preserved and treasured in the Rome of St. Mark's day, (pp.315/6). A sane approach even if I cannot agree with some of his conclusions.

Across the distance of two thousand years we learn of a great man who dared to say, Let the mighty keep that what symbolises their might – the symbol which is *external* to them; and let him who bears the vision of perfection in his mind, give himself to that vision – which is *within* him. It is one of the tragic ironies of human history that this profound saying has been turned into its reverse by the midgets who crowd around the memory of that supreme man.

Do not speak evil of thy rulers

Hardly had Jesus been destroyed by those in power than his followers were exhorted to give unconditional obedience to their worldly rulers and to all authority. Jesus' clear injunction to give Caesar what is Caesar's and to God what is God's appears to have been forgotten by the early Church for reasons of well-considered expediency. The result was shameless obsequiousness and servility. Paul tells us, 'Slaves, be obedient to them that are your masters, according to the flesh, . . . with good will doing service' (*Eph.* 6:5 to 8); and 'Slaves, obey in all things your masters according to the flesh, not with eyeservice as menpleasers, but in singleness of heart, fearing God . . . for ye serve the Lord Jesus Christ' (*Col.* 3:22 to 24). With slight sarcasm prompted by the occasion, he nevertheless acknowledges the dictum of the Old Testament: 'Thou shalt not speak evil of the ruler of thy people' (*Acts* 23:5). He writes to Timothy: 'Exhort therefore that first of all supplications, prayers, intercessions, and giving of thanks be made for all men: for kings, and for all that are in authority' (*1 Tim.* 2:1/2); and to Titus, 'Exhort slaves to be obedient unto their own masters, and to please them well in all things, not answering back, not purloining, but showing all good fidelity' (*Titus* 3:1), and, 'Put them in mind to be subject to principalities and powers, to obey magistrates, to be ready to every good work' (*Titus* 3:1).

Peter is not outdone by Paul: 'Submit yourselves,' he writes, 'to every ordinance of man for the Lord's sake: whether it be the king as supreme: or unto governors as unto them that are sent by him for the punishment of evil-doers,' (*I Peter* 2:13/17), and 'The Lord knoweth how to reserve the unjust unto the day of judgment to be punished . . . but chiefly them that walk after the flesh in the lust of uncleanness, and despise government. Presumptuous are they, self-willed, they are not afraid to speak evil of dignities' (*2 Peter* 2:9/10). And Jude also threatens with 'the vengeance of eternal fire . . . these filthy dreamers who defile the flesh, despise dominion, and speak evil of dignities' (*Jude* 7/8). [It is known that several letters of Paul, as well as those of Peter and Jude, are of doubtful authenticity.]

However, it *is* Paul [the authentic Paul] who reaches the lowest level of servility. His is the apotheosis of conformity, a lesson to all who still believe that early Christianity was a rebellious creed. In *Romans* he writes: 'Let every soul be subject to the higher powers. For there is no power but of God: the powers that be are ordained of God. Whosoever therefore resisteth the power, resisteth the ordinance of God, and they that resist receive to themselves damnation. For rulers are not a terror to good works, but to the evil. Wilt thou then not be afraid of power? do that which is good and thou shalt have praise of the same. For he is the minister of God to thee for good. But if thou do that which is evil, be afraid for he beareth not the sword in vain: for he is the minister of God, a revenger to execute wrath upon him that doeth evil. Wherefore ye must need be subject not only for wrath, but also for conscience sake. For this cause pay ye tribute also: for they are God's ministers, attending continually upon this very thing. Render therefore to all their due: tribute to whom tribute is due: custom to whom custom; fear to whom fear; honour to whom honour' (*Rom.* 13:1 to 7).

Jesus himself is not to blame: nowhere do his words display this submission, nowhere does he impress upon his listeners the political duties of the citizen, nowhere does he glorify obedience to any earthly master, and nowhere does he recommend his followers to pray for those in authority. Indeed, he believes that their rulers receive their authority from superhuman sources: 'Satan, tempting him, says: All this power will I give thee: for that is delivered unto me: and to whomsoever I will give it' (*Luke* 4:6). On several occasions Jesus refers to Satan as 'the prince of this world' (*John* 12:31, 14:30, 16:11). He explicitly condemns the Gentile practice of worldly kingship and warns his followers to avoid its pitfalls (*Matthew* 20:25/8), (*Mark* 10:42/4) (*Luke* 22:25/6). Speaking of his way as the only one for the sheep to follow, he warns that 'All that ever came before me, are thieves and robbers' (*John* 10:8). And his accusers, when they take him before Pilate, exclaim: 'We found this fellow perverting the nation, and forbidding to give tribute to Caesar, saying that he himself is Christ, the king. [Probably, the anointed king] . . . He stirreth up the people, teaching throughout all Jewry, beginning from Galilee to this place (*Luke* 23:2/5).

In Martin Luther, the 'great reformer', the Pauline doctrine of subservience to the State found a powerful new advocate. Discussing the fourth commandment in his *Large Catechism* he lays down his teaching concerning authority and submission: 'God speaks to you and demands obedience. If you obey him, you are his dear child, if you despise this commandment, then take shame, misery and grief for your reward. The same may be said of obedience to the civil government which . . . is to be classed with the estate of fatherhood, the most comprehensive of all relations. In this case a man is father not of a single family, but of as many people as he has inhabitants, citizens or subjects. Through civil rulers, God gives us food, house and home, protection and security. Therefore, since they bear his name and title with all honour as their chief glory, it is our duty to honour and magnify them as the most precious treasure and jewel on earth. He who is obedient, willing, ready to serve, and cheerfully gives honour where it is due, knows that he pleases God and receives joy and happiness for his reward. On the other hand, if he will not do so in love, but despises and rebelliously resists authority, let him know that he shall have no favour or blessing from God . . . Why do you think is the world now so full of unfaithfulness, shame, misery and murder? It is because everyone wishes to be his own master, be free from authority, care nothing for anyone, and do whatever he pleases . . . ' (pp.29/30). To make sure that we understand him, Luther emphasises, 'We have three kinds of fathers, presented in this commandment: fathers by blood, fathers of the household, and fathers of the nation' (p.31). And he calls obliquely for a greater measure of repression: 'Because this commandment is disregarded, God terribly punishes the world: hence there is no longer any civil order, peace or respect for authority. We all complain about this state of things, but we do not see that it is our own fault. Because of the way we train them, we have unruly and disobedient subjects!' (p.33)

Even more revealing are the records of *Luther's Table-Talk*: 'Christ did not come to us to disband the State but to start a new spiritual kingdom. Just as he commanded, 'Eat such things as are set before you' (*Luke* 10:8), so one must abide by the laws of the State in which one lives' (*Luther's Table-Talk* V:5196). His social ideas are simple: 'Human society is, in the words of Aristotle, not an end, but a means to an end. Aristotle says: 'Society is not composed of physician and physician, farmer and farmer. There are three ways of life: people must work, fight and govern. The State combines these three classes . . . '(ibid., IV 3993). For Luther government is a miraculous function of God-inspired men: 'The world is but the world, people do not love justice nor even tolerate it. Yet in a miraculous fashion the world is ruled by a few heroic men, in the same way as hundreds of sheep can be herded by a boy of seven. In this way the world is governed – supernaturally' (ibid., IV 4348).

'Luther's political ethic,' writes Polanyi, 'was particularly flagrant in its moral confusion upon this point, for he enjoined the purest pacifism upon the citizen in his relation to the State, while he absolved the rulers of every moral scruple in their use of violence. He declared, "I will always side *with* him, however unjust, who suffers rebellion, and *against* him who rebels, however justly." Calvin was hardly less confused. "If we are cruelly vexed by an inhuman Prince" he said, "or robbed and plundered by one prodigal and avaricious – let us remember our own offences against God which doubtless are chastised by these plagues," Calvin follows Luther also in enjoining a pure Christian ethic of non- resistance upon the subjects, and allowing the ruler *carte blanche* in the use of the sword. "The use of the sword ought not to be permitted any private individual, to make resistance to evil; for the arms of the Christians are prayer and meekness, to possess their lives in patience and to overcome evil by doing good according to the doctrine of the gospel. But to condemn the public use of the sword, which God hath ordained for our protection, is blasphemy against God Himself. The sword is placed in his hand to punish malefactors. Since God orders him to do this, who are we to hinder him?"' (*Christianity and Social Revolution,* pp.451/2).

In an age when many people exchange their religious allegiances for political loyalties and convictions, it is not surprising that the Pauline doctrine of the State has found enthusiastic response among contemporary Christians.

The *CC* is cautious in its attitude towards *Romans* 13:1/7. Professor Theissen discusses the passage and says that the apostle summarises here the Christian's duties towards the State, such as submission and obedience to the ruling government, which is divine law. Disobedience towards a divinely appointed authority would be a sin, 'which would not be left unpunished'. The Christian must act in this manner in pursuance of his conscience and not for fear of being found out. Theissen finishes his comments: 'The duty of obedience towards the

State and its laws is clearly stated to be a duty imposed by God' (pp. 1074/5). Commenting on *Eph.* 6:5/8, Professor Leahy admits that Paul does not denounce the system of slavery openly, but he believes that the apostle advocates principles preparing the way for its abolition. The slave depends on Jesus Christ and possesses the key to eternal happiness in heaven (p. 1125). Concerning *Col. 3:11,* Leahy even claims that 'with regard to slaves – to the sanction of reward for good is added that of punishment' (p. 1136). *1 Tim.* 2:1/2 is discussed by Professor Foster: 'Kings and those in high station are mentioned because their attitude is fraught with grave consequences for the well-being of the Church and the individual. The command gains force when we bear in mind that the ruler then in power was Nero. The injunction to pray for those responsible for the guidance of the State is more urgent today than ever, since society is now so highly organised and controlled that the individual is liable to be at the mercy of some form of totalitarian control' (p. 1146). An interesting thought: had Jesus followed the Pauline teaching he might have escaped crucifixion!

Regarding Titus 2:9/10 Foster admits without embarrassment that 'Slaves are again urged to be submissive to their masters and indeed to give such good service that they bring credit upon the Christian religion' (p. 1150). So much for the frequent claim that early Christianity was in the forefront of the fight against slavery. The commentary of *Titus* 3:1 rounds off neatly the statement of the Christian position with regard to authority: 'The apostle calls upon the Christians to fulfil their duties as members of society, civic and municipal. Far from weakening loyalty to the State, faith in Christ is rather a guarantee of its strength, because the nation as such is derived from God . . . and in consequence must be loyally served by the Christian as a matter of duty' (ibid.) Professor Wilmering writes on *1 Peter* 2:13/7: 'Christians are to accept the established form of government and to submit to those in authority "for the sake of the Lord", i.e. Christ, in order not to bring discredit upon his teaching and Church [sic] . . . Submission to their authority is indirectly obedience to God, the source of all authority. It has a very practical side, since it silences those who through ignorance or malice slander the Christian way of life' (p. 1179). And *2 Peter* 2:10 draws this comment: 'Such summary punishment in the past should be a warning to those who disregard the moral law and legitimate authority' (p. 1183). *Jude* 7/8 is said to concern false teachers. 'These in their dreams i.e. dreaming in the sleep of sin, defile the flesh, by giving themselves over to immorality, like the Sodomites: and despise dominion, i.e. scorn authority, like the disgruntled Israelites, and revile Majesty, speak ill of those who exercise authority' (p. 1192).

The attitude towards slavery is also glossed over in the Protestant *PC*. Much space is devoted, however, to the Christians' duty towards authority. Professor Manson, the commentator on *Rom.* 13:1, writes: 'In counselling obedience to the imperial government St. Paul may be held to imply obedience to the spiritual powers behind it, but . . . such obedience can be given by Christians to these authorities whatever kind they may be, only in so far as their commands are consistent with the rule of Christ. God is the supreme Power . . . All other power or authority is derivative, either authorised or permitted by Him. Hence resistance to legitimate authority legitimately exercised, is wrong. It is assumed in these verses that the State is doing its appointed task of maintaining order and administering justice, and when *Romans* was written a case could be made that the Roman Empire was doing its duty by its subjects' (p. 950).

The Epistle to the Romans was probably written in A.D. 57 or 58 (*Halley's Bible Handbook*, p. 530), during the rule of the Emperor Nero. We need not dwell upon the character of that period. It was an age when the horrors of the reigns of Tiberius (died 37) and Caligula (died 41) were still living memory. Every one of the emperors, Tiberius, Caligula and the ageing Claudius (died 54) were assassinated, and a similar fate awaited Nero himself. Claudius, a weakling of good intentions, was unable to prevent the preposterous mismanagement of imperial affairs by the favourites of his lascivious wife, Messalina. When he learnt of her unruly life, he had her executed, only to replace her by an equally unscrupulous woman, Agrippina, who eventually became the instigator of her husband's assassination. It was during the reign of Tiberius that Jesus was crucified, and during the reign of Claudius that the Jews were expelled from Rome' (Suetonius, *Vita Claudii*, 15:4). Such was the background against which the epistles of Paul were written and of which modern ecclesiastics write with such glowing praise.

After this diversion let us continue with Professor Manson's commentary: 'It is to be noted that St. Paul regards the State in its punishment of evil-doers as an agent of God's wrath. This sounds strange considering the punishment meted out by Nero to the Christians. The motive for obedience must be something more and better than fear of punishment; there must be an awareness of personal responsibility which may not be evaded.' On reading this passage a student of Suetonius may be excused for laughing heartily. 'The obligations of a Christian to the State include payment of taxes, direct and indirect, since the civil rulers are in God's service (whether they know it or not) and busy with their proper task, the encouragement of good and repression of evil. They have a right both to your material and moral support' (p.950). Shades of Tiberius, Caligula, Claudius and Nero!

A more realistic assessment of the situation in Judaea may be gained from an account given by Agrippa I whom Philo of Alexandria quotes with approval: 'Pilate "was cruel by nature and in his harsh-heartedness entirely lacking in remorse."' Philo relates that under Pilate's rule the country was full of 'bribes, vainglorious and insolent conduct, robbery, oppression, humiliations, men often sent to death untried, and incessant and unmitigated cruelty' (*Embassy to Caius,* para. 38). Klausner mentions how of all their provinces, Judaea was the least comprehensible to the Roman rulers who, as a result, often unnecessarily and sometimes unintentionally, offended the Jews, provoking a bitter and violent reaction.

Soon after the Epistle to the Romans was written, the Christians became victims of the most senseless and cruel acts of persecution. In the wake of the Great Fire of Rome in A.D. 64, Nero sought a scapegoat and found it in the Christian community. As is known, they were displayed in Rome as live torches to die in an excruciating manner. Soon after the writing of the First Epistle of Peter, the Emperor Domitian introduced another period of ruthless persecution.

Bishop Barnes states that the persecution under Domitian 'led to the half-mad resentment which we find in Revelation. Typical of the writer's fury . . . is the passage in which, as he dare not name Rome, he denounces "Babylon, the great, the mother of harlots and abominations of the earth. And I saw a woman drunken with the blood of the saints, and with the blood of the martyrs of Jesus"' (*Rev.* 17:5/6), (*The Rise of Christianity,* p.304). This may strike the reader as language somewhat different from the ignorant babblings about the 'great and benevolent empire'.

The truth is that the Roman rulers were in the habit of squeezing out every penny from their subject peoples. They considered themselves as owners of all conquered land and regarded taxes as rent to be paid by the indigenous population whose continued presence was tolerated in the subjugated territories. They also imposed compulsory services and other public obligations, and often caused famines by the removal of grain and stocks. The historian Paterculus ironically says of a certain procurator that 'he entered a rich province as a poor man, and left a poor province as a rich man.'

He shall be put to death

A primitive people needs severe laws to secure its cohesion and its power to resist perils within and without. If the same primitive people has a caste of literate priests and judges, it is likely that their severe laws will be codified to give guidance to the scribes present and future. Such a primitive people were the Jews of the eighth century B.C., who codified their laws in some of the books of their Bible (known to Christians as the Old Testament). Today few people would take these laws seriously, yet the moral principles underlying that code are still effective in the social customs and ideals of our own age.

The laws themselves have little in common with the social and ethical theories current among modern men, and certainly nothing with the permissive views of the twentieth century. The value of human life was acknowledged only in the encouragement of procreation (within wedlock), but not at all in dealing with offenders against the accepted moral code. But capital punishment was also decreed for those who hit or cursed their parents, who committed murder, who kidnapped a person, who 'defiled' the sabbath, who were engaged in adulterous, incestuous or homoerotic relationships, who were heretics, witches or wizards, who had a 'familiar spirit', and for many other 'offences'. A city in which the 'abomination' of serving gods other than Jehovah was practised was to be smitten 'with the edge of the sword, destroying it utterly, and all that is therein, and the cattle thereof' (*Deut.* 13:15). These laws had to be enforced even against one's own mother, son, daughter, wife or friend (*Deut.* 13:6). In many cases the death penalty was pronounced also on those who came too near the holy tabernacle, or entered a forbidden place in the Temple, who came too close to the officiating priest, or who blasphemed the name of the Lord, and on women who lost their virginity prior to marriage. The strangest of all these savage laws was the one which decreed death for him who would 'do presumptuously' (*Deut.* 17:12), a crime which can easily be visited upon a man by his adversaries. It is still a matter of debate whether the expression 'Shall be cut off from his people' meant the death penalty, or mere banishment. In either case it is interesting to list the 'crimes' which were subject to this form of punishment. The offender may be cut off for doing 'aught presumptuously' (*Num.* 15:30), for not observing the passover ritual, for eating or drinking blood, for not having been circumcised after birth, for not being purified, for unauthorised slaughter of cattle, for offering sacrifice without the aid of clergy, and for many similar 'transgressions'.

The 'impulse to punish' (Nietzsche's telling expression) has always been a feature of Judeo-Christian attitudes. Although Jesus said, 'Judge not that ye may not be judged' (*Matthew* 7:1) and 'Judge not, and ye shall not be judged; condemn not and yet shall not be condemned, forgive and ye shall be forgiven' (*Luke* 6:37), the desire to give vent to righteous anger in the name of the Lord soon overcame his followers. St. Paul, in *Rom.* 1/3, writes on this problem, and it is clear that the 'moralic acid' which prompted him [St. Paul] to heights of fury and indignation, made him thirst for revenge and judgment, even if their execution was left to the Lord. It is unnecessary to present here the record of the Church's persecution of 'evildoers', but we may well consult the Roman Catholic *QB* about the attitude of Christians to punishment by authority.

'The Catholic Church has always taught that the State has a right to inflict death for grievous crime, and thereby to preserve public order and security . . . The New Testament takes it for granted that the State has the right to put criminals to death.' Here the *QB* quotes the encounter between Jesus and Pilate which, as we know, was followed by the sentence, and the execution of the former. 'Then saith Pilate unto him, Speakest thou not unto me? knowest thou not that I have power to crucify thee, and have power to release thee? Jesus answered, Thou couldst have no power at all against me, except it were given thee from above, therefore he that delivered me unto thee hath the greater sin' (*John* 19:10/11). The other passage quoted by the *QB* reads; 'For if I [Paul] be an offender, or have committed anything worthy of death, I refuse not to die, but if there be none of these things whereof these accuse me, no man may deliver me unto them. I appeal unto Caesar' (*Acts* 15:11). The citation of these passages is in itself preposterous. In the first instant, Jesus is the 'criminal' and the State which has 'the right' to put him to death is represented by Pontius Pilate during Jesus' cross-examination. In the second example, Paul asserts his right as Roman citizen to be properly tried and to appeal to Caesar. If he had been a 'criminal' without the privilege of Roman citizenship, he might have been condemned by the State which 'had the right' to judge him.

The *QB* continues: 'While clearly asserting the right of capital punishment, the Church has never demanded its infliction as the only possible deterrent of crime, however heinous. That she leaves to the judgment of the individual citizens. Her bishops have often called upon the State to be merciful to criminals . . . ' [It is interesting to note that after the Spanish Civil War, when the victorious régime executed tens of thousands of its enemies, the only authority which could have halted the massacre, did not call upon the State 'to be *merciful*'.]

'That one convincing argument,' says the *QB* 'for capital punishment is the State's right of self-defence. Just as the individual has the right to defend his life against the attacks of an unjust aggressor, so the State has the right to defend itself against external (war) and internal (capital punishment) enemies, who by their crimes undermine the very foundations of the social order . . . Many today deny the right of capital punishment, because they deny the freedom of will, and consider the crime as a disease due to heredity or environment. They would segregate the criminal indeed as one segregates a man afflicted with smallpox in a pesthouse, but they deem imprisonment ample punishment even for the most heinous murder . . . It is certainly more in harmony with the Gospel to limit the death penalty to certain grave crimes like murder, piracy and treason . . . ' (pp.420/1).

In the Christian world there have always been ardent defenders of capital punishment. The most important thinker of the Church, Thomas Aquinas, himself pronounced on the death penalty meted out by the authorities, that 'such killing is not murder' (S.T IIae Q 100 art.8), and he explicitly stated: 'The slaying of an evildoer is lawful inasmuch as it is directed to the welfare of the whole community' (ibid., Q 64 art.3). Pope Innocent III, speaking about the Waldensian 'heretics' said that 'the secular power could inflict the death penalty without grievous sin'. The Catechism of the Council of Trent declared (1545): 'The magistrates who condemn to death . . . are not only not guilty of murder, but eminently obey this law [the fifth commandment] which prohibits murder' (Pt.iii chap.6 Q4).

Article 37 of the Church of England is also explicit on the subject. Its penultimate sentence reads: Leges regni possunt Christianos, propter capitalia et gravia crimina, morte punire (the Laws of the Realm may punish Christians with death, for heinous and grievous offences). It must be said in praise of the Anglican bishops that in the historic debate in the House of Lords most of them voted for the permanent abolition of the death penalty.

Martin Luther who was after all an inspiration for the authors of the Articles, was not quite so squeamish. And he certainly was not amongst those who questioned the legitimacy of capital punishment. This 'great Christian' was adamant in his desire to punish: 'Once upon a time, under the papacy, the authorities were afraid to pass a sentence, because they were unable to distinguish between the public and the private aspect of a person. The hangman had to repent and ask the condemned man's forgiveness for what he was going to do, as if he were guilty for dealing with the offender, while he was only fulfilling his special function. St. Paul said "He beareth not the sword in vain, for he is the minister of God" (*Rom.* 13:4). God Himself acts likewise. It is as if I handed over my son into the care of a schoolmaster. If he beats him with a cane, I am well pleased and it is as if I had done it myself. If on the other hand, someone attempted to castigate my son without my commission, I would not tolerate it. Prince-Elector Frederick used to be timid when he punished, and said "Well, he might yet become God-fearing!" As a consequence the country was full of evil-doers. But Prince and Magistrate should not be merciful. Look at God, the Most Merciful, did He not give a strict commandment when he said: "He that curseth his father, or his mother, shall surely be put to death" (*Exod.* 21:17). That means: off with his head so that the earth should not be full of godless men! That way authority has a chance to become just. The men of law themselves take life when they teach, invoke the law and pass sentence. After all, the hangman cannot execute anyone unless he be the first sentenced to death. Yet, Dr. Schurff, an eminent lawyer and a good Christian, was never able to pass a death sentence with a clear conscience' (*Luther im Tischgespräch* (Luther's Tabletalk) III, 2910).

More than anything else, the revolt of the oppressed and starving peasants aroused the wrath of the learned Doctor. He fulminated against the rebels in a style which would do honour to the most fanatical misanthropist. He called upon the princes to act 'against the murderous robber bands of the peasants', exhorting the rulers of Germany to 'smash them, strike at them, strangle them openly or by ruse, as best as you can. Remember that there is nothing more poisonous, more devilish than the rebel – just like a mad dog – if you don't kill him, he will kill you and the whole land with you . . . And I would not prevent even those powers who do not suffer the Gospel [he meant the Roman Catholics] from beating down these peasants; they have a good right to do so, for the peasants no longer fight for the Gospel; but they are treacherous, disobedient traitors, murderers, robbers and blasphemers whom even heathen Lords have a right to punish – nay they have a duty to punish such rogues, for therefore do they carry the sword, and are God's ministers, revengers to execute wrath upon him that does evil. As for the evangelical princes [meaning the Protestants] they are certainly fighting in a good cause and in the execution of their office, so that when the lord can punish and does not, though it be with murder and bloodshed, he makes himself guilty of all the murder and evil that these rogues do' (Quoted from B. Lunn, *Martin Luther*, p.222).

Luther also acted as recruiting agent for the princes: 'Here is the advantage: the peasants have a bad conscience and a bad cause, and any peasant who is killed therein is lost body and soul, and is the devil's for eternity. But the higher powers have a good conscience and a good cause, and can say to God in all sureness of heart: "See, my God, Thou hast appointed me to be a prince or lord, and Thou hast commanded me to use the sword against evildoers" *Rom.* 13 . . . Therefore it may well be that he who falls on the side of the higher powers is a true martyr to God . . . They die secure, who are found dead in the office of their sword, and leave to the devil the kingdom of the world, gaining instead the eternal kingdom. We live in such strange times . . . that a prince may earn heaven by shedding blood, while others get nowhere with praying' (ibid., p.223).

The righteous certainty of his cause overwhelmed him to such a degree that he exclaimed: 'Indeed I think the preachers are the worst of all murderers! They must continually call upon authority to carry out its office with all severity and punish the guilty. And so it was I, Martin Luther, who slew all the peasants during the rising, for I commanded them to be slaughtered. All their blood be on my head! But I pass on the responsibility to our Lord God, who instructed me to give this order. If the killing is done by the devil, then of course it is wrong. Anyone pondering this has indeed learnt something' (*Luther im Tischgespräch*, III, 2910/1).

I cannot but heartily agree. I have indeed learnt something! Even Luther's admiring biographer, Brian Lunn, feels constrained to admit: 'The effect of Luther's outburst was catastrophic. It is computed that a hundred thousand peasants were slaughtered. Had Luther used his immense influence on the side of moderation, he might have enfranchised the peasants in very important liberties. As it was, the rebellion left the peasantry with the shackles of serfdom so firmly riveted that more than two centuries later German princes were able to sell their able- bodied men to fill the ranks in the English war against the American colonists' (*Martin Luther,* pp.224/5).

Thou art fair my love, there is no spot in thee

These words taken from one of the most beautiful and deeply erotic love-poems (Song of Songs, 4:7) which have been despoiled by the Christians, like so many other things of tender beauty. Solomon's Song has not been given an X-certificate, instead, we find this superscription in the Authorised Version: 'Christ setteth forth the graces of the Church. He showeth His love to her.' The attempt to turn these verses into symbolic images, depicting the dialogue between Christ and 'his Church' is indecent, to say the least. The lyrical passage 'Thy two breasts are like two young roes that are twins, which feed among the lilies' demonstrates the facetious hypocrisy behind the Christian endeavour to turn this great poetry into pseudo-religious cant.

But let us accept for the sake of argument that Jesus indeed tells the Church: 'there is no spot in thee'. He must be singularly blind, or else it must be our own eyesight which deceives us when we discover spots on the leopard's skin.

When did the Church develop these ungainly spots? I would suggest that it was born with them, and in the Pauline doctrine there is already more than one sign of the things to come. The abyss between Jesus and the Church which claims to be his, became manifest when it established its lasting links with the State. Since then, there has always been the problem of the relation between Church and State which has little to do with the teaching of Jesus. It has very much to do, though, with the power struggle between two mighty organisations living side by side.

There has been no period in history when the Church did not woo the State, first to gain toleration, then influence and finally dominance. The teachings of the Pauline doctrine were calculated to secure the goodwill of the Roman State. The part played by the Romans in the trial and execution of Jesus was deliberately trivialised. Pontius Pilate, a greedy and malevolent tyrant was whitewashed, and the Roman domination of Judaea was presented as an idyllic and benign rule.

I shall attempt to show how, throughout history, this trend maintained itself in the activities of the Church, and how the relations between Church and State eventually undermined completely the influence of Jesus' ideas. This subject can, unfortunately, only be dealt with in a cursory manner, otherwise it alone would fill a great number of volumes.

The Pauline School maintained its subservient attitude throughout the ruthless persecutions under Claudius, Nero, Domitian and others. Christianity was not generally known before the second century. One of the first Romans to mention it was the historian Tacitus who wrote about 115: 'Those people who were held in abhorrence for their crimes, and were commonly known by the name of Christians. They had their name from one Christus who had been put to death by the procurator Pontius Pilate in the reign of Tiberius. This pernicious superstition, checked for a while . . .' (*Annals,* 15:44). A few years earlier Pliny the Younger had asked the Emperor Trajan whether it was desirable to punish Christians in performing his duties as proconsul. He called Christianity 'a crazy and unrestrained superstition' (superstitionem pravam et immodicam) (Letters, 10:97). At about the same time the historian Suetonius mentioned the Christians. In his *Life of Claudius* he tells us how the Jews were banished from Rome because of their rebelliousness instigated by 'Chrestos'. In the *Life of Nero* he refers to the Christians as 'a race of men of a new and villainous superstition' (genus hominum superstitionis novae et malificae). In the *Life of Vespasian* Suetonius refers to the Messianic aspiration of the Jews aiming at world dominion. Uncomplimentary allusions to the Christians appear in the writings on the Emperors Hadrian (134) and Marcus Aurelius (180); and of Lukianus (176). The persecution of the growing Church continued in the third century under the emperors Decius, Valerianus and Diocletian. The first sign of a changing attitude on the part of Rome is the Edict of Toleration given by Constantine and the dying co-emperor Galerius in 311. The Edict was recorded by Lactantius in *De mortibus persecutorum* (XXXIV). It was followed by the Edict of Milan in March 313, signed by the Emperors Constantine and Licinius, a document of favour rather than toleration, and preserved in chapters XIV and XVIII of the same work. Eusebius and others record the various Letters and Ordinances of the Emperor Constantine who restored Church property, subsidised the clergy exempting it from all public duties (313), adjudicated in Church disputes (316), suppressed pagan soothsayers, i.e. non-Christian priests (319), and recognised the Church Sunday as a universal day of rest (321). His successor, Emperor Constantius, was a militant Arian and an avowed enemy of Athanasius and his trinitarian ideas. By now the emperor and the State machine has become so intertwined with Christianity that it was nearly impossible to distinguish between the State and the favoured Church. A saying of Constantius is recorded, which he addressed to the Western bishops: 'Let my will be deemed a canon among you as it is among the Syrian bishops' (355). An injunction, the spirit of which inspired the utterances of innumerable sovereigns throughout history.

The successor of Constantius, Emperor Julian, a man of exceptional drive and culture, was the last great enemy of Christianity. He attempted to reverse the process initiated by his predecessors, trying to halt the growth of the Church and to replace Christianity by a mixture of Greek philosophy and Mithraic sun-worship. This sovereign, no mean writer himself, coined the phrase: 'The Christians are more dangerous enemies to one another than wild beasts.'

It is moving to read some of the writings of this last great 'pagan'. It is a sad fact of history that his light was extinguished after a very short life to give way to the darkness of an epoch known to us as 'Dark Ages', although we should more correctly refer to them as the Christian centuries.

This is what Julian wrote on our subject, Jesus versus Christianity: 'But you, unfortunately, do not abide by the tradition of the apostles, which in the hands of their successors deteriorated into greater blasphemy. Neither Paul, nor Matthew, nor Luke, nor Mark had the audacity to say Jesus *was* God. But the worthy John, realising that by that time a vast number of people in many of the Greek and Italian cities was infected with the disease and hearing that the tombs of Peter and Paul were being worshipped (privately, no doubt, but still worshipped), John, I say, was the first to have the impudence to make this assertion. This evil was inaugurated by John. But who can find a fitting denunciation of this innovation of yours, the introduction of many recent dead bodies (as objects of worship) besides that original dead body? You have filled all places with tombs and monuments . . . You think that not even the words of Jesus are to be listened to on this question . . . Jesus says (*Matthew* 23:27) that sepulchres are full of uncleanness. How is it then that you invoke God upon them,' (Quoted by Cyril of Alexandria in his *Contra Julianum,* 9:326).

To Cyril we owe also the record of another significant statement made by the Emperor: 'If anyone should wish to know the truth with respect to you Christians he will find your impiety to be made up partly of the audacity of the Jews, and partly of the indifference and confusion of the Gentiles, and that ye have put together not the best but the worst characteristics of them both' (ibid., 2).

In 352 the Emperor wrote: 'I had imagined the prelates of the Galileans were under greater obligation to me than to my predecessor. For in his reign many of them were banished, persecuted and imprisoned, and many of the so-called heretics were executed . . . All this has been reversed in my reign; the banished have been allowed to return, and confiscated property has been restored to the owners. But such is their folly and madness that, because they can no longer be despots, or carry out their designs first against their own brethren and then against us, the worshippers of the gods, they are inflamed with fury and stop at nothing in their unprincipled attempts to arm and enrage the people. They are . . . disobedient to our edicts, however lenient they may be. For we allow none of them to be dragged to the altars unwillingly . . . people must not abet the seditions of the clergy . . . They may hold their meetings, if they wish, and offer prayer according to their established usage . . . And for the future let the people live in harmony. Let no one be at variance, or do wrong to an other; neither you that are in error, to those who worship the gods as is right and proper, in the manner handed down from earliest antiquity; nor let the worshippers of the gods destroy or plunder the house of those who are misled by ignorance rather than by deliberate choice. Men should be taught and won over by reason, not by blows, insults and corporal punishments. I therefore most earnestly admonish the adherents of the true religion not to injure and insult the Galileans in any way, either by physical attacks or by reproaches. Those who are in the wrong in matters of supreme importance are objects of pity rather than hate!' (*Epistle* III). It is this great man whom Christian-inspired history calls 'Julian the Apostate'.

After the young Emperor's death the Church was reinstated in its now dominant position. The Emperor Gratianus endowed it with statutory powers in ecclesiastical matters (376), while Theodosius I, East Roman emperor, outlawed heretics and made the Creed of Nicaea the official Creed of the Empire. Valentinian III decreed the primacy of the bishop of Rome as head (Pope) of the whole Church. This explains why even today it is the Bishop of Rome who heads the whole universal Church: a Roman emperor willed it so more than fifteen centuries ago.

The disintegration of the Empire did not leave a complete power-vacuum. Centres of authority came into existence and attempted to act as heirs and perpetuators of imperial might. The East Roman Empire (Byzantium) continued until 1453, while in Western Europe the Frank-Roman Empire established itself lasting until the ninth century to be replaced by the German-Roman Empire which survived until the beginning of the 19th century. During those periods many other powerful nations and dynasties came into existence, some of which survived to the present. Wherever power was concentrated, a parasitical Church fastened itself onto its holders, and created a close liaison between its own institutions and the State.

The Frank-Roman Empire owed its might to the skill and diplomacy of Clovis I who, in his battle against the Alemans (496), vowed that in the case of his victory he would accept the God of the Christians. He conquered and was baptised, setting an example for all his subjects. This at least is the legend – the fact is that he made Christianity the religion of his realm, seeing that the Church and its influence was a safeguard of his newly established dominion. This cynical view was, of course, refuted by the grateful clergy: at the ceremony of Clovis' baptism at Reims a white dove appeared bringing in its beak the little flask to be used at the baptism of crowned heads. The many murders committed by this Christian sovereign may have cost him the halo: he was not canonised in spite of his incalculable services to the Church.

King Dagobert I, a malevolent and treacherous monarch, is highly praised in Christian annals, because he too favoured the clergy and became himself founder of a number of monasteries. The great king, Carolus, known to history by the name Charlemagne, was encouraged to fight his wars (772 to 785). These wars, which were pursued with utter ruthlessness and alternating success and failure, ended in Charlemagne's victory and the forcible conversion of the defeated Saxons. In 783, in the wake of a decisive battle, this great Christian sovereign ordered the beheading of 4,500 Saxon prisoners of war. The height of Charlemagne's success was the baptism of the Saxon leader Widukind, and the incorporation of Saxony into the Frankish Empire. The Church was not ungrateful. On Christmas Eve of the year 800, in Rome, Pope Leo III himself placed the crown of the Roman Empire on the head of Charlemagne who henceforth bore the title Holy Roman Emperor.

The clerics surrounded every powerful ruler. They induced King Sisebut of the Visigoths to initiate the first savage persecution of the Jews in Christendom. This otherwise able and circumspect monarch enforced 90,000 conversion of Jews to which they submitted in order to escape death. One of his successors, King Wamba, was a tolerant and independent man: he invoked the anger of the Church: he lost his throne as a result of the clerics' conspiracy.

Nowhere did the Church make a greater effort to gain dominance and establish itself as a permanent influence than in Constantinople, the centre of the East Roman Empire. It was so powerful as to be able to dispose even a ruthless tyrant like Justinian II when he incurred its displeasure. It also fought with all its might against the iconoclasts, the Emperors Leo II and his son, Constantine V. It prevailed in the end, and all its demands were met by the Dowager Empress Theodora and her son, Michael III. The cult of the holy icons, sculptures and relics was restored (845), after a bitter struggle which lasted well over a century.

In Britain, clerical influence began about 600 at the court of the Kentish king Ethelbert, who was converted and baptised by the abbot Augustine, the Pope's emissary. Augustine was soon able to baptise another 10,000 Anglo-Saxons. When Egbert, king of Wessex (802 to 839) united the seven Anglo-Saxon kingdoms, the power of the clergy was established throughout the new realm. Egbert's son and successor, Thelwolf (839 to 858) introduced the 'Peter's Penny', a church tax which preceded the later tithe. But it was not until the Norman conquest, that the Church whose representatives accompanied the invader, became a powerful and decisive factor in the policies of the realm.

By winning the support of the most powerful rulers, the Church also gained influence in Scandinavia. After the first abortive attempt under King Sigurd Ring (about 700) Christianity was adopted in Denmark by the joint kings Harald and Eric I (about 820). In spite of initial successes, in which Bishop Anscar, 'the Apostle of the North', played a dominant part, a pagan rebellion broke out and Anscar had to flee to Sweden. There, with the help of the king, Björn II (about 830), he introduced the Christian faith. The Church soon took roots in Southern Scandinavia but suffered a temporary eclipse during the rule of the great King Gorm the Old in Denmark. This avowed enemy of the Christians lived to the immense age of over 100 years, and resisted any attempt to reintroduce Christianity in his realm, although his wife Thyra was, without his knowing, a convert to the new faith. Thyra succeeded in winning her son, Gorm's successor, Harald, for the Christian religion. Harald's son once again turned against the clergy, shut their churches and banished their missionaries. Not until the rule of Canut I, king of Denmark and England, was it possible for the Church to gain a firm foothold and ultimately lasting dominion in the North of Europe.

Waik, the ruling prince of Hungary, himself son of a Christian woman, won in marriage the hand of Gisela, the German emperor's sister, after accepting the Christian faith and baptism. When she joined her husband in his pagan principality, she brought with her six hundred clergymen, and the forcible conversion of the Magyar people began. Waik was crowned king under the name Stephen. The uprising of the Magyars under Kupa was defeated in 999, and the leaders of the rebellion died under dreadful torture. The king's brother, Almos, who had sided with the 'heathens' was executed by having molten lead poured into his ears. The zealous Christian king soon introduced legislation under which attendance at mass became compulsory, and absence from the church service save for a good reason (certified sickness etc) was severely punished, sometimes even by death. The services of this ruler were greatly appreciated by the Church, and Stephen was canonised. All the successors of the Saint King Stephen bore the title 'Apostolic King of Hungary', which only expired in 1918 when Hungary lost its last King. The gratitude of the Church was so pronounced that even Stephen's son Emeric, who died at the age of 15, was eventually made a Saint.

During the Middle Ages the influence of the Church in Europe did not spread through the acceptance of Christianity by the people: it was almost always the sovereigns and their courts who accepted or rejected the clergy. The fortunes of the Church varied with the attitude of the worldly rulers. The German Emperor's favour very often decided who should be chosen for the Holy See. A typical example is the election of Gregory V at the behest of Emperor Otto III (St. Stephen's brother-in-law). After the departure of the emperor from Italy Gregory was replaced by John XVII. The emperor, angered by this show of ecclesiastical disobedience, returned to Italy and reinstated Gregory. It was left to the latter to deal with his rival and indeed, the end of John XVII is one of the most appalling stories of man's inhumanity to man. He was tied to a donkey's back, face backwards and led through the streets of Rome before being mutilated by cutting off his nose, ears and hands. A little later Emperor Henry II, a willing tool of the clergy, renounced all rights secured by one of his predecessors, Otto I, for the State in its relation to the Church. However, towards the end of the 11th century, a remarkable man, the monk Hildebrand, literally made himself Pope of Rome. Under the name Gregory VII he became a decisive influence in Europe. Even his opponent, the equally remarkable Emperor Henry IV of Germany, had to knuckle under to the will of this powerful Pope. Henry was forced, on the occasion of his famous 'pilgrimage' to Canossa (1077), into abject submission. A few years later he treacherously turned against Gregory, beleaguering Rome, and after a siege of three years, forcing the Pope to flee (1083). Shortly before his death in Salerno (1085), Gregory spoke these noble words: 'I loved justice and hated injustice, that is why I must die in exile.'

In 1137 a man appeared in Brescia, Italy, who proclaimed that the teachings of Jesus required a Church without power and possessions. Arnold of Brescia found following and response throughout Italy. The enraged princes of the Church invoked their anathema against them. In 1139 Pope Innocent II excommunicated him, and Arnold had to flee, first to France, then to Zurich. Partly under the influence of his teaching, the citizens of Rome declared their independence from the Pope (who was their secular ruler) and proclaimed the Roman Republic. In vain fulminated the Popes, first Eugene III, then Hadrian IV, against Arnold, they had to call the aid of the German Emperor, Frederick I, who destroyed the Roman Republic and delivered the captured Arnold to Pope Hadrian. On the self-same night, before anyone could intervene, Arnold was burnt at the stake.

The most powerful pope of that period arose in Innocent III, an Italian nobleman who continued the policy of Gregory VII, trying to unite Christendom under papal influence. He declared the papal throne to be supreme in the Christian world, and above any secular sovereign. In his famous statement *Sicus universitatis conditor,* commonly called the 'Sun and Moon Declaration' (1198), he laid down his political creed which deserves to be quoted here: 'The Creator of the Universe set up two great luminaries in the firmament of heaven: the greater light to rule the day, the lesser light to rule the night. In the same way for the firmament of the universal Church, which is spoken of as heaven, he appointed two great dignities: the greater to bear rule over the souls (these being as it were days), the lesser to bear rule over bodies (these being as it were nights). These dignities are the pontifical authority and the royal power. Furthermore, the moon derives its light from the sun, and is in truth inferior to the sun in both size and quality, in position as well as effect. In the same way the secular power derives its dignity from the pontifical authority: and the more closely it cleaves to the sphere of that authority, the less is the light with which it is adorned; the further it is removed, the more it increases in splendour' (*Documents of the Christian Church,* p.155). In 1202 he claimed the right to 'vet' secular rulers and throughout his reign he interfered successfully in the internal affairs of kingdoms as powerful as England and France.

The thirteenth century saw the zenith of papal power. Able men like Gregory IX and Boniface VIII knew how to maintain the power of Rome on the level established by Innocent III. Gregory tarnished his record by the ruthless persecution of 'heretics' and by creating the so-called 'heresy- courts' which later developed into the infamous Inquisition. Boniface was the author of the papal bull *Clericis Laicos* of 1296 which forbade the taxing of clergy and thereby lay the foundation of the fabulous wealth of the Church. It contains the fateful words: 'Truly he who denies that the temporal sword is in the power of Peter, misunderstands the words of a Lord, "Put up thy sword into the sheath" (*Luke* 22:38). Both are in the power of the Church, the spiritual sword and the material. But the latter is to be used for the Church, the former by her; the former by the priest, the latter by kings and captains but at the will and by permission of the priest. The one sword then should be under the other, and temporal authority subject to spiritual'. He finishes with the words: 'We declare, define and pronounce that it is altogether necessary to salvation for every human creature to be subject to the Roman Pontiff (ibid., pp.160/1).

Proud words, these. They were followed by centuries of decline of papal supremacy.

Hubris led to immediate retribution. After the death of Boniface (1303), at the behest of King Philip of France, Pope Clement V, realising that spiritual power must lean on willing material swords, called the Council of Avignon to pass judgment on the acts and ordinances of his imperious predecessor. The outcome was a sorry surrender to the irate king, and all edicts and bulls of Boniface were declared null and void.

In the wake of this setback to the Church, secular power began to assert itself everywhere. At the demand of Philip, the papal see moved from Rome to Avignon (1303) where it remained until 1377 when Gregory XI returned to the City by the Tiber. In was then that the derelict Lateran was replaced by the Vatican which has remained the papal residence ever since. The main reason for the return of the Pope was the continued existence of the Papal State (the secular State) which, in the absence of the Pope, was governed by a Regent, and threatened to disintegrate. However, after the return of Gregory the Church split, and some bishops recognised the Pope of Rome while others declared their allegiance to a rival Pope elected by the College of Cardinals in Avignon. There was a period when three popes contested the throne of Peter (1410 to 1415). Eventually the Council of Constance (1415) settled the problem by persuading Gregory XII to abdicate, deposing the Avignon Pope, Benedict XIII, and putting in the dock the third, Pope John XXIII (the first!) indicted of tyranny, simony, murder, incest and debauchery with three hundred nuns. His papacy was declared null and void and that is why the recent Pope John was counted to be twenty-third of that name. Martin V became the only and universal pontiff. Even this did not resolve the difficulties of the Church. Benedict refused to budge from Avignon, and after his death in 1424 the French Cardinals elected a new rival pontiff, Clement VIII. Only when Clement abdicated in 1429, was Martin universally acknowledged. Most of the subsequent popes were instrumental in bringing the papacy into disrepute, thus paving the way for the Reformation. The epoch was crowned by the term of office of Alexander VI Borgia who openly lived 'in sin' with a beautiful Roman, Rosa Vanozza, and had four illegitimate children: John, Caesar, Godfrey and Lucretia. He is said to have indulged in every possible form of sexual gratification, organising semi-public orgies and being contemptuous of any counsel of moderation. He has another claim to our lasting attention: He was the first ruler to introduce official censorship, that most infamous of anti-libertarian institutions.

It is not surprising that all over Europe voices were raised to condemn the desertion of Jesus' teaching by a powerful and unscrupulous organisation claiming to act in his name. Very soon, however, the enemies of the papacy and their crowned supporters took the 'evangelical' movement under their wings, and utilised them for their own political purposes. As we have seen above, the most influential of evangelical preachers became the protégés of certain princes who used

Luther in their quarrels with the German Emperor. Luther started with his ninety-five theses (1517), a diatribe against papal indulgences, including the statement: 'The Pope's riches at this day far exceeds the wealth of the richest of the rich (86th thesis), and ending with a malediction against the rebellious peasants. Other figures of the Reformation were no less unequivocal in their 'subjection to authority'. Ulrich Zwingli wrote in 1523: 'Wordly power has its strength and affirmation in the teaching and actions of Christ' (Thesis No. 35). Philip Melanchton claimed; 'It is the Christian's duty to be subject to authority and to its ordinances and laws insofar as this can be done one without sin. Where it cannot be done without sin, one should obey God rather than man' (*Augsburg Confession,* Art. 16, 1530). 'There are those' he wrote elsewhere, 'who say the secular authority should not be arbiter in doctrinal disputes, to which the true and complete answer should state that it is the Church who judges such things following the guidance of the gospels. Since, however, a god-fearing authority is in fact part of the Church, it is itself entitled to judge alongside with all the pious and learnéd men in accordance with the afore-mentioned guidance' (*Loci theologici*).

Finally, we may hear Calvin: 'We owe a respectful and devout attitude towards all our superiors, even to the very last, whatever their character may be. I repeat this so that we should learn not to examine the person, but be satisfied that their position is held by the will of the Lord who has given it [their position] an indelible and inviolable majesty . . . If therefore we are cruelly vexed by a severe prince or greedily exploited by a mean or extravagant one, neglected by an indifferent one or even maltreated for our god-fearing faith by a godless and blasphemous one; we must always remember our own misdeeds and realise that no doubt the Lord is chastising us through such scourges' (*Institutio,* 4:B:20:k). We see that the 'return to the New Testament' meant a return not to Jesus, but to Paul. It may not surprise us then that Calvin, after having established a dictatorial regime in Geneva, zealously burnt at the stake those who happened to differ from his own opinions and interpretations of Christian doctrine. Among his victims was the unitarian philosopher and writer Miguel Servetus whom he condemned to death in 1553 because Servetus dared to teach that the trinitarian doctrine was erroneous and non-scriptural. Calvin's reign of terror in Geneva is just one example of the atrocities committed against human beings where Christian (or any other) zealots attain absolute power.

A free Church in a free State

It would be a gargantuan task to describe the misdeeds of the Christian clergy throughout history, and it is not the aim of this book to attempt it. It is intended, however, to trace the exercise of authority by the Church in her relation to the State. It would be foolish to complain about the 'wicked deeds of the Church': the Church is an institution, and it is always man who acts and not the institution. On the other hand, the interest and expediency of institutions to which man belongs often prompt him to act in an unethical, inhuman manner. Seen in this context it is fascinating to observe the conflict and co-operation between the two most powerful institutions which dominated the history of Europe for nearly two thousand years. When political theory was reborn, many centuries after Aristotle, its basic problem was, and remained for a long time, the relationship between ecclesiastical and secular power. The Catholic apologists are right when they claim that the idea of political authority and power by divine right was foreign to mediaeval thinkers, although God's consent to the exercise of authority was always taken for granted. It did not occur to Christian scholastics to use it as a justifying social principle. 'Human dominions and princedoms, said Thomas Aquinas, are by human not by divine right' (S.T. IIa IIae Q10:10 and 12:2).

The rebirth of political theory in the 16th century also produced its Catholic representatives. The most distinguished of them, Cardinal Robert Bellarmine, a Jesuit theologian, came out in defence of the idea of popular sovereignty against the concept of divine right still upheld by English theologians. The cardinal wrote in support of the English sovereigns who wished to unite in their hands both political and ecclesiastical power. According to Bellarmine the ruler's privileges are not vested in any system of government, but in the population itself. 'It depends on the consent of the multitude', he said, 'to place over themselves a king, consul or magistrate and if there be a legitimate reason, the multitude can change the government into an aristocracy or democracy' (*De laicis,* 3:6). If we compare the attitude of this contemporary of the Reformation with that of most of its [the Reformation's] spokesmen, we must admit that it shows considerably more vision and broadmindedness. Another Jesuit theologian, Francisco Suarez, attacked the English political theology which was, according to him, 'new and singular, invented to exaggerate the temporal and minimise the spiritual power' (*Defensio Fidei Catholicae,* 3:2 and 5).

Lest Bellarmine's ideas prompt the reader to relate them to those of Rousseau, the Catholic *QB* hastens to the reader's rescue to prevent such sacrilege: 'There is a fundamental difference between the doctrines of Bellarmine and Rousseau. Bellarmine held that political power is a natural and divine institution, necessary for the good of society, while Rousseau held that it was a mere human convenience, existing solely by the agreement of men. Bellarmine derived political power immediately from the people as a whole, but ultimately from God, while Rousseau rested it solely on the contract between ruler and subject. Bellarmine held that men were bound in conscience to obey all lawful authority, while Rousseau declared "each one is united to all, but obeys only himself, and remains as free as before". While therefore, Rousseau made the French Revolution possible, Bellarmine made the democracy of the United States a reality. Catholic moralists, unlike the divine right theorists, declare that rebellion is lawful when the people are oppressed by a lasting and intolerable tyranny; when legal and pacific means of reform have proved useless; when the revolt has a reasonable chance of success; and when it is approved by the larger and better [sic] portion of the people' (p.417). (Anybody interested in the source of this unspeakable inanity should look up the Roman Catholic conditions for a war to be 'just' (see chapter on 'War and Violence').

Of course, Catholics will readily admit that their concept of an ideal State cannot and should not identified with the 'actual' situation which prevailed throughout the Middle Ages, when there was a close connection between temporal and spiritual power. The *QB* quotes with approval a Dr. Pohl who says: 'The intimate connection of both powers during the Middle Ages was only a passing and temporary phenomenon, arising neither from the essential nature of the State nor from that of the Church. The Church is free to enter into a more or less close association with the State, but she can also endure actual separation from the State, and given favourable circumstances, may even prosper under such conditions, as for example in the United States.' To this the *QB* adds: 'The liberal formula "A free Church in a free State" has in countries like France and Italy been made the pretext for bitter attacks upon the Church . . . In the United States . . . the country has never identified itself in any way with intolerance. The separation has been honourably maintained. That is why Cardinal Gibbons, a true Catholic and a loyal American, could write: "American Catholics rejoice in our separation of Church and State: and I can conceive of no combination of circumstances likely to arise which should make a union desirable either for Church or State. We know the blessings of our present arrangement, it gives us liberty and binds together priest and people in a union better than that of church and State. Other countries (Protestant England or Catholic Italy), other manners; we do not believe our system is adapted to all countries; we leave it to Church and State in other lands to solve their problem for their own best interests. For ourselves we thank God we live in America, "in this happy land of ours", to quote Roosevelt, "where liberty and religion are natural allies"' (pp. 188/9).

In hoc regno Angliae

The relation between Church and State in England is carefully defined in Article 37 of the Church of England, and the full text is given below:

De civilibus magistratibus	*Of the civil magistrates*
Regia Majestas in hoc Angliae regno ac caeteris ejus dominiis, summam habet potestatem, ad quam omnium statuum hujus regni, sive illi Ecclesiastici sint sive Civiles, in omnibus causis suprema gubernatio pertinet, et nulli externae dictioni est subjecta, nec esse debet.	The Queen's Majesty hath the chief power in this realm of England, and other her dominions, unto whom the chief government of all estates of this realm, whether they are Ecclesiastical or Civil, in all causes doth appertain, and is not, nor ought to be, subject to any foreign jurisdiction.

Cum Regiae Majestati summam gubernationem tribuimus, quibus titulis intelligimus animos quorundam calumniatorem offendi, non damus Regibus nostris aut verbi Dei, aut Sacramentorum administrationem; quod etiam Injunctiones, ab Elizabetha Regina nostra nuper editae, apertissime testantur; sed eam tantum praerogativam, quam in Sacris Scripturis a Deo ipso omnibus piis Principibus videmus semper fuisse attributam: hoc est, ut omnes status atque ordines fidei suae a Deo commissos, sive illi Ecclesiastici sint sive Civiles, in officio contineant et contumaces ac delinquentes gladio civili coercant.	Where we attribute to the Queen's Majesty the chief government, by which titles we understand the minds of some slanderous folks to be offended, we give not to our Princes the ministering either of God's Word or of the Sacraments, the which thing the Injunctions also lately set forth by Elizabeth our Queen, do most plainly testify; but that only prerogative, which we see to have been given always to all godly Princes in Holy Scriptures by God Himself; that is, that they should rule all states and decrees committed to their charge by God, whether they be Ecclesiastical or Temporal, and restrain with the civil sword the stubborn and evildoers.
Romanus Pontifex habet nullam jurisdictionem in hoc regno Angliae.	The Bishop of Rome has no jurisdiction in this realm of England.
Leges regni possunt Christianos, propter capitalia and gravia crimina, morte punire.	The Laws of the Realm may punish Christians for heinous and grievous offences, with death.
Christianis licet, ex mandato Magistratus, arma portare, et just bella administrare.	It is lawful for Christian men, at the command of the Magistrate, to carry arms, and serve in just wars.

We have considered the last two paragraphs in the sub-chapter 'He shall be put to death' above. Here we are only concerned with the relationship established between Church and State: the inseparable bond which finds expression in the 'personal union' vested in the head of the two institutions. The original document described the sovereign as 'Supreme Head of the Church'. Possibly in deference to the words of the New Testament, 'Christ is the head of the Church' (*Eph. 5:23*), *Queen Elizabeth* I changed the title to Supreme Governor. The Article also makes clear that the Sovereign may not administer the Word of the Sacraments, but has full powers over the administration of both

Church and State. Parliament too can alter official publications, such as the Prayer Book, but it has not the right to interfere with doctrine or ritual.

It is noteworthy that the reformers' zeal and their hatred of Rome blinded them to the fact that by depriving the Roman hierarchy, a distant despot, of its powers, they invested with the same powers the tyrant on their own doorstep. This may be the reason why the process of reformation never came to completion in England, but has continued through the centuries; and why the Protestant character of the Church of England was never unequivocal. Even today there are Catholic and Evangelical extremes within the Church. Only now when the centralised might of the State is unchallenged, and the power of the Church practically non-existent, can voices be raised which call for ecumenism.

The Church of England frequently encounters the criticism that, being national, it cannot fulfil its role as universal Church. Another point raised is that the influence of the State, always doubtful, may become injurious to doctrine if not countered by an independent spiritual authority. To this accusation the British theologian replies: 'Establishment is cherished by many because of its essential value as national testimony to God. It must never be forgotten that Church and State are equally divine in their proper places, though the distinction between them is vital and fundamental. As the State is based upon the law of compulsion involving outward adherence only, and the Church is based upon the law of love expressive of an inward willingness, it can easily be seen that with weapons so different the two can never be formally one. Indeed, they never have been, and whether we believe in Establishment or not, the precise spiritual relations of Church and State are clearly laid down in Holy Scripture' (Griffith Thomas, *Principles of Theology,* p.469).

With this argument we are, of course, left high and dry. It presupposes that we accept the bold statement that Holy Scripture clearly defines the relation between Church and State. It presupposes that we believe that the Church is based on the law of love. And, finally, it presupposes that we think its integrity so great even as an institution 'established' by temporal authority, it will retain its role, its character, and the principle of love, whatever pressure its worldly masters might exert over it. For if its fails to do so, it will inevitably become part of that which Satan declared to be his – 'for that is delivered unto me, and whomsoever I will give it'. A considerable danger for a body which claims to be the Church of Jesus, based on Holy Scripture.

8
Jesus And Riches

Blessed are the poor

Matthew tells us how it happened that a crowd gathered around Jesus and his disciples, waiting for him to speak. From the fact that the scene is set in a mountain from where he addressed his audience, Graves and Podro conclude that the sermon on the Mount is really a speech from the throne, delivered by Jesus on assuming his rightful title as King of Israel. However that may be, on this occasion he gave a 'sermon' which began with the customary ten beatitudes, probably followed by ten woes, which are lost in Matthew's report. Some of the woes have been preserved in the Gospel according to Luke. What interests us here is the first of the beatitudes: 'Blessed are the poor in spirit: for theirs is the kingdom of heaven' (*Matthew* 5:4). We find the same saying in Luke, in its shorter form: 'Blessed are ye poor: for yours is the kingdom of God' (*Luke* 6:20).

Those who accept the version of Matthew in its entirety with its emphasis on the poverty 'in spirit', can find its origin in the Old Testament. David's psalm reads: 'The sacrifices of God are a broken spirit; a broken and contrite heart . . . (*Psalm* 51:19). In the Proverbs we find the sayings, 'Better is it to be of an humble spirit with the lowly, than to divide the spoil with the proud' (16:19); and, 'A man's pride shall bring him low: but honour shall uphold the humble in spirit' (29:23). In Isaiah we read: 'I dwell with him . . . that is of contrite spirit' (57:15); and, 'To this man will I look, to him that is poor and of a contrite spirit' (66:2).

The Greek text of Matthew is as follows: . . . Μακάριοι οἱ πτωχοὶ τῷ πνεύματι. The similar saying in Luke is more succinct: . . . Μακάριοι οἱ πτωχοὶ. There is ample evidence that the latter thought was also prevalent in the Old Testament. 'God raises up the poor out of the dust' (*1 Sam.* 2:8 and

Psalm 132:15); 'This poor man cried, and the Lord heard him, and saved him out of all his troubles' (*Psalm* 34:6); and 'Thou, O God, has prepared of thy goodness for the poor' (*Psalm* 68:10); 'Yet setteth God the poor on high from affliction' (*Psalm* 107:41); and, 'I will abundantly bless her provision: I will satisfy the poor with bread' (*Psalm* 132:15).

Most Christians prefer the rendering of Matthew, since they wish to present material poverty as a God-willed condition. Professor Fenton says that 'the poor in spirit' was an expression used of the pious in the Old Testament. [He means the above-quoted examples – nowhere do we find the expression 'poor in spirit]'. He adds: 'In spirit' may mean 'willingly', voluntarily', i.e. those who have renounced their possessions to follow Jesus' (*the Gospel of St. Matthew*, p.80). William Barclay maintains that the expression indicates a man who is resigned to his complete helplessness when confronted with the might of God. He argues that poverty being an undesirable thing 'Jesus would never have called a state blessed where people live in slums and have not enough to eat . . .'. With emphasis Barclay asserts that not this kind of poverty but *poverty of the spirit* was acclaimed by Jesus, a spirit which surrenders to God without reservation (*The Gospel of St. Matthew*, pp.86/7). An earlier commentator, Dummelow claims that 'the poor in spirit' are those who 'approach God as penitents and supplicants'. He too protests that the poverty meant here is not material want (*OVBC*, p.639). The same line of approach is taken by the Catholic Professor Jones, according to whom 'poor' in bible-language [sic] means those who, whether rich or poor, turn to God in adversity (*CC*, p.861). In the same volume, discussing Luke's version, Professor Ginns says that Luke's poor really means 'poor in spirit', and emphasises that Jesus is not teaching social revolution (ibid., p.949). In *PC*, Professor Stendahl's approach is cautious. He considers that the words 'poor' and 'meek' should not be over-elaborated, and mentions that Godspeed's translation 'feel their spiritual need' goes beyond the limits of interpretation (p.775). After this admission it is disappointing to read Professor Lampe's comment on Luke's version: 'Matthew's "poor in spirit" well expresses the meaning of "poor" here (ibid., p.830). Dummelow goes farthest in disclaiming any 'communist' content: 'By the "poor" and the "hungry" St. Luke does not mean the literally such . . . also St. Luke "Rich", prosperous and well-fed persons are not simply the well-to-do, but those who have the vices of their station. Our Lord never approves poverty or condemns riches as such' (*OVBC*, p.748).

We may observe here the unanimity with which the reverend

gentlemen reject the suggestion that Jesus *may* have meant those who actually suffered the scourge of poverty (slums, malnutrition, disease, lack of purpose) rather than the meek and the humble. It would not do to present Jesus as an advocate of social justice who took up the cudgel for the dispossessed. In order to clear him of any suspicion of 'teaching social revolution' many commentators distort his words beyond recognition. Yet it may be that his indignation was aroused when he saw that the just often were poor while the dishonest and the vile were frequently the ones who enjoy riches. It is refreshing to read Professor Caird who is prepared to present Jesus as a person with social conscience and political courage: 'We might suppose from the Matthean Beatitudes that Jesus was setting an ethical standard for entry into the kingdom, and that men must earn their blessedness by being humble, merciful and pure of heart. Luke's simpler version guards against this misrepresentation. The one thing Jesus requires in his disciples is an emptiness that God can fill, a discontent with the world which will lead them to wealth: the satisfaction, the consolation, the comradeship of the kingdom' (*Saint Luke,* p. 102).

It is, of course, impossible to say what Jesus '*meant*' but I suspect the answer to be simpler than expected. Maybe his words, on this occasion at least, were exactly as recorded. In verbal diction as in the Greek script the comma is merely implicit. May Jesus not have said: 'Blessed are the poor, in spirit'? in which case his meaning would have been that the poor are deprived of, and not blessed with, the good things of the earth, yet they are blessed in spirit. I have no reason to think that Jesus saw the poor in a similar light as Brueghel did in his amazing 'Sermon on the Mount', each peasant being a grotesque caricature of humanity. It is much more likely that in the embracing vision of Jesus they were all like St. Paul's 'little children' whom he loved. Even the blessing is in the eye of the beholder.

Woe unto you that are rich

It was, as has already been mentioned, a device of Jewish religious poetry to confront ten blessings (beatitudes) with ten woes (curses). Everywhere ten was a sacred number of mystics: the Egyptians employed it, the Pythagoreans glorified it, and the Jewish mystical schools used it frequently: the ten commandments, the ten plagues, the ten lost tribes, ten men constitute an independent religious community, tithes of one tenth, etc. Matthew uses the ten blessings in the fifth chapter of his gospel, but omits the woes. In Luke's report the beatitudes are incomplete, but we find three of the complementary woes. It is the first of these that concerns us here: 'But woe unto you that are rich!' (*Luke* 6:24), an unequivocal condemnation of those 'who have laid up treasures for themselves upon earth'.

The Old Testament is full of unfavourable references to the materially rich. 'The rich ruleth over the poor, and the borrower is servant to the lender' (*Prov.* 22:7); 'Better is he that walketh in his uprightness, than he that is perverse in his ways, though he be rich' (*Prov.* 28:6); 'If thou seest the oppression of the poor, and violent perverting of judgment and justice in the province . . .' (*Eccles.* 5:8); 'There is a sore evil which I have seen under the sun, riches kept for their owners to their hurt' (*Eccles.* 5:13) which text continues:" But those riches perish by evil travail . . . ' (*Eccles.* 5:14). Acquisitiveness is condemned: 'Better is little with righteousness than great income through injustice' (*Prov.* 16:18); and 'Woe unto them that join house to house, that lay field to field' (*Isaiah* 5:8).

Luke's words are an embarrassment for many commentators. Writing in *PC*, Professor Lampe avoids any mention of them. So does Bishop Wordsworth in his edition of the New Testament with detailed commentary. Dummelow says the words refer to 'those who possessing wealth, trust in it, or spend it in selfish luxury like Dives, and despise the poor and oppress them' (*OVBC*, p.748). He is also at pains to point out that 'St. Luke's sermon is much less striking than St. Matthew's . . . Some critics profess to find in St. Luke's sermon an Ebionitic, or as we should now say, a socialistic or communistic tendency. Probably wrongly . . . ' (ibid.).

Even Professor Caird disappoints us in his *Saint Luke*. He wonders whether the Woes should be ascribed to Jesus at all. According to him they interrupt the address and necessitate a clumsy resumption of the flow of the sermon. He believes that they are more likely to be commentaries of the early Church than the original words of Jesus. (p.101).

Treasures upon earth

Also in the Sermon on the Mount Jesus said: 'Lay not up for yourselves treasures upon earth, where moth and dust does corrupt, and where thieves break through and steal: But lay up for yourselves treasures in heaven, where neither moth nor dust doth corrupt, and where thieves do not break through and steal: for where your treasure is there will your heart be also' (*Matthew* 6:19/21). The same idea is recorded, somewhat differently, in Jesus' saying: 'Sell ye that ye have, and give alms, provide yourselves with bags which wax not old, a treasure in heaven that faileth not, where no thief approaches, neither moth corrupteth. For where your treasure is, there will your heart be also' (*Luke* 12:33/4). *Luke* 12:21, too, comes near to this idea: 'So is he that layeth up treasure for himself, and is not rich toward God!'.

Proverbs provide the Scriptural sources of the sayings: 'Labour not to be rich: cease from thine own wisdom' (23:4); and 'A faithful man shall abound with blessings; but he that maketh haste to be rich shall not be unpunished' (28:20). Similar passages are to be found in non-canonical books: 'His kinfolk said: Thy father gathered treasure, which thou hast squandered. He replied: My father laid up treasures upon earth, but I lay them up in heaven . . . ' (*Baba Batra* 11a); 'by righteousness lay up riches in the heavenly palace, in bags that wax not old, and where thieves do not break through nor steal' (*Testament of Levy,* 13:5); and 'If thou hast abundance, give almost accordingly: if thou hast but little, be not afraid to give according to that little: For thou layest up a good treasure for thyself against the day of necessity' (*Tobit,* 4:8/9).

Professor Lampe in *PC* suggests that alms seemed to the followers of Jesus not only a means to acquire merit but also a means to enter into the kingdom, 'the primary object of endeavour'. In his view, Luke may have considered these sayings as encouragement to the sharing of property which was obligatory in the early Church (*PC*, p.835). Professor Ginns volunteers this profound observation:'Luke's verses are well placed here where our Lord tells 'the Jews' [surprisingly not the *Chinese*] why they fail to see what is staring them in the face: their dispositions are evil' (*CC*, p.955). Dummelow talks of the 'right use of wealth' which results in the laying up of treasure in heaven! (*OVBC*, p.648).

On the whole, the commentators tend to present the saying not as an attack on riches, but rather as a call to charity, to alms, and to the sustenance of the poor. While Jesus deplored poverty, his alleged disciples present him as one anxious to perpetuate it while calling upon the rich to be more charitable. The similarity with the attitude of a great number of country vicars is undeniable.

Ye cannot serve God and Mammon

In the Sermon on the Mount we find also these momentous words: 'Ye cannot serve God and Mammon' (*Matthew* 6:24). The same words are quoted in *Luke* 16:13, both gospels presumably drawing on a common source known as 'Q'.

Mammon is said to be the Aramaic word for wealth or 'property'.

The Syriac 'mamunai' is translated by 'riches', the origin of the word seems to be 'hamon' i.e. abundance. The Scriptural origin of both imagery and saying is unknown. There is a possibility that it originates from *1 Kings* 18:21, 'How long halt ye between two opinions, if the Lord God, follow Him: but if Baal, then follow him.' The thought frequently appears in New Testament scripture, albeit in different wording: 'Do I seek to please men? for if I yet please men, I should not be the servant of Christ' (*Gal.* 1:10); 'Be not highminded, nor trust in uncertain riches, but in the living God . . . ' (*1 Tim.* 6:17); 'Whosoever . . . therefore will be a friend of the world is the enemy of God . . . ' (*James* 4:4); 'If any man love the world, the love of the Father is not in him' (*1 John* 2:15); but none of these equals in power and succinctness the saying of Jesus.

It is difficult to equivocate about this saying. Professor Jones admits it means that man must choose between God and gold, 'Each is in practice a jealous master. We must recognise that their interests will inevitably clash, and we must therefore declare for God or for Mammon' (*CC*, p.863). Professor Stendahl cautiously says, 'Mammon is used in rabbinic texts without any bad connotation, e.g. in legal texts like Mishna Sanhedrin, a fact which adds sharpness to this antithesis of Jesus' (*PC*, p.779). Professor Barclay, too, hastens to assure us that originally Mammon was not a bad word. He quotes a rabbinical writing (unnamed) which says: 'Let the mammon of thy neighbour be as dear to thee as thine own'. Eventually, however, Barclay claims, people began to put their trust in it, in fact it became their god. his conclusion is: 'Wealth is always subordinate good [sic] . . . the possession of wealth, money, material things is not a sin, but it is a grave responsibility . . . ' (*Gospel of St. Matthew*, pp.250/7). There are, according to Barclay, two decisive questions to be asked: How did a man gain his possessions? and, How does he use his possessions? And once more, he reassures us: 'A man will not go far wrong, if he uses his possessions to see how much happiness he can bring to others'.

I have so arranged these comments as to show how easy it is to quote the words of Jesus and yet to move farther away from their spirit. The justification of the apologists is to be found not in the teaching of Jesus, but in that of Paul: 'The *love of money* is the source of all evil' (*1 Tim.* 6:10). The commentators also prefer the modified 'them that trust in riches' of Mark, to the straightforward 'they that have riches' in Luke. Most of them forget the intractable saying: 'The care of this world, and the deceitfulness of riches, choke the word' (*Matthew* 13:22).

Many commentators seem to be concerned lest they offend the rich and powerful members of their congregations, the ones that provide all the money for institutional religion and for the material requirements of an organised clergy. How could they confront their benefactors with the words of the Teacher who condemned riches and believed that the service of God (spiritual values) inevitably conflicts with the service of Mammon (material values)?

The uppermost seats in the synagogues

Luke describes how Jesus, having accepted a Pharisee's invitation for dinner, enters the house of his host, sits down to a meal without performing the required act of courtesy and religious custom (the washing of hands – oriental people eat with their hands from a common dish) and proceeds to upbraid his host and his host's friends in a most ungracious manner: "Woe, unto you, Pharisees! for ye tithe mint and rue and all manner of herbs, and pass over judgment and the love of God: these ought ye have done and not to leave the other undone. Woe unto you, Pharisees! For ye love the uppermost seats in the synagogues, and greetings in the markets . . . ' (*Luke* 11:42/3). In another tirade against the Pharisees he exclaims: 'Woe unto you, scribes and Pharisees, hypocrites!' and in the course of his speech he says of them that they 'love the uppermost rooms at feasts, and the chief seats in the synagogues' (*Matthew* 23:6). During a discourse in the Temple, he warns: 'Beware of the scribes, which love to go in long clothing, and love salutations in the marketplaces, and the chief seats in the synagogues, and the uppermost rooms at feasts, which devour widow's houses . . .' (*Mark* 12:38/40). The 'devouring of widows' houses is also mentioned in *Matthew* 23:14. Luke likewise records the righteous anger of Jesus in the Temple, and his warning: 'Beware of the scribes, which desire to walk in long robes, and love greetings in the markets, and the highest seats in the synagogues, and the chief rooms at the feasts, which devour widows' houses . . .' (*Luke* 20:46/7).

The preoccupation with the 'uppermost rooms and chief seats' seems to have been general, and in the Epistle of James we encounter it again: 'For if there come unto your synagogue a man with a gold ring, in goodly apparel, and there come also a poor in vile raiment; And ye have respect to him that weareth the gay clothing, and say unto him, Sit thou here in a good place; and say to the poor, Stand thou there, or sit here under my footstool, Are ye not the partial in yourselves, and are become judges of evil thoughts? Hath not God chosen the poor of this world rich in faith . . . ? But ye have despised the poor. Do not rich men oppress you . . . ?' (*James* 2:3/6).

In the *CC* Professor Ginns glosses over the situation and the strange words of *Luke* 11:42/3, neither does he comment closely on 20:46/7. In the same volume Professor Jones has not much to say about *Matthew* 23:6 either: 'The whole chapter is a warning to those who are or may be deceived by the worst element in Phariseeism. It is with this in view that our Lord mercilessly exposes them' (p.892). A little more is said by Professor O'Flynn, commenting on *Mark* 12:38/40. According to him, the scribes had failed as teachers, and given the people a bad example which is the more reprehensible because they are supposed to be strict followers of the divine Law. Jesus condemns their greed and vanity, and their ruses to deceive the most defenceless members of the community, the widows, by their pretence of charitable piety (p.924). Professor Willmering, the commentator on James, is somewhat more daring. He points out that the Church should show respect for people regardless of their wealth, and not indulge in 'snobbish and unjust judgment'. And alone among the commentators, he has the courage to say: 'The rich, as a class, are enemies of Christ and of his followers' (p.1175).

We will be disappointed if we expected more from the Protestant *PC*. Professor Lampe, who commenting on *Luke* 11:42/3, complains that 'justice and the love of God have been subordinated to legalism' (p.835), an inconsequential remark. About *Luke* 20:42/3 we hear the usual clichés. The scribes are examples of the Jewish leaders' complacency and worldliness, and 'the saying shows how the poor are vindicated in contrast with the self-righteous rulers of Israel' (p.839). Any specific comment on *Matthew* 23:6 is avoided, but *Mark* 12:38/40 is discussed by R.M. Wilson who states that Jesus condemns the practices of the scribes, accusing them of vanity and ostentation as well as hypocrisy. Their greed in exploiting the poor is in direct contradiction to the Old Testament which frequently enjoins care for the widows and fatherless. 'The scribes are charged with violation of the Law they profess to expound'(p.813).

According to Professor Fenton the aim of the saying is to warn the disciples against attitudes of scribes and Pharisees (*St. Matthew* p.367), while Professor Nineham thinks that the scribes extorted large sums from old women under the pretext of piety (*Saint Mark*, p.333). Here again Nineham shows a discernment unusual among Christian commentators in stating: 'We have no reason to think that . . . "devouring widows houses" was common among the scribes . . . there was also a very large number of good ones' (ibid., p.334). And he continues by quoting Vincent Taylor who wrote: 'A hostile attitude to Judaism and to the rabbis is reflected in the choice and use of these sayings, despite the probability that they represent actual utterance of Jesus.'

Professor Caird goes even further in expressing doubt whether Jesus did deliver 'a single great harangue such as this against the Pharisees, and still more unlikely that he did it while a guest in a Pharisee's house' (*Luke* p. 158). Only Professor Barclay states unequivocally that the religion of the Pharisees was a religion of ostentation, trying to impress people with their demonstrative observance of rules, while insisting that they should be shown every respect for their piety in the manner of address and in their seating at feasts (op cit., pp. 316/7).

From these examples it may be seen that many Christian commentators assert that Jesus generally condemned the scribes and Pharisees (in most languages spoken by Christian peoples the word 'Pharisee' has come to mean 'hypocrite'.) They are being held up as examples of religious *mauvaise foi*. The truth is probably far removed from this assumption.

Who were the Pharisees? Who were the scribes? Perhaps we can leave aside for the moment the testimony of the gospels. After the return from Babylonian captivity there was a strong trend among the Jews toward a stricter observance of the Law. It originated in the circles of the prophets Ezra and Nehemiah, and eventually led to the resistance against the hellenising efforts of the Seleucids. The movement in the vanguard of this trend was called the Hasidim, the 'pious ones', even today known as Hasideans or Chassidim. They insisted on the strictest observance of religious and ritual laws, down to the smallest detail, and were prepared to go to any length to achieve this end. They are frequently mentioned in the Old Testament: 'Then there united with them a company of Hasideans, mighty warriors of Israel, every one who offered himself willingly for the law' (*Macc.* 2:42); and, 'Then a group of scribes appeared . . . to ask for just terms. The Hasideans were the first among the sons of Israel to seek peace . . .' (*Macc.* 7:12/3). Their zeal and righteousness singled them out among their fellows, from whom they became increasingly 'separated', which word is the etymological origin of the term 'Pharisee'. Some of their number were of course full of overbearing pride and casuistry, but then have there ever existed fanatics who were not self-righteous, over-confident and humourless? There is every reason to believe that Jesus himself had been for a time a member of, or at least in full sympathy with, the Pharisee party; and we certainly know of Paul that prior to his 'conversion' he was himself a fanatical Pharisee. The new Testament speaks with great respect of well-known Pharisees such as

Nicodemus, Simon and Gamaliel. In fact, it is recorded that Jesus called upon his disciples to *exceed* the righteousness of the Pharisees: 'Except your righteousness shall exceed the righteousness of the scribes and pharisees, ye shall in no case enter the kingdom of Heaven' (*Matthew* 5:20). He uttered this saying after having assured his listeners that 'one jot or one tittle shall in no wise pass from the Law' (*Matthew* 5:18), a principle which we may consider as the basic doctrine of Phariseeism. It is also recorded that he was addressed as 'Rabbi', a title used to honour scribes and Pharisees.

The famous bible-scholar, Julius Wellhausen, emphasised that Jesus based his teaching on the Bible referred to by Christians as *The Old Testament*, and never denied his Judaic faith (*Israelitische and jüdische Geschichte*, p.360). A nineteenth-century work by an anonymous Jew claims that hypocrisy was not widespread among the Pharisees at the time of Jesus: far from paying lip service to ritual laws rather than practising charity and the love of mankind, most Pharisees were themselves contemptuous of their hypocritical colleagues. Even the words of Jesus show that his strictures were aimed at insincere Pharisees and not at the true Pharisees (Klausner, *JN* p. 113). Another Jewish author, M. Friedländer, is quoted by Klausner: 'At first Jesus favoured the ceremonial law . . . then he rose in opposition only against insincere Pharisees . . . the more disreputable among them whom the Talmud itself blames and doubts "the plague of Pharisees"; not till later times did the evangelists generalise Jesus' strictures and repeat them as though they were aimed at the Pharisees as a whole' (ibid., p. 117). Daniel Chwolson was yet more explicit: 'Jesus said and taught nothing which the true Pharisee could not have subscribed to, and did nothing with which they could find fault' (*Das letzte Passamahl Christi*, pp.95/6).

The Old Testament calls the Pharisees 'mighty warriors of Israel', and indeed it is recorded by Josephus that in the first decade B.C. many Pharisees refused to swear allegiance to the Roman Emperor and to King Herod, and were slain (*Ant.* 17:2:4). While the Saducees were willing collaborators of Rome, the Pharisees, even if they did not advocate open defiance like the Zealots, always maintained an attitude of passive resistance.

An interesting description of the Pharisees is given by Klausner: 'These were the popular party, the representatives of the middle classes . . . and to some extent in the villages . . . and of the enlightened nationalists whose education consisted of the national Torah (Law) and its interpretations . . . they represented that national democracy in Maccabean times and in the time of Jesus . . . They were remarkable also for their high ethical standards and their aloofness from the pleasures of life, and for this reason Josephus likens them to the Greek stoics. The Tannaim and Amoraim and Jews as a whole are all of them no more than the successive generations of the disciples of the Pharisees who perpetuated the work of the "Scribes" and laid the foundation of the Talmud and all later Jewish literature . . . ' (*JN*, p.212).

The strictures of the New Testament were certainly not undeserved as far as some Pharisees were concerned. Josephus himself records that the Pharisees were 'Jews who valued themselves highly upon the exact skill they had in the Law of their fathers . . . and made men believe they were highly favoured by God' (*Ant.* 17:2:4). But the Talmud is also critical of the false and hypocritical individuals among them: 'A stupid hasid, a cunning knave, a female devotee and the plague of the Pharisees are they who destroy the world' (*Mishna Sota* 3:4); and, 'There are seven kinds of Pharisees; the shoulder Pharisee, the bookkeeper, the mock- humility pestle, the dutiful observer, the doom-fearing Pharisee, and then the seventh, the true, out-of-love Pharisee' (*Merakoth* 9:5/7). Jesus himself, Klausner says, may not have been wholly a Pharisee – he was like any 'Rab', much more of a Pharisee than a Saducee. The Essenes and Zealots were . . . the exponents of certain extreme aspects of Phariseeism' (op. cit., p.215).

The scribes were originally high State officials, secretaries of the king. 'And Zadok the son of Ahitub, and Akimeleh the son of Abiathar were the priests; and Seraiah was the scribe . . . '(*2 Sam.* 8:17); 'and Sheva was a scribe . . . ' (*2 Sam.* 20:25); 'the king's scribe and the high priest came up . . . ' (*2 Kings* 12:10); 'And he sent Eliakim who was over the household, and Shebna the scribe to the House of the Lord . . . ' (*2 Kings* 19:2); and, 'This is the copy of the words of the commandments of the Lord and of the statutes to Israel . . . ' (*Ezra* 7:11). The word recurs in Jeremiah where it seems, the prophet deplores the attitude of 'the wise men and the scribes: How do ye say, we are wise, and the Law of the Lord is with us: Lo, certainly in vain made he it, the pen of the scribes is in vain.. The wise men are ashamed, they are dismayed and taken, lo, they have rejected the word of the Lord: and what wisdom is in them?' (*Jer.* 8:8/9). This passage may of course be read as a failure of the word of God and the work of the scribes to enter into the hearts of the foolish wise. We shall never know which interpretation is correct.

In any case, Pharisees and scribes were by no means identical. The Pharisees constituted a political faction, or at least displayed a certain political attitude. The scribes were men learned in Scripture, 'doctors of the Law', teachers of legal and traditional writings. They taught in the Temple, in the synagogues, and even in private houses. Their pupils sat on the ground, committing to memory their teachers' words, learning by question and answer, and by discussion. The most famous of the teachers in the period preceding Jesus were Hillel and Shammai, by no means hypocrites but men counted among the greatest ethical teachers of all times. Jesus probably disagreed with many scribes, as a man of faith and learning inevitably would, but he would not have indulged in diatribes against '*the* scribes and *the* Pharisees', that is, the learned men of Israel.

It is not my intention here to prove that Pharisees who shared many of Jesus' view on religion and social conditions, or scribes who may have belonged to any political or religious group, were not responsible for the passion and death of Jesus. There have been many outstanding scholars during the past hundred years who have performed that task. I am trying to show that Jesus himself is unlikely to have abused and attacked '*the* scribes and *the* Pharisees.'

We may consider once again *James* 2:2/6 in conjunction with two other passages from James' Epistles, remembering that James was very close to Jesus, probably his brother. "But the rich in that he is made low: because as the flower of the grass he shall pass away. For the sun is no sooner risen with a burning heat, but it withereth the grass, and the flower thereof falleth, and the grace of the fashion thereof perisheth: so also shall the rich man fade away in his ways" (*James* 1:10/11); and, "Go to now, ye rich men, weep and howl for your miseries that shall come upon you. Your riches are corrupted, and your garments are moth-eaten. Your gold and silver is cankered, and the rust of them shall be witness against you, and shall eat your flesh as it were fire. Ye have reaped treasure together for the last days. Behold, the hire of the labourers, who have reaped down your fields, which is kept of you back by fraud, crieth: and the cries of them, which have reaped are entered in the ears of the Lord . . . Ye have lived in pleasure on earth, and been wanton; ye have nourished your hearts, as in a day of slaughter, ye have condemned and killed the just, and he doth not resist you . . . " (*James* 5:1.6). Take these passages and relate them to James' complaint that the rich take "the uppermost seats in the synagogues", and you may see the attitude which has probably prevailed among the closest associates of Jesus.

I do not claim that this view can be proven or substantiated by Scripture. I merely suggest the likelihood that the accusations against 'the scribes and the Pharisees' were in the original sayings, tirades against the rich. Probably much of the teaching of Jesus was directed against the rich rulers of Judaea, and indeed it is much more likely that his words, now regarded as critical of his own kind, were really addressed to those who were natural enemies of his doctrine: the rich and powerful. Let us, therefore, see how some of the sayings would read if they were altered in accordance with this hypothesis.

'Woe unto you, ye rich men! for ye tithe the mint and rue and all manner of herbs, and pass over judgment and the love of God: these ought ye have done and not to leave the other undone. Woe unto you, ye rich men! for ye love the uppermost seats in the synagogues and greetings in the market . . . '. Since the Pharisees could not be accused of tithing the herbs and little luxuries of cooking, which they did not and could not do, it is possible that the rich and powerful were exposed here who might have done these things. It would also explain Jesus' behaviour which would indeed have been reprehensible if he had entered into a tirade against *the* Pharisees while being the guest of one. 'Woe unto you, ye rich men, hypocrites! For ye devour widows' houses and for a pretence make long prayer: therefore ye shall receive the greater damnation.' It is difficult to explain why Pharisees should have 'devoured widows' houses': it becomes quite clear if the words did refer to the rich. 'Beware of the rich who love to go in long clothing, and love salutations in the market place, And the chief seats in the synagogues and the uppermost rooms at feasts. Which devour widows' houses, and for a pretence make long prayers: these shall receive greater damnation.' The corresponding passage in *Mark* 12:38/30 is followed by a confrontation of the alms given by the rich, and by the poor widow. And it is after this event that Jesus tells the parable about 'a certain rich man' and Lazarus, the beggar.

Admittedly only circumstantial evidence supports my assumption. I realise also that Jesus' outbursts against hypocritical Pharisees are usually interpolated with tirades against the rich. My suspicion is merely that – for expedient reasons – the early Church transposed many of the diatribes as being attacks on 'the scribes and the Pharisees'. After all there were many rich people among the new believers, some of whom were willing to make considerable sacrifices, while there was no need to consider the sensitivities of the scribes and Pharisees.

We shall never know whether this assumption is correct or not. The earliest manuscripts of the New Testament fragments we possess, with one notable six-line exception, are from the second century. Their writers were Greeks or hellenised Jews, believers, who based their accounts on verbal tradition. It is impossible to say what changes occurred in the evangelical texts during the intervening years, and whether the tradition was preserved in writing or only verbally.

The camel and the needle's eye

Everybody knows the story of the young man who came to Jesus for advice on how to attain 'eternal life'. Jesus recommends the keeping of the commandments. In the words of Matthew: 'The young man saith unto him, All these things I have kept from my youth up: what lack I yet? Jesus said unto him: if thou wilt be perfect, go and sell that thou hast, and give to the poor, and thou shalt have treasure in heaven: and come and follow me. But when the young man heard that saying, he went away sorrowful: for he had great possessions. Then said Jesus unto his disciples, Verily I say unto you, That a rich man shall hardly enter into the kingdom of heaven. And again I say unto you, It is easier for a camel to go through the eye of a needle, than for a rich man to enter into the kingdom of God. When his disciples heard it, they were exceedingly amazed, saying, Who then can be saved? But Jesus beheld them, and said unto them, With men this is impossible, but with God all things are possible' (*Matthew* 19:20/6). We find almost the same text with slight changes in *Mark* 10:20/7 and *Luke* 18:21/7.

Only part of these texts has its origin in Jewish Scripture. The 'camel' passage may be related to some jocular words of the Talmud, 'Are you not from Pumpeditha where they draw elephants through a needle's eye?' (*Baba Mazia* 38b); but the saying that 'with God everything is possible' is definitely Old Testament 'Is anything too hard for the Lord?' (*Gen.* 18:14); 'I know that thou canst do everything' (*Job* 42:2); and, 'There is nothing too hard for thee' (*Jer.* 32:17). Mark's words 'trust in riches' may be related to 'This is the man that made not God his strength, but trusted in the abundance of his riches' (*Psalm* 52:7); 'If riches increase, set not your heart upon them' (*Psalm* 62:10); and, 'He that trusteth in his riches, shall fall . . . ' (*Prov.* 11:28). On the whole, however, the text shows an original approach by Jesus who despised riches and exalted voluntary poverty.

In the *CC* Professor Jones draws the conclusion that 'it is *with difficulty* [his italics] that the rich shall enter the kingdom of heaven' and asserts that Jesus here is talking of 'not impossibility but of difficulty'. He continues by saying that Jesus 'did not condemn the rich young man but illustrates from his case how riches may grip and even suffocate the heart'. And he draws the moral of the story by stating that 'our Lord explains that divine grace accomplishes the humanly impossible', thus turning the rider of the story into its intent (p.886). As we seen, this, and many other commentaries demonstrate how easy it is to interpret any doctrine in accordance with one's own preferences and prejudices. Professor O'Flynn says about the Marcan passage that riches are not evil in themselves but worldly goods are merely placed in trust into human hands by God, and therefore exaggerated love of wealth can be compared to idolatry. He adds, 'What is humanly impossible does not exceed the power of God. With the aid of grace . . . the rich man can be saved' (p.921). Commenting on the text of Luke, Professor Ginns also emphasises that 'riches in themselves are neither good nor bad', and that only attachment to riches is reprehensible. God can save even him who does not give away his riches 'provided he acts like a good steward in the sense of the parable of 16:1 to 9' (p.961).

After allowing that riches 'are an almost insuperable barrier to Christian discipleship' the Protestant Professor Nineham points out that the Christian's right to keep his property depends on his willingness to achieve inner detachment from worldly things.' Nineham too is anxious to show that the 'apparent contradiction . . . is resolved in this saying of Jesus that all things are possible with God . . . ' (*PC*, p.271/2). The Luke commentator, Professor Caird, believes that 'the peril of possessions is that they stand in the way of . . . receptive faith.' The rich and powerful man 'must cast himself simply on the divine compassion' (both *PC*, p.205).

In the commentary on Matthew by Professor Barclay we find the spurious view that by camel (kamélos) really a ship's hawser (kamilos) may have been meant, and that the 'needle's eye' was possibly the little gate within the big main gate of Jerusalem. Barclay enumerates the ways in which riches may endanger a man's entry into the kingdom: riches may encourage a false independence, it may shackle a man to this earth and it may tend to make him selfish. Afraid that he has gone too far already, Barclay hastens to add: 'Jesus did not say that it was impossible for a rich man to enter the kingdom of Heaven . . . it is not that those who have riches are shut out. It is not that riches are a sin – they are a danger' (*The Gospel of St. Matthew,* pp.239/42).

It is noteworthy that the commentators (including, unfortunately, Professor Nineham, who often shows discernment and integrity) agree on describing riches as a burden or 'danger', but they are quite unwilling to admit that Jesus condemned riches without reservation. They also point out that non-attachment to riches or the 'right use of wealth' can redeem the rich man from this dangerous involvement. They seem to take their cue from the Church Father, St. Hilary, who writes: 'It is not a sin to be rich, for how can a man give largely without means? But it is a sin to covet wealth and to dote upon it.' The apologists try to play down the severe judgment of Jesus, making much of the saying that 'with God everything is possible', by which

Jesus may have implied that by the grace of God a rich man may even abandon his riches. Most of them repudiate the hoary and discredited interpretation concerning ropes and small gates, yet some still find it necessary to mention the possibility of such argument. Glancing through many commentaries I have not found one which goes along with Jesus in his unconditional condemnation of great wealth. With near-unanimity they impose upon Jesus their own view that 'It is not a sin to be rich'. Graves and Podro mention the possibility that *Matthew* 10:24 'who trust their riches' was an interpolation to reassure wealthy Christians that prayer, faith and good works may enable the rich man to enter the Kingdom (*NGR*, p. 521)

In this context we may note that one of the apocryphal gospels, the one 'According to the Hebrews' contains this passage: 'The second of the rich men said unto him: Master what good things can I do and live? He said unto him, O Man fulfil the law and the prophets. He answered him, I have kept them. He said unto him: Good, sell all that thou ownest, and distribute it unto the poor, and come follow me. But the rich man began to scratch his head, and it pleased him not. And the Lord said unto him: How sayest thou, I have kept the law and the prophets? For it is written in the law: Thou shalt love thy neighbour as thyself, and lo, many of thy brethren, sons of Abraham, are clad in filth, dying for hunger, and thine house if full of many good things, and nought at all goeth out of it to them. And he turned and said unto Simon his disciple who was sitting by him: Simon son of Jonah, it is easier for a camel to enter in by a needle's eye than for a rich man to enter into the kingdom of heaven' (*The Apocryphal New Testament* p. 6). There does not seem to be any mention of the usual escape clause: 'With God everything is possible'.

The manuscript has been lost and the text is spurious. It shows, however, that the early Church considered the saying as referring to the effect of worldly riches.

I may mention that the *Holy Koran*, too, uses this metaphor: 'Lo! they who deny Our revelation and scorn it, for them the Gates of heaven will not be opened nor will they enter the Garden until the camel goeth through the needle's eye' (7:40, Mentor edition p. 124).

From each according to his ability

The community, in the days after the death of Jesus, lived in a form of primitive communism. 'All that believed were together, and had all things in common. And sold their possessions and goods, and parted them to all men, as every man had need' (*Acts* 2:44/5). 'Their principles were; 'Every man according to his ability' (*Acts* 11:29) and 'unto every man according as he had need' (*Acts* 4:35). The result was a congregation of believers that 'were of one heart and one soul: neither said any of them that ought of the things which he possessed was his own: but they had all things common. Neither was there any of them that lacked: for as many as were possessors of lands or houses sold them, and brought the prices of the things that were sold . . . ' (*Acts* 4:32/34). We are told what happened to those who tried to keep back part of the proceeds for their own personal benefit: the story of the tragic end of Ananias and Saphira, his wife, who tried to lie 'to the living God' is well-known.

It seems that until the advent of Saulus of Tarsus, the community of the followers under the leadership of James, 'the brother of the Lord', developed communistic tendencies in the wake of the doctrine of Jesus. When, however, Saulus appeared on the scene, and as the self-styled Apostle Paul began the demolition of the Law and the introduction of new religious principles, the original disciples resisted him. Those who would not fit into the eventually triumphant Pauline organisation, withdrew and became a 'sect' under the name Ebionites. They were persecuted by Romans, Jews and Pauline Christians alike, and later withdrew beyond the river Jordan. Their last traces disappear about two centuries later in the rock-city of Petra.

Speculation has been rife as to whether or not Jesus was a Communist of ancient stamp; a social reformer intending to transform the people of Judaea according to a preconceived pattern. It seems he did not share two important assumptions of modern Communism: (a) that people can, through an act of mere reasoning, change the human condition; and (b) that the order of things can be changed through social ordinance. For Jesus the problem was how to project the kingdom of heaven which is potentially within us, into the external world: and, secondly, how to bring about a complete reorientation of the human being and not merely a change in his thinking.

Some outstanding scholars disagree with this assessment. George Bernard Shaw, always a great simplifier, states unequivocally that Jesus 'was a communist; that he regarded much of what we call law and order as machinery for robbing the poor under legal forms; that he thought domestic ties a snare for the soul; that he agreed with the proverb "The nearer the Church, the farther from God"; that he saw plainly that the masters of the community should be its servants and not its oppressors and parasites; and that though he did not tell us to fight our enemies, he did tell us to love them, and warned us that they who draw the sword shall perish by the sword' (*Androcles and the Lion*, p.38). I might agree that Jesus, with some important reservations, believed all these things: what I am not willing to accept it that the 'Communists' believe them.

A statement by Professor Lewis is rather apt: 'The Gospel is rich in social morality, in egalitarian and revolutionary ethics. It is amazing with what obtuseness scholars and preachers move unheeding through its pages, or with heavy insensitiveness busy themselves with taking the edge off the Sermon on the Mount' (*Christianity and Social Revolution*, p.92).

Discussing Karl Kautsky's writing, the well-known American writer on psychology, Erich Fromm, says: 'Kautsky, in *Vorläufer des neuen Sozialismus,* and later in *Foundations of Christianity,* has set forth the view that Christianity is a proletarian class-movement, that in essence, however, its significance lay in its practical activity, that is, in its charitable work and not in its pious fanaticism. Kautsky overlooks the fact that a movement may have a class- origin without the existence of social and economic motives in the consciousness of its instigators. Although Kautsky misses the real problem, the class foundation of early Christianity are nevertheless so clear that the tortuous attempts . . . to explain them away and weaken them, betrays the political tendencies of the writers concerned' (*The Dogma of Christ,* p.34). The same accusation, even if it is true, may of course be levelled against Fromm himself: any thorough study of the origins of Christianity would show that it is very difficult, if not impossible, to discern any definite 'class foundation' in its beginnings. This would save Fromm the trouble of analysing works such as those of Kautsky.

To all men according to their need

There has always been a 'communist' trend among Christians. The majority and the Church(es) never shared it, but it raised its head again and again, and led to the foundation of monastic orders. The outsider, however, was never quite sure whether the communist trend was decisive or not, and this uncertainty resulted in persecution by those who wished to suppress it. The Emperor Hadrian, himself anxious to alleviate the lot of the small man, regarded the Christians as meddlesome extremists and, in spite of his otherwise liberal views, persecuted them. And indeed, the hatred of the poor for the rich, of the maltreated slave for his master, of the uneducated for the learned Pharisee, of the Sicari rebel for the conformist – they all found their way into the newly organised Christianity. Far more than the doctrine of love, taught by Jesus, it was the hate for the oppressor which led to the rapid influx of new supporters. Once in the Church, their antagonisms were transformed by the Pauline doctrine into a strange kind of submissiveness and 'domestication'. Eventually, in the fourth century, the Roman State recognised that the Church did not represent a 'communist' threat, but offered the greatest security for the *status quo* of power and wealth. Christianity became the State-religion.

One of the great conformists of Christian thought, Martin Luther, gave forceful expression to this particular role of the Church. He became the favourite of powerful German princes and wealthy landowners because of his doctrines which masqueraded as unequivocal interpretations of Christian ideas: 'Riches are the slightest thing on earth, the smallest gift which God can bestow upon a man,' said Luther in one of his recorded discourses. 'What is it, compared with the gifts of the Spirit? What indeed, compared with the word of God? And yet people are so eagerly after it! . . . That is why our Lord God bestows riches on Asses whom He would not grant anything the better' (*Luther im Gespräch* (Luther's Table Talk V 5559, p. 288). I am certain the Asses are quite satisfied with that particular gift, while those without it feel completely content at being recipients of the Word, Beauty and the Spirit.

'I am not interested in mining shares,' exclaimed Luther, 'They are like chips which profit you nothing, like gambling money. And it's not even a gamble. If it were, it would depend on our will whether we risk winning or losing. But I am told that the whole thing is full of deception and injustice. I have often been tempted to have such shares, but I've never succumbed to the temptation' (ibid., V 5675, p. 293). It is interesting to learn of the reasons which made Luther abstain from gambling in mining shares, at a period of history when child labour in mines was taken for granted.

'Community of possessions is not natural law,' he said in another context. 'Neither is it decreed, merely permitted. If it were decreed, that decree could not be lived up to, owing to our sinful nature. There would always be some who consumed more than they produced, and this would result in confusion' (ibid., IV 4007, p. 197). But the way in which this allegedly great mind worked is best manifested in his dicta concerning the Great Peasant War: 'A God who is merciful is not the God suitable for these peasants. He who sends war and pestilence, He is just right for them' (ibid., III 3094, p. 133).

Luther is indignant that the clerics should not receive the material support to which they are 'entitled': 'Peasants and citizens are so impious that they are not prepared to support even one preacher. If that were not done by the princes and noblemen, we would not last long. For this reason Isaiah was right when he said "And kings shall be thy nursing fathers, and their queens thy nursing mothers" (*Isaiah* 49:23). Peasants certainly will not do so, as our present troubles with this ungrateful breed show us' (ibid., IV 4007, p. 192). [In *Isaiah* 49 God addresses these words to Zion!]

Another typical episode which reveals the 'great' reformer's thinking, is told by the recorder of his table talk: 'A speculator in Wittenberg bought a house for 30 florins, redecorated and sold it for 400. When this case was discussed, Luther said: "Does that scoundrel think that rotten beams are as valuable as useful commodities? If he persists in his shameful enterprise he should be excommunicated from the Christian community and, in any case, do not let him think that he belongs in heaven! It would be more than enough if he had sold it for 150 florins. But if he finds a buyer who pays him the exorbitant price of 400 *I* shall excommunicate him. It's high time excommunication were re-introduced!" (ibid., III 2958, p. 105).

The Catholic *QB* is very careful in its approach to the delicate problem of material possessions. Of the communism of the early Christians it says that it resembled the communal life of monastic orders but 'in no way implied a denial of private ownership'. The authors believe that it was based on voluntary agreement and not on any demand the Church made on its members. As a proof of this view Peter is quoted as saying to Ananias: 'Whilst it remained, did it not remain to thee? And after it was sold, was it not in thy power?' (*Acts* 5:4). There is forceful support for the opinion upheld by the Church Fathers which proclaims the right to own private property. They are said to have denounced the unlawful acquisition of wealth, but were not against lawful riches, and indeed some of them retained personal ownership of several estates (St. Basil, St. Ambrose). In fact, St. Jerome taught that 'wealth is not an obstacle to the rich man, if he uses it well' (p. 415). Apropos, what happened to Ananias?

The Catholic Church claims that it does not side with the rich, but upholds the right of private property and therefore condemns what it calls 'socialism'. Its approach to these problems led to the famous encyclical *Rerum Novarum* of 1891 in which Pope Leo XIII declared 'the proposals of Socialism are emphatically unjust because, by destroying private property, they would rob the lawful possessor, bring the State into a sphere that is not its own, and cause complete confusion in the community. Note, how, just like Luther, the modern Pontiff is afraid of economic confusion. What would happen, we may ask ourselves, if, what some like to call the 'counsel of perfection' of Jesus were acted upon by most people? One is constrained to think that the Luthers and

Popes of this world would fear nothing more than a change of heart among Christians which would prompt them to *act* in the spirit of the Teacher. Also revealing is the following ambiguous passage in *Rerum Novarum:* 'Whenever the general interest of any particular class suffers or is threatened with injury, which can in no other way be met or prevented, it is the duty of the public authority to intervene.'

We read in the *QB* that 'Catholic moralists have always admitted the evil of modern capitalism, its excessive love of gambling and speculation, its shrinking of personal responsibility, its manipulations of the press and the like. But while fully admitting these evils, they hold that they are less than the evils attendant upon Socialism. For Socialism is a quack cure, worse than the disease ... Catholic moralists, again, teach that the right of property in material things is a moral right, founded in human nature. It belongs not merely to the community at large, but to private corporations, families and individuals. Every man has the right, not only to a general use of nature's bounty but to the possession of goods as his own. 'This right extends not only over objects consumed in production, such as land, mines, railroads, factories, stores, banks, etc.' (p. 417).

Which is not surprising if we consider that one of the largest Italian banking corporations, the Banco di Santo Spirito (Bank of the Holy Ghost) [which may be just a coincidence of names, but how significant!] is owned mainly by the Catholic Church. In those countries where the Church still wields considerable influence, it owns a large part of landed estates. The Churches of the Reformation were no exception either. The Church of England, as everyone knows, retains enormous property in the form of land, real estate, bonds and shares. After all, clergymen must live, and the teaching of Jesus most imprudently did not provide for sources of substantial income: he did not envisage the survival of priestly caste. It was up to the Church to see that the Teacher's omission was duly corrected.

All these things shall be added unto you

In the Sermon on the Mount, Jesus assured his listeners: 'Seek ye first the kingdom of God, and his righteousness; and all these things shall be added unto you' (*Matthew* 6:33). We meet the same saying – a proof of its Q origin – in Luke: 'Seek ye the kingdom of God, and all these things shall be added unto you' (*Luke* 12:31). This phrase is the nearest Jesus ever came to giving a political or social testimony, and indeed it is perhaps one of the most important passages in the Gospels. Its scriptural origin is doubtful, it may be related in spirit to the text: 'If ye busy yourselves with the words of the Law, God will provide such food for you also' (*Mekilta* 2:126).

Christian commentators have been unable to make much of this important saying. In the *CC* Professor Jones merely remarks that 'Provided man calmly pursues his labour, God will provide' (p.864). *PC* commentator Professor Stendahl, says inconsequentially that 'Matthew brings the "righteousness of God" into parallelism with the kingdom. Both are the objects of man's undivided concern and both are about to be given' (p.779). Professor Fenton's remark is even more inane: 'The prayer which Jesus had taught the disciples did not include petitions for clothing, and even the petition for food may have been a petition for the kingdom. That is what the disciples are to pray for, and to trust God to give them *all these things* as well. Even the verbose Professor Barclay finds nothing worthy of special attention in this passage. Dummelow completely ignores it. So does the otherwise highly conscientious Bishop Wordsworth. Not wanting to think that the disregard for this important saying is intentional, I can only conclude that its significance has escaped the commentators.

Strangely enough, it was one of the 'rebel priests', Conrad Noel, sometime vicar of Thaxted, who discerned the meaning of this key to the doctrine of Jesus: 'It is the basic law of the New World Order of which Jesus says: "Seek ye first the kingdom of God and His justice, and all these things will be added unto you". These things, it will be seen from the context, refer not to blessings in the sky, but to material things such as food, clothing and shelter' (*Christianity and Social Revolution,* p.64). He continues relevantly: 'Amongst Christians who do not deny what they lamely call the "social implications of the Gospels", there often exists an assumption that Jesus Christ gave certain persons their immense wealth, or their more modest incomes, to use in his service and for the advancement of his kingdom. It is asserted not only of individuals, but of countries with their God-given "civilising mission" to "lesser breeds without the law" . . . A delightful, if somewhat blasphemous example of this may be seen in a recent prayer published by the authority of Church of England officials. It begins as follows: "Almighty God, who rulest in the kingdom of men, and hast given our sovereign Lord, King George, a great dominion in all parts of the earth . . . ". When we consider how our Empire has been obtained – by fraud, trickery and violence – the unctuous assumption that God has bestowed it upon His chosen Englishmen is almost British-Israelite in its pharisaic naïveté' (ibid.).

A writer who recognised the saying's true significance is J. Middleton Murry: 'Men were to become sons of God; if they became sons of God, they and all things would be changed. Not gently changed, in the sense that bad men would become good, but radically, catastrophically changed. A new kind of life, a new order of consciousness would begin, as different from that which men have now, as human life and consciousness are different from animal life and consciousness. Between these two is an abyss. Such an abyss mankind would have leaped when they became sons of God' (*Life of Jesus*, p.70).

On the whole, we may say that the full weight of the saying has hardly been noticed by most Christians. The words somehow complement that other momentous text: 'Why call me Lord, Lord, and do not the things that I say?!' Merging the two passages, Jesus thought may be reconstructed in this way: 'Do the things that I have told and taught you, and you will transform the world around you. The kingdom of Heaven which is within you will become manifest in the world; and following my teaching you will show consideration and trust for one another, greed and violence will disappear; and working together in mutual respect, men will share the fruits of their experience and in their labour – creating plenty for all.' This dream of a truly great man is alien to his self-styled followers, and this is perhaps the reason why his call has remained 'a voice crying in the wilderness'.

9
War And Violence

I came not to send peace

Many Christians and, understandably, their enemies also, like to quote these words: 'Think not that I am come to send peace on earth: I came not to send peace but a sword' (*Matthew* 10:34). However, the sequel is readily forgotten: 'For I came to set a man at variance against his father, and a daughter against her mother, and a daughter-in-law against her mother-in-law. And a man's foe shall be they of his own household'. In the Gospel according to Luke we read: 'Suppose ye that I am come to give peace on earth? I tell you, Nay but rather division. For from henceforth there shall be five in one house divided, three against two and two against three. A father shall be divided against the son, and the son against the father; the mother against the daughter and the daughter against the mother; and the mother-in-law against the daughter-in- law, and the daughter-in-law against the mother-in-law' (*Luke* 12:51/53). We see that Jesus did not mean tribal or national war, nor *any* murderous group- conflict, but the mental conflict which sets his followers at variance with their nearest and dearest. The saying itself has its origin in the Old Testament: 'For the son dishonoureth the father, the daughter rises up against her mother, the daughter-in-law against her mother-in- law,: a man's enemies are the men of his own house' (*Micah* 7:6). This verse of Micah was frequently quoted among the Jews to show the impact of the Messiah will have on people, and the divisions caused by his coming. It is in fact an echo of the words attributed to the revered teacher Moses: 'Who said unto his father and his mother, I have not seen you: neither did he acknowledge his brethren, nor knew his own children; for they have observed thy word, and kept the covenant' (*Deut.* 33:9). All this implies that the disciples endangers his relations with his family. The 'two against three' in Luke confronts the two members of the younger generation with the three members of the older one.

Of course, Christian apologists will comment on these saying without touching upon the essential point. Dummelow, for instance, argues: 'Christ could not expect that His claims to absolute dominion over the soul of man and all human institutions would be accepted without a bitter struggle. But knowing such a struggle to be necessary for the establishment of peace with God and of permanent peace on earth, He deliberately willed it. "The sword" stands for persecution and for all kinds of social and domestic dissensions!' (*OVBC*, p.663). Professor Fenton considers the saying as another example for the Messianic claim made by Jesus: 'The popular Jewish belief was that when the Messiah came, he would bring *peace* to the earth, though suffering will increase in the days immediately before his arrival. Jesus contradicts these ideas: he has indeed come, but the woes and tribulations will still increase . . . Jesus is saying, *I have come* to inaugurate the woes before the Messianic age, of which Micah has spoken' (*Saint Matthew*, p.165). Barclay says: 'When some great cause emerges, it is bound to divide people; there are bound to be those who answer and those who refuse the challenge . . . The world is always divided into those who have accepted Christ and those who have not . . . It has happened that a man has refused God's call to some adventurous bit of service because he allowed personal attachments to immobilise him . . . it is seldom that any man is confronted with this choice; a man will go through life and never be confronted with it; but the fact remains that it is possible for a man's loved ones to become in effect his enemies, if the thought of them keeps him from doing what he knows God wishes and wants him to do' (*Gospel of St. Matthew*, pp.406/7).

It is true that the Old Testament abounds in passages which show that the God of Israel approved of war. 'The Lord hath sworn that the Lord will have war with Amalek from generation to generation' (*Exod.* 17:16); 'And the Lord hearkened to the voice of Israel, and delivered up the Canaanites, and they utterly destroyed them and their cities' (*Num.* 21:3); 'When the Lord thy God shall bring thee into the land whither thou goest to possess it, and hath cast out many nations before . . . seven nations greater and mightier than thou; and when the Lord thy God deliver them before thee, thou shalt smite them, and utterly destroy them, thou shalt make no covenant with them, nor show mercy unto them' (*Deut.* 7:1/2); 'And the spirit of the Lord came upon him, and he judged Israel and went out to war' (*Judges* 3:10); 'The Lord God of Israel commanded, Go and draw toward Mount Tabor, and take with thee ten thousand men . . . and I will draw unto thee . . . the captain of Jabin's army, with his chariots and his multitude and I will deliver him into they hand' (*Judges* 4:6/10). His chosen ones rely upon Him to work miracles for their victory. 'And blessed be the most High God, which hath delivered thine enemies into thy hand' (*Gen.* 14:20); 'As they fled from before Israel . . . the Lord cast down great stones from heaven . . . and they died . . . more died with hailstones than they whom the children of Israel slew with the sword' (*Josh.* 10:11); 'And the sun stood still and the moon stayed, until the people had avenged themselves upon their enemies . . . for the Lord fought for Israel' (*Josh.* 10:13/4). 'And the Lord discomfited Sisera and all his chariots, and all his host, with the edge of the sword . . . so that Sisera lighted down off his chariot, and fled away on his feet' (*Judges* 4:15); 'But when the battle waxed strong, there appeared unto the enemies from heaven five comely men upon horses with bridles of gold, and two of them led the Jews, And took Maccabeus betwixt them and covered him on every side with their weapons, and kept him safe, but shot arrows and lightnings against the enemies: so that being confounded with blindness, and full of trouble, they were killed. And there were slain of footmen twenty thousand and five hundred, and six hundred horsemen' (*2 Macc.* 1:29/31). God chastised men's sins by sending war: 'Then I will walk contrary unto you, and will punish you yet seven times for your sins. And I will bring a sword upon you' (*Lev.* 26:24/5); 'The Lord shall cause thee to be smitten before thine enemies' (*Deut.* 28:25): 'I will bring a nation upon you from far . . . a mighty nation . . . an ancient nation . . . and they shall eat up thine harvest and thy bread . . . they shall eat up thy flocks and thine herds, they shall eat up thy vines and thy fig trees: they shall impoverish thy fenced cities, wherein thou trustedst, with the sword' (*Jer.* 5:15 to 17). God is called the 'Lord of Hosts' (*Isaiah* 3:1, 5:7, *Hos.* 15:5, *Amos* 5:14).

Blessed are the peacemakers

In the Gospels a very different atmosphere prevails. Not a single word can be found to condone war or command group violence. It is obvious that Jesus and his followers thought that war, organised violence and any mortal feud are contrary to the will of God. This point is made several times in the Sermon on the Mount. The Beatitudes contain this passage, 'Blessed are the peacemakers: for they shall be called the children of God' (*Matthew* 5:9). The Greek words are υἱοὶ Θεοῦ (sons of God) but this expression is suppressed to give greater emphasis to the uniqueness of Jesus as 'Son': The Vulgate, the Revised Version, the *NEB* and some other translations. The Syriac New Testament, French, Italian and Spanish use the correct word 'sons', while the Authorised Version, Luther's translation, the Roman Catholic text in English and many other translations (Swedish, Norwegian) prefer to speak of God's 'children'. In *Hos.* 1:10 the children of Israel are promised that they shall be called the 'sons of the living God'.

It is not surprising that many Christian commentators try to minimise the impact of this saying. In the *CC* Professor Jones assures us that the term peacemakers denotes those who 'spread their own inward peace about them'. They will reflect the spirit of "the Lord of peace", whose Father is necessarily the God of Peace. (p.861). Professor Stendahl in *PC* is no less evasive. According to him peace here does not have the full meaning of the Hebrew 'shalom', but merely refers to the non-militant attitude of those who became true disciples. He even suggests that the word 'peace' may be a mistranslation altogether, and the correct term should read perfect or honest. [I admit that in a number of languages the translation reads 'the peaceful ones', but the English translation renders the Greek original with admirable exactitude.] Stendahl continues with the emphatic words: 'The beatitudes in 8 and 9 are not to be understood as consciously ethical statements' (*PC* p.775). According to Dummelow, peacemakers are those who reconcile antagonists, whether they be individuals, or employer and employees in conflict [sic], or even nations. He adds, 'those who strive to reconcile men to God and so bring peace to their souls' (*OVBC*, p.640).

Professor Barclay goes yet further, and it is worth while quoting him in full: 'It must be . . . noted . . . the blessing is on the peace-*makers*, not necessarily on the peace-*lovers*. It . . . happens that if a man loves peace in the wrong way, he succeeds in making trouble and not peace. We may . . . allow a threatening and dangerous situation to develop . . . and for peace's sake . . . do not want any action. There is many a person who thinks that he is loving peace, because he is refusing to face the situation and to take the action which the situation demands . . . what this beatitude demands is not the passive acceptance of things because we are afraid of doing anything about them, but the active facing of things, and the making of peace, even when the way to peace is through struggle . . . the highest task which a man can perform is to establish right relationships between man and man' (*Gospel of St. Matthew*, pp.103/6).

The above quoted commentators seem to agree that Jesus cannot have meant what the contemporary 'pacifist', Christian or otherwise, takes the beatitude to signify. The 'child of God' or 'son of God' is, according to them, an arbiter, a mediator between nations or between employer and worker, and, if necessary, a fighter for peace with guns and bombs.

Thou shalt not kill

Another passage in the Sermon on the Mount is even more explicit: 'Ye have heard that it was said by them of old time: Thou shalt not kill; and whosoever shall kill shall be in danger of the judgment, but I say unto you, That whosoever is angry with his brother shall be in danger of the judgment' (*Matthew* 5:21/2). The *NEB* uses the expression: 'Do not commit murder', instead of 'Thou shalt not kill', with some justification, as the Greek word φονεύω means murder, kill, slay; keeping in mind that the word 'kill' may indicate the putting to death of an animal, while the word and verb 'murder' is reserved for the killing of human beings, and thus an ambiguity is avoided. However, it may be added that 'Do not commit murder' was probably not understood by Jesus as a commandment in the sense of the secular statutory law, but as a demand not to harm our fellowmen by violence – or even by giving expression to anger!

Professor Jones makes an effort to give the injunction the weight it deserves (*CC,* p.861), but in *PC* there is much equivocation. Professor Stendahl speculates whether the word 'brother' meant fellow man, or fellow Israelite or indeed internal relationships within a community. Discussing the Ten Commandments, and especially *Exod.* 20:13 ('Thou shalt not kill'), the Reverend David Stalker makes it clear: the commandment refers to murder, not to killing in war or capital punishment. Both of these the Old Testament sanctions unequivocally' (*PC*, p.229). The Old Testament texts quoted are: 'When thou goest out to battle against thine enemies . . . be not afraid of them: for the Lord thy God is with thee' (*Deut.* 20:1ff.), and 'He that smiteth a man, so that he die, shall be surely put to death' (*Exod.* 21:12). The words of Jesus, 'But I say unto you . . . ' are conveniently forgotten.

Professor Fenton remarks upon technicalities concerning the numbering of the commandments, without wasting his breath over the passage itself. Professor Barclay considers the text in great detail, but mainly from the point of view of anger. The problem that the commandment contains a total prohibition of taking another person's life – to the extent that even hostile anger is deplored – is only touched upon cursorily (*The Gospel of St. Matthew*, pp.135/6).

Professor Barclay, too, uses the philological argument, devoting much attention to the differences between stergein, philein and agapan, from which he draws the conclusion that 'Jesus never asked us to love our enemies in the same way we love our loved ones . . . The very word is different, to love our enemies in the same way . . . would neither be possible nor right. This is a different kind of love . . . No one would say that a parent really loves his child if he lets the child do as he likes. If we regard a person with invincible goodwill, it will often mean that we must punish him, that we must restrain him, that we must discipline him. That we must protect him against himself. But it will also mean that all Christian discipline and all Christian punishment [sic] must be aimed, not at vengeance but at cure. Punishment will never be merely retributive, it will always be remedial' (*The Gospel of St. Matthew*, pp. 172/3).

Barclay is determined to divest the saying of any 'pacifist' tone: 'It must be noted that Jesus laid this love down as a basis for personal relationships. People use this passage as a basis for pacifism and as a text on which to speak about international relationships. Of course it includes that, but first and foremost it deals with our personal relationships . . . It is very much easier to go about declaring that there should be no such thing as war between nation and nation, than to live a life in which we personally never allow such thing as bitterness to invade our relationship with those we meet every day' (ibid., p. 173).

What is the origin of the remarkable sayings concerning peace and non-violence in the Sermon of the Mount? The most important source is, once again, the Old Testament. The expression 'sons of God' occurs frequently. It is said of Israel: 'It shall be said unto them, Ye are the sons of the living God' (*Hos.* 1:10).

The famous injunction, 'Love thy neighbour as thyself', is a word for word quotation from *Lev.* 19:18. The statement in *Matthew* 5:43 to the effect 'that it hath been said . . . hate thine enemy', is based on error. Nowhere in the Old Testament or in talmudic literature is there a commandment calling upon man to hate his enemies. On the contrary, there are injunctions commanding the Jew to help even his enemy: 'If thou meet thine enemy's ox or ass going astray, thou shalt surely bring it back to him again. If thou see the ass of him that hateth thee, lying under his burden, and wouldst or bear to help him, thou shalt surely help with him' (*Exod.* 23:4/5); 'Rejoice not when thine enemy falleth, and let not thine heart be glad when he stumbleth' (*Prov.* 24:17); and, 'If thine enemy be hungry, give him bread to eat, and if he be thirsty give him water to drink' (*Prov.* 25:21), followed by the mysterious words, 'For thou shalt heap coals of fire upon his head' (*Prov.* 25:22), the whole saying being quoted in the Epistle to the (*Romans* 12:20).

A similar sentiment is expressed in the saying: 'The discretion of a man deferreth his anger; and it is his glory to pass over a transgression' (*Prov.* 19:11). In other writings the same theme appears. In the *Letter of Aristeas,* an apocryphal work written by an Alexandrian Greek (Jew?) in the first century B.C., we read: 'All men hold that we should return good to them that do good unto us; but should we not also open our hand with gifts to those that show enmity, that thereby we may draw them to righteousness?' (p.227). There are other examples: 'If any man seek to do you evil, do ye well unto him, and pray for him, and the Lord shall redeem you from evil' (*Testament of the Twelve Patriarchs, Josh.* 18:2); 'Love ye one another from the heart. If a man sin against thee, speak peaceably unto him, and hold no guile in thy soul' (ibid. Gd. 6:3); 'Say not thou, I will recompense evil, but wait on the Lord' (*Prov.* 20:22), 'Say not, I will do so to him as he hath done to me' (*Prov.* 24:29); and, 'He giveth his cheek to him that smiteth him' (*Lam.* 3:30)!

Talmudic injunctions reveal the same spirit: 'Who is the mightiest among the powerful? He who wins the love of his enemies' (*Abo. RN* 23); 'May it please you, O God of my fathers, to keep men's hearts free of hatred against us, and our own hearts free of hatred against anybody' (*Ber.* 4:2); 'Forgive your neighbour the injustice he hath done you and then, when you pray, your sins will be forgiven' (*Sir.* 28:2 to 5); 'My soul should meet with silence him who curseth me' (*Ber.* 17a); and 'May everyone who hath done me injustice be forgiven' (*Megilla* 28a). The last two are of Babylonian Jewish origin and date from about 400 B.C.

Resist not evil

Jesus exclaims: 'Ye have heard that it hath been said, An eye for an eye, and a tooth for a tooth: but I say unto you, That ye resist not evil: but whosoever shall smite thee on the right cheek turn to him the other also' (*Matthew* 5:38/9). The Revised Version says: 'Resist not him that is evil.' The *NEB* goes further: 'Do not set yourself against the man who wrongs you.'

The Catholic *QB* dismisses this sentence with the remark: 'Christ's words . . . are a counsel of perfection addressed to the individual' (p.426), an expression always used when Catholic apologists imply that Jesus' words are 'impracticable'. Professor Stendahl, in *PC*, is careful not to draw any 'pacifist' conclusions from this saying; on the contrary, his interpretation is followed by a comment on 5:41 ('And whosoever shall compel the to go a mile, go with him twain') stating:

'41 refers to the right of the government or the army to demand services. The 'mile' is a Roman measurement; the Roman soldier had the right to require non-Roman subjects to carry his equipment one mile, cf.27:32 ['And as they came out, they found a man of Cyrene, Simon by name: him they compelled to bear his cross']. Hence the anti-zealotic note in the Sermon on the Mount is apparent' (p.777). Is it possible, indeed, to comment on this comment?

Equally 'amusing' is Dummelow's interpretation: 'Christians are not to resent injuries . . . to retaliate . . . they are to turn the cheek to the smiter. Does this forbid us on fitting occasions to expostulate with the wrong-doer, or bring him to punishment? By no means. There are occasions when, in the interest of Society, and in the interest of the criminal himself, it is necessary to resist evil and to bring the wrong-doer to justice. Our Lord elsewhere fully recognises this (*Matthew* 18:5) 'Moreover if thy brother shall trespass against thee, go and tell him his fault between thee and him alone: if he shall hear thee, thou hast gained thy brother' [Another amazing reference!] (*OVBC*, p.643).

Professor Fenton only comments in passing, but Professor Barclay is more obliging: 'Retaliation, however, controlled and restricted, has no place in Christian life'. He goes on to say that a Christian should resent no insult and seek no vengeance for any slight (*Commentary to St. Matthew*, pp.163/4). One would applaud, if, continuing to read Barclay, one did not come across the text quoted in the following sub-chapter.

Love your enemies

'Ye have heard that it hath been said, Thou shalt love thy neighbour, and hate thine enemy: but I say unto you, love your enemies, bless them that cure you, do good to them that they hate you, and pray for them which despitefully use you and persecute you' (*Matthew* 5:43/4). In accordance with the best manuscripts, the Revised Version is shorter: 'Love your enemies and pray for your persecutors.' The same injunction is found in the Gospel according to St. Luke: 'Love your enemies, do good to them which hate you, bless them that curse you, and pray for them which despitefully use you' (*Luke* 6:27/8). Luke continues: 'And to him that smiteth thee on one cheek, offer also the other' (6:39), a passage which Matthew puts before the words concerning the love for our enemies (5:39).

In *PC*, Professor Stendahl weakens the appeal: He points out that whilst the statement could be interpreted in the light of non-resistance and hope for the vengeance of God, the saying concerns itself with the question of hate and its sharp language. 'The attitude of Jesus is grounded in God's concern for both good and evil without restrictions for repentance shown by the unrighteous.' By not mentioning the significance of Jesus' refusal to feel enmity, Stendahl takes the sting out of the saying and, indeed, compares it with *Matthew* 5:20 in which Jesus calls for 'the righteousness which exceeds that of the Pharisees' (p.777).

Dummelow applies the philological method. 'The word for "love" is carefully chosen,' he says. 'It is not demanded that we should love our enemies with a natural and spontaneous affection (philein), but with the supernatural Christian love that comes by grace (agapan)' (*OVBC*, p.644).

The words in *Matthew* 5:43/4 cannot refer to traditional ethical commandments. It is more likely that they express opposition to the Qumran approach which called for hatred against the enemy. According to Josephus, the Essenes had to swear an initiation oath which promised 'that he will always hate the wicked; and assist the righteous' (*Bell*. 2:8:7). In the 'Community Rule' of the Dead Sea Scrolls, the Master demands that the disciples 'may love all that God hath chosen and hate all that He hath rejected' and that they 'may love all the sons of light and hate all the sons of darkness' (Vermes, *The Dead Sea Scrolls*, p.72).

It cannot be denied that similar sentiments can be found in the Old Testament, although never in the form of an injunction. 'When he shall be judged, let him be condemned, and let his prayer become sin. Let his days be few, and let another take his office. Let his children be fatherless, and his wife a widow. Let his children be vagabonds and beg . . . let strangers spoil his labour. Let there be none to extend mercy unto him: neither let there be any to favour his fatherless children . . . Let this be the reward of mine adversaries from the Lord, and of them that speak evil against my soul' (*Psalm* 109:7/20); 'Thou hast maintained my right and my cause . . . thou hast destroyed the wicked, thou hast put out their name for ever and ever' (*Psalm* 9:4/5); 'Be not merciful to any wicked transgressor . . . God shall let me see my desire upon my enemies . . . scatter them by thy power and bring them down. O Lord . . . Consume them in wrath, consume them that they may not be' (*Psalm* 59: 5/13). 'Let their table become a snare and their welfare a trap. Let their eyes be darkened and their loins to shake . . . Let their habitations be desolate and none dwell in their tents . . . Let them be blotted out of the book of the living' (*Psalm* 69:22/8); 'O daughter of Babylon who art to be destroyed, happy shall he be that rewardeth thee as thou hast served us, happy shall he be that taketh and dasheth thy little ones against the stones (*Psalm* 137:8/9); and 'Every one that is found shall be thrust through: and every one that is joined unto them shall fall by the sword. Their children also shall be dashed to pieces before their eyes, their houses shall be spoilt and their wives ravished . . . they shall have no pity on the fruit of the womb, their eyes shall not spare children' (*Isaiah* 13:15/6). This is the 'great' Isaiah speaking of the destruction of Babylon. Yet these quotations cannot be instanced to disprove the very high ethical demands which permeated Jewish thought at the time of Jesus.

In ancient world it was not only Jewish teachers who asked for mercy and love to be shown towards the enemy. St. Augustine himself says: 'The substance of what is called Christianity today, was already to be found among the ancients and was never absent from the very beginnings of humanity, until Christ appeared in the flesh, and now the true religion which always existed is named after him Christianity' (*Retractiones*, 1:12/3).

The *Egyptian Book of the Dead* which originated from the sixteenth century B.C. contains a passage where the Dead Soul assures the Judge: 'Never have I caused suffering to any man'. On the clay table made for Assurbanipal's library in the seventh century B.C., we read Xisuthros' commandment to humanity: 'Do not evil to your adversary. If someone harms you, recompense him with good.' Assyrian sayings from the fourth century B.C. record the words of the wise Achikar: 'My son, if thine enemy meeteth thee with evil, thou shalt meet him with good.' Taoist literature abounds with examples: 'Arms are implements of ill-omen. Where armies are quartered, thorns and brambles grow. Great wars cause years of misery. The man of Truth uses arms only when he cannot avoid it. In his conquests he takes no delight, for he does not enjoy the slaughter of men. He who enjoys the slaughter of men does not rejoice in the world.' (*Tao te-King*, Ch'u Takao's modified translation, p.42). 'As if there were no enemies he will not . . . when opposing armies meet in the field, the compassionate will win' (ibid., p.82); 'the violent do not die a natural death' (ibid., p.55); 'the way for a vital man to go is not the way of the soldier, in time of war men . . . turn from their higher nature to their lower nature . . . arms are an instrument of evil . . . one with a will to kill shall never prevail in the world . . . Regard your triumph as a funeral' (Witter Bynner's translation, pp.42/3). 'Open your hand and show no weapon. Bear your breast and find no foe . . . But as long as there be foe . . . respect him, measure him, be humble towards him; Let him however strong he may be, not deprive you of compassion, the only one of your possessions which can conquer him' (ibid., p.68), and 'He who . . .

tries to live by force shall die thereby' (ibid. p.51). These sentences were written five hundred years before Christ. At about the same time Buddha was recorded to have told a story to the quarrelling monks: 'There was once a prince whose parents had been brutally murdered. After many years the murderer fell into the hands of the prince who, however, was not prepared to exact vengeance. If I took your life now, your friends would take mine, and my friends would take theirs in revenge. Thus our enmity would continue to create enmity without end. As it is I forgive you and you may live. In this way through forgiveness, our enmity has ceased forever.' Not much later in history, the ruler of Rhodos, Kleobulos, exclaimed: 'Let there be an end of all enmity!' Even Plato warns in his *Eighth Letter* against the continuation of hostilities which can only lead to the extermination of Greeks in Sicily. In the year 256 B.C. King Ashoka had these words carved into a rock: 'In the eighth year of his rule, the King, the friend of the Gods . . . conquered Kalinga. Of its inhabitants, 150,000 were deported and 100,000 killed . . . Since that conquest the King's heart has been full of remorse. The conquest of an independent country means misery, death and captivity for its inhabitants . . . Let there be a change of heart and a end to killing . . . These words are being carved into the rock so that our sons and grandsons . . . shall not hanker after new conquests.'

Of course, Jesus did not derive his words from these distant sources, but from the Old Testament and other Jewish scriptures. Klausner rightly says that 'throughout the Gospels there is not an item of ethical teaching which cannot be paralleled either in the Old Testament, the Apocrypha, or in the talmudic or midrashic literature of the period near the time of Jesus' (*JN* p.384). These then, are the origin of New Testament ethics: a very strict and demanding code, assiduously ignored by official Christendom past and present.

They that take the sword

There are many passages advocating non-violence in the Sermon on the Mount. At the time of his arrest, Jesus said: 'Put up again thy sword into its place: for all they that take the sword shall perish with the sword' (*Matthew* 26:52). An echo of this passage is found in Revelation: 'He that killeth with the sword must be killed with the sword' (*Rev.* 13:10). Its origin is probably, 'Whoso sheddeth a man's blood, by man shall his blood be shed: for in the image of God made He man' (*Gen.* 9:6); 'He that smiteth a man, so that he die, shall be surely put to death' (*Exod.* 21:12); and 'He that killeth an man shall surely be put to death' (*Lev.* 24:17).

In *PC* Professor Stendahl ignores this saying. Dummelow rightly remarks that 'it discourages violence on the part of Christ's followers, and recommends instead the meek endurance of injuries'. Dummelow adds, however, 'Another interpretation has been given, "All that take the sword", that is, rashly and on their own authority, "shall perish by the sword" of the magistrate' (*OVBC*, p.713). To Walsham How we owe this ingenuous statement: 'The sheath is the proper place of the sword, except when the sword is drawn in accordance with the will of God, in a righteous cause' (*Commentary to the New Testament*). Professor Barclay applies a strange twist in his interpretation of the saying: 'History proved Jesus right: for those Jews who took him with violence, and who gloried in violence, and who would gladly have dipped their swords in Roman blood, saw forty years later their City destroyed for ever, while the man who would not fight is enthroned for ever in the hearts of men' (*The Gospel of St. Matthew* p.388). Is it possible to comment on such barbarous nonsense?!

Another relevant saying: 'Forgive if ye have aught against any: that your Father which is in heaven, forgive your trespasses' (*Mark* 11:25/6). The *NEB* puts it in modern English: 'If you have a grievance against anyone, forgive him so that your Father in heaven forgive you the wrongs you have done' The saying is glossed over by Fenton and Wilson in *PC*.

Professor Griffith Thomas argues that those who wish to base their pacifist argument on the words of Jesus in *Matthew* 26:52, are historically wrong. Once again we learn what Jesus 'really meant': those who take the sword, that is, those who act in a spirit of militarism and aggression for conquest, will perish. 'We conclude therefore,' continues the Professor 'that it is not, and cannot be, a sin to be a soldier, for not only do we find today many of the most earnest Christians in the ranks, but the Bible nowhere condemns a soldier's life. Indeed, God Himself appeared before Joshua in military form (*Josh.* 5:21/3) . . . there are many aspects of war . . . A Christian man voluntarily becoming a soldier . . . must judge for himself according to his conscience in the light of the Holy Scripture' (*Principles of Theology*, p.477).

I should like to refrain from commenting on this repulsive cant, yet I must point out two inaccuracies: There is no *explicit* condemnation of war in the New Testament, nor indeed of soldiers as such. But John the Baptist, speaking to soldiers, does say: 'Do violence to no man' (*Luke* 3:14), which injunction, if obeyed, would make 'a soldier's life' impossible and soon land him to being courtmarshalled for mutiny. It is a charitable understatement to say that the reference to *Josh.* 21 is an inaccuracy. The test reads: 'And it came to pass, when Joshua was by Jericho, that he lifted up his eyes and looked and behold, there stood a man over against him with his sword drawn in his hand: and Joshua went unto him and said unto him, Art thou for us of for our adversaries? And he said, Nay: but as captain of the host of the Lord am I now come. And Joshua fell on his face to the earth and did worship, and said unto him, what says my Lord unto his servant, And the captain of the Lord's host said unto Joshua, Loose thy shoe off from thy foot; for the place whereon thou standest is holy. And Joshua did so'. It is arbitrary to claim that the captain of the host of the Lord was God Himself, and indeed some Christian commentators merely speak of an angel who appeared to Joshua (Professor May in *PC* (p.293), Dummelow, *OVBC* (p.145) and others. On the other hand, the Anglican Bishop Wordsworth in his exhaustive *Commentary* (II, pp.16/7) and, more recently, Professor Power in *CC* (p.282) consider the possibility that the 'captain' was none other than Jehovah himself. The Authorised Version presents the captain as an angel.

The Golden Rule

In *Mark* 11:25/6 we have encountered the idea that we should forgive our adversaries if we ourselves wish to be forgiven. In the Gospel according to Luke we find 'the Golden Rule' in its most *positive* form: 'As you would that man should do to you, do ye also to them likewise' (*Luke* 6:31). Similarly, in Matthew we read: 'All things whatsoever ye would that men should do to you, do ye even so to them: for this is the law and the prophets' (*Matthew* 7:12). This means presumably that the Golden Rule is the substance of the Law and the prophets.

The Golden Rule is to be found in almost all great religions. The Jain scriptures say that 'a man should go about treating all creatures as he himself would be treated', and that 'we should refrain from inflicting upon others such injury as would appear undesirable to us if inflicted upon us' (Pike, *Ethics of the Great Religions,* p.123). The *Granth Sahib* of the Sikhs contains the Golden Rule in these words: 'Treat others as thou wouldst be treated thyself' (ibid., p.129). In the Confucian *Chung Yung* we read: 'What you do not like when done to yourself, do not do to others' (ibid., p.226). Buddha teaches: 'Hurt not others with that which pains thyself.' The *Zend Avesta* of the Zoroastrians formulates the rule thus: 'Do not do unto others all that which is not well for thyself'. In the Hindu Mahabharata we are called upon 'Do naught to others which if done to thee would cause thee pain'. And Plato says: 'May I do to others as I would that they should do unto me' (ibid., p.242).

Jewish literature abounds in passages containing the Golden Rule: it is to Rabbi Hillel that the saying is attributed: 'What you do not like yourself, you shall not do to your neighbour.' He is reported to have added: 'That is the whole of the Torah (Law), and the remainder is but commentary.' How very reminiscent of the words of Jesus in *Matthew* 7:12! A paraphrase of the same thought is found in the Talmud: 'Do not to others as thou wouldst not have them do unto thee' (*Shab.* 31a). In an apocryphal book of Jewish scripture, dating from the first century B.C., we find the words, 'Do that to no man which thou hatest (*Tobit*, 4:15).

In *PC* much is made of the *negative* character of Hillel's formulation (. . . do not . . .) in comparison with the *positive* injunction of Jesus. However, we have seen that the Golden Rule finds its positive formulation in the sayings of many religious teachers. Dummelow also asserts that the Golden Rule is usually negative, while Jesus' words command active benevolence. He tells an anecdote of Aristotle who formulated the rule close to the form given by Jesus, but applied it merely to friends. Asked how we should act towards our friends, the sage answered: 'As we would that they should act towards us' (*OVBC*, p.650).

Professor Barclay goes out of his way to assure us that this is 'very probably the most universally famous thing that Jesus ever said. With this commandment the Sermon on the Mount reaches its summit . . . This saying is the topmost peak of social ethics, and the Everest of all ethical teaching. It is possible to quote rabbinic parallels for almost everything that Jesus said in the Sermon on the Mount; but there is no real parallel to this saying. This is something which had never been said before [sic]. It is a new teaching, and a new way of life and of life's obligations' (*The Gospel of St. Matthew*, pp.266/7). It is strange that almost immediately after stating this, the Professor goes on describing the antecedents of the saying, quoting Hillel, Tobit and Aristeas. He even cites Confucius and Buddhist hymns containing the negative formulation, but – like other Christian commentators – insists that 'no one but Jesus ever put it in its positive form' (ibid., p.278).

Mercy, peace and salvation

Insistence on mercy is another point continually made by Jesus and his disciples. 'Be ye merciful, as your Father is also merciful' (*Luke* 6:36).

The saying originates from David's psalm recorded in *2 Sam.* 22:26: 'With the merciful thou wilt show thyself merciful'. Suffice it to confront this passage with a saying of that great Christian Martin Luther: 'A merciful God is not for these peasants, but He who sends plague and war, He is the God they need!' (*Luther im Tischgespräch*, III, 3094).

Another text from Luke's Gospel is worth noting: 'For the Son of man is not come to destroy men's lives but to save them' (*Luke* 9:56). This saying is of doubtful origin, most Greek manuscripts do not contain it, and the Revised Version omits it altogether. It is probably a Johannite passage that found its way into Luke's Gospel: 'For God sent not his Son into the world to condemn the world; but the world through him might be saved' (*John* 3:17); and, 'I come not to judge the world, but to save the world' (*John* 12:47).

The disciples, too, are emphatic in their condemnation of the enemies of peace. Paul castigates them in his Epistle to the Romans: 'With their tongues they have used deceit; the poison of asps is under their lips: whose mouth is full of cursing and bitterness: their feet are swift to shed blood: and the ways of peace have they not known' (*Rom.* 3:13/7).

Magnificent words, but let us trace their origin,

EPISTLE TO THE ROMANS		OLD TESTAMENT
3:13	Their throat is an open sepulchre with their tongues they have used deceit	Ps. 5:9 Their throat is an open sepulchre
		Ps. 10:7 His mouth is full of deceit
		Ps. 140:2 . . . continually are they gathered together for war. They have sharpened their tongues like a serpent;
	the poison of asps is under their lips.	adders poison is under their lips.
3:14	Whose mouth is full of cursing and bitterness	Ps. 10:7 His mouth is full of cursing and deceit and fraud.
3:15	Their feet are swift	Isa. 59:7 Their feet are running to evil and they make haste
	to shed blood	to shed innocent blood.
3:16	Destruction and misery are in their ways	Wasting and destruction are in their path.
3:17	And the way of peace have they not known . . .	The way of peace they know not.

A similar surprise awaits us when, in the same epistle, we read with admiration: 'If thine enemy hunger, feed him; if he thirst, give him drink,' followed by the words, 'for in doing so thou shalt heap coals of fire on his head' (*Rom.* 12:20). Compare this with *Prov.* 25:21/2; 'If thine enemy by hungry, give him bread to eat; and if he be thirsty, give him water to drink: for thou shalt heap coals of fire upon his head . . .'; or the injunction: 'Let us therefore follow after the things which make for peace' (*Rom.* 14:19), comparing it with, 'Depart from evil and do good, seek peace and pursue it' (*Psalm* 34:14).

Writing in *PC*, Professor Manson shows his awareness of these strange coincidences, without expressing any surprise. He enlightens us, however, about the obscure passage concerning the heaping of coals of fire: 'It is a reference to an Egyptian ritual in which a penitent shows his repentance by carrying on his head a dish burning charcoal on a layer of ashes . . . the English equivalent would be . . . by showing kindness to your enemies, you will make them ashamed of themselves before God' (p.950). Dummelow, too, knows Paul's source. 'Coals of fire' according to him, means that 'one should melt him into shame, as a furnace melts metals (*ovbc*, p.884).

Against all the weight of evidence the only two passages which may be quoted against my argument that none of Jesus' saying justifies armed conflict, are to be found in the Gospel according to Luke, after the account of the Last Supper: 'He that hath no sword, let him sell his garment and buy one' (*Luke* 22:36); and, "They said, Lord, behold, here are two swords. And he said unto them, 'It is enough' (*Luke* 22:38).

In *PC*, Professor Lampe says that these words cancel the previous instruction given to the disciples, and grants them permission to bear a sword freely and to fight in a crisis. He did not want, however, says the commentator with emphasis, to encourage an act of assassination or fight on the side of revolutionary 'transgressors' (p.841).

This would not satisfy Dummelow. He believes the controversial passage served to make the disciples aware of the dangers awaiting them: probably they would need their swords more than anything else (*OVBC*, p.767). And this is what Dummelow has to say about *Luke* 22:38): 'The disciples thought that Jesus advised them to buy swords to protect Him from arrest. They pointed out therefore that they had two already with which they were prepared to defend him. Seeing Himself misunderstood, Jesus abruptly closed the conversation with the words, "It is enough", i.e. "Enough of the trifling". He had intended the disciples to "buy swords" (i.e. take measures) for their own safety, not for His. He Himself was resolved to die, but He wishes their lives to be preserved. Professor Ginns, in the *CC* also thinks that Jesus altered his injunction regarding violence in view of 'a situation of the utmost gravity'. Times have changed and they must be prepared to practise self-defence (*CC*, p.966). It seems to be the general view of

Christian apologists that force and violence are sometimes justified, and the words of Jesus are quoted to prove that even he condoned violence in face of provocation.

Klausner believes that Jesus did not expect his imminent death, and thinking that a small skirmish was to be feared, commended a minimum of armed force to avert a greater catastrophe (*JN*, p.331). There is, however, nothing to support this speculation, and we must agree with the ancient view of Christian theologians: if Jesus had in mind material weapons, a hundred swords would not have been enough; if he meant spiritual weapons, two swords would be too many. The saying is, and remains, a mystery. It might be an interpolation to justify the use of the sword in 'a situation of utmost gravity'.

Visions of war

To justify their readiness to fight wars Christian thinkers often quote the words of Jesus: 'And ye shall hear of wars and rumours of wars: see that ye not be troubled: for all these things must come to pass, but the end is not yet. For nation shall rise against nation, and kingdom against kingdom, and there shall be famines and pestilence, and earthquakes, in divers places. All these are the beginning of sorrows' (*Matthew* 24:6 to 8). Almost the same words are to be found in *Mark* 13:8 and *Luke* 21:10.

The origin of these passages may be traced to an apocryphal book, 2 *Baruch*, written in the days of Jesus and, therefore, prior to the books of the New Testament. In chapter 27 we read of the 'Pangs of the Messiah' which will come with great commotion, massacre and sudden death, the appearance of the sword (war), famine, earthquakes, demons, oppression and confusion.

Professor Stendahl thinks that 'the war' for Matthew may have meant the Jewish war A.D. 66 to 70 which was preceded by a famine (*PC*, p.793). And in his comments on Mark, R.M. Wilson says that 'wars and rumours of wars' followed by earthquakes and famine as prophesied by Jesus, were common apocalyptic expectations (*PC*, p.813), while the passage in Luke is discussed by Professor Lampe: 'Luke substitutes tumults for Mark's rumours of war'. Such disturbances are probably only part of the general apocalyptic imagery, and not to be identified with the event in A.D. 68 . . . Luke adds pestilences to the famines and earthquakes, probably under the influence of literary convention and assonance in Greek. All three are part of the apocalyptic imagery and not to be identified with particular events' (ibid., 839). The Greek assonance referred to is λιμοί καὶ λοιμόι. Dummelow calls the passage 'the great prophesy of Christ' (*OVBC*, p.731), and asserts that it does refer to the fall of Jerusalem (ibid., p.766). Fenton and Barclay are of the same opinion.

However that may be, the problem is really whether the words of Jesus constitute a permission for Christians to fight wars. If it is argued that this utterance gives absolution to the followers for partaking in war, it could be reasoned in similar fashion that, since Jesus foretold the coming of famine and pestilence, the Christian is allowed to be instrumental in the causing of these disasters. And how are we to interpret Jesus' words in St. John's Gospel: 'These things I have spoken unto you, that in me ye may have peace. In the world ye shall have tribulation; but be of good cheer, I have overcome the world' (*John* 16:33) 'My kingdom is not of this world, if my kingdom were of this world, then would my servants fight' (*John* 18:36)? Or the significant words in Luke's Gospel: 'It is impossible but that offences will come: but woe unto him through whom they come' (*Luke* 17:1)?

This passage must be read in conjunction with the 'apocalyptic prophesy' of Jesus ('wars and rumours of wars') to understand the total immorality of those who take meaning and menace out of the mighty words in *Luke* 17:1. Tribulations and dreadful sufferings are inevitable, but woe unto him who causes these tribulations and sufferings!

Let us see what some commentators make of Jesus' bitter threat? Professor Lampe says: 'Temptations to sin are inevitable, but those who cause ordinary believers to go astray will be punished . . . Luke . . . probably applies to saying to the apostles' exercise of Church discipline' (*PC*, p.837). Dummelow speaks of the offence 'as causing others to sin' (*OVBC*, p.762). In the *CC* Professor Ginns arrives at the conclusion that it is impossible to avoid 'scandals' altogether (*CC*, p.960). Walsham How defines offences as 'occasions to fall, or temptations to sin. To tempt others, especially the young and weak, to sin, is verily to do the devil's work'. It seems that not even Jesus can disturb the good conscience and smugness of some commentators. They have indeed overcome the world and are of good cheer. Lightfoot's comment on *John* 16:33 is particularly reassuring. 'Although the world is the object of God's love, it remains to the end – and must remain – a battlefield; however, victory already lies with the Lord, and is therefore guaranteed also to His followers' (*A Commentary to St. John's Gospel*, p.294). And his comment on Jesus' powerful words in *John* 18:36 is simpler still: 'The kingdom . . . can only be seen and entered by those who undergo spiritual rebirth' (ibid., p.324).

Professor Barrett's comment on *John* 16:33 carefully avoids the issue. 'This devastating disclosure is not . . . made with the purpose of destroying but establishing their peace. "These things" might refer simply to the preceding prediction; they will be reassured when they recall that Jesus himself foretold their desertion. More probably it refers to the contents of the discourses as a whole, which interpret both the sufferings of Christ and the sufferings of the Church in such a way as to make peace possible. The ultimate ground of peace is the fact that Christ has overcome the world. It is overcome (a) through being redeemed, and (b) through the overthrow of the Ruler of this world [Satan] who is responsible for the transformation of God's creature in His enemy' (*PC*). About *John* 18:36 Barrett says: 'The reply is not direct. A kingdom may be 'of this world' or not. If Jesus' kingdom were of this world, his followers would take appropriate action against *the* Jews [sic] but this they have not done. It follows that his kingdom has a different origin' (*PC*, p.865).

The Catholic Professor Leonard sees in *John* 16:33 merely a promise of victory to the disciples, while in the comment on 18:36 we meet a Jesus anxious to prove that 'he is not a Palestinian rival of the majesty of Roman Tiberius' (*CC* pp.1009 and 1012).

It does not surprise me that the Catholic apologists compete with their Protestant counterparts in their endeavour to show how remote any 'pacifist' idea was from the mind of Jesus. Pope Pius XI spoke of a 'just war' in which Christians may have to fight, and the *QB* volunteers this information: 'The Bible never declares war intrinsically immoral. On the contrary, in hundreds of passages [here many of the above-quoted Old Testament passages follow as examples of divine approval] . . . Our Lord's chief commandment was the love of God and the love of the neighbour for God's sake. If the world were faithful to it, war would become impossible. But a pagan nationalism often sets to naught the Christian principles of justice and charity . . . Our Lord praises highly the faith of the centurion, but neither asks he the soldier to abandon his calling as immoral . . . Christ's words in the Sermon on the Mount are a counsel of perfection [sic], addressed to the individual, while St. Paul forbids private vengeance as a grievous sin . . . The early Fathers never condemned war as intrinsically immoral . . . While recognising that war is one of the greatest evils that can confront a nation, the Catholic Church has always held that a just war is licit and moral. She condemns the pacifism of the Quaker who declares all wars incompatible with Christianity . . . A nation goes to war in self-defence. For a war to be just, Catholic moralists insist upon the following conditions: A State can rightly declare war only when it is morally certain that its rights are being actually violated, or are in certain and imminent danger; when the cause of war is in proportion to the evils incident to the war; when every peaceful method of settlement has proved inadequate; when there is a well-grounded hope of bettering conditions by the conflict. If these conditions were fulfilled – they rarely have been in history – wars would rarely happen' (pp.426/7).

Against this flood of hypocritical sophistry I can only refer the reader to the dignified and simple words of Jesus: 'Love your enemies . . .' And let us remember here that forgiveness, so alien to the advocates of war, violence and revenge, was extolled by Jesus in the famous episode when Peter asked him: 'Lord, how oft shall my brother sin against me and I forgive him? till seven times?' Jesus' answer was: 'I say not unto thee, until seven times: but, Until seventy times seven' (*Matthew* 18:21/2). Variations on the theme of this moving dialogue are also to be found in *Mark* 11:25/6, and *Luke* 17:3/4).

When his hostility was aroused, Martin Luther, the father of Protestant thought, no more displayed the spirit of Jesus than did his Catholic opponents. In another context I have mentioned his remark about the merciful God and the rebellious peasants. To the same category belong his meditations on the 'Turkish Peril' (compare Yellow Peril, Red Peril, etc.): 'Thinking about the Turks I have come to the conclusion that if I were Samson I could slay a thousand Turks daily, that is three hundred and fifty thousand Turks in a year . . .' (*Luther im Gespräch,* I, 289); and, 'Anyone who thinks it possible to conquer the Turks with humane methods will himself be conquered . . .' (ibid., II, 2548).

The same avowed Christian wrote the following commentary on the commandment 'Thou shalt not kill': 'Neither God nor the government is included in this commandment . . . their right to take human life is not abrogated. God has delegated his authority to punish evildoers to civil magistrates in the place of parents; in early times, we read in Moses (*Deut.* 21:18) parents had to bring their own children to judgment and sentence them to death. Therefore, what is forbidden here applies to private individuals, not to governments. This commandment is simple enough . . . in *Matthew* 5:3, where Christ himself explains and summarises it: We must not kill, either by hand, heart or word, by sign or gesture, or by aiding and abetting. It forbids anger except, as we have said, to persons who occupy the place of God, that is, parents and rulers. Anger, reproof and punishment are the prerogatives of God and his representatives, and they are to be exercised upon those who transgress this or the other commandments. The occasion and need for this commandment is that, as God well knows, the world is evil and this life full of misery. He has therefore placed this and other commandments as a boundary between good and evil . . . We must live among many people who do us harm, and so we have reason to be at enmity with them. For instance your neighbour, envious that you have received from God a better house and estate or greater wealth and good fortune than he, gives vent to his irritation and envy by speaking ill of you. Thus by the devil's prompting you acquire many enemies . . . When we see such people, our hearts in turn are enraged, and we are ready to shed blood and take revenge. Then follow curses and blows, and eventually calamity and murder. Here God, like a kind father, steps in and intervenes to settle the quarrel for the safety of all concerned . . . He wishes to have all people defended, delivered and protected from the wickedness and violence of others, and he has set up this commandment as a wall, fortress and refuge about our neighbour so that no one may do him bodily harm or injury. In the second place, this commandment is violated not only when a person actually does evil, but also when he fails to do good to his neighbour . . . if you send a person away naked when you could clothe him, you have let him freeze to death. If you see anyone suffer hunger and do not feed him, you let him starve . . . Therefore God rightly calls all persons murderers who do not offer counsel and aid to men in need and in peril of body and life . . . it is God's real intention that we should allow no man to suffer harm, but show to everyone all kindness and love' (*The Large Catechism,* p.34).

Among these laudable sentiments it passes almost unnoticed that Luther has succeeded in smuggling into the argument the condoning of murder and capital punishment when practised by authority. The importance of this argument in Luther's thinking can be seen in greater detail in the preceding chapter on 'Authority'.

At the bidding of the Magistrate

The Protestant State was not slow to see the value of this argument. Articles 37 of the Church of England makes it clear that Royal Supremacy is entitled to hold sway over life and death. It speaks of the lawfulness of capital punishment and military service. It claims that the exercise of violence is sometimes necessary and sometimes inevitable, and that it 'is lawful for Christians to carry arms and serve in wars at the bidding of the Magistrate'.

Discussing this Article, Griffith Thomas says that its truth has been seriously questioned in recent times. But, he claims, the distinction between wars of aggression and defence remains valid, and 'the teaching of the Article . . . is undoubtedly in accord with the

Christians' relation and duty to the State' (*The Principles of Theology*, p.476). He argues that the Christian has an interest and a stake in the life of the nation. 'When it is said that Christians are "not of this world", it does not mean "Not of this nation", for world and nation are not interchangeable,' (ibid.). Grace upholds the family and the State, and being "under grace" is not incompatible with being "under government", since God is the supreme ruler of the nations.' [What a self-defeating argument!] Griffith Thomas quotes Paul as an example who showed patriotism for Israel (*Rom.* 9:14, 10:1), and respect for his Roman citizenship (*Acts* 16:37 and 22:25/8), yet he was not disloyal to his citizenship of Heaven.

Hatred, malice and vengeance, the Professor argues, are as wrong between nations as between individuals. 'But when violence, aggression and tyrannical cruelty are seen, the question . . . arises as to what Christianity requires of Christians . . . The Christian is responsible for others. The difficulty in some minds is due to a confusion between retaliation and resistance. The former is unchristian, the latter is not. Resistance to evil may be and often is a positive duty . . . There is also no essential difference between police force and military force, because in both instances force is exercised to resist evil. The kind and degree of resistance, or of the force required to overcome it, are quite irrelevant to the issue, and if, when the burglar resists or gets maimed or killed, the householder or the policeman is not regarded as guilty of murder any more than the soldier is considered guilty on the battlefield. The contention that "Thou shalt not kill" as a prohibition of war is impossible, because the Jewish nation, to which this command was given, had a military organisation by virtue of the same Authority as the one which issued the commandment' (ibid., pp.476/7).

It is rewarding to continue the analysis of Griffith Thomas' book since it demonstrates clearly, more clearly than most other works, how much the amoral State and established Christianity have in common. He goes on to discuss the injunction of Jesus, 'Resist not evil' which, according to him, was merely a proverbial form for stating a general principle to guide the individual. 'We have no right to condone the wrong done to others, even if we ourselves are prepared to endure the wrong done to us. *Matthew* 5:39 ("Turn the other cheek") is to be understood as a piece of *personal* advice which does not refer to war at all, neither does it affect civic affairs. In a world not guided by Christian principles, some form of force is indispensable and in the interest of the community those who are brutal and aggressive must be resisted. Whenever therefore compulsory military service is the law of the land, it is impossible to doubt [sic] that Christians are justified in responding to the claim of the government to take up arms in defence of the country. Government is still as much as ever the Divine method of maintaining order and putting down evil (*Rom.* 13)' (ibid.p.477).

According to the Professor, 'under certain conditions a Christian ought to be ready to draw and use the sword'. The Christian is justified in fighting when the righteousness of a cause is clear, and when the social order for which we are all responsible, is endangered. Ingenuously he remarks: 'Tyranny in its attempt to override liberty is manifestly wrong in the sight of God' (ibid.).

In the same way as the Catholic *QB*, the Protestant Professor argues that for a Christian war is justifiable when everything has been tried to preserve peace, 'and the enemy still refuses to lay aside his tyranny and hatred' (ibid., p.478). Our individual conscience must be clear, and based on Holy Scripture – we must decide in all sincerity. "Love your enemies" applies to personal relationships and enmities, but the case is altogether different when the world is applied to an organised community, for other elements then enter into the problem which prevent us from using the precept to avoid hostility against national wrongdoing' [sic]! (ibid.).

At the end of the relevant chapter of the *Principles of Theology,* Griffith Thomas sums up his conclusions: Force 'is often the only weapon that man can use to further his purpose. It is only the unnecessary and cruel use of force that can be called wrong. It has to be used to slay an animal for food, and no one can say that this is wrong in itself, so long as it is done in a humane fashion. *The same is obviously true in social, civic and national affairs.* [My italics.] For this reason it is contended that a war of defence for the sake of righteousness and, as it has been well said the true conclusion is not "peace at any price", but righteousness at any cost' (pp.478/9).

In a letter to the *Spectator,* a former Bishop of Durham wrote: 'There is no approach to a complete analogy between an organised community and a person, however much we may "personify" the community. The State is not at all a personality: it is a great complex of personalities. It is such a complex that its organisation largely exists on purpose that the community may safeguard its personal components in their several interests and liberties, particularly its weaker components. From this point of view the State is morally right, is morally bound, to take indignant and resolute action when its members' lawful interests of peace, security, liberty, are violated or forcibly threatened by another State. We are nowhere commanded by our Lord to love other people's enemies as such. Where others are concerned, as victims of wrong, a wholly new element enters the scene. We see a ruffian maltreat a woman or a child. He is an evil, to be, by all possible means, quelled and also punished. And the State, when its member suffers violence or wrong, is called to act thus, as the third party interposing to protect and avenge another party' (Quoted from ibid., p.478).

An article published by the New York *Outlook*, written by R.C. Cabot in April 1917, justified the entry of the United States in the First World War. Under the title *America's Duty*, the Protestant author affirmed: 'We are Christians, servants of a religion of love which expresses itself equally by gentleness and by force, never by supineness, never by hate. Is a Christian less loving when he seizes the bridle of a runaway horse, to save innocent bystanders from being trampled under its hooves? He gives all for love, force and reason freely flung into the service of right. Has one forgotten Christ when one risks one's life to restrain a maniac crazed with disease and near to throttling an innocent neighbour? Could one's love, one's Christianity, be other than hypocrisy if one was not faithful unto death, withholding no service called for? Force directed to noble ends is not base. Tiny forces that wag tongue or pen in reasoning and persuasion are no more Christian than the brutal elemental force that launches a lifeboat. Our religion may call for any power we may possess. He who holds back any service in the hour of need does but lipservice to his God' (Quoted from ibid., p.479).

A few years ago the Chaplain-General of the Church of England rebuked an obstreperous clergyman who advocated civil disobedience against nuclear armament, for 'trying to embarrass those who sought to guide us'. And in the same Convocation the offending priest was accused of 'pure pacifism'.

The then Bishop of Rochester had this to say in 1958: 'For the Christian, aggressive war is always wrong. But defensive war, or war to preserve order to save others from oppression, is a very different matter. As such, in an evil world, war can be the lesser evil.' No less a dignitary than the former Archbishop of Canterbury said in the same year: 'All war is detestable, horrible and sinful in the sight of God. But in a sinful world, good people have to do sinful things sometimes. You have to obey Caesar and God, and the task of humanity is to reconcile the two. Very often in a sinful world you have to support Caesar, even though it is far less than the complete will of God'.

This statement can be confronted with some passages of the New Testament. 'And be not conformed to this world; but be ye transformed by the renewing of your mind, that ye may prove what is that good and acceptable and perfect will of God' (*Rom.* 12:2); 'For such are false apostles, deceitful workers, transforming themselves into the

Apostles of Christ. And no marvel: for Satan himself is transformed into an angel of light. Therefore it is no great thing if his ministers also be transformed as the ministers of righteousness' (*2 Cor.* 11:13/15). 'If any man preach any other gospel unto you than that you have received, let him be accursed' (*Gal. 1:9*), not 'as being lords over God's heritage, but being examples to the flock' (*1 Peter* 5:3). 'He that saith I know him, and keepeth not his commandments, is a liar and the truth is not in him' (*1 John* 2:4); and, 'Thou has tried them which say they are apostles, and are not, and hast found them liars' (*Rev.* 2:2).

Karl Barth, in a letter to a fellow clergyman, wrote in September 1938 of 'the strange times in which . . . for the sake of one's faith . . . one has to give priority to one's fear of injustice and love of freedom over one's fear of violence and love of peace . . . '.

Bishop Barnes, who in the twenties caused a great uproar with his *Rise of Christianity*, an attempt to take the teaching of Jesus seriously, expressed the view that Jesus' doctrine was indeed 'pure pacifism'. 'Of all Roman virtues . . . patriotism . . . was the most highly esteemed. By the bravery of her citizens . . . Rome had conquered the civilised world, as it was then known . . . A refusal to fight was treachery to the beloved and eternal city. Unfortunately for their happiness, such refusal was part of the creed which Christians held and taught.

'The passage in Matthew, in which Jesus said that he could summon legions of angels, amplifies the corresponding story in Mark (14:17/50). There can be little doubt that it was intended to emphasise the pacifism inherent in the teaching of Christ, a pacifism which the Gospels derive from Q. Obviously a sect which took seriously such passages as "Blessed are the peacemakers"; "Resist not him that is evil", "Love your enemies and pray for them that persecute you", could not countenance the doing of evil that good might come, which is the essence of war. The Christian attitude to war is crystallized by Matthew in the sentence, "put up again thy sword into its place, for all they that take the sword shall perish with the sword". Somewhat surprisingly, it recurs in the Apocalypse (13:10): "If any man shall kill with the sword, with the sword must he be killed". Here is the patience and the faith of saints.

'Although the pacifism of the Christians was regarded with angry contempt, it was probably not the main cause of the detestation in which they were held. The Roman government does not seem to have needed, during the period covered by the first two centuries of the Christian movement, to have recourse to conscription in order to maintain the armies on the frontiers at full strength. The population of the Empire at the end of the first century of our era is estimated to have numbered seventy million: the strength of the army varied, but may have averaged six hundred thousand, less than one per cent of the population. The Civil Wars at the end of the Roman Republic had largely eliminated the good fighting material of Italy; and increasingly troops were recruited on the frontiers. The urban proletariat, among which Christianity made headway most effectively, was not promising military material.

'But though Christian pacifism was in all probability not a source of serious trouble to the army authorities, the Christian attitude towards enemies who were always threatening the frontiers, must have been deemed both absurd and mischievous. The barbarians beyond the frontiers were regarded as being little better than savages, whose existence was a perpetual menace. But the Christians affirmed that to them also the Gospel should be preached: they also were children of God the Father. In Christ, as we read in *Col.* 3:11, there should be no Greek or Jew, circumcision or uncircumcision, barbarian, Scythian, bondman, freeman: but Christ is all, and in all' (pp. 299/300).

Conclusion

The voice of the great teachers of peace, the voice of Jesus, of Ashoka, of Gandhi, is still alive in the world. Christians and non-Christians alike give expression to the spirit which was once preached by 'a voice in the wilderness'. We owe the following small collection to Stauffer who quotes these statements in his remarkable little book, *Die Botschaft Jesu* (The Message of Jesus).

A few hours before his execution by the German Army, the Belgian airforce captain, de la Lindi, wrote: 'There is no need to tell you that I forgive all who wronged me, even my enemies . . . '. After dreadful torture by his captors, Torleif Tellesen, a Norwegian partisan, wrote before being put to death: 'Do not repay with hatred that which is done against us: that would merely create new hatred.' About to be executed by the blackshirts, Dr. Passavalli wrote: 'I forgive those who sentenced me, they did not know what they were doing.' The evening before his death by shooting, Hendrik Hos, a Dutch physician, penned these words: 'I beg of you, and this is my last wish, do not allow yourselves to feel hatred . . . '. Twenty-two-year-old van Beek, a German pottery artist, wrote the following, soon after she heard the court pronounce her death sentence for anti- Nazi activities: 'I am free of any sentiment of anger or hatred . . . I feel only love for my fellow men, for all of them . . . '. Before his execution, Manouchian, an Armenian journalist in Paris, wrote to his wife: 'In the face of death I declare that I feel no hatred towards the German people'. The last letter of Fucik, a Czech communist leader, reads: 'You must know that I have never felt any antagonism towards the German people.' The Dutch communist Pstma, also writing to his wife, warned in his last letter, 'Do not allow our son to grow up hating the German people. If he wants to revenge his father, let him fight a corrupt social order which causes war and all its consequences. The people of Germany are themselves victims of these consequences.' Before being shot, Ernest Omer, a Belgian worker, signed his last letter to his mother: 'Your son begs you to bear no anger or hatred in your heart.' Upon hearing his death sentence, the Italian Socialist Pietro Benedetti, wrote to his children: 'Make your love for people your religion,' and to his wife: 'Forgive, as I myself forgive them.'

Distant echoes of the teaching of the Nazarene.

10
Jesus And Women

Introduction

'See, I shall lead her, so that I will make her a living spirit resembling you males. For every woman who makes herself male will enter the kingdom of Heaven.' This cryptic sentence appears in the apocryphal *Gospel of Thomas* (Logion 114).

Jesus could have said, without his message being misunderstood; 'See, I shall lead him and make him a living spirit resembling you females. For every man who makes himself female will enter the kingdom.' Perhaps we understand the logion better in 2 Clement of Rome 5:7: 'For the Lord himself, being asked by a certain person, when the kingdom would come?, answered, When the two shall be one, and that which is without is as that within; and the male with the female, neither male nor female.'

Akhnaton, king of Egypt, was to my knowledge the first who taught the worship of one universal God whose work we see in the life-giving sun, and without whom there would be no light but impenetrable darkness. After his death the priests of the old gods regained their power, and those who remained true to the teaching of Akhnaton had to flee the country. Their leader was an Egyptian prince who used only one of his names: Moses. (Usually the name of a heathen god was prefixed, Ra-Moses, Tuth-moses etc.)

The refugees stayed together, wandering in the desert for a long time and remaining faithful to the idea of one omnipotent God. They called themselves the tribes of Israel and after Moses's death, finding Canaan, a fertile country, conquered it after a long struggle. The God of Akhnaton was transformed into the tribal war-god of the Hebrews.

Among the legends of the Jewish people was one promising them that in time of need a Messiah would arise. He would be an anointed king of the Jews, a mighty warrior, a son of God. During the oppressive rule of the Romans many Jews expected that the time of the Messiah was approaching.

Some believed that the Messiah had already arrived in the person of a simple, wise and profound teacher, and called him the Christ (Greek for 'the Anointed One'), the eternal son of God. In fact Jesus of Nazareth was very different from the expected Messiah, he was the son of a poor carpenter, and instead of a conquering hero he was a preacher with great poetic imagination, a man of peace.

The Women's Bible — or is it?

One of the first obstacles Jesus had to overcome, among the conventions which existed in his society, was a patriarchal system based on the domination of men over women. It had established itself after nomadic men had settled down to till the soil, build a home, cultivate grain, fruit and vegetables, breed cattle: the beginning of property. During the first period of this development man was still a hunter and warrior. While men and women led a nomadic existence, they shared all vicissitudes of life equally. This changed radically when man became a chattel owner. Hunting and war remained his pursuits, woman became part of his stationary wealth, confined to serving her husband, and bearing children which were recognisably his own. They were to inherit and continue to cultivate his property after his death.

The patriarchal society often treated women as the inferior sex; and early Christianity, the evangelists, the apostles the Church Fathers and religious teachers of later periods continued the effort to keep women in servitude, an attitude which prevails to the present.

It is perhaps strange that so many women have accepted Christianity; how, in the name of Jesus, they are deprived here on earth and even in 'the kingdom' of all dignity and due respect.

1 Cor. 7:1ff	It is good for a man not to touch a woman. Nevertheless, to avoid fornication, let every man have his own wife, and let every woman to have her own husband . . . For I would that all men were even as myself . . . I say therefore to the unmarried and widowed, it is good for them if they abide even as I. But if they cannot contain, let them marry: for it is better to marry than to burn . . .
1 Cor. 7:34-40	There is a difference also between a wife and a virgin. The married woman careth for the things

of the world, how she may please her husband . . . Nevertheless he that standeth stedfast in his heart, having no necessity that he will keep his virgin, doeth well. So then, he that giveth her in marriage, doeth well, but he that giveth her not in marriage doeth better. The wife is bound by the Law as long as her husband liveth but if her husband is dead, she is at liberty to be married to whom she will; only in the Lord. But she is happier if she so abide, after my judgment . . .

1 Cor. 11:3ff. But I would have you know, that the head of every man is Christ; and that the head of the woman is the man; and the head of Christ is God . . . But every woman that prayeth and prophesieth, having her head uncovered dishonoureth her head: for that is even all one as if she were shaven . . . For the man is not of the woman, but woman is of the man . . . (Then Paul says the opposite) . . . For as the woman is of the man, so is the man also by the woman, but all things of God . . . Judge for yourselves: is it comely that a woman pray unto God uncovered?

1 Cor. 14:34-35 Let your women keep silence in the churches: for it is not permitted for them to speak; but they are commanded to be under obedience, as also says the Law. And if they learn anything, let them ask their husband at home: for it is a shame for women to speak in the church.

Col. 3:18 to 4:1 Wives, submit yourselves unto your own husbands, as it is fit in the Lord. Husbands, love your wives and be not bitter against them. For the husband is the head of the wife, even as Christ is the head of the Church, and he is the saviour of the body. Therefore, as the Church is subject unto Christ, so let the wives be to their own husbands in everything . . . Nevertheless, let every one in particular so love his wife even as himself, and the wife see that she reverence her husband . . .

1 Timothy 9:15ff In like manner also, that women adorn themselves in modest apparel, with shamefacedness and sobriety, not with broided hair, or gold, or pearls, or costly array. But which becometh women pro-

fessing godliness with good works. Let the woman learn in silence with all subjection. But I suffer not a woman to teach, nor to usurp authority over men, but to be in silence. Adam was first formed, then Eve. Adam was not deceived, but the woman being deceived was in the transgression. Notwithstanding she shall be saved in childbearing, if they continue in faith and charity and holiness with sobriety.

1 Timothy 3:11   Even so must the (deacon's) wives be grave, not slandererous, sober and faithful in all things.

1 Peter 3:1 to 6   Likewise, ye wives, be in subjection to your own husbands; that, if any obey not the word, they also may without the word in the conversation of the wives; While they behold your chaste conversation coupled with fear . . . For after this manner in the old time the holy women also, who trusted in God, adorned themselves, being in subjection to their own husbands . . .

I shall refrain from quoting other passages from the Bible, the apostolic fathers, the Church Fathers and other luminaries of the church that show the hostility prevailing against women. These examples are sufficient to demonstrate the atmosphere in which the child Jesus grew up: the patriarchal disregard and contempt for the female sex. It is to his credit that Jesus by his teaching revised this social prejudice showing himself as a brother to every human being: man or woman.

The child Jesus

Jesus' early years were of course strongly influenced by the religion of his fathers. God himself was a male figure; the Lord of Hosts leading the Jews even in their military adventures; strict, vengeful, possessive, jealous, dominant, the Father of all. Almost all important figures for the Israelites were men: Abraham, Jacob, Moses, Aaron, Joshua, David, the Maccabees and the prophets. The priesthood, unlike the heathen priests was exclusively male.

In the temple women had their own Court; they were forbidden to enter the Inner Courts. Learning was discouraged; if they wanted to know anything their husbands were supposed to provide the answer. Man was allowed to divorce his wife if he no longer desired her, without any excuse or question. A writ of divorce was enough to deprive her of her home and even of her children. She could not practise certain professions or become a priestess. Nor could she offer sacrifices in the company of men. She was 'defiled' and 'unclean' on the occasions of childbirth and menstruation, and had to be 'purified'. The Law dealt with women with greater severity, in practice also judges were often more lenient with man's sexual behaviour. Women, slaves and minors were not included in 'common grace'.

There were many Jews who doubted that women had a soul at all. To the biblical Eve they attributed the cause of sin and death, and believed as a consequence that woman should be kept in 'apartheid' so that she could not act as a temptress and occasion of sin. Many Church Fathers inherited that belief and held the view that woman was the originator of sin.

Jesus was undoubtedly well versed in scripture and influenced by it. He read the passage in which the Lord commanded: 'Slay utterly old and young, both males and little children, and women . . . And he said unto them, 'Defile the house and fill the courts with the slain, Go ye forth!' And they went forth and slew in the city.' (Ezekiel 9:5-6) 'And if a husband accused his spouse that she was not a virgin on her wedding night and it turned out that it was true and the tokens of virginity be not found for the damsel, then they shall bring out the damsel to the door of her father's house, and the men of the city shall stone her with stones that she die . . . ' (Deuteronomy 22:20-21)

And what did Jesus learn about sexual relations? 'The woman also with whom man shall lie with seed of copulation, they shall both bathe themselves with water, and be unclean until the even . . . ' (Leviticus 15:1) Many sexual relations, modes and irregularities were to be punished by death (Leviticus 20). Perhaps the most uncompromisingly prejudiced is Exodus 22:18 for which many innocent women have paid with their lives in the course of centuries: 'Thou shalt not suffer a witch to live.'

A fine line leads from violence to sex in Moses's speech to the Israelites after their battle with Midian: 'Now therefore kill every male among the little ones, and kill every woman that hath known man by lying with him. But all the women children that have not known a man by lying with him, keep alive for yourselves . . . ' (Numbers 31:17). And the thread assumed a note of tenderness when Jesus read the Song of Songs, the ecstatic hymn on the love of man and woman.

Jesus, the young Israelite

It is likely that he experienced the bitter-sweet impulse of erotic desire which may have only confirmed his patriarchal outlook. Seventeen years of his youth are undocumented and sexual inexperience would have aroused the contempt of his Jewish environment and even of his immediate relatives. Abstinence in a young man was something the ancient Hebrews considered abnormal and against the will of God.

Some claim that Jesus was homoerotic; a theory which I consider unlikely. It is true that he appears to have resisted environmental pressure to marry. This was unusual in his society. It is true that among the three temptations the erotic experience was not even mentioned. And it is also true that he surrounded himself with men whose age is unknown to us. Finally, there is the attempt of John (in the gospel written by those who seemed to have shared his style and tradition) to present himself as 'the disciple whom Jesus loved'. This may indicate a special relationship with his master: but this is no evidence to show that Jesus' erotic desire was polarized to his own sex. It merely suggests that in the service of his mission the company of young men was preferable, and he himself may have been that rare phenomenon, one of the men 'who made themselves eunuchs for the sake of the kingdom of Heaven' (Matthew 19:12)

Nothing is known of Jesus' life between his twelfth and thirtieth years and it is surprising that so few writers of fiction have dared to fill in this gap with imaginative speculation. Enquiry into Jesus' youth remains one of the most guarded taboos of the Christian religion.

Before the great change

In considering the role of women in the New Testament I need not mention Jesus' relation to Mary, his mother. Two chapters in this book deal with his attitude towards her. The first feminine name mentioned in the New Testament is that of the Old Testament Rachel: 'A voice was heard in Ramah, lamentation and bitter weeping: Rachel weeping for her children, because they were not.' (Jeremiah 31:15) This passage was regarded by Matthew as an example of 'fulfilled prophesies', although it is not clear to me what the alleged 'murder of the innocents' has to do with the words of Jeremiah.

Anna, a wise woman of 84, appeared in Jerusalem speaking about the birth of the Saviour. Another woman was Elizabeth, a cousin of Mary who, when about to give birth to John the Baptist, 'was filled with the Holy Ghost'. Her encounter with Mary is one of the most lyrical passages of the New Testament and, indeed, most of these accounts show a reverential treatment of the much maligned female sex.

Most of the women who attested to Jesus' miraculous powers during his ministry were Israelites. In the fable of the miracle curing Peter's mother-in-law, Jesus healed her of an incapacitating fever (Matthew 8:14). A woman who was consumed by an issue of blood for twelve years, dared to touch Jesus' garment. He turned round and said to her: 'Daughter, be of good comfort, thy faith hath made thee whole' (Matthew 9:20).

At the request of a man called Jairus, Jesus went into his house where mourning relatives were gathered round the bed of Jairus's dead daughter. But Jesus said: 'The maid is not dead but sleepeth.' Despite the doubt and scorn of those present, the young woman opened her eyes and rose from her bed. (Matthew 9:18- 26).

The turning point in Jesus' attitude to women came when he travelled in Samaria (John 4:5-42). The Samaritans were despised by the Jews. Jesus who was thirsty had to overcome two prejudices – one against women and one against Samaritans – when he asked a Samaritan woman who was drawing water from the famous Jacob's Well, for a drink. A dialogue ensued between the domineering Jewish male and the Samaritan woman; a confrontation which was perhaps one of the first steps Jesus made towards the realisation of his true self. All his Jewish paternalistic arrogance disappeared and his eyes filled with tears. The dialogue contains some of Jesus' most profound thoughts, and he certainly *won* the argument. Yet, the outcome realized the humiliated woman's victory over the Son of David. He had overcome both his prejudices, against foreigners and against women.

This decisive change of attitude was preceded by another meeting with a foreign woman which must also have deeply impressed him. It happened on the coast of Tyre, where 'a woman of Canaan came out and cried unto him saying, Sir, have mercy on me, thou Son of David; my daughter is grievously vexed with a devil. But he answered and said, 'I am not sent but after the lost sheep of Israel.' Then came she and begged him, 'Sir, help me.' But he answered and said, 'It is not meet to take the children's bread and to cast it to dogs.' And she said, 'Truth Sir, yet the dogs eat of the crumbs which fall from their master's table.' Then Jesus answered and said unto her, 'O woman, great is thy faith, be it unto thee even as thou wilt.' And her daughter was made whole from that very hour.' (Matthew 15:22-28).

These were the women who had a lasting effect on Jesus' ideas. It became clear to him that women, who were despised, are human beings imbued with the Holy Spirit.

An unnamed woman, a great sinner (often confused with Mary Magdalene) came and washed Jesus' feet, wiping and kissing them, and using a precious ointment in her devotion. When those present reproached him for allowing a notorious sinner to continue with her action, he said, 'I say unto thee, Her sins which are many, are forgiven for she loved much: but to whom little is forgiven, the same loveth little. And he said unto her, "Thy sins are forgiven . . . Thy faith hath saved thee; go in peace."

The growing contrast between the old laws and Jesus' new understanding became obvious when an irate crowd came to Jesus with a woman caught in adultery. They came to him as to a rabbi, to condemn her to death. The adulterer had got away, but the adulteress was brought to justice. In their anger the crowd were betraying their own hidden desires.

Was he, a rabbi, entitled to ignore the law which demands her execution by stoning? Was he, realising the patriarchal undertones of law and vengeance, to pronounce sentence? In order to gain time, he wrote on the sand. Then he said, 'You judge according to the flesh, I do not judge anybody.' Eventually he ruled: 'He who is without sin, let him throw the first stone.' The crowd dispersed, only the woman lay prostrate in the sand. Jesus asked: 'Woman, where are the men who accused you? Is no one left?' The woman answered: 'No one, Sir.' 'Neither do I sentence you. Go and sin no more.' (John 8:4-11)

If you are untouched by evil, the desire to punish is no longer there.

Martha and Mary of Bethany

In Luke 10:38-42 we are told: 'Now it came to pass as they went, that he entered in a certain village (Bethany – AR) and a certain woman named Martha received him into her home. And she had a sister called Mary which also sat at Jesus' feet and heard his word. But Martha was cumbered with much serving, and came to him and said, Sir, doest thou not care that my sister hath left me to serve alone? Bid her therefore that she help me. And Jesus answered and said unto her: Martha, Martha, thou art careful and troubled about many things: but one thing is needful, and Mary hath chosen that good part which shall not be taken away from her.'

There has been much discussion about this saying, apparently proving that woman's spirituality should be more highly valued than her domesticity. Some believe it was not intended as a reproach, merely a hint at the importance of reason. Others again say that Martha's domesticity was on a lower plane than her other virtues. Martha had all the virtues which are expected from a good hostess in a patriarchal society, whilst Mary preferred listening to the Word. At a later date Mary proved her awareness of Jesus' divine ministry by washing his feet and pouring a vial of precious oil over his head. Some critics were not accommodating. Meister Eckhart for instance claimed that Mary listened to Jesus more for pleasure than for spiritual enlightenment.

Be this as it may, a later passage shows Martha's significance by recognising Jesus as he *wished* to be known. Perhaps she even anticipated Peter's speaking those significant words at Caesarea Philippi. 'Then Martha, as soon as she heard that Jesus was coming, went and met him, but Mary still sat in the house. Then said Martha unto Jesus, Sir, if thou hadst been here, my brother (Lazarus) had not died. But I know that even now, whatsoever thou wilt ask of God, God will give it thee. Jesus saith unto her, Thy brother shall rise again. Martha saith unto him, I know that he shall rise again at the last day. Jesus saith unto her, I am (he probably said, God is . . . AR) the resurrection and the life, he that believeth in me (in him . . . AR) though he were dead, yet shall he live. Believest thou this? She saith unto him: I believe that thou art the Christ, the Son of God, which should come into the world. And when she had so said, she went her way . . .' (John 11:20-28) This episode presents Martha in a more favourable light and shows that without having sat at Jesus' feet and without being prompted, she made Peter's proclamation spontaneously and simply.

Bultmann remarks that Martha was possessed by a certainty that even her sister did not have. It is obvious that Jesus loved and respected the sisters of Bethany and gained from them the insight and understanding of woman's spiritual depth.

Mary Magdalene

Another woman disciple, and probably a close friend of Jesus' was Mary Magdalene. She is often confused with Mary of Bethany, and even with the Magna Peccatrix whom the crowd had wanted to stone. Their friendship developed after Jesus had cured her disturbed mind (seven devils) as related in Luke 8:2. Possibly she was a woman of great beauty and dignity who engaged the Teacher's interest and benevolence. Of all the women who surrounded him, he showed her most affection. John claims that Jesus' mother and Mary Magdalene stood with him at the foot of the cross while all the apostles and disciples had fled and were in hiding.

After her recovery, Mary Magdalene, deeply touched by Jesus' words and deeds, attached herself to the little group of disciples. She liked to be near him and probably became one of his confidential companions. There is no indication of any physical relationship, although several modern writers like to present her as Jesus' lover and even wife. A venerable inquirer, St. Augustine, called her the 'apostle of apostles'. And Mary Magdalene was described as the first person to whom Jesus appeared after his resurrection.

I am convinced that the resurrection story is a symbolic tale, but I have to admit that the reports in the gospels claiming that women were the first to encounter the resurrected Jesus cannot be ignored.

The Russian writer, Merezhkovsky, a Christian, wrote this moving tribute "The faith of those women was stronger than the faith of men. Peter, the ever faithful rock, ran away like sand. The love of men proved powerless, the love of women endured. The sun of men's love sets in death, the sun of women rises in resurrection."

The situation of women

Did Jesus propose change in the role of women? Under the Jewish law only man could separate from his wife by giving her a Bill of Divorce. Jesus proclaimed that man cannot divorce his wife arbitrarily: 'But I say unto you that man cannot divorce his wife either . . . whosoever shall put away his wife . . . causeth her to commit adultery, and whosoever shall marry her that is divorced committeth adultery' (Matthew 13:22). Mark 10:12 goes even further: ' . . . the Pharisees came unto him and asked him, is it lawful for a man to put away his wife, tempting him. And he answered and said unto them: What did Moses command you? And they said, Moses suffered to write a Bill of Divorcement to put her away. And Jesus answered and said unto them, for the hardness of your hearts he wrote this precept. But from the beginning of creation God made them male and female. For this cause shall a man leave his father and mother and cleave to his wife. And they twain shall be one flesh: so then they are no more twain, but one flesh. What God therefore hath joined together, let no man put asunder.'

While I do not agree with strictures against divorce, the saying shows that Jesus tried to establish equal rights for the sexes.

Jesus showed forbearance and refused to condemn the adulterous woman. He chose friends and followers among women whom he treated with great respect. He learned to understand their ways and needs and abandoned, or at least modified, his patriarchal values. He took the union between the sexes seriously, to the extent that he expected woman to relinquish part of her (assumed) female element, and man to recognise and conquer his own male element, so that the two shall be one spiritual entity.

In her *'Die Weiblichkeit Gottes'* Christa Mulack puts this point very succinctly: 'As long as man has not integrated his feminine character, he needs a woman onto whom to project the inferior 'feminine traits.' (p. 277).

And now the passage of the *Gospel of Thomas* which I quoted at the opening of this chapter reveals its wisdom: 'See, I shall lead her, so that I will make her a living spirit, resembling you males. For every woman who makes herself male, will enter the kingdom of Heaven.' Clement's sentence reinforces this: 'The two will become one, the external and the internal, the male element and the female element, and there will be no male and no female.'

The aim of Jesus was to incorporate all human beings of different tribal, national, party, class and sex into an all-embracing oneness with himself and to unite himself with God, in mutual devotion and love.

'Let us love one another, for the love is of God; and anyone that loveth is born of God and knoweth God . . . God dwelleth in us and his love is perfect. Hereby we know that we dwell in him and he is in us . . . because he hath given us of his spirit; he that dwelleth in love dwelleth in God and God in him . . . ' (1 John 3:7-16).

11
Jesus Lived And Died A Jew

The Jewishness of Jesus

It is likely that Jesus never thought of his doctrine as one to be carried into the world among the nations. Where the English translation of the Gospels speaks of Gentiles (whenever the context is flattering) or of heathens (where the context implies contempt), the Greek original always employs the word ἔθνοι (nations). The Jews thought of themselves as the 'House of Israel', while all the others were the 'nations'. This distinction was similar to the Greeks' way of thinking, who referred to themselves as 'Hellenes' and all the others were 'barbarians' (strangers, foreigners).

Originally, Jesus thought and taught that his disciples should not 'go into the way of the nations', and should not 'enter into any city of the Samaritans'; but 'go rather to the lost sheep of the house of Israel' (*Matthew* 10:5). In ordinary language this could be summarised as saying that his disciples should not worry about teaching foreigners but concern themselves with non-believing Jews. The derivation of these words is not far to seek: 'My people hath been lost sheep: their shepherds have caused them to go astray . . . ' (*Jer.* 50:6). It is the same prophet who exclaims in despair: 'Israel is a scattered sheep . . . (*Jer.* 50:17). And speaking of Israel, Jehovah himself says: ' . . . they were scattered because there is no shepherd . . . my flock was scattered upon all the face of the earth and none did search or seek after them . . . I will seek that which is lost . . . ' (*Ezek.* 34:5/6). This chapter of Ezekiel is full of 'feed my flock' references.

Neither can Jesus be said to have rejected the Jewish Law. On the contrary, he made it clear that it was the basis of all his aspirations. How else could his momentous statement be explained: 'Think not that I am come to destroy the law, or the prophets: I am not come to destroy, but to fulfil. For verily I say unto you, Till heaven and earth pass, one jot or one tittle shall in no wise pass from the law, till all be fulfilled. Whosoever therefore shall break one of these least commandments, and shall teach men so, he shall be called the least in the kingdom of heaven: but whosoever shall do and teach them: the same shall be called great in the kingdom of heaven' (*Matthew* 5:17/19). We find the same attitude expressed in Luke: 'It is easier for heaven and earth to pass than one tittle of the law to fail' (*Luke* 16:17). Here again Jesus was merely paraphrasing Old Testament scripture: 'The grass withereth, the flower fadeth: but the word of our God shall stand for ever' (*Isaiah* 40:8); and, 'The heaven shall vanish away like smoke, and the earth shall wax old like a garment . . . but my salvation shall be for ever . . . ' (*Isaiah* 51:6).

Even where Jesus castigates the errors of the scribes (the rabbis) and the Pharisees (the orthodox) – should my speculation be mistaken that those words were addressed to the rich – he calls upon his followers to distinguish between the commandments of God and those who unworthily proclaim them: 'The scribes and Pharisees sit in Moses's seat: All therefore whatsoever they bid you observe and do; but do not ye after their works: for they say and do not' (*Matthew* 23:2/3).

On many occasions Jesus clearly insisted upon the observance of Mosaic law. To the leper he cured he said: 'Show yourself to the priest and offer for thy cleansing those things which Moses commanded . . . ' (*Matthew* 8:4, *Mark* 1:44, *Luke* 5:14), a reference to *Lev.* 14:2ff, where the ceremonial laws for recovery from the dread disease are described in detail.

In the chapter on 'prayer' I discuss Jesus' views on public prayer as expressed in *Matthew* 6:5/6, a view also to be found in the Old Testament: 'He went in therefore and shut the door . . . and prayed unto the Lord' (*2 Kings* 4:33). His words on fasting in *Matthew* 6:16/18 are reminiscent of *Isaiah* 58:5/6. The saying concerning prayer is followed by the injunction: 'But when ye pray use not vain repetitions, as the heathens [foreigners] do: for they think that they shall be heard for their much speaking' (*Matthew* 6:7). The Old Testament origin is: 'Let thy words be few . . . a fool's voice is known by multitude of words . . . (*Eccles.* 5:2/3), and, 'They called on the name of Baal from morning even until noon, saying, O Baal, hear us . . . ' (*1 Kings* 18:26).

We may also examine the attitude of Jesus to the Jewish ceremonial of sacrifice and burnt offerings: 'Woe unto you, scribes and Pharisees, hypocrites! for ye pay tithe of mint and anise and cummin, and have omitted the weightier matters of the Law: judgment, mercy and faith: these ought ye have done, and not to leave the others undone' (*Matthew*

23:23). Similar words are reported in *Luke* 11:42. The same idea appears in its simplest and most impressive form in Matthew: 'I will have mercy and not sacrifice' (*Matthew* 9:13). The Old Testament is equally explicit: 'Hath the Lord as great delight in burnt offerings and sacrifices, as in obeying the voice of the Lord? (*1 Sam.* 15:22); 'Will the Lord be pleased with thousands of rams, or with ten thousand rivers of oil? and what does the Lord require of thee, but to do justly and love mercy, and to walk humbly with God' (*Micah.* 6:7/8); 'For I desire mercy, and not sacrifice, and the knowledge of God more than burnt offerings' (*Hos.* 6:6).

The forgiveness of sin is an aspect of Jesus' teaching which is quoted by many Christians to show that he overruled the Jewish idea of such forgiveness as the prerogative of the Father. They quote the critics of Jesus, who exclaimed: 'Who can forgive sins but God only?' (*Mark* 2:7 and *Luke* 5:21). The critics had a good authority in the Old Testament: 'I, even I, am he that blotteth out thy transgressions for mine own sake and will not remember thy sins' (*Isaiah* 43:25). and 'I have blotted out . . . thy transgressions and . . . thy sins; for I have redeemed thee' (*Isaiah* 44:22). There are other passages where God promises pardon for sins and iniquity: 'I will pardon them . . . ' (*Jer.* 50:20). 'Though your sins be scarlet, they shall be white as snow; though they be red as crimson, they shall be as wool' (*Isaiah* 1:18); 'I will forgive their iniquity, whereby they have sinned, and whereby they have transgressed against me' (*Jer.* 33:8), and, 'God pardoneth iniquity' (*Micah* 7:18). It is not surprising that the notion of a man pardoning the sin and iniquity of his fellows was offensive to Jesus' listeners. His answer, recorded in the three synoptic gospels, is revealing and dignified: 'The Son of men hath power on earth to forgive sins . . . (*Matthew* 9:6, *Mark* 2:10 and *Luke* 5:24). The Greek term used by the three evangelists is ἐξουσίαν ἔχει, that is, 'has authority'. Yet the Revised Version retains the word 'power', and even the *NEB* uses the word 'right'. However, it is significant that Jesus used the word 'authority' which implies that there is someone to give authority, to endow with authority. The suggestion here is that God has endowed the Son of man with authority, and in this sense, the right, to forgive sins. It is strange that most translations avoid the obvious rendering of the word ἐξουσία as 'authority', an exception being the Revised Standard Version of the Roman Catholic Bible. The Latin translation still retained the original term 'habere autoritatem', and is followed by the translations into Romance languages. The Protestant Bibles in the various Germanic languages, such as English, use Luther's translation of the word as 'Macht' (power).

The reluctance to translate ἐξουσία as authority is the more remarkable since in another context the same Greek word is correctly rendered by the word 'authority' (*Matt.* 7:29 and *Mark* 1:22).

Graves and Podro are doubtful of Jesus having used even the word 'authority'. They maintain that such terminology would amount to a public declaration of his Messiahship, and that Jesus showed himself anxious, even at a later date, to impress upon his disciples the need to keep his claim a close secret. 'The incident has,' they say, 'been rewritten to assure Gentile doubters that Jesus plainly declared himself, and showed himself to be, God; and that the Pharisees knew well what they were doing when they subsequently rejected his claim' (*NGR*, p.277).

The God of Jesus

When asked which is the greatest commandment of all, Jesus answered: 'The first of all commandments is, Hear, O Israel; the Lord our God is One Lord. And thou shalt love the Lord thy God with all thy heart, and with all thy soul, and with all thy strength: this is the first commandment' (*Mark* 12:29). This commandment which is also found in *Luke* 10:27, has its origin in the Old Testament, it is in fact a verbatim quotation from *Deut.* 6:4/5. It is an affirmation of the Oneness of God, and of his indivisibility, of the refusal to entertain the idea of any divinity other than the One. The clear and honest distinction between himself and God was not even motivated by a desire to show that he himself did not claim divinity: such arrogance and presumption would not have occurred to a God-fearing pious Jew. He made the distinction to show that his strength, his knowledge and his goodness are not really his own, but a gift of God to his humble servant. 'Why callest thou me good, there is none good but one, that is, God' (*Mark* 10:8, *Matthew* 19:17 and *Luke* 18:19). As I mentioned earlier, even this self-effacing humility is being exploited by some commentators who try to show that this remark was a sophisticated way of saying, 'You think I am good? Don't you see if I am good then I must be God!'

It is not only in goodness that Jesus does not claim to share the power of God. He disclaims any knowledge of divine intentions when he says: 'But of that day and hour knoweth no man, neither the angels of the heavens, nor the Son, but my Father only' (*Matthew* 24:36, *Mark* 13:32).

Finally, Jesus made it quite clear that his powers and deeds are not his own, he being merely a tool of the divine will which acts through him: 'The Son can do nothing of himself . . . ' (*John* 5:30); 'I do nothing of myself, but as my Father hath taught me . . . (*John* 8:28), 'I have not spoken of myself, but the Father which sent me . . . '(*John* 12:49); and, 'I speak not of myself, but the Father that dwelleth in me, he doeth the works' (*John* 14:10).

Israel, my firstborn son

The God Jehovah says that 'Israel is my firstborn son . . . (*Exod.* 4:22). He grows quite sentimental over his firstborn: 'When Israel was a child, I loved him and called my son out of Egypt' (*Hos.* 11:1). He affirms his paternity: 'I am father to Israel, and Ephraim is my firstborn' (*Jer.* 31:9). From these passages we can see the relationship that existed between the house of Israel and its God: the relationship of father and son.

It was customary among Jews to call God 'Father', and Jesus merely conforms to this widespread usage of referring to God as Father. There are many passages in which the English translation reads 'my father', while Jesus merely used the definite article 'the Father'. (See chapter 'The Lord Jesus Christ'.)

Passages of Jewish scripture may contribute to our understanding of the relationship of ancient Israel to God, their Father. We have already quoted the words, 'Israel is my firstborn son . . . ' which merely means that all peoples are children of God, but Israel is the firstborn. We also find passages in the Old Testament which assure Israel: 'Ye are children of the Lord your God' (*Deut.* 14:1); and, 'I have said, ye are gods: and all of you are children of the Most High' (*Psalm* 82:6). Elsewhere we read: 'And God shall call thee son . . . (*Ben Sira* 5:10); 'Beloved are Israel, for they are called sons of the Highest' (*Abo.* 3:3) and, 'Even if they are foolish, even if they transgress, they are still called sons . . . (*Sifre on Deut.*).

It is from Klausner's remarkable *JN* that I quote: 'In Judaism God is regarded as Father even in the sense of begetter and creator of the Jewish nation; and so the Jews use "Father" and "King" in the same breath (Abinu Malkenu = our father and king)! (p.104).

The Jewish teacher

The Gospels present Jesus as a great teacher of Jewish thought, well versed in scripture and the prophets, able to quote long passages word for word and to comment aptly on some of the most difficult writings. He uses parables often borrowed from the Old Testament and early talmudic texts which were, at the time, only a verbal tradition, and enhances them with his poetic power. Klausner says, 'throughout the gospels there is not one item of ethical teaching which can not be paralleled either in the Old Testament, or in the talmudic or midrashic literature of the period near to the time of Jesus' (ibid., p.384).

I have chosen a selection of the words of Jesus from just one of the Gospels, the first. A similar selection could be compiled from any other gospel, and indeed from the whole text and imagery of the New Testament where it does not record Jesus' own sayings.

Gospel according to St. Matthew	*Jewish writings*
'Man shall not live by bread alone, but by every word that proceedeth out of the mouth of God.' (4:4) – Acknowledged –	'Man doth not live by bread alone, but by every word that proceedeth out of the mouth of the Lord doth man live.' (Deut. 8:3)
'Thou shalt not tempt the Lord thy God' – Acknowledged – (4:7)	*Ye shall not tempt the Lord your God* (Deut. 6:13)
'Thou shalt worship the Lord thy God, and him alone shalt thou serve' –Acknowledged– (4:10)	*'Thou shalt fear the Lord thy God, and serve him'* (Deut. 6:13) (Deut:10:20)
[Narrator: 'The people which sat in the darkness saw great light; and to them which sat in the region and shadow of death light is sprung up] (4:16)	*{The people that walked in the darkness have seen a great light: they that dwell in the land of the shadow of death, upon them hath the light shined}* (Isaiah 9:2)
'The kingdom of heaven is at hand'(4:17)	*'The kingdom under the whole heaven shall be given to the saints')* Deut. 6: (Dan. 7:27)
'Blessed are the poor in spirit' (5:3)	*'Saith the Lord: to this man will I look . . . to him that is poor and of a contrite spirit . . .'* (Isaiah 6:2)
'Blessed are they that mourn for they shall be comforted' (5:4)	*' . . . to comfort all that mourn'* (Isaiah 61:2)
'Blessed are the meek: for they shall inherit the earth' (5:5)	*'the meek shall inherit the earth'* (Psalm 37:11)
'Blessed are they which do hunger and thirst for righteousness: for they shall be filled' (5:6)	*'Behold my servants shall eat . . . behold my servants shall drink'* (Isaiah 65:13)
'Blessed are the merciful: for they shall obtain mercy' (5:7)	*'Blessed is he who has mercy upon the poor'* (Psalm 41:1)
Blessed are the pure in heart: for they shall see God' (5:8)	*'He that hath . . . a pure heart . . . shall receive a blessing from the Lord.'* (Psalm 24:3/5) *'The upright behold his countenance'* (Psalm 11:7)
'Blessed are the peacemakers: for they shall be called the children of God' (5:9)	*'Come ye children . . . seek peace and pursue it . . . the eyes of the Lord are upon the righteous'* (Psalm 34:11/15)

JESUS LIVED AND DIED A JEW

Gospel according to St. Matthew	*Jewish writings*
'Ye are the salt of the earth' (5:13)	'... statute for ever: it is a covenant of salt for ever' (Num. 18:19) 'God gave the kingdom over Israel to David for ever, to him and to his sons by a covenant of salt' (2 Chr. 13:5)
'Ye are the light of the world' (5:14)	*'The path of the just is as the shining light'* (Prov. 4:18)
'Think not that I am come to destroy the law, or the prophets: I am not come to destroy but to fulfil' (5:17)	*'I am not come to take away from the law of Moses but to add ...'* (Shab. 116a & b)
'Till heaven and earth shall pass, one jot and one tittle shall in no wise pass from the law till all be fulfilled' (5:18)	*'Ye shall not add unto the word which I command you, neither shall ye diminish ought from it'* (Deut. 4:2)
'Whosoever shall break one of these least commandments ... shall be called the least in the kingdom of heaven' (5:19)	*'Ye cannot know how great and how small the sin will be reckoned that proceedeth from the breach of any commandment: be ye wise therefore and obey all'* (Aboth 2:1)
'First be reconciled to your brother' (5:24)	'... *for trespass against the neighbour brings forth not forgiveness until a man shall be reconciled with him'* (Yoma 8:9)
'Agree with thine adversary quickly' (5:25)	*'Go not forth hastily to strive'* (Prov. 25:8)
'Whosoever looketh on a woman to lust after her hath committed adultery with her already in his heart' (5:28)	*'he that committeth adultery with his eyes is also to be called an adulterer'* (R. Shimeon, Lev. R.23) *'Unchaste imagination is more injurious than the sin itself'* (Yoma 29a)
'It is profitable for thee that one of thy members should perish, and not that the whole body should be cast in hell' (5:30)	*'Better that his belly burst that he go not down to the pit of destruction'* (Niddah 13b)
'saving for the cause of fornication' (5:32)	*'except ye have found in her a matter of lewdness'* (Gitt. 9:19)
'Ye have heard that it hath been said by them of old time, Thou shalt not forswear thyself, but shalt perform unto the Lord thine oaths: But I say unto you, Swear not at all, neither by heaven, for it is God's throne ... But let your communication be, Yea, yea: Nay, nay' (5:33ff)	*'I will swear no single oath either by heaven or by earth, or by any creature which God hath made. If there be truth in men, let them swear by a word: Yea, yea or Nay, nay.'* (Sifra Lev. 19:36 quoting Secrets of Enoch 49:1)
'Heaven is God's throne' (5:34)	*'The heaven is my throne'* (Isaiah 66:1)
'the earth is his footstool' (5:35)	*'and the earth my footstool'* (ibid.)
'[Jerusalem is] the city of the great King' (5:35)	*'the city of the great King'* (Psalm 48:2)
'Resist not evil' (5:39)	*'Say not thou: I will recompense evil; but wait on the Lord'* (Prov. 20:22)

Gospel according to St. Matthew	Jewish writings
'Whosoever shall smite thee on thy right cheek, turn to him the other also' (5:39)	'He giveth his cheek to him who smiteth him' (Lam. 3:30)
'Give to him that asketh thee and from him that would borrow of thee turn not thou away' (5:42)	'Thou shalt not . . . shut thine hand from thy poor brother; but thou shalt open thy hand, and shall surely lend him sufficient for his need, in that which he wanteth' (Deut. 7:8)
'Love your enemies, bless them that curse you . . .' (5:44)	'Heed not them that counsel thee: Let it be thy prayer that poverty and sickness be the lot of thine enemies' (Berak. 10a)
'He maketh the sun rise on the evil and on the good' (5:45)	'And upon whom doth not his light arise?' (Job 25:3)
'and sendeth rain on the just and on the unjust' (5:45)	'The rain falls equally for the righteous and for the sinful' (Taanith 7a)
'Be ye therefore perfect, even as your Father which is in heaven is perfect' (5:48)	'Say unto them, Ye shall be holy: for I the Lord your God am holy' (Lev. 19:2)
'When thou doest thine alms do not sound a trumpet before thee, as the hypocrites do . . . Verily . . . they have their reward' (6:2)	'He who ostentatiously gives alms to the poor – for this God will bring him to judgment' (Hagigah 5a)
'But when thou doest alms, let not thy left hand know what thy right hand doeth' (6:3)	'He giveth and knoweth not to whom he giveth or taketh and knoweth not from whom he taketh' (Baba Bathra 10b)
'That thy alms may be in secret' (6:4)	'He who giveth alms in secret' (ibid. 9b)
'Pray to your Father . . . in secret' (6:6)	'He that prays so that his words can be heard by them that stand by, is of small faith' (Berak. 24b)
'Use not vain repetitions, as the heathens do: for they think that they shall be heard for their much speaking' (6:7)	When you pray "Let thy words be few . . . a fool's voice is known by multitude of words' (Eccles. 5:2/3) {The heathens}, called on the name of Baal from morning until noon, saying, O Baal, hear us, But there was no voice or any that answered' (1 Kings 18:26)
'Our Father which art in heaven . . .' (6:9)	General address to God in liturgy: Yoma, Sotah, Abot etc.
'Hallowed be thy name . . .' (6:9)	'Hallowed be thy exalted name' (Kadish)
'Thy kingdom come . . .' (6:10)	'May thy kingdom and thy dominion come' (Kedusha)
'Thy will be done in earth, as it is in heaven . . .' (6:10)	'Do thy will in heaven above and give comfort to them here below . . . and do what is good in thine eye' (Berak. 29b)
'Give us this day our daily bread' (6:11)	'Give me . . . the bread appointed to me' (Prov. 30:8)
'And forgive us our debts as we forgive our debtors' (6:12)	'Forgive thy neighbour's sins and then thy sins will be forgiven' (Ben Sira 28)

Gospel according to St. Matthew

'And lead us not into temptation' (6:13)

'But deliver us from evil' (6:13)

'For thine is the kingdom, and the power and the glory, for ever' (6:13)

'When ye fast, be not, as the hypocrites are, of a sad countenance: for they disfigure their faces, that they may appear unto men to fast' (6:16)

'Anoint thy head and wash thy face' (6:17)

'Lay not up for yourselves treasures upon earth . . . but lay up for yourselves treasures in heaven' (6:19/20)

'Take no thought for your life, what ye shall eat and what ye shall drink, nor yet for your body, what ye shall put on' (6:25)

'O, ye of little faith' (6:30)

'Behold the fowls of the air . . . Your heavenly Father feedeth them' (6:26)

'Behold the fowls of the air, for they sow not, neither do they reap, nor gather into barns, yet your heavenly father feedeth them' (6:26)

'Take no thought, saying, What shall we eat? What shall we drink?' (6:31)

'Seek ye first the kingdom of God, and his righteousness; and all these things shall be added unto you' (6:33)

'Take no thought for the morrow . . . sufficient unto the day is the evil thereof' (6:34)

'Judge not that ye be not judged. For with what judgment ye judge: and with what measure ye mete, it shall be measured to you again' (7:1/2)

'And why beholdest thou the mote that is in thy brother's eye, but considerest not the beam that is in thine own eye?' (7:3)

'Give not that which is holy unto the pigs, neither cast ye your pearls before

Jewish writings

'Lead us not into the power of sin and temptation' Morning prayer

'The evil in our thoughts — Be it thy will to deliver us therefrom' (Sanhedrin 107a)

'Thine, O Lord, is the greatness, and the power, and the glory . . . for ever and ever' (1 Chr. 29:10/11)

'Wherefore have ye fasted, and thou seest not? have we afflicted our soul and thou takest no knowledge, Behold, in the day of your fast ye find pleasure . . . wilt thou call this a fast?' (Isaiah 58:3 to 5)

'Wash thyself therefore and anoint thee' (Ruth 3:3)

'My father laid up treasure below; I have laid it up above' (Baba Bathra 11a)

'Everyone who hath a morsel of bread in his basket and says, What shall I eat to-morrow?' (Sota 48b)

. . . 'is of little faith'

. . . 'He giveth to the beast his food, and to the young ravens which cry' (Psalm 147:9)
'Who provideth for the raven his food when his young ones cry unto God? (Job 38:41)

'I have never seen a gazelle a fruit gatherer . . . a fox a shopkeeper, or a wolf a jarseller, but they get their food without care' (Qidd. 2b)

'Trust the Lord and do good . . . and verily thou shalt be fed' (Psalm 37:3)
'If you busy yourselves with the words of the Law, God will provide such food for you also' (Mekhilta 2:126)

'Boast not thyself of tomorrow; for thou knowest not what a day may bring forth' (Prov. 27:1)

'The judgment is God's: and the cause that is too hard for you, bring it unto me' (Deut. 1:17)

'If a judge commanded a man: Remove the splinter from between thy teeth! he would answer: first do thou remove the beam from between thy eyes!' (Baba Bathra 15b)

'Speak not into the ears of a fool, for he will despise the wisdom of thy words' (Prov.23.9)

Gospel according to St. Matthew	Jewish writings
swine . . . lest they trample them under their feet' (7:6)	
'He that seeketh findeth' (7:8)	'Those that seek me shall find me' (Prov. 8:17)
	'Ye shall seek me and find me' (Jer. 29:13)
'All things whatsoever ye would that men should do to you, do you even so to them' (7:12)	'Do not unto others as thou wouldst not have them do unto thee' (Shab. 31a)
'Beware of false prophets' (7:15)	'Thou shalt not hearken unto the words of that prophet' (Deut. 13:3)
	'Hearken not unto the words of the prophet that prophesy unto you' (Jer. 23:26)
'Inwardly they are ravening wolves' 7:15)	'The prophets that make my people err, they bite with their teeth' (Mic. 3:5)
'Do men gather grapes of thorns, or figs of thistles?' (7:16)	'He hath laid my vine waste, and barked my fig tree' (Joel 1:7)
	'There shall be no grapes on the vine, nor figs on the fig tree' (Jer. 8:13)
'Depart from me, ye that work iniquity' (7:23)	'Depart from me all ye workers of iniquity' (Psalm 6:8)
'Himself took our infirmities, and bare our sicknesses' (8:17)	'He hath borne our griefs, and carried our sorrows: yet we did not esteem him stricken, smitten of God, and afflicted' (Isaiah 53:4)
– Acknowledged –	
'And behold, there arose a great tempest in the sea insomuch that the ship was covered with the waves: but he was asleep' (8:24)	'But the Lord sent out a great wind into the sea . . . so that the ship was like to be broken . . . but Jonah was gone down into the sides of the ship, and he lay, and was fast asleep' (Jon. 1:4/5)
'But go and learn what that meaneth, I will have mercy and not sacrifice; for I am not come to call the righteous, but the sinners to repentance' (9:3)	'For I desired mercy and not sacrifice and the knowledge of God more than burnt offerings' (Hos. 6:6)
'But go rather to the lost sheep of Israel' (10:6)	'All we like sheep have gone astray' (Isaiah 53:6)
	'My people hath been lost sheep' (Jer. 50:6)
	'And they were scattered because there is no shepherd' (Ezek. 34:5)
'Freely have ye received, freely give' (10:8)	Spiritual services should be rendered free. See story of Gehazi. (2 Kings 5:20ff)
	'I will love them freely' (Hos. 14:4)
'But when they deliver you up, take no thought how or what ye shall speak: for it shall be given you in that same hour what ye shall speak. For it is not ye that speak but the spirit of your Father which speaketh in you' (10:19/20)	'How therefore go, and I will be with thy mouth, and teach thee what thou shalt say' (Exod. 4:12)
	'Thou shalt go to all that I shall command thee thou shalt speak . . . behold I have put my words into thy mouth' (Jer. 1:7-9)
'The spirit of the Lord spake by me, and his word was in my tongue'	(2 Sam. 23:2)

Gospel according to St. Matthew	Jewish writings
'And the brother shall deliver up the brother to death, and the father the child: and the children rise up against their parents' (10:21)	'For the son dishonoureth the father, the daughter riseth up against her mother, and the daughter-in-law against her mother-in-law: a man's enemies are the men of his own house' (Micah 7:6)
'But he that endureth to the end, shall be saved' (10.22)	'But go thy way till the end: for thou shalt rest, and stand in thy lot at the end of the days' (Dan. 12:13)
'And fear not them which kill the body, but are not able to kill the soul: but rather fear him which is able to destroy both body and soul in hell' (10.28)	'What people feareth shall ye not fear, and be not terrified thereat. The Lord of Hosts, him shall ye sanctify and let him be your fear, and let him be your terror' (Isaiah 8:12/3)
'For I am come to set a man at variance against his father, and the daughter against the mother, and the daughter-in-law against her mother-in-law. And a man's foes shall be they of his own household.' (10:35/6)	'For the son dishonoureth the father, the daughter riseth up against the mother, the daughter-in-law against her mother-in-law: a man's enemies are the men of his own house' Micah. 7:6)
'The blind receive their sight, and the lame walk, the lepers are cleansed, and the deaf hear, the dead are raised up, and the poor have the gospel preached to them' (11:5)	'And in that day shall the deaf hear the words of the book, and the eyes of the blind shall see out of obscurity, and out of darkness . . . and the poor among men shall rejoice' (Isaiah 29:18/9)
	'Then the eyes of the blind shall be opened, and the ears of the deaf shall be unstopped. Then shall the lame man leap as an hart, and the tongue of the dumb sing . . . and the ransomed of the Lord . . . shall obtain joy and gladness' (Isaiah 35:5/10)
'Behold, I send my messenger before thy face, which shall prepare thy way for thee' – Acknowledged – (11:10)	'Behold, I will send my messenger, and he shall prepare the way before me' (Mal. 3:1)
'And if he will receive it, this is Elias which was for to come' (11:14)	'Behold I will send you Elias the prophet' (Mal. 4:5)
'Ye shall be brought before . . . kings for my sake . . . for a testimony' (10:18)	'I will speak of thy testimonies also before kings . . .' (Psalm 119:46)
'Wisdom is justified of her children' (11:19)	'Wisdom exalteth her children' (Ecclec. 4:11)
'Which art exalted unto heaven, shalt be brought down to hell' (11:23)	'I will exalt my throne above the stars of God . . . Yet thou shalt be brought down to hell' (Isaiah 14:13/15)
'Thou hast hid these things from the wise and prudent, and hast revealed them unto babes' (11:25)	'Since the Temple was destroyed, prophecy was taken from the prophets and given to the foolish and the babes' (Baba Bathra 12b)

Gospel according to St. Matthew	*Jewish writings*
	'Out of the mouth of babes and sucklings hast thou ordained strength' (Psalm 8:2)
'And ye shall find rest unto your souls' (11:29)	'And ye shall find rest for your souls' (Jer. 6-16)
'For my yoke is easy, and my burden is light' (11:30)	'Whosoever taketh unto himself the yoke of the Law, from him shall the yoke of government and the yoke of earthly cares be removed' (Aboth 3:6)
'Have ye not read what David did, when he was an hungred, and they that were with him; how they entered into the house of God, and did eat the shewbread, which was not lawful for him to eat, neither for them which were with him, but only for the priests' – Acknowledged – (12:3/4)	'And it {the showbread} shall be Aaron's and his sons, and they shall eat in the holy place: for it is most holy' (Lev. 24:9) 'So the priests gave David hallowed bread for there was no bread there but the showbread, that was taken from before the Lord' (1 Sam. 21:6) 'A stranger shall not eat thereof because they are holy' (Exod. 29:33)
'Or have ye not read the law, how that on the sabbath days the priests in the Temple profane the sabbath and are blameless' – Acknowledged – (12:5)	'And on the sabbath day two lambs of the first year without spot, and two tenths deals of flour for a meat offering, mingled with oil, and the drink offering thereof' (Num. 28:9)
'In this place is one greater than the Temple' (12:6)	'Behold, heaven . . . cannot contain thee; how much less this house which I have built' (2 Chr. 6:18)
'If ye had known what this meaneth, I will have mercy and not sacrifice' (12:17)	'For I have desired mercy and not sacrifice' (Hos. 6:6)
'For the son of Man is Lord even of the sabbath day' (12:8)	'The Sabbath was given for you: ye were not given for the Sabbath' (R. Shimeon – Mech. on Exod. 31:14) 'God delivered the Sabbath unto you, not you unto the Sabbath' (Yoma 85b) 'A man may break the Sabbath so that another may keep many' (ibid.)
'Why speakest thou unto them in parables? (13:10)	'Then said I, O Lord God, they say of me, Doth he not speak in parables?' (Ezek. 20:49)
'Behold my servant, whom I have chosen; my beloved, in whom my soul is well pleased: I will put my spirit upon him, and he shall show judgment to the Gentiles. He shall not strive nor cry; neither shall any man hear his voice in the streets. A bruised reed shall he not break, and smoking flax shall he not quench, till he sent forth judgment into victory. And in his name shall the Gentiles trust.' – Acknowledged – (12:18/21)	'Behold my servant, whom I uphold; mine elect, in whom my soul delighteth, I have put my spirit upon him, he shall bring forth judgment to the Gentiles. He shall not cry, nor lift up, nor cause his voice to be heard in the streets. A bruised reed shall he not break, and the smoking flax shall he not quench: he shall bring forth judgment unto truth . . . (Isaiah 42:1 to 3) 'And the Gentiles shall come to thy light' (Isaiah 60:3)

Gospel according to St. Matthew

'... they seeing see not; and hearing they hear not, neither do they understand.' (13:13)

'I will open my mouth in parables, I will utter things which have been kept secret from the foundation of the world' (13:35)

[The miracle of the five thousand loaves] He said: Bring them hither to me ...' (14:18)

'This people draweth nigh unto me with their mouth, and honoureth me with their lips; but their heart is far from me. But in vain do they worship me, teaching for doctrines the commandments of men'
– Acknowledged – (15:8/9)

'They be blind leaders of the blind, And if the blind lead the blind, both shall fall into the ditch' (15:14)

'Out of the heart proceed evil thought, murders, adulteries, fornications, thefts, false witness, blasphemies' (15:19)

'Every man according to his work' (16:27)

God's voice: 'In whom I am well pleased' (17:5)

'God's voice: 'Hear ye him' (17:5)
'Elias truly shall first come, and restore all things' – Acknowledged – (17:11)

'It is better for thee to enter into life with one eye than having two eyes to be cast into hell fire' (18:9)

'If thy brother shall trespass against thee, go and tell him his fault between thee and him alone: if he shall hear thee, thou hast gained a brother' (18:15)

'Where two or three are gathered together in my name, there I am in the midst of them' (18:15)

'In the mouth of two or three witnesses every word may be established' (18:16)

Jewish writings

'... hear ye indeed, but understand not; and see ye indeed, but perceive not' (Isaiah 6:9)

'I will open my mouth in a parable: I will utter dark sayings of old' (Psalm 78:2)

'But he said: 'Then bring meal ... a man ... brought the man of God bread, twenty loaves of barley ...' (2 Kings 4:41/2)

'This people draw near me with their mouth and with their lips do honour me, but have removed their heart far from me, and their fear toward me is taught by the precepts of men' (Isaiah 29:13)

'The leaders of this people cause them to err; and they that are led of them are destroyed' (Isaiah 9:16)

'The imagination of man's heart is evil' (Gen. 8:21)

'God saw the wickedness of man ... and that every imagination of the thoughts of his heart was only evil' (Gen. 6:5)
'The heart is deceitful above all things and desperately wicked' (Jer. 17:9)

'Every man according to his works' (Prov. 24:12)

'In whom my soul delighteth' (Isaiah 42:1)
'In whom I am well pleased' (Testament of Levy, 17:2/14)

'Unto him shall ye hearken' (Deut. 18:15)
'I will send you Elias the prophet before the coming of the great and dreadful day of the Lord' (Mal. 4:5)

'Better that his belly burst that he go not down to the pit of destruction' (Niddah 13b)

'If a man sin against thee, speak peaceably to him and in thy soul hold no guile, and if he repent and confess, forgive him' (Gad. 6:2)

'Where two are seated together intent upon the Law, glory {God} is in the midst of them' (R. Chananiah)

'At the mouth of two witnesses, or at the mouth of three witnesses, shall the matter be

Gospel according to St. Matthew	*Jewish writings*
	established' (Deut. 19:15)
'He which made them at the beginning made them male and female' (19:4) – Acknowledged –	'Male and female created he them' (Gen. 1:27) (Gen. 5:1)
'For this cause shall a man leave father and mother, and shall cleave to his wife; and they twain shall be one flesh' (19:5) – Acknowledged –	'Therefore shall a man leave his father and mother, and shall cleave to his wife and they shall be one flesh' (Gen. 2:24)
'Whosoever shall put away his wife . . . and shall marry an other, committeth adultery' (19:9)	'The very altar sheds tears for him that divorceth his first wife' (Gittin 19b)
'Suffer little children . . . to come to me: for of such is the kingdom of heaven' (19:14)	'Children receive the presence of the Shekinah' (Kallah Rabati 2 Bar)
'Thou shalt love thy neighbour as thyself' (19:19)	'Thou shalt love thy neighbour as thyself' (Lev. 19:18)
'It is easier for a camel to go through the eye of a needle, than for a rich man to enter the kingdom of God' (19:23)	'Are you not from Pumpeditha where they draw elephants through a needle's eye' (Baba Mezi'a 38b)
'With men this is impossible: but with God all things are possible' (19:26)	'Is anything too hard for the Lord?' (Gen. 18:14) 'There is nothing too hard for thee' (Jer. 32:17)
'Is thine eye evil because I am good?' (20:15)	'His eye shall be evil toward his brother' (Deut. 28:54)
'For many be called, but few chosen' (20:16)	'There be many created, but few shall be saved' (2 Esd. 7:3)
'Tell ye the daughter of Zion, Behold thy King cometh unto thee, meek and sitting upon an ass, and a colt, the foal of an ass' (21:5) – Acknowledged –	'Rejoice greatly, O daughter of Zion, Behold thy King cometh unto thee . . . lowly, and riding upon an ass, and upon a colt the foal of an ass' (Isaiah 62:11 and Zec. 9:9)
'My house shall be called the house of prayer' (acknowledged) (21:13)	'Mine house shall be called a house of prayer' (Isaiah 56:7)
'but ye have made it a den of thieves' (21:13)	'Is this house which is called by my name become a den of robbers?' (Jer. 7:11)
'Out of the mouth of babes and sucklings thou hast perfected praise' – Acknowledged – (21:16)	'Out of the mouth of babes and sucklings hast thou ordained strength' (Psalm 8:2)
'Let no fruit grow on thee henceforward for ever. And presently the figtree withered away' (21:19)	'He hath . . . barked my figtree . . . he hath made it clean bare . . . the branches thereof are made white' (Joel 1:7)
'The stone which the builders rejected, the same is become the head of the corner: this is the Lord's doing, it is marvellous in our eyes' – Acknowledged – (21:42)	'The stone which the builders refused is become the headstone of the corner. This is the Lord's doing: it is marvellous in our eyes' (Psalm 118:22/3)

Gospel according to St. Matthew	Jewish writings
'Thou shalt love the Lord thy God with all thy heart, and with all thy soul, and with all thy mind' – Acknowledged – (22:37)	'Thou shalt love the Lord thy God with all thine heart, and with all thy soul, and with all thy might' (Deut. 6:5)
'The Lord said unto my Lord, Sit thou on my right hand, till I make thine enemies thy footstool' (22:44) – Acknowledged –	'The Lord said unto my Lord, Sit thou at my right hand, until I make thine enemies thy footstool' (Psalm 10:1)
'One is your Father which is in heaven . . . and one is your master ['master' in the sense of 'teacher], the Messiah' (23:9/10)	'A son honoureth his father and a servant his master' (Mal. 1:6)
'Whosoever shall exalt himself shall be abased; and he that shall humble himself shall be exalted' (23:12)	'A man's pride shall bring him low: but honour shall uphold the humble in spirit' (Prov. 29:23) 'The mighty man shall be humbled, and the eyes of the lofty shall be humbled' (Isaiah 5:15)
'Ye devour widows' houses' (23:14)	'Ye shall not afflict any widow' (Exod. 22:22)
'[You] have omitted the weightier matters of the Law: judgment, mercy and faith: these ought ye have done and not to leave the other undone' (23:23)	'Hath the Lord as great delight in burnt offerings and sacrifices, as in obeying the voice of the Lord?' (1 Sam. 15:22) 'Will the Lord be pleased with thousands of rams, or with ten thousand rivers of oil? and what doeth the Lord require of thee but to do justly, and to love mercy and to walk humbly with God?' (Micah 6:7/8)
'Ye make clean the outside of the cup and platter, but within they are full of extortion and excess' (23:25)	'Let no disciple who is not inwardly as outwardly enter the lecture hall' (Berakoth 28a)
'I have gathered thy children together, even as the hen gathereth her chickens under her wings' (23:37)	'I gathered you together, as the hen gathereth her chickens under wings' (2 Esd. 1:30)
'Your house is left unto you desolate' (23:38)	'Your house is desolate' (2 Esd. 1:33)
'There shall not be left here one stone upon another, that shall not be thrown down' (24:2)	'Therefore shall Zion . . . be plowed as a field, and Jerusalem shall become heaps' (Micah 3:12)
'Nation shall rise against nation, and kingdom against kingdom' (24.7)	They shall fight . . . against his neighbour, city against city, and kingdom against kingdom' (Isaiah 19:2)
'The beginning of sorrows' (24:8)	'The beginning of sorrows' (2 Esd. 16:18)
'For wheresoever the carcase is, there will be the eagles gathered together' (24:28)	'The eagle's young ones also suck up blood: and where the slain are, there is she' (Job 39:30)
'Those days shall the sun be darkened, and the moon shall not give her light,	'The earth shall quake before them; the heavens shall tremble: the sun and the moon shall

Gospel according to St. Matthew	*Jewish writings*
and the stars shall fall from heaven, and the powers of the heavens be shaken' (24:29)	be dark, and the stars will withdraw their shining' (Joel 2:10) Similar passages: Isaiah 13:10; Ezek. 32:7; Joel 3:15, Baruch 3.
'They shall see the Son of man coming in the clouds of heaven with power and great glory' (24:30)	'The Son of man came with the clouds of heaven . . . and there was given him dominion, and glory, and kingdom' (Dan. 7:13/14)
'Heaven and earth shall pass away, but my word will not pass away' (24:35)	'The heavens shall vanish away . . . and the earth shall wax cold . . . but my salvation shall be for ever' (Isaiah 51:6)
'But of that day and hour knoweth no man' (24:36)	'It shall be one day which shall be known to the Lord' (Zec. 14:7)
'He shall separate them one from another, as a shepherd divideth sheep from the goats' (24:32)	'Thus saith the Lord God: Behold, I judge between cattle and cattle, between the rams and the goats' (Ezek. 34:17)
'The kingdom prepared for you from the foundation of the world' (25:34)	'The kingdom is already prepared for you' (2 Esd. 2:13)
'I was sick and ye visited me' (25:36)	'Be not slow to visit the sick' (Eccles. 7:35)
'Depart from me ye cursèd' (25:41)	'Depart from me all ye workers of iniquity' (Psalm 6:8)
'And all these shall go away into everlasting punishment: but the righteous into life eternal' (25:46)	'And many shall awake . . . some to everlasting life, and some to shame and everlasting contempt' (Dan. 12:2)
'For ye have the poor always with you.' (26:11)	'For the poor shall never cease out of the land' (Deut. 15:11)
'For this is the blood of the New Testament' (26:28)	'Behold the blood of the covenant which the Lord hath made with you' (Exod. 24:8)
'I shall smite the shepherd and the sheep shall be scattered abroad' – Acknowledged –	'Smite the shepherd and the sheep shall be scattered' (Zec. 13:7)
'My blood which is shed for the remission of sins' (26:28)	'He hath poured out his soul unto death . . . and he bare the sins of many' (Isaiah 53:12)
'For all they that take the sword shall perish with the sword' (26:52)	'Whoso sheddeth man's blood, by man shall his blood be shed' (Gen. 9-6)
'My God, my God, why hast thou forsaken me?' (27:46)	'My God, my God, why hast thou forsaken me?' (Psalm 22:1)

This impressive list shows that Jesus was (or the writers of the New Testament were) well versed in scripture, both canonical and talmudic, and knew when to quote appropriate passages. Since he could not have drawn upon any other source of inspiration, it may be said that he was a deeply faithful, able and skilled teacher of Jewish doctrine throughout the time of his ministry. I would ask the reader not to regard the above list as an accusation of plagiarism, but as an indication how deeply the Teacher and the writers involved were steeped in the doctrinal and moral teaching of Judaism.

Most of the modern Jewish critics recognise the strong influence Mosaic thought and scripture had on the ideas of Jesus, and scholars like Klausner believe that his influence explains almost every aspect of his teaching. I must mention, however, that another eminent Jewish student of the Christian religion, Samuel Sandmel, claims that a fair analysis would show considerable differences as well as similarities. He remarks scathingly that attempts such as mine, trying to confront excerpts from Scriptural and rabbinical sources with the sayings of Jesus 'have encouraged both the imprudent and, one must say, the impudent' (*A Jewish Understanding of the New Testament,* p.199). With alacrity he asserts that the parallels established often result from 'predisposition and partisanship' (p.202). Yet even he admits that the presentation of the material, especially in the Fourth Gospel, often leads to a minimising of the Jewish character of Jesus' teaching, and even to an overt encouragement of anti-Jewish feeling.

We may safely assume that Jesus never thought of himself in terms other than a servant of God and a teacher of the Jewish law. It is possible that he believed eventually that he *was* the Messiah, the anointed servant of the Lord God of Israel. It is probably for this reason that he referred to himself as the Son of man (ben adam), a Messianic title frequently applied by Daniel. Hans-Joachim Schoeps points to Jesus' use of this title in preference to the term Son of God, widely known in the pagan world (*The Jewish-Christian Argument,* p.26).

Thinking of himself as the Messiah, it is likely that Jesus believed he would fulfil the destiny of God's Messenger: become the King of the Jews (perhaps only in the spiritual sense as the supreme Messenger of God), free the Jewish people and establish peace on earth in order to hand over a spiritually free world to God, the Lord of Israel. Perhaps it was this vision which haunted him from the moment Peter spoke those fateful words at Caesarea Philippi, until the hour when, nailed to the cross he realised that he would never fulfil the Messianic destiny and cried out: 'My God, my God, why hast thou forsaken me?' (*Matthew* 27:46). This heart-rending cry, quoting *Psalm* 22:1, can be understood only in this context. It is certain that he never thought of himself as the Suffering Servant of *Isaiah* 53, whom every Jew understood to be Israel itself. It was only Christian theology, no longer confident of the Second Coming, which introduced the Suffering Servant as a Messianic concept fulfilled by Jesus of Nazareth.

Summarising the ministry of Jesus I may say that he attempted to meet the enormous challenge of Rabbi Hillel: 'Be of the disciples of Aaron, loving peace and pursuing peace, loving mankind, and bringing them nigh to the Law' (*Shabbath* 127A and *Aboth* 1:12).

'His blood be on us and our children,' they exclaim, while Pilate washes his hands (*Matthew* 27:24/5) to dissociate himself from guilt: an old Jewish custom no high-ranking Roman would ever perform. The apocryphal gospel of Peter is yet more explicit in allocating the responsibility for Jesus' death to the 'the Jews', and similar allusions occur in every gospel. Some texts are worth recording here: 'The Jews' exclaim "Woe upon our sins, judgment and the end of Jerusalem are at hand" (*Peter* 7:25); 'The sons of the Kingdom are cast out' (*Peter* 8:12); 'The Kingdom hath been taken from them and given to another people' (*Peter 21:43);* and, since 'they have not accepted the invitation to the Son's marriage feast, the King hath destroyed their city' (*Peter* 22:7). In the Gospel according to John Jesus calls those Jews who do not follow him, 'sons of the devil', who persist in unbelief (*John* 8:43/4). To 'the Jews who sought to kill him' Jesus says that they stand accused by him, by God and by Moses himself (*John* 5:44/5). On another occasion he accuses them of a blindness which outraged no less a prophet than Isaiah.

A few more examples from Pauline writings. The Epistles show that at one time the point was reached when no reconciliation was possible and when the 'Church of Christ' was inevitably set against 'the Jews'. The Jews are said to have failed to attain righteousness and stumbled through unbelief (*Rom.* 9:31/3). They are ignorant of God's will (*Rom.* 10:3) and invoke His severe stricture (*Rom.* 10:21). Straying from the path of righteousness, they have sinned through blindness and stubbornness' (*Rom.* 11). Although 'the Jews' have 'both killed the Lord Jesus and their own prophets, and . . . please not God, and are contrary to all men, (*1 Tess.* 2:15), 'God hath not abandoned them utterly, but in His infinite mercy reserved to Himself some of their number (*Rom.* 11:1/4). Thus it becomes understandable that Pauline Christianity soon came to regard itself as the new Israel, inheriting the status of the old, and replacing it in God's esteem. Johannes Weiss shows how the early Church developed the view that, the Jews being outside the Church of Christ, a new race has arisen out of Gentiles and

Jews which is taking the place of Israel in sacred history (*Earliest Christianity*, II, p.662).

Playing on the words of Hosea: 'Then said God . . . ye are not my people, and I will not be your God (*Hos.* 1:9) and, 'I will say to them which were not my people, Thou art my people, and they shall say, 'Thou art my God' (*Hos.* 2:23), we find in an Epistle of Peter: 'Which in the past were not my people, but are now the people of God' (*1 Pet.* 2:10). It is conveniently forgotten that Hosea's prophecy continues: 'Yet the number of the children of Israel shall be as the sand of the sea, which cannot be measured nor numbered; and it shall come to pass that in the place where it was said unto them, Ye are not my people, there it shall be said unto them, Ye are the sons of the living God. Then shall the children of Judah and the children of Israel be gathered together, and . . . great shall be the day of Jezreel' (*Hos.* 1:10/1). A happy ending, for everyone to see, except for those who were interested in believing that the Jewish people had been abandoned in favour of a New Israel. This is the meaning of many allusions in the Pauline Epistles: 'Give none offense, neither to the Jew, nor to the Gentiles [correctly translated 'the foreigners'], nor to the Church of God (*1 Cor.* 10:32). Three distinct groups are listed here: by 'the Israel of God' (*Gal.* 6:16) the Christian Church is meant; and the claim to regard Abraham as the father of all Christians 'not . . . through the law, but through the righteousness of faith' (*Rom.* 4:13). The Epistles of Peter go one step further: there the Christians are called 'a chosen generation, a royal priesthood, an holy nation, a peculiar people . . . the people of God' (*1 Peter* 2:9/10), and Christian women are 'the daughters of Sarah' (*1 Peter 3:6)*. Even the Old Testament, as the Bible the holy Scripture of the Jews, becomes the spiritual property of the Christians: it belongs to the new people (*Barn.* 5:7, 7:5), the holy people (*Justin Dial.* 119). Justin states unequivocally: 'The true, spiritual Israelite people, the people of Judah, and Jacob and Isaac and Abraham who in the beginning received a witness of their faith in God by circumcision, and who were blessed and called the fathers of many people *are ourselves* who through this crucified Christ were brought to God' (*Dial.* 11). In another dialogue Justin says to the Jews: 'In your scripture, or rather not yours but ours'.

The gap widens between Israel and Christianity

Authorities disagree as to which of the four Gospels is the most unfavourable to 'the Jews,', and indeed each one contains a strong anti-Jewish bias. Nevertheless, it has been thought for a long time that the author of Matthew was pre-eminently Jewish and compiled his work with the Jewish reader or listener in mind. Stauffer rejects the whole Gospel according to Matthew as an unreliable Jewish portrait of the Teacher and his message (*Die Botschaft Jesu*, pp. 38/9, p. 83 and other passages). Other scholars think, however, that anti-Jewish sentiment is stronger in Matthew than anywhere else.

Ever since the Jewish people became dispersed over the face of the earth, and became a national and religious minority living among other peoples, anti-Jewish attitudes have appeared in the wake of their settlement. We owe one of the earliest vivid descriptions of this phenomenon to the historian Josephus, who records events which took place in the Greek city of Scythopolis in Syria (*Wars*, 2:18:3). After some friction with the local Jews, the people of Scythopolis demanded that the Jews should leave the city with their families and possessions and settle in a nearby area. The Jews complied and were lulled into a feeling of false security. Suddenly, one night, they were attacked and wiped out by a raiding force from the town. These and similar events were not uncommon, and it is not surprising that Jesus and his disciples preferred to teach in areas and cities which were predominantly Jewish.

Johannes Weiss mentions that in *Luke* 24:47 Jesus calls for the carrying of his message 'to all nations', and that the original destination of the Twelve is no longer mentioned. In *Acts* 1:8 the disciples are sent 'to the uttermost part of the earth', and in a later document, attributed to Justin Martyr (*Apol.* 1:39), the message is addressed to 'the whole race of men' (*Earliest Christianity*, II, p. 661).

The process of dissociation from Judaism was slow and painful. Paul still acknowledged his debt to the Jewish Law (*1 Cor.* 9:20), and hoped for the eventual 'redemption' of the Jews (*Rom.* 11:25). He looked forward to the 'unity between Israel and the nations' (*Eph.* 2:14). He admitted that the apostles James, Peter and John wished to remain faithful to the task of bringing salvation to Israel (*Gal.* 2:9), and that a remnant of Israel should be among the chosen (*Rom.* 9:27). On his journeys Paul used the synagogues as starting points for his missionary work and his 'kinsmen' were specially remembered (*Rom.* 16 and *Col.* 4). Judging from the anger and persecution engendered by his movements it appears that his mission was wholly successful.

So much for the oldest writings, the Epistles of Paul. The Gospels, of a somewhat later date, show a similar development. The Twelve are explicitly sent to Israel (*Matthew* 10:6, *Mark* 6:7, *Luke* 9:1), Jesus shows signs of national pride (*Mark* 7:25), he shows regard for the Jewish Law (*Matthew* 5:17 to 19), and enjoins his listeners to observe the Sabbath and the commands of the scribes (*Matthew* 23:3). Even *Revelation* draws a distinction between the multitudes and the 144,000 'sealed servants of God' (7:3/4). However, the trend changed and was eventually reversed.

In the Gospels we read more and more frequently about the Jewish people being reluctant to accept Jesus as the Messiah. He speaks to his Jewish audiences about 'your Law' as if it were not the same Law which he acknowledges and lives by. He grieves for the 'hardness of the hearts' of the Jewish congregation (*Mark* 3:5). We read about the Jewish people having been 'moved against' Jesus by the priests (*Mark* 15:11), and as a result Pilate takes action against an innocent man to placate the hostile Jews (*Mark* 15:15). The later gospels are even more adamant in their condemnation of 'the Jews'. The story of the trial of Jesus is heavily weighted against them. Pilate finds 'no fault in him' (*Luke* 23:3), but Jewish pressure prevails and compels the powerful Roman official to sentence Jesus to death (*Luke* 23:23). In John's Gospel Pilate is yet more reluctant to pass sentence and makes a great effort to secure the release of Jesus (*John* 18:38/40). He asserts the prisoner's innocence (*John* 19:4/6), and only the insistence of 'the Jews' prompts him to deliver Jesus to his executioners. Reading this story in the Gospel of John, one might even get the impression that the executioners in question *were* Jews, although the only form of execution used by the Jews was stoning; crucifixion, the Roman form of carrying out a death sentence, filled them with horror.

Anyone glancing through the titles of old Testament chapters in Christian bibles may see for himself to what extremes this pilfering from the holy Scriptures of another religion has gone. The effect of this looting is sometimes quite ludicrous. The Song of Solomon, one of the earliest and most beautiful examples of erotic poetry in the literature of the world, has been provided with annotations in the Authorised Version: *Chapter 1.* The Church's love unto Christ, She confeseth her deformity and prayeth to be directed to his flock. Christ directeth her to the shepherd's tent: and showing his love giveth her gracious promises. The Church and Christ congratulate one another. *Chapter 2.* The mutual love of Christ and the Church. *Chapter 3.* The Church's fight and victory in temptation. The Church glorieth in Christ. *Chapter 4.* Christ setteth forth the graces of the Church [Thy two breasts are like two young roes that are twins]. He shows his love to her. The Church prayeth to be made fit for his presence. *Chapter 5.* Christ awaketh the Church with his calling. The Church having a taste of Christ's love is sick of love. A description of Christ by his graces. *Chapter 6.* The Church professeth her faith in Christ. Christ sheweth the graces of the Church and his love towards her. *Chapter 7.* A further description of the Church's graces. The Church professeth her faith and desire. *Chapter 8.* Love of the Church to Christ. Calling of the gentiles. The Church prayeth for Christ's coming. (Perhaps it is superfluous to point out that in these beautiful, but rather voluptuous love-poems there is no mention of Christ or of whatever is called 'his Church'.)

The expropriation of the Old Testament was followed by an uneasy polemic against Judaic laws and doctrines, which reached its climax in Justin's *Dialogue* with Tripho the Jew. The apocryphal Epistle of Barnabas describes circumcision as a stupid misunderstanding of the will of God, a consequence of a too literal interpretation engineered by a malevolent angel – God has merely asked for a circumcision of the heart [sic], an expression often used in the Pauline Epistles. This reflects the general Christian view that the law of Moses was not really the law of God, but a temporary system of restrictions, abolished and superseded by the appearance and doctrine of Jesus Christ. The Gospels do not justify this approach and, as we have shown above, Jesus himself had demanded that his disciples should give meticulous attention to the Mosaic law. This was initially confirmed by Paul who himself had carried out the circumcision of his disciple Timothy, a Greek by birth (*Acts* 16:3). The great apologist of Judaism, Isaac Troki, rightly stated that 'those who assert that there are two laws, that of Moses and that of Jesus, are in error, since Jesus gave no law, but rather commanded that the law of Moses be observed' (*Hizzuk Emunah*, 1:20).

One more point should be kept in mind when the anti-Jewish trends of Christianity are assessed. It seems that for a long time Jesus did not wish to be recognised as the Messiah, be it on account of his own doubts in his mission, be it for the realisation that 'his time hath not yet come'. We read that he rebukes the devils for revealing him as the 'Son of God' (*Mark* 1:25, 34 and 3:2; *Luke* 4:34/5 and 41); that he conceals his miracles (*Matthew* 8:4, 9:30; *Mark* 1:44, 5:43, 12:16 and *Luke* 5:14); that he refuses to give a sign (*Mark* 8:12) and finally, the important fact that he warns his disciples not to tell any man that he is the Christ (*Matthew* 16:20). Thus the people of Judaea cannot be blamed for being unaware of the presence among them of a divine miracle-maker, a Son of God, who is none other than the long-awaited Messiah. How should they have known when even his own disciples, the men who were always in his company, did not seem to realise it (before *Matthew* 16:16) and then only through the perspicacity of one of their number.

The Jewish Teacher and the Church claiming to have been founded by him have parted company. His teaching and his life have become sticks with which to beat his people; the law he had lived by has been abandoned without being replaced by his love. Known by a Greek name, son of an emigrant God, he is condemned to lend his authority to organisations which teach doctrines he abhorred, and ignore doctrines he taught. 'Why call me Lord, Lord, and do not the things which I say' was a cry of despair – in our own days it has become a cry of resignation. 'Sufficient unto the day is the evil thereof'.

12
Genealogies – the seed of David

The shadow of the Most High or the seed of David?

If Jesus was not the son of Joseph, he did not spring from the seed of David according to the flesh, which was one of the prerequisites of Christhood. The two New Testament genealogies, *Matthew* 1:17ff, and *Luke* 3:23ff., endeavour to show that Jesus was indeed the seed of David, in order to establish his claim as Messiah. However, both genealogies demonstrate Joseph's descent from King David, since the evangelists thought it sufficient to describe the origin of Jesus' father. In the current Bibles the genealogies are followed by the story of the Virgin Birth which renders the genealogies completely irrelevant.

The Old Testament prophesy upon which the promise of the Messiah is supposed to be based (according to Christian doctrine) merely says that the Wonderful Counsellor of God, the Everlasting Father, will sit on the throne of David (*Isaiah* 9). Compare the Jews' apposite translation with the Christian version:

Holy Scripture translated by I. Leser, Bloch Publ. Company, New York, 1914.	*The Holy Bible, Authorised Version, Oxford University Press, New York.*
His name is called the wonderful counsellor of the Mighty God, of the everlasting Father, the Prince of Peace.	His name shall be called, Wonderful, Counsellor, the Mighty God, the Everlasting Father, the Prince of Peace.

Of course, there are many more Old Testament passages promising that God's blessing will be forever with the descendants of David:

'And thine house and thy kingdom shall be established for ever before thee: thy throne will be established for ever.' *2 Sam.* 7:16

GENEALOGIES – THE SEED OF DAVID

'I will establish the throne of thy kingdom upon Israel for ever'
1 Kings 9:5

'I have made a covenant with my chosen, I have sworn unto David my servant, Thy seed will be established for ever, and build up thy throne to all generations'
Psalm 89:3/4

'His [David's] seed also will I make to endure for ever, and his throne as the days of heaven'
Psalm 89:29

'His seed shall endure for ever, and his throne as the sun before me'
Psalm 89:36

'The Lord hath sworn in truth unto David; he will not turn from it; Of the fruit of thy body will I set upon thy throne'
Psalm 132:11

'There shall come forth a rod out of the stem of Jesse [David's father] and a branch will grow out of his roots'
Isaiah 11:1

'I will raise unto David a righteous Branch, and a King shall reign and prosper, and shall execute judgment and justice on earth'
Jer. 23:5

'Thou Bethlehem [the town of David] . . . out of thee shall come forth . . . that is to be the ruler of Israel'
Micah 5:2

'The house of David shall be as God'
Zec. 12:8

In the Jewish translation of the Old Testament this last sentence is rendered as 'the house of David shall be as divine beings' and not 'as God'. The Greek text of the Septuagint says ὁ δὲ οἰκος Δαυεὶδ ὡς οἰκοσ Θεοῦ which means that the house of David shall be as the house of God. By no stretch of imagination can it be conceded that Zachariah wrote 'shall be as God'. This is just one more example of tendentious translation.

The New Testament contains many passages which refer to the Davidic descent of Jesus, which is meant to prove the legitimacy of his claim to the throne of David. Apart from the genealogies themselves, we find two decisive texts which show that Jesus was thought to be 'of the seed of David according to the flesh'.

'Jesus Christ our Lord which was made of the seed of David according to the flesh'
Rom. 1:3

'God hath sworn with an oath to him [David] that of the fruit of his loins, according to the flesh, he would raise up Christ to sit on his throne'
Acts 2:30

On many occasions Jesus is called the son or the seed of David (*Matthew* 1:1, 9:27, *Luke* 1:32, *John* 7:41/3, *Acts* 13:23, *2 Tim.* 2:8, *Rev.* 5:5, 22:16). Several of these were obviously inspired by the *Isaiah* 11 passage quoted above. It is also mentioned that 'Jesus' father, Joseph, was a descendant of the great King. 'Joseph . . . was of the house and lineage of David' (*Luke* 2:4).

From these texts we may conclude that Jesus was either the son of Joseph in which case he might have been the Christ (Messiah) of the seed of David, but could not have been the Son of God in the literal sense; or else, he might have been the Son of God in the literal sense, in which case he could not have been the Christ of the seed of David.

The argument that Mary was of the seed of David need not even by considered. There is no Scriptural hint or evidence connecting Mary to the seed of David. The only old writing which claims for her Davidic descent, is the so-called Protevangelium, an apocryphal gospel of the second century, which relates the conception and birth of Mary: 'And the priests called to mind the child Mary, that she was of the tribe of David' (10:1), and some apocryphal copies inspired by the Protevangelium.

If David call him Lord

A strange utterance, put in the mouth of Jesus, must be considered here: 'What think ye of Christ? whose son is he? They [the Pharisees] say unto him, The son of David. He saith unto them, How then doth David in spirit call him Lord, saying, THE LORD said unto my Lord, Sit thou at my right hand, till I make thine enemies thy footstool? If David then call him Lord, how is he his son,' (*Matthew* 22:41/4, *Mark* 12:35/7 and *Luke* 20:39/44).

The scriptural origin of his argument is to be found in *Psalm* 110:1: THE LORD said unto my Lord, Sit thou at my right hand, until I make thine enemies thy footstool'. For the benefit of the reader I am quoting here the full text of this psalm, as it reads in the Jewish Bible:

'The Eternal saith unto my Lord, Sit thou at my right hand, until I place thine enemies as a stool for thy feet. The staff of thy strength will the Eternal stretch forth out of Zion: rule thou in the midst of thine enemies. Thy people will bring free-will gifts on the day of thy power, in the ornaments of holiness: as out of the bosom of the morning-dawn, so is thine the dew of thy youth, after the order of Melchizedek. THE LORD at thy right hand crusheth kings at the day of his wrath. He shall judge among the nations – there shall be a fullness of corpses – he crusheth heads on a wide spread land. From the brook will he drink on the way: therefore will he lift up the head.'

Graves and Podro advance this explanation: 'The saying which refers to *Psalm* 110:1, has been wrongly reported. Jesus could not have quibbled in a sense contrary to Pharisaic doctrine. The quibble must have been introduced by the Saddusaic lawyers with whom, according to Mark and Luke, the conversation took place; an obtuse editor of

Matthew here copied from *Luke* 20 and misread the "they" in verse 41.' Much the same point is discussed in *Yalkut Shimeoni* 2:869 where Abraham's face is darkened because, in *Psalm* 110:1, the Messiah was placed on God's right hand and thus given greater honour than himself, although he is his own remote descendant. Graves and Podro suggest the following text: 'Then certain of the scribes answered, Master, thou hast well said. But the same Sadducee asked again, By what authority sayest thou that the Anointed One, the Son of David, will come to judge the world? He answered and said, though ye Sadducees reject the prophets, yet sing ye the psalm of David which saith: THE LORD said unto my Lord: sit thou on my right hand till I make thine enemies thy footstool. But the Sadducee laughed him to scorn, saying, If David calleth him Lord, how is he then his son? And if he is David's son, how shall he be given greater honour than David? Jesus' reply, as in *Yalkut Shimeoni,* would have been to refer the questioner to verse 5 of the same psalm: The Lord at thy right hand shall strike through kings in the day of His wrath. Therefore shall David sit on the left hand, for something of sin was found in him, but his son shall be perfected and shall sit on the right hand' (*NGR*, pp.207/8).

I suggest a much simpler solution to this tricky, contrived argument: Most of the psalms, if not all, were written by the courtpoets (poets laureate) of David, and that God is referred to as the Eternal or THE LORD, while 'my Lord' merely means David.

In any case, the contradiction was resolved finally and irrevocably by no less an authority than Paul who wrote that Jesus was 'made of the seed of David according to the flesh, and declared to be the son of God with power according to the spirit . . . ' (*Rom.* 1:3/4).

The genealogies

Many attempts have been made to explain away the glaring differences between the two genealogies: *Matthew* 1:1ff. and *Luke* 3:23ff. That of Matthew enumerates twenty-six generations linking Jesus to David, while Luke shows forty-one generations between David and Jesus. Matthew names Jacob as the father of Joseph, 'the husband' of Mary. In Luke's genealogy Joseph's father is called Heli. A number of other discrepancies can be found.

The Catholic *QB* refers to a theory of Julius Africanus, advanced about A.D. 220 and known to us through a quotation by Eusebius (*Eccl. History* 1:7), which claims that Jacob was the 'real father of Joseph, while Heli was his 'legal' father under the Jewish law of the levirate. This law, laid down in *Deut.* 25:5/6, provides that where a childless widow marries the brother of her deceased husband, the firstborn of the union should bear the name of the first husband, so that 'his name should not be put out of Israel'. The second theory, attributed to Annius of Viterbo (died 1502), suggests that we find Joseph's genealogy in Matthew while Luke's text shows the descent of Mary. The *QB* claims this theory had the support of authorities like Bishop Le Camus and Rose, but with laudable honesty adds that there are strong arguments against it, especially the fact that generally the Jews were concerned with paternal descent only. The authors of the *QB* favour a third theory, according to which Matthew presents the royal line which establishes the legitimate succession to the throne of David, while Luke is concerned with the real line of descent. They seem to regard the following as an adequate explanation: 'The genealogies of St. Matthew and St. Luke satisfy both points of view. The Davidic rights descended to Joseph and his legal son Jesus through Solomon (*Matthew* 1:6/7), whereas Jesus' true Davidic ancestry was traced through Nathan (*Luke* 3:31)'. I should also quote the concluding remark in the *QB*: 'Whatever theory we hold – and we admit that no theory is absolutely satisfactory, Catholics accept the two genealogies as part of the Sacred Scriptures, guaranteed them by the divine infallible voice of an authoritative teaching Church. The rationalist critic is unscholarly [sic] and unfair, because he starts out with the set purpose of denying the historical value of a document which goes contrary to his personal views' (pp.357/8).

The rationalist critic might remark that he need not argue against two documents which most effectively argue against each other, apart from the inner contradiction contained in each of them.

Another Catholic commentary which is used as a Scripture textbook for schools, is the *Study of the Gospels* by T.E. Bird. It is distressing that young children are presented with didactic statements of this kind: 'But there was one who was reticent although she treasured up every detail of that wonderful night – Mary the Mother. Later she told it all to St. Luke. We thank her for telling him, and us' (p.61). The theory that the genealogy given by Luke is *really* Mary's is usually supported by the evidence that no one but Mary could have told Luke the details recorded in his Gospel. Speculation is presented as fact, and in the impressionable mind of the child it remains imprinted as fact. The book goes on in this vein: 'On the eighth day the child was circumcised, and St. Joseph had the honour of giving him the holy name Jesus. To the outside world he was the child's father, whereas in reality he was only His foster-father' (ibid.). The discrepancy between the two genealogies is also dealt with. Joseph's genealogy is given by St. Matthew, no one disputes this. Writing for the Jews, Matthew produced Joseph's pedigree. Bird then proceeds to develop (for the benefit of children!) the argument of the levirate law, as advanced by Eusebius. Bird admits that if these speculations are correct, this would be the only known case where the Levirate Law is applied to half-brothers. This honest admission is followed, however, by his own contrived and sophisticated view. 'It is admitted by all [sic] that St. Luke went, directly or indirectly, to Mary for the matter in the first two chapters of this Gospel. Surely he would ask her about *her* pedigree. Jesus was her child, and Joseph was only His foster-father . . . So thoughtful a woman, who pondered things over in her mind, would hardly have been ignorant of her father's pedigree . . . ' Should one be angry or amused at the obvious dishonesty of the argument that Mary knew that her father 'belonged to the House of David, as it is clear from Gabriel's words "The Lord shall give unto him the throne of David, His father", and from Luke's statement that Mary, espoused to Joseph, was of the House of David.' In order to substantiate this barefaced untruth, this book (which influences the minds of many thousand children) brackets the references of *Luke* 1:27 and 1:32. The former reads: 'to a virgin espoused to a man whose name was Joseph, of the house of David; and the virgin's name was Mary.' *Luke* 1:32 says: 'He shall be great, and shall be called the Son of the Highest, and the Lord God shall give unto Him the throne of His father David.' I wonder if the reader can find in these passages any proof that Luke claimed Davidic descent for Mary? Bird crowns his argument with the inane statement: 'The words "supposed son of Joseph" hint that it is not the genealogy of Joseph that Luke is about to give, but that of the Virgin Mother' (pp.47/50).

The commentators of the Church of England present similar arguments. Professor Stendahl speaks of the difference between the two genealogies, but claims that the author of Matthew followed information found in *1 Chr.* 2 and 3, and *Ruth* 4, in its Greek form and that, from Zerubabel on, there are no biblical records. However, Jewish genealogies were current and highly valued. It seemed of great importance to the disciples to prove the Davidic descent of Jesus. 'Among the three Messianic figures of the Qumran community, the Prophet, the Messiah of Aaron and the Messiah of Israel (*1 QS* 9:10/11), the genealogy identifies Jesus with the last, non-priestly Messiah' [who was not even born yet!] Here the author presents an interesting speculation: 'While Matthew reports three times 14 generations, it is striking that the third group contains only 13. It is as hard to believe that one link should have been completely lost in the transmission of the text, as it is to think that Matthew just could not count. Is it totally excluded that Matthew counts the Messiah as the fourteenth, while Jesus is the thirteenth? 'Christ' should then refer to Jesus in his risen state and/or at his coming (parousia) at the end of time. We should then have here the strong futuristic eschatology of the primitive Church' (*PC*, pp.770/1).

Dummelow admits that both genealogies are those of Joseph and that neither relates to Mary. This, he says, is due to the fact that the Jews did not take account of female descent, and because Jesus' Davidic descent could only be established through his foster-father. On the other hand, he claims that the genealogies were not inspired documents but well-meaning concoctions of Jewish pedigree-makers. He goes even so far as to say that, although 'our Lord's Davidic descent through Joseph may be regarded as established', it is probable that Jesus descended from David through Mary as well. This is, according to Dummelow, supported by *Luke* 1:32 and 1:69 (God . . . hath raised up an horn of salvation for us in the house of his servant David'] which suggests that the child *is* of the House of David. The amazing argument from conclusion to premise proceeds: 'The Old Testament prophesies and the Apostolic Church regards Christ as descended from David according to the flesh . . . and if Jesus were born of a virgin, His actual descent could only be on his Mother's side' (*OVBC*, p.622).

R.H. Lightfoot also mentions the dispute concerning Jesus' Davidic descent, but he concludes from the silence of St. John on this subject that, to John, the Davidic descent and the birth in Bethlehem were so obvious that the objections raised could only be mentioned but left unrefuted' (*St. John's Gospel*, p.184).

Walsham How prefers to be taken in by the argument that one of the genealogies is that of Joseph, the other of Mary. Both belong, he says, to 'Joseph as the legal (though not the real) father of Jesus.' However, he adds, we know 'in other ways' [sic] that Mary *was* of David's line. The proof is once again produced by an intellectual somersault, by reference to *Luke* 1:32 and, rather ludicrously, to *Luke* 2:5 ('to be taxed with Mary, his espoused wife').

Professor Fenton cautiously remarks that Matthew believed both in Jesus' Davidic descent and his conception through the Holy Spirit. 'He therefore shows that Joseph, who married Mary, was the son of David; and that Jesus was conceived before they came together. Joseph thus became the legal father of Jesus, and Jesus was in this way both the son of David and miraculously conceived' (*Commentary to St. Matthew*, p.40).

Professor Caird states that 'Luke . . . substantiates Jesus' Messianic claim by adducing evidence of his Davidic descent. By tracing his ancestry back to Adam, he reminds his readers that Jesus was bound by ties of kinship not only to Israel, but to humanity, and that his mission was ultimately to all mankind. By calling Adam son of God he makes a link between the baptism and God's purpose in creation. Man was designed for that close filial relationship with God which was exemplified in Jesus and which Jesus was to share with those who became his disciples (*Saint Luke,* pp.77/89).

It is significant that a passage in the Scriptures where a father-in-law's almost customary reference to his daughter's husband as 'son' and the son-in-law's reference to his wife's father as 'father' should serve as yet another explanation for the different names of Joseph's father in the gospels of Mark and Luke. Many fundamentalists accept this form of special pleading in gospel interpretation. The statement is then followed by the puerile assertion: 'There is little in Christ's life prior to His public ministry to indicate His royalty, except that His whole being, in spite of His humble occupation, even then must have revealed Him to be a king amongst men,' and, 'Although uncrowned, many people recognised His literal kingship, as was evident from the fact that not infrequently He was called the son of David'. These quotations are from a fundamentalist pamphlet, author unknown.

No rational argument can be advanced against such unquestioning faith.

The son of Joseph

It is not only the genealogies which allow us to believe that the evangelists regarded Joseph as the father of Jesus 'according to the flesh'. There is a passage quoting the words of the Apostle Philip: 'Jesus of Nazareth, the son of Joseph' (*John* 1:45). After an address by Jesus 'the Jews murmured at him,' and said, 'Is not this Jesus, the son of Joseph, whose father and mother we know' (*John* 6:42). In this context we should note that the Gospel of John never mentions the Virgin Birth, and its author probably did regard Joseph as the father of Jesus.

But even the Gospel according to Luke contains passages like: 'When the parents brought in the child Jesus, to do for him after the custom of the Law' (that is, circumcise him) (*Luke* 1:27); and another one, an obviously manipulated text quoting the words of the Apostle Philip: 'And Joseph and his [Jesus'] mother marvelled' (*Luke* 2:33). Most Greek manuscripts read: "And his father and mother marvelled', which did not deter the editors of the Authorised Version from misleading their readers. The Revised Version corrects this mistake.

There are other passages: 'Now his parents went to Jerusalem every year' (*Luke* 2:41); 'The child Jesus tarried behind in Jerusalem, and Joseph and his [Jesus'] mother knew not of it' (*Luke* 2:43). (Greek original: . . . and his parents knew not of it.) Mary is scolding the child: 'Thy father and I have sought thee' (*Luke* 2:48). In *Matthew* 13:55 the people of Nazareth ask: 'Is not this the carpenter's son?' In *Mark* 6:3 the same question is reworded: 'Is not this the carpenter, the son of Mary?' As this question is followed immediately by the enumeration of his brothers, and the mention of his sisters, it is unlikely that Jewish people would have worded the question in this form – it would only be conceivable in the case of an illegitimate child, a very rare occurrence in their midst, and certainly not applicable in this case where (younger) brothers and sisters are mentioned. Finally, in *Luke* 3:23 we find this text: 'Being, as was supposed, the son of Joseph', followed by the genealogy. There is every reason to believe that the 'as was supposed' is an interpolation, since if Jesus was *not* the son of Joseph, the genealogy is completely irrelevant.

Nearly a century ago two Englishwomen, Mrs. Smith-Lewis and Mrs. Gibson, found an old Syriac manuscript of the Gospels in St. Catherine's monastery in Sinai. In that manuscript the Matthew genealogy 1:16 reads: 'And Joseph to whom was espoused the virgin Mary, begot Jesus who was called the Messiah.' Professor Kenyon, otherwise a dogmatic Christian, volunteers the information that there is also a manuscript (No. 346 Sod.E. 1024) from the 12th century and found in Milan, which renders *Matthew* 1:16 as follows: Ἰωσὴφ, ὁ μνηστεύθεισεν παρθένος Μαρίαν ἐγεννησεν Ἰησοῦν τὸν λεγόμενον Χριστόν.

An outstanding scholar of early Church history, Johannes Weiss, suggests that 'the Jewish-Christian author of the first Gospel himself advocated with absolute conviction the virgin birth of Jesus by the Spirit . . . But that such family-trees were to be found at all, points to a Christology which knew as little about the superhuman birth of Jesus, as did St. Paul (*Gal.* 4:4)' (*Earliest Christianity*, II, pp.732/3). This celebrated passage of the Pauline Epistle reads: 'But when the fullness of time was come, God sent forth his son, made of a woman, made under the Law'. Berguer confirms that there is no doubt that St. Paul was completely ignorant of the tradition that Jesus was born of a virgin, he does not speak of it. Nor do the two oldest sources, Mark and the *Logia*, breathe a word of it' (*The Life of Jesus*, p.103).

A daring misrepresentation of the Pauline doctrine appears in the

CC. Its General Editor, the Rev. D.B. Orchard himself, mentions 'a very important verse from which we learn of the pre-existence of the Son, of His taking flesh from a Woman . . . at a time pre-determined by God, and of His further condescension in His submission to the Law' (p.1117). And this is what Luther has to say about this Pauline passage: 'In that he [Paul] nameth the sex, he signifieth that Christ was made true and very man of womankind, saying 'made of a woman', it is as if he had said, made of a virgin' (*Commentary on Galatians,* p.333). Luther states furthermore: 'Although he be the Lord of the Law, and therefore the Law has no authority or power over him, for he is the Son of God, yet of his own accord he maketh himself subject to the law' (ibid., p.335). According to Luther, the words of this verse 'declare that the Son of God, being made under this Law, did not only perform one or two works with the Law, that is to say, has not only been circumcised and presented in the Temple, or went up to Jerusalem . . . at the time appointed, or only lived civilly under the Law; but he suffered all the tyranny of the Law . . . So Christ, a divine and human person, begotten of God without beginning, and born of the Virgin at the time appointed, came not to make Law, but to feel and suffer the terrors of the Law with all extremity, and to overcome the same, so that he might utterly abolish the Law' (ibid. p.337/8). Far more modestly, the Rev. J.N. Sanders comments in our own time: 'Then, at the time which God had appointed, we attained to our inheritance. "God sent forth his Son", a man born like other men, and being a Jew, subject to the Law' (*PC,* p.977). What a refreshing statement – 'a man born like other men', I wonder if the reverend gentleman meant what he said?

Concerning Philip's designation of Jesus as 'son of Joseph' there is a very skilful way of warding off the impact of that 'slip of the tongue' in Walsham How's *Commentary to the New Testament.* Alone of all the commentators I know, he mentions here the words of Jesus: 'Have I been so long time with you, and yet hast thou not known me, Philip?' (*John* 14:9).

Graves and Podro are of the opinion that Matthew's shorter genealogy is the more distinguished of the two, since it follows the royal line of Solomon down to Josiah, the last independent king of Judah before the captivity; but they consider Luke's genealogy more credible because it run through Nathan, a son of David, who never became king. They also quote Eusebius (*E.H.*, 3:20:1/2), who mentions the testimony of Hegesippus, according to which the grandsons of Jude, a brother of Jesus, Galilean smallholders, admitted before the Emperor Domitian that they were descendants of the royal house of David.

Graves and Podro accept that Joseph was considered to have been of the seed of David. In fact, a great number of poor Jews were in the direct male line of the Great King (*NGR*, pp.65/6).

Dr. Klausner contends that 'the account in Matthew and Luke about the birth of Jesus . . . stands on the same footing as the story of Celsus' Jew, and of the Toldoth Yeshu and the Talmud which regard Jesus as illegitimate (basing their stories on Christian assertions), and the son of Pandera or Pantera. So long as Jesus was regarded only as the Messiah, it was necessary to show that his father Joseph was of the stock of Jesse, but as the Son of God it was not possible for him to have a human father . . . The truth is that Jesus was as legitimate as any other Jewish child in Galilee where strict supervision was exercised over espoused maidens . . . Jesus' father was an artisan, a carpenter, and as was the custom . . . the son learnt the father's trade. A happy chance preserved the talmudic expression, "a carpenter and the son of a carpenter" (*Ab.Zar.* 3b, *J. Yebam* 8:2). Justin Martyr records how Joseph and Jesus made goads and ploughs which were still extant in Justin's day. Jesus thus came from the ranks of the simple classes . . . who laboured with the sweat of their brow: he had experienced their troubles, their poverty and their labour' (*JN*, pp.232/3).

However, this approach to the problem of Joseph's fatherhood has always been severely discouraged by the Church. The early Fathers were indignant about the Ebionites who 'suppose that Jesus was from Mary and Joseph' (Origen, *Matt.tom.* 17:12), who believe that he was a plain and common man who alone was justified because of the advancement of his ways, born of intercourse of Mary and a man' (Eusebius, *E.H.*, 3;27); who claim 'that Christ was born of Joseph and Mary . . . a mere man' (ibid., 6:17); and that 'Christ was born of intercourse and of the seed of a man, i.e., Joseph' (*Epiphanius* 30:2). Irenaeus speaks of a heretic, a certain Carpocrates who 'suggested that Jesus was not born of a virgin, but was the son of Joseph and Mary, just like all other men, and that he had been more powerful than all in righteousness and intelligence and wisdom' (*Irenaeus* 1:26:2).

It is likely that the Ebionite tradition (to which, in all probability, James, 'the brother of the Lord', adhered) was an unadulterated following of Jesus, free from all the fanciful idolatry and mythology that had grown around his memory in the Christian Church. Those who agree with this view may conclude that the Ebionites preserved the original view that Joseph, the man of the seed of David, was Jesus' father 'according to the flesh'. This was perhaps taken for granted when the gospels were launched, and I myself believe that in Matthew and Luke, or rather in their common source, the hypothetical 'Q' document, the story of the virgin birth (and some other things) were interpolated under foreign influence. The interpolators did not realise that, by allowing the genealogies to stand and terminate in Joseph, they created a contradiction which two thousand years of theology would try to resolve in vain.

The origin and ancestry of Mary

Nothing is known about the origin and ancestry of Mary. There is no clue in the New Testament. She was the cousin of Elisabeth, the wife of Zacharias and mother of John the Baptist [*Luke* 1:36). Of Elisabeth we are told that she was a descendant of Aaron, i.e., a Levite, and not of Judah, like David. This single pointer does not, of course, establish the descent of Mary who might have been a cousin of Elisabeth on her mother's side.

There are, however, some apocryphal writings which are of later origin, and which attempt to establish that Mary *was* of Davidic descent, in order to circumvent the awkward contradiction between the descent of Jesus in accordance with assumed prophesy on the one hand, and the legend of the virgin birth on the other.

In the Protevangelium we read that Mary was the daughter of a very rich man, Ioacim, whose wife Anna did not bear him a child until both were well advanced in years. This is a recurring theme in Jewish narratives – Sarah, Hannah, Elisabeth – and in every case prayer softens the heart of the Lord, and the ageing woman has 'her womb opened'. At the birth of the child, Anna said, 'My soul is magnified this day, and she laid herself down. And when the days were fulfilled, Anna purified herself and gave suck to the child and called her name Mary' (5:2). Father and mother decided that 'Mary will be brought into the temple of the Lord' upon reaching the required age. At the age of three she danced in the temple [sic] and received food from the hand of an angel' (7:2 and 8:1). Mary remained in the temple until she was twelve when she was placed in the care of Joseph, an old man with sons of his first marriage, who took her to his house, but 'did not come unto her'. Soon after this a veil was needed for the temple and the priests decided that it must be spun by 'a pure virgin of the tribe of David' (10:1). When they remembered the virgin Mary, she was entrusted with this task. While she was working on the veil, an angel visited her and here the Protevangelium repeats the story of Luke 1. It continues by relating Luke's narrative about the visit to Elisabeth. At the age of sixteen, still a virgin, Mary gives birth to a male child, Jesus. Joseph, returning home, finds Mary pregnant and bitterly reproaches her. The dream (14:1) follows, in which the angel reassures Joseph. Annas, the scribe, notices that the young virgin who was entrusted to Joseph is 'great with child'. Annas and the priests rebuke Joseph who tells the accusers that the child is of the Holy Ghost. Joseph and Mary are subjected to an ordeal by poison (16:1 to 3), but they return 'whole'. The priests marvel and release them.

The story continues about the birth and childhood of Jesus which is of no interest here. Suffice it to say that the Protevangelium is a concoction of details convenient to the Church: Mary's origin and Davidic descent, her proven virginity, Joseph as an old man with sons of a prior marriage. All the ingredients for a successful apology are here, and it is to the credit of the early Church that they did not avail themselves of this spurious document.

The *Liber de Infantia,* or Gospel of Pseudo-Matthew, another apocryphal infancy gospel, is a Latin compilation of the 7th or 8th century, and follows very much the same story. A further apocryphal document is the Gospel of the Birth of Mary, attributed to St. Jerome, which is a reiteration of Pseudo- Matthew, presented in a more elegant Latin. The Virgin's birth is also described in the Armenian Gospel of the Infancy, an extended version of the Protevangelium, of very late origin. Finally, there is the history of Joseph the Carpenter, or Death of Joseph, an Egyptian writing of the 4th or 5th century. Its influence on Coptic beliefs about the Virgin and Joseph was decisive. It claims that Joseph was of Bethlehem and had four sons of an earlier marriage, Judas, Josetos (or Justus), James and Simon, as well as two daughters Lysia and Lydia. Joseph lived to the age of 111. Mary was brought up in the Temple and given to Joseph when she was twelve years of age. She educated his small son James and became 'great with child' two years after she had gone to live with Joseph. Much of the story is told by Jesus in the first person. Among other things he is quoted as saying: 'I took flesh in the Holy Virgin Mary' (Chapter 25). There is also a number of Coptic Lives of the Virgin, mostly stories vaguely based on the Protevangelium.

According to the *Discourse* of Demetrius of Antioch, Ioacim's (or Joakim's) wife was called Susanna. Details of Mary's idyll with her baby-son are supplied in the *Discourse* by Cyril of Alexandria: 'She used to take hold of his hand and led him along the roads saying, 'My sweet son, walk a little way', in the same manner as all other babes are taught to walk. And he, Jesus, the very God, followed after her untroubled. He clung to her with his little fingers, he stopped from time to time, and he hung onto the skirt of Mary his mother, he upon whom 'the whole universe hangeth'. He would lift up his eyes to her face . . . and she would catch him up in her arms, and walk along with him' (*The Apocryphal New Testament*, p.89).

Substitution may be responsible for the expression: 'Is not this the carpenter, the son of Mary, the brother of James? . . . (*Mark* 6:3), which is the more likely because Mark does not seem to know anything about the Virgin Mary and the corresponding legends. The original text was probably similar to *Matthew* 13:55 and read: 'Is not this the son of the carpenter and of Mary?'

In the early centuries the Church habitually referred to Jesus as Son of Mary, which explains the Holy Koran's expression: 'The Messiah, son of Mary, is but an apostle . . . ' (*Holy Koran*, 5:75).

The levirate marriage

Christian apologists often quote the custom of levirate marriage to eliminate a number of contradictions arising in connection with the genealogies and the descent of Jesus.

The Law ordained that 'if brothers dwell together, and one of them die, and have no child, the wife of the dead shall not marry without unto a stranger: her husband's brother shall go in unto her, and take her to him to wife, and perform the duty of an husband's brother unto her. And it shall be, that the firstborn which she beareth shall succeed in the name of his brother which is dead, that his name shall not be put out of Israel' (*Deut.* 25:5/6). The Old Testament relates a number of episodes in which this law was invoked: 'And Judah took a wife for Er his firstborn, whose name was Tamar, and Er, Judah's firstborn, was wicked in sight of the Lord: and the Lord slew him. And Judah said unto Onan, Go in unto thy brother's wife, and marry her, and raise up seed to thy brother. And Onan knew that the seed should not be his; and it came to pass, when he went in unto his brother's wife, that he spilled it on the ground, lest that he should give seed to his brother. And the thing which he did displeased the Lord: therefore he slew him also' (*Gen.* 38:6/10); 'Moreover Ruth, the Moabitess, the wife of Mahlon, have I purchased to be my wife, to raise up the name of the dead upon his inheritance, that the name of the dead be not cut off among his brethren, and of the gate of his place . . . So Boaz took Ruth, and she was his wife: and when he went in unto her, the Lord gave her conception, and she bare a son' (*Ruth* 4:10/13). This son was Obed, the grandfather of David. The reader will note that in *Matthew* 1:5, in spite of all the talk of levirate marriage, Boaz is named as the father of Obed, and not Ruth's first husband, Mahlon!

The widow was only under a moral, and not a legal, obligation to comply with this ordinance, and the brother of the deceased could also refuse to comply. Boaz says to Ruth: 'And now . . . fear not; I will do to thee all that thou requirest . . . It is true that I am thy near kinsman: howbeit there is a kinsman nearer than I. Tarry this night, and it shall be in the morning, that if he will perform unto thee the part of a kinsman, well; let him do the kinsman's part: but if he will not do the part of a kinsman to thee, then I will do the part of a kinsman to thee, as the Lord liveth: lie down until the morning' (*Ruth* 3:11/13).

It is likely that it was difficult for a righteous Jew to avoid the obligation the law imposed upon the brother of the dead man. *Deut.* 25:7/10 provides: 'If a man like not to take his brother's wife, then let his brother's wife go up to the gate unto the elders, and say, My husband's brother refuseth to raise up unto his brother a name in Israel, he will not perform the duty of my husband's brother. Then the elders of his city shall call him and speak unto him: and if he stand to it, and say, I like not to take her; then shall his brother's wife come unto him in the presence of the elders, and loose his shoe off his foot, and spit in his face, and shall answer and say, So shall it be done unto that man that will not build up his brother's house. And his name shall be called in Israel, The house of him that hath his shoe loosed.'

In this context it should be mentioned that sexual union between a man and his sister-in-law was considered punishable incest while his brother was still alive. 'And if a man shall take his brother's wife, it is an unclean thing: he hath uncovered his brother's nakedness; they shall be childless' (*Lev.* 20:21).

An amusing sidelight on the levirate law is the fact that it is 'the subject of a long commentary in the Mishnah, which sets down the procedure to the extent of fixing the amount of saliva that the widow who has been refused may eject, at the sandal- removing ceremony' (W. Corswant, *Life in Bible Times*, p. 181).

The argument about the application of the levirate law to the genealogies probably originated with Eusebius (*H.E.* 1:7:16). He supported the view that the different names attributed to the father of Joseph in the genealogies (Jacob in *Matthew*, Heli in Luke) are due to a levirate marriage which, Heli and Jacob having been brothers, was concluded between the surviving brother and the deceased man's widow. According to Dummelow, the view that they were indeed brothers is strengthened by the similarity of their respective fathers, Mathat and Mathan. With surprising honesty Dummelow admits that Mathat's father was Levi, and Mathan's father Eleazar, which circumstance would prompt speculation about yet another levirate marriage (*OVBC*, pp.622/3).

The mystery of the genealogies

A comparison between the two genealogies shows obvious dissimilarities. In Matthew we find twenty-eight generations between David and Jesus, in *Luke* forty-one. Assuming that twenty years count as a generation, Matthew covers about 650 years, while Luke covers about 1025 years, which is about correct if, as is thought, David's kingdom flourished around 1000 B.C.

As I have already mentioned, Matthew divides his genealogy starting with Abraham into three parts of fourteen generations each: Abraham to David, David to the Captivity, and from the Captivity to Jesus. Luke begins with Jesus and proceeds backward in time, until Adam, 'the son of God'.

The genealogy of Matthew was probably divided into groups of fourteen for easier memorising. The figure 14 was mystically derived from the name DAVID written DVD in Hebrew – D stands for 4 and W for 6: 4 plus 6 plus 4 = 14. The evangelist shows that Jesus was a true son of Abraham, the ancestor of all Jews. Luke indicates that he was a true son of Adam the son of God, the ancestor of all men. Both genealogies are based on the Greek translation of the Bible, the Septuagint, since there are further discrepancies in the Hebrew original.

The first group in the Gospel according to Matthew may be called the 'List of Patriarchs', from Abraham to King David. The second, the 'List of Kings', from David to Jechoniah, the eighteen-year-old king at the time of the deportation to Babylon (598 B.C.). The exiles returned in 537 B.C., and the third list may be called the 'List of the Dethroned Royal Family', covering the period from Jechoniah to Joseph. Bishop Wordsworth says that 'the names inserted after Jechoniah are the names of those who would have reigned if the Monarchy had continued, who were kings of the Jews *de jure* though not *de facto*' (*Greek New Testament*, I, p.3). This is, of course, incorrect since the descendants indicated are not necessarily first-born sons who would have inherited the throne. In the days of Jesus many Jews claimed Davidic descent.

While it is generally true that the Jews did not record the female members of any family in their ancestral charts, the genealogy of Matthew does mention four women as wives of male descendants, through whom the seed passes: Thamar, Rahab, Ruth and Bathsheba. By some strange coincidence (or is there an explicit reason?) these four were not Israelites by birth, the first two being Canaanites, Ruth a

Moabite, and Bathsheba probably a Hittite. We shall never know how and why these women were included in the genealogy presented by Matthew at the beginning of his gospel.

Christian commentators often suggest that Matthew's genealogy gives the *legal*, the official descent of Jesus from David the King through Solomon the King; while Luke's genealogy provides the human, the *personal* descent from David the King, but through Nathan, who never became king.

Another claim frequently made is the already mentioned speculation that Luke's account shows the descent of Mary. Since none of the Church Fathers mention this possibility (which would have served their arguments well indeed), it is likely that the early Church was unaware of such a theory. It is first encountered in an argument put forward by Annius of Viterbo in the 15th century, whose views were later adopted by many Catholic and Protestant theologians.

While it has always been acknowledged by a majority of students of Christianity that both genealogies show the descent of Joseph, it was mostly taken for granted that Mary too was of Davidic descent. St. Jerome himself stated: 'It may be asked why the genealogy of Christ is traced through Joseph? We reply that it is not usual to trace genealogies from women; and that Joseph and Mary were of the same tribe and house.' Eusebius also argues that Joseph and Mary were of the same lineage. Bishop Wordsworth who quotes these examples, himself believes this, and that the marriage was, in fact, *jure agnationis,* i.e., Mary was given in marriage to Joseph as her next of kin. He argues that they had almost all ancestors in common, and although the genealogies *are* traced through Joseph, they were truly the genealogies of Jesus through both his parents. Wordsworth takes it for granted that Scripture proves Mary's Davidic origin, and quotes *2 Tim.* 2:8 as evidence (*Greek New Testament*, I, p.2/3). *2 Tim.* 2:8 reads: 'Remember that Jesus Christ of the seed of David was raised from the dead according to my Gospel.'

In his *Philology of the Gospels,* F. Blass says that it seems to him an unfounded supposition that the genealogy in Luke's Gospel is Mary's and not Joseph's. The claim is based on a manuscript which speaks of Joseph going to Bethlehem with his wife because *they* were of the house and lineage of David.' According to Blass, the wording of the genealogy itself leaves no doubt that the lineage is that of Joseph's forefathers (pp.170/1).

In a scholarly and remarkably unbiased book Professor Sandmel has this to say about the controversy: 'Matthew begins with a genealogy which starts with Abraham and leads up to Joseph. The latter part of the genealogy is found in varying forms in the ancient manuscripts, as a result of conscious changes found necessary in the divergent views of the Church. Joseph is described in some of the texts as the husband of Mary, of whom Jesus was born; in at least one he is described as the father of Jesus. The relevance of the genealogy would disappear if it did not in some way include Jesus; but the inclusion of Jesus would contradict the virgin birth which immediately ensues. Hence the texts vary in the end of the genealogy. The insoluble problem for the modern reader is whether or not Matthew was aware of the inconsistency of beginning with a genealogy of men, and then proceeding to the virgin birth. Whatever may be the truly proper end of the genealogy, Matthew exhibits no awareness of the inconsistency between his genealogy and his account of the virgin birth' (*A Jewish Understanding of the New Testament,* p. 147).

This need not surprise us. The original author was probably unaware of the Virgin Birth which would have made nonsense of his meticulous effort to trace the origin of Jesus. The Virgin Birth and the corresponding adaptations in both gospels are, in my opinion, later modifications affecting *Matthew,* 1:18/25 and *Luke,* 1:34/7, also necessitating some minor adjustments elsewhere. The Greek-speaking authors of the New Testament were acquainted with the Old Testament only in its Greek translation and, as a consequence, misinterpreted *Isaiah* 7:14. This is quite obvious from the text of *Matthew* 1:23, 'Behold a virgin shall conceive . . .' which is clearly based on the erroneous translation in the Septuagint.

In this way Christian theology has deprived Jesus of his Messianic claim and of his Davidic descent through his father Joseph; it has rendered doubtful the legitimacy of his birth, and Joseph's fatherhood; it has turned his mother into a sexless virgin who lived by the side of the husband without fulfilling her matrimonial duties; and it has denied him the brothers and sisters whom his mother bore. All this happened in the endeavour to turn him into God: the theologian 'thought it robbery to be equal with men', to paraphrase *Phil.* 2:6.

The question whether Jesus was of Davidic descent or not, is after all not so important. The great King was probably not a very savoury character. In the Old Testament he was a killer (*1 Sam.* 27:8/9); a robber (ibid.); a traitor and adulterer (*2 Sam.* 11:2/15); a torturer (*1 Chr.* 20:3 and *2 Sam.* 12:31); and, an intractable hater unto death (*1 Kings* 2:6 to 9), even if he was, for some mysterious reason, 'a man after God's own heart' (*1 Sam.* 13:14 and *Acts* 13.22).

There have been many despicable tyrants like David, there has only been one Teacher who taught that the kingdom of Heaven is within us.

13
Miscellany

Public worship

'And when thou prayest, thou shalt not be as the hypocrites are: for they love to pray standing in the synagogues and in the corners of the street, that they may be seen of men. Verily I say unto you, they have had their reward. But thou when thou prayest, enter into thy closet, and when thou hast shut the door, pray to thy father which is in secret, and thy father which seeth in secret shall reward thee . . . ' (*Matthew* 6:5.6).

Once again I ask the reader *not* to interpret this passage. The meaning is clear: prayer is a personal affair between a man and his God. Ostentation in prayer is calculated to give the appearance of piety, and the reputation of the pious is their 'reward'. Jesus says it is hypocritical *to be seen* praying, and advises his followers to turn to their God unseen by men.

Desperate attempts have been made to ignore these words and their implications. The reason is obvious. From time immemorial, the priests of the crocodile god, and of all other forms of belief, depended on the act of public worship to assess and perpetuate the influence of priestcraft among the people. Without public worship the profession of the priests would go under and disappear.

Let us see what the commentators make of this uncomfortable injunction. Professor Stendahl states that 'neither Matthew nor Jesus criticised public worship as such, but he was aware of its temptations' (*PC*. p.778). The Catholic *QB* says that Jesus was 'condemning the Pharisees 'who loved to stand in the corners of the street that they may be seen of men''' (*QB*, p.367). Note how carefully any reference to the synagogues are omitted. Another Catholic, Professor Jones is quite categorical: 'Jesus does not condemn the practice of praying in public assemblies (*Luke* 18:10), the words . . . are hyperbolic . . . Nor does he condemn the practice (in use among Moslems) of praying in the streets. He condemns the practice of deliberately striking a pious attitude for public notice' (*CC*, p.863).

Dummelow's *OVBC* speaks of those 'who . . . understand what prayer is' and who 'will not pray like the hypocrites or like the heathen. They will pray in secret as well as in public, from the mere delight of praying' (*OVBC*. p.645). He adds: 'There is no disparagement here of public worship which our Lord elsewhere emphatically commends by precept and practice' (ibid.). I wish Dummelow had quoted chapter and verse so that one could find this 'elsewhere' in the New Testament.

A more modern commentary by Professor Barclay deals with the issue, or rather, evades the issue, over a number of pages. The desperate attempt to skip over the decisive point is obvious: Jesus 'insists that all true prayer must be offered to God. The real fault of the people whom Jesus was criticising was that they were praying to men and not to God' (*The Gospel of St. Matthew*, p.197). Professor Fenton also avoids the question and merely states: 'The Jews practised private prayer, as well as public prayer in the temple and the synagogues. This private prayer is under consideration here and in the next verse; the early church did not abandon corporate prayer' (*Commentary to St. Matthew*, p.100). Walsham How's *Commentary* provides another interesting example of saying something without saying anything: 'Standing in the synagogues, that is, making a public show of their devotion . . . To put on sanctity of manner or devoutness of attitude, without the inward spirit of devotion . . . is to be guilty of the hypocrisy of the Jewish Pharisees. A devout manner and posture is the right thing and a great help to devotion, when it is the simple and natural expression of the inward feelings. Enter into thy closet. This may be fulfilled both literally, by withdrawal to some secret place for private prayer, by entering at any time into the secret chamber of the heart, and there holding communion with God'.

Is it a coincidence that all commentators keep silent about the emphasis Jesus placed on the question of private prayer? Is it merely an oversight that the literal, obvious, non- interpretative content of Jesus' injunction is ignored, left unmentioned, and *never included in doctrine or practice?*

Many Christians argue that these words do not imply a prohibition of public prayer, merely a depreciation of the manner in which some Pharisees used to pray. This seems to be the general line of the commentators, too, who regard *Matthew* 6:5/6 merely as a criticism of hypocritical prayer. However, the Sermon on the Mount contains another two similar injunctions:

'Take heed that ye do not your alms before men, to be seen of them, otherwise ye have no reward of your Father which is in heaven. Therefore, when thou doest thine alms, do not sound a trumpet before thee, as the hypocrites do in the synagogue and in the street, that they nay have glory of men. Verily I say unto you, they have their rewards. But when thou doest alms, let not thy left hand know what thy right hand doeth: That thy alms may be in secret: And thy Father, which seeth in secret, shall reward thee . . . ' (*Matthew* 6:1/4).

'When ye fast, be not as the hypocrites, of a sad countenance: for they disfigure their faces, that they may appear unto men to fast: Verily I say unto you, they have their reward. But thou, when thou fastest, anoint thy head and wash thy face that thou appear not unto men to fast, but unto thy Father, which seeth in secret, shall reward thee . . . ' (*Matthew* 6:16/18).

The three passages, with their obvious formal similarity framed into the same speech, show that Jesus considered prayer, almsgiving and fasting as being matters between God and man, and that these actions should be performed without witness. He does not only tell his disciples *what not to do*, he says quite explicitly *what* he expects them *to do*.

Yet, does not Dummelow claim that Jesus himself practised public worship? This misconception is based on two factors. Firstly, it is often mentioned in the New Testament that he prayed to his Father. Secondly, it is recorded that on several occasions he entered a synagogue.

Passages in which Jesus is said to have been praying abound indeed; but there is no record anywhere that he ever prayed in public. We read that 'he left them', 'he departed', 'he went a little further', 'withdrew himself' to pray (*Matthew* 26:39, 26:42, 26:44; *Mark* 1:35, 6:46, 14:32, 14:34/5, 14:39; *Luke* 5:16, 6:12, 22:41). He also prayed, not publicly, but in the presence of his disciples in *John* 11:41/2, 12:27/8 and 17:1 to 26).

The commentaries I have consulted pay no attention whatsoever to this consistent pattern of behaviour, prompted by Jesus' honesty and his desire to act in harmony with his beliefs. Only in *PC* have I found a brief sentence: 'Such withdrawals are characteristic of Jesus; in the solitude he sought renewal of strength in communion with the Father' (*PC*, p.801). The authors of the Synoptic Gospels conscientiously recorded Jesus' insistence on private prayer in word and deed: most modern Christians do not even notice it.

And what was Jesus doing in the synagogues which he is said to have visited on several occasions?

The ancient Jews knew only one 'House of Prayer', the Temple in Jerusalem. They prayed in its courts opposite the Sanctuary, standing upright, reciting formalised prayers and singing rhythmic hymns. Their prayers were addressed direct to the Almighty; the idea of intercession, angelic and heavenly, appeared only at a later date, probably long after the Exile; it was certainly current in New Testament times. The notion of substituting the local synagogue for the Temple appeared during the Exile when the deported Jews in Babylon were unable to attend the Temple service. They created its counterpart in the foreign land and the synagogue was born. Turning in the direction of the Holy City they prayed fervently to be allowed to return to their homeland. The first trace of a historical synagogue was found in Schidia, near Alexandria, Egypt. It was probably built during the reign of Ptolemy II. Later synagogues were built in all foreign countries where Jewish communities lived, and eventually in Palestine itself.

The word synagogue is Greek (συνάγειν means to gather together, to assemble). Philo and Josephus mistakenly believed that the first synagogues were founded by Moses himself. The first mention of such a meeting place in *Psalm* 74:8, believed to have originated in Maccabean times, when synagogues existed already all over the country.

While it is true that the synagogue was first used as a house of prayer when the Temple did not exist or was inaccessible, it gradually became a substitute for the restored distant Temple. Later its main purpose was no longer to serve as a place of prayer and worship. It became a court of justice, a school, a debating forum and even a simple meeting place. Corswant writes: 'It does not appear that at the time of the New Testament there was an official appointed for the reading, the exposition and the prayer; however, already at that time we know there was a chief of the synagogue (who chose the reader and the commentator), a receiver of alms, and a 'sexton' who carried the Scriptures, taught the children to read, and meted out punishments' (*A Dictionary of Life in Bible Times*, p.267).

The synagogue served as a religious and cultural centre of Jewish life in areas where the people had no easy access to the Temple in Jerusalem. The practice of praying in the synagogues, still widespread, was frowned upon by Jesus, and indeed, every passage recording his visits to synagogues tells us that he taught, read, preached and debated – never is it said that he prayed there (*Mark* 11:17; *Luke* 4:15/6, 4:44, 13:10; *John* 6:59, 18:20).

The above-cited passage in the Gospel according to Matthew

continues: 'But when ye pray, use not vain repetitions as the heathens [nations] do. For they think that they shall be heard for their much speaking' (*Matthew* 6:7). Jubilantly, Protestant theologians use this injunction as a stick to beat the Roman Catholic with. The endless litanies of the Catholic ritual, the rosary repetitions, the prayers recited as penance – all these practices are condemned by these words of Jesus.

The Catholic Church is aware of the dangers involved. The *QB* bravely confronts them: 'Christ never condemned repetition in prayer, for He repeated the self-same prayer thrice in the Garden of Gethsemane and He granted the gift of sight to the repeated prayers of the blind men (*Matthew* 20:31). Repeated prayers are not necessarily mechanical. A pianist like Paderewski may play the same concerto over and over again and always play it with perfect interpretation . . . ' (*QB*, pp. 367/8). It is true that Jesus is recorded to have prayed in the same words thrice in the Garden of Gethsemane [*Matthew* 26:39/44], but it remains a mystery how the evangelist knows this, since Jesus left his disciples and prayed on his own! To call the words of the blind men in *Matthew* 20:31 a 'prayer' shows only the commentator's utter disregard for the word and concept of prayer. The comparison with Paderewski is also contrived, since Jesus did not suggest that a prayer should not be said several times, but that it should not be composed of repetitions.

In fact, Jesus himself gave a formula for prayer, a formula which has survived into our days and is still an archetype for true prayer. 'After this manner therefore pray ye: Our father which art in heaven, hallowed by thy name. Thy kingdom come. Thy will be done in earth as it is in heaven. Give us this day our daily bread. And forgive us our debts, as we forgive our debtors. And lead us not into temptation, but deliver us from evil' (*Matthew* 6:9/13). The Revised Version introduces one significant change, in *Matthew* 6:13: ' . . . deliver us from the Evil One'. The *NEB*, too, alters the text: 'Forgive us the wrong we have done, as we have forgiven those who have wronged us. And do not bring us to the test, but save us from the evil one.' The Greek original is most conscientiously rendered in the Authorised Version, although the question whether πονηρός meant 'evil' or 'the evil one' cannot be decisively answered. The mere noun evil is mostly πονηρία (f.).

Klausner calls the Lord's Prayer 'a remarkable prayer, universal in its appeal, it is earnest, brief and full of devotion' (*JN*, p. 387), He adds, however, that every single clause in it can be traced to Jewish prayers and sayings. It seems that the authors of the gospel merely combined ritual words of Jewish liturgy into a string of requests and blessings which constitute this prototype of a prayer. When, during the persecution in Hadrian's reign, the reciting of the main Jewish prayer, the Shemá, was forbidden, the new prayer was substituted in those synagogues where Christian influence was predominant.

Here is a brief analysis of the Lord's Prayer to enable the reader to trace its origins:

'Our father which art in heaven' is one of the three general forms of address. For the benefit of the assembled farmers, prayers were said in the synagogues on the market days, and parts of the Pentateuch were read. When the Scroll of the Law was returned to the Ark, an ancient prayer was recited with the recurring words; 'May it be thy will, O our Father which art in heaven'.

'Hallowed by thy name. They kingdom come.' These words are from the *Kedusha*, the *Amidah*, and the *Kadish*, a widespread prayer still recited by modern Jews. Graves and Podro reconstitute it as follows: 'Hallowed be thine exalted name in the world which thou didst create according to thy will. May the kingdom and thy dominion come speedily: and many it be acknowledged by all the world that thy name shall be praised in all eternity' (*NGR*, p.237).

'Thy will be done, in earth, as it is in heaven.' This is part of the famous 'Short Prayer' of the early Tanna, R Eliezer, who said: 'What is the shortest prayer? Do thy will in heaven, and on earth give comfort to them that fear thee. In all things do what is right in thy sight' (*Tosephta Berakhot 3:7*).

'Give us this day our daily bread,' is a variant of the Old Testament 'Give me the bread that is needful for me' (*Prov.* 30:8). R. Eliezer prayed: 'May is be thy will, O our God, to give every one his needs and to every being sufficient for his lack' (*Tosephta Berakhot* 3:11, *Berakhot* 29b).

'And forgive us our debts, as we forgive our debtors.' In the *Amidah* we find: 'Father forgive us our trespasses'; 'Forgive us our debts' is the sixth blessing in the *Shemonah Esreh*. The nearest to the Lord's Prayer is, however, a text from *Ben Sirs*: 'Forgive thy neighbour's sin and then, when thou prayest, thy sins will be forgiven' (28:2/5). In the *Megillah*, too, the words occur: ' . . . all who have trespassed against us', and 'even as we also forgive all' (28a).

'And lead us not into temptation' is part of a talmudic prayer: 'Lead us not into sin or iniquity or temptation' (*Berakoth* 60b). To the present day Jews use it as a morning prayer. Even the 'optional' addition to the Lord's Prayer: 'For thine is the kingdom, and the power, and the glory, for ever' (*Matthew* 6:13) is a contraction of *1 Chr*, 29:11/13, and appears as a Jewish evening prayer in the following form: 'For thine is the Kingdom, for ever wilt thou reign in glory.'

Most Christian apologists attempt to gloss over the origins of the Lord's Prayer and present it as a completely original gospel-passage. Dummelow goes as far as to state: 'The originality of the Lord's Prayer has sometimes been called in question, but without reason. The parallels adduced from rabbinical prayers are for the most part superficial, and prove no more than that our Lord availed himself of current Jewish forms of expression' (*OVBC*, p.645). It must be left to the reader to decide whether, in view of the examples quoted, the parallels are superficial, or whether the Lord's Prayer is but a contraction of several important Jewish prayers?

Similar criteria may, perhaps, be applied to the injunction quoted at the opening of this chapter. Was criticism of, and opposition to, public worship and ostentatious almsgiving unknown before Jesus expressed it? By no means: in *1 Kings* 18:28 we read of the false prophets of Baal who cried aloud to their god, which prompted the talmudic commentator to remark: 'He that prays so that his words can be heard by them that stand by, is of small faith; he that crieth aloud in prayer is of the false prophet' (*Berakoth* 24b). And another Talmud passage has a familiar ring: 'He that giveth, it were better that he knew not to whom he giveth; and he that receiveth, it were better that he knew not from whom he receiveth' (*Baba Bathra* 10b).

The pattern of prayer and worship practised in Christianity are Judaic in origin and form. Any attempt to deny this can only cast doubt on the sincerity of the apologist concerned.

Oaths

Jesus forbade the swearing of any oaths: 'Ye have heard that it hath been said by them of old time, Thou shalt not forswear thyself, but shall perform unto the Lord thine oaths: But I say unto you, Swear not at all, neither by heaven . . . nor by the earth . . . neither by Jerusalem . . . But let your communications be, Yea, yea, Nay, nay: for whatsoever is more than these cometh of evil' (*Matthew* 5:33/7). Here, too, the Revised Version speaks of 'the evil one'. The *NEB* renders this passage thus: 'You have learned that they were told, Do not break your oaths, and, Oaths sworn to the Lord must be kept. But what I tell you is this: You are not to swear at all – not by heaven . . . nor by earth . . . nor by Jerusalem . . . Plain "Yes" and "No" is all you need to say; anything beyond that comes from the devil'. Further emphasis was given to this injunction in James's Epistle: 'Swear not, neither by heaven, neither by earth, neither by any other oath; but let your yea be yea, and your nay, nay; lest ye fall into condemnation' (*James* 5:12).

The Old Testament passage to which Jesus refers is probably, 'Ye shall not swear by my name falsely' (*Lev.* 19:12). That God's name should not be taken in vain, is a frequent injunction, *Exo.* 20:7, *Deut.* 5:11 are two of many examples. According to Graves and Podro, Jesus may have been quoting an original Hebrew text, no longer extant, of the *Secrets of Enoch* 49:1. The words are preserved in *Sifra Leviticus* 19:36 which probably shares a common source with *Matthew* 5:33/7. They think the saying was originally a midrash on the Third Commandment (*Exod.* 20:7), and that Jesus could not have forbidden the swearing of oaths which was sanctioned by law. According to the Mishna (*Shebuoth* 4:13), however, oaths rendered by heaven, earth or Jerusalem, were invalid unless they were sworn in the name of God. Thus Jesus is held to have condemned idle oaths only, although warning his disciples about swearing generally, because of the attendant danger of forswearing themselves. This approach is traditional in the Talmud: 'Beware of swearing, even on a truth' (*Gittin* 35a); 'Let thy Nay be an honest nay, and thy Yea an honest yea – and say not a thing with thine heart but another with thy mouth' (*Sifra Lev.* 19:36); and, 'Knowest thou not that the whole world shook when the Holy One, blessed be he, pronounced on Sinai: "Thou shalt not take the name of thy God in vain"' (*Shebuoth* 38b/39a).

Flavius Josephus records: 'Whatsoever they [the Essenes] say also is firmer than an oath, but swearing is avoided by them, and they esteem it worse than perjury, for they say that he who cannot be believed without [swearing] God, is already condemned' (*Wars* 2:8:6). The reason given by Josephus for the Essene aversion to oaths is probably the full interpretation of the saying of Jesus. It must be admitted though, that both Josephus (*Wars* 2:8:7) and the Qumran *Manual of Discipline* show that the taking of oaths was an important part of Essene initiation rites. According to *PC* the prohibition is mainly an extension of the warning that God's name should not be taken in vain, and a reminder that the irresponsible swearing of oaths 'may result in irreverence or in a debased sense of truth as something which need not be observed unless supported by an oath (p. 1025).

A very interesting aspect of the swearing of oaths is pointed out by Graves and Podro. They say that according to the Mishna a pious Jew was allowed to tell untruth to robbers, murderers and tax collectors! The School of Hillel goes so far as to say that in such cases a false declaration may even take the form of an oath, if it protects an honest man from victimisation. this principle was called 'tikkun ha'olam', improvement of the social order, i.e. mitigation of the literal severity of the Mosaic Law (*NGR*, pp.217/8).

Antiquity, so rich in oaths, always showed great weariness in permitting them. Plutarch speaks of the 'peril of perjury' which would reach the whole commonwealth', and the great danger involved in a wicked, godless and forsworn person being in charge of prayers, vows and sacrifices' (*Quaestiones Romanae*, p.44).

Aulus Gellius reports that Vestal Virgins were not allowed to take an oath (*Noctes Atticae*, 10:15:31). Later in history there were may religious bodies, which were forbidden oaths.

The attitude of the ancients towards the swearing of oaths (the Anglo-Saxon 'ath' equals solemn affirmation) can be explained by their view that the oath is a kind of curse, calling upon God to destroy the speaker if he does not tell the truth. 'As the Lord liveth' (*1 Sam.* 19:6) is an example of the calling of God as witness to the truth of the statement. It implies that any falsehood would inevitably result in dire punishment. The oath releases a fearful chain of consequences which might lead to the destruction of the perjurer.

The oath is taken by the name of God (*Deut.* 6:13), or by calling upon God as witness (*Gen.* 21:23), raising the hand towards heaven (*Gen.* 14:22, *Deut.* 32:40), or even by placing one's hand under the other person's thigh (*Gen.* 24:2. 47:29).

Geza Vermes emphasises that the initiation of the Qumran sect involved the taking of an oath: 'Candidates for admission to the sect required to be native Israelites and were obliged to undergo a preliminary scrutiny by the Guardian so that he might assess their mental and moral capacities. If they passed muster, they were then permitted to enter the Covenant of God in the presence of the whole community, freely pledging themselves "by abiding oath" to return with all their heart and soul "to every commandment of the Law of Moses in accordance with all that hath been revealed to the sons of Zadok, the Keepers of the Covenant and Seekers of His will"' (*The Dead Sea Scrolls*, p.26). It may be seen that the swearing of oath was reserved for the weightiest occasions, otherwise it was scrupulously avoided.

In view of the fears and apprehensions of the ancient Jews and Gentiles, it is surprising how lightly this problem is taken by most practising Jews and Christians of our days.

The problem is clearly stated by Sandmel: 'The old law enjoined complete honesty in oaths, but the new law forbids an oath under any circumstances, since recognised honesty can satisfy with a simple yes or no' (*A Jewish Understanding of the New Testament*, p.149).

The Catholic *QB* reassures the faithful; 'Did not Christ and St. James forbid the taking of oaths in any form? No, the literal interpretation of Christ's word held by the medieval Cathari and the modern Quakers is contrary to the Church's divine tradition and practice from the beginning. In counselling his followers "not to swear at all", Christ desired them to be so truthful and sincere that all oaths confirming their words would be unnecessary. Our Lord himself replied to the solemn adjuration of the high Priest at His trial' (*Matthew* 26:63). St. Paul often called 'God witness to what he said' (*Rom*, 1:9,2 *Cor*. 1:23, 11:31; Phil. 1:8; *Gal*. 1:20), and declared that 'an oath for confirmation is the end of all controversy' (*Heb*. 6:16). St. Jerome, citing *Jeremiah* 4:2, asserts that three conditions are required for a lawful oath: it must be truthful stating things as they are, and honestly intending to keep the promise made; it must relate to a matter of some importance for the welfare of either soul or body, whether it be public or private; it must not go counter to the moral law' (p.408).

Concerning the New Testament passages quoted above I can only say that nothing but rampant imagination or perhaps embarrassment can present *Matthew* 26:63 ('The High Priest answered and said unto him, I adjure thee by the living God, that thou tell us whether thou be the Christ, the Son of God') as an example of Jesus swearing an oath. The other examples are in the Pauline Epistles, the beginning of the decline of Jesus' teaching, as I have attempted to show on several occasions.

Professor Jones indulges in cautious casuistry when he writes: 'Jesus is not attacking juridical procedure in which oaths are calmly and respectfully taken. Yet even here the necessity for such oaths issues from a defect which, though characteristic of human societies, should be absent from the kingdom whose charter our Lord defines' (*CC*, p.862). Another Catholic book, by T.E. Bird, intended for use in schools, goes as far as to say: 'Christ is referring to ordinary conversation. Oaths may be taken when God's honour or our neighbour's good require them' (*Study of the Gospels*, p.105).

It is not only the Catholic commentators who desire to invalidate the words of Jesus. In *PC* we learn that 'what is condemned is the *vain* use of the name of God or a too ready resort to it' (p.1025). Professor Barclay, too, refers to *Matthew* 26:63 and to the oaths of St. Paul. His argument is a masterpiece of unscrupulous sophistry: 'It is necessary to take an oath from a man, that necessity arises from the evil that is in man. If there was no evil in man, no oath would be necessary. That is to say, the fact that it is sometimes necessary to make a man take an oath is a demonstration of the evil in Christless human nature. The fact that it is necessary to put a man on oath on certain occasions arises from the fact that this is an evil world. In a perfect world, which was the kingdom of God, no taking of oath would ever be necessary. It is necessary only because of the evil in the world.' [The reader should note that this master of the English language and style was a university professor!] 'What Jesus is saying is this: the truly good man will never need to take an oath, the truth of his sayings and the reality of his promises need no such guarantee. But the fact that oaths are still sometimes necessary is the proof that men are not good men and that this is not a good world' (*Matthew*, pp. 159/160).

Griffiths Thomas' authoritative commentary on the Articles of the Church of England contains the usual reference to Jesus' oath in *Matthew* 26:63 and Paul's affirmations. The commentator goes on to say that the words of Jesus and St. James 'abundantly vindicate the practice of oath-taking in Courts of Justice, solemnly appealing to the presence of God in support of the statements made. The reference at the end of the Article lays down the principle of such taking of oaths . . . The allusion is to the words of *Jeremiah* (4:2). Granted these conditions, an oath is perfectly legitimate. It is no doubt correct that if men were always strictly truthful, oaths would not be required, but in view of the presence of evil in the world, the necessity of some solemn attestation seems inevitable, and for this purpose is to be regarded as quite lawful and right for a Christian' (*Principles of Theology*, p.484).

Let us now consult the source itself, Article 39 of the Church of England: 'Of a Christian Man's Oath. As we confess that vain and rash swearing is forbidden Christian men by out Lord Jesus Christ, and James His Apostle; so we judge that Christian religion doth not prohibit, but that a man may swear when the Magistrate requireth in a cause of faith and charity, so it be done, according to the Prophet's [Jeremiah] teaching: in justice, judgement and truth.' This article dates from 1533, but its original text said 'Christian men may take an oath.' This was directed against the Anabaptists who opposed any form of oath, even in Courts of Justice.

There seems to be unanimity concerning the disregard in which the words of Jesus and James are to be held. These are a few examples which show up more clearly the cleavage between the Teacher and his 'interpreters'.

14
Jesus did not found a Church

Introduction

It was a great moment in the life of Jesus when one of his disciples, a simple and devout fisherman, said to him: 'Thou are the Christ [Messiah], the Son of the living God' (*Matthew* 16:16). Perhaps it was the first time Jesus became aware that he might indeed be the Messiah, the Messenger of God, the apocalyptic hope of Israel.

His whole life, past, present and future, arranged itself into a new pattern. No longer was he a vagrant teacher, the son of a poor Galilean carpenter: he was the rightful heir to the throne of David. His father *was* of the seed of David, and his cousin John who had baptised him in the river Jordan was none other than the prophet Elijah himself. Simon, the son of Jonah, suddenly became the revealer of a sublime secret: the man who recognised him as the Christ of God.

Jesus was exultant, overwhelmed. He blessed Simon, saying: 'Blessed art thou, Simon Barjonah, for flesh and blood hath not revealed it unto thee, but my Father which is in heaven.' And following this up with the fateful words: 'And I say unto you, Thou art Peter, and upon this rock will I build my church: and the gates of hell shall not prevail against it' (*Matthew* 16:17/8).

Later this saying became the basis of the claim of the Christian Church to have been founded by Jesus. In fact, he said nothing of the sort. The text itself reads: Σὺ εἶ Πέτρος, καὶ ἐπι ταύτῃ τῇ πέτρᾳ οἰκοδομήσω μοῦ τὴν ἐκκλησίαν. The word ἐκκλησία did not mean Church, but 'assembly', 'gathering', those 'called forth'. It came to mean Church in the modern sense only at a much later date. In Jesus' days the concept of 'a Church' did not even exist. The quotation itself shows that Jesus may have foreseen the possibility of his death, and entrusted the leadership of his *minneh* (a Jewish religious group of at least ten men, being allowed to practice their faith independently of any religious authority), his little community, to his oldest apostle.

From that day onward Simon was called Kephas (Aramaic for 'stone') or, in Greek Πέτρος (stone). This is of course only the account of Matthew. Much shorter versions are to be found in *Mark* 8:29, *Luke* 9:20 and *John* 6:69. In fact John reports that the name Kephas was given to Simon by Jesus when they first met (*John* 1:42).

The scene which took place near Caesarea Philippi, some time during the second year of Jesus' ministry, made a profound and lasting impression on his mind and attitude. It is likely that the deep-rooted belief in his Messianic role did not leave him until the hour of crucifixion. The evangelists record that Jesus wished this revelation to be kept secret. He probably thought that Israel would need a period of preparation to meet the impact of the tremendous claim of an unknown teacher 'without authority.'.

He was quite aware of the greatness of the task he had accepted. He would claim the throne of David and restore the might of the Great King. He would reign in Jerusalem which was in his eyes the centre of the world, and all the tribes and sons of Israel would return from the Dispersion to settle once more in the Land of Promise. He would overcome the enemies of God, and make the Lord of Israel the Lord of the Earth. (By the Lord of Israel, he meant of course, God the Father Almighty.) Supernatural powers would aid him, the Messenger, and the word of his mouth would render his enemies helpless. His exaltation would not be political, nor revolutionary, but the irresistible unfolding of the divine will. Somewhere along this line of thought it may even have occurred to him that a spiritual reality (the kingdom of heaven) would be superimposed on the physical reality of earthly things, and the events of the future would take place with all-pervading power in this new dimension. The 'Shekinah', the shadow of the Divine Presence, would cover everything, and in this shadow the real would become dream and dream reality. It is in this sense that his kingdom would not be of this world.

As his wisdom and understanding increased, so he realised that the 'kingdom of God' was not something external but an experience to be achieved 'within us'. The idea of political or military victory disappeared altogether. The 'ecclesia' lost its fighting character and became a spiritual community. As head of such a community, Jesus had to translate the Messiah (the idea of Christhood) into terms of spiritual kingship, liberation and world-wide supremacy. All the same, the 'ecclesia' was not the wider context of his dream, but the practical community of purpose uniting him with the circle of his followers.

According to the Gospels, Jesus used the word 'ecclesia' only twice. Although theologians are aware of this, yet they base their claim for the foundation of the Church on these two short passages. There are other doubtful points. Petros means stone rather than rock, or 'rock of stone' at best. The text shows Jesus playing with the words, and suggesting that Peter (Simon) was a rock of loyalty and steadfastness, an opinion belied by events immediately following and by events of later date. Peter, indeed, appears in the records as a timid and cautious person who, in his endeavour to disguise his association with Jesus, denied him several times after he (Jesus) was taken prisoner. It is also unlikely that Jesus, a pious and learned Jew, would have used the word rock, a title reserved exclusively for the Almighty: 'He is the rock, his work is perfect' (*Deut.* 32.4); 'For their Rock is not as our Rock' (*Deut.* 32:31) 'Neither is there any Rock like our God' (*1 Sam.* 2:2); 'The Lord is my Rock' (*2 Sam.* 22:2); and, 'Who is Rock save our God?' (*Psalm* 18:31). At the most, the metaphor would be applied to Abraham, and the rabbis were supposed to have a saying 'When the Holy One saw Abraham who was going to arise, He said, Lo, I have discovered a rock to found the world upon' (Quoted from Barclay, *The Gospel of St. Matthew*, 1 p.155) Another confusing fact: as I have mentioned, in the Fourth Gospel, Jesus called Simon 'Kephas' on the very first day of their encounter (*John* 1:42). But then, according to the Gospels, Kephas meant stone, like Petros, and *not* rock. However, the expression ἡ πέτρα may mean rock.

The text in Matthew is followed by the words: 'Whatsoever thou shalt bind on earth shall be bound in heaven: and whatsoever thou shalt loose on earth shall be loosed in heaven' (*Matthew* 16:19). It is claimed by scholars that the Aramaic language used the expression 'to bind' to denote something that is forbidden and unlawful, while 'to loose' meant that something is not binding. Dummelow quotes two interesting examples for this usage: 'Rabbi Meir loosed (that is, permitted) the mixing of wine and oil, and the anointing of a sick man on the Sabbath', and 'Rabbi Jochanan said, They necessarily 'loose' (that is, permit) saluting on the Sabbath'; and, 'Concerning gathering wood on a feast day, the School of Shammai binds (forbids) it, the School of Hillel looses (permits) it' (*OVBC*, p.682).

Yet, whatever their reservations, almost all Christian writers accept the theory that the foundation of a Church was the intention of Jesus. Perhaps the most tortured of these speculations is expressed by the Russian novelist, Merezhkovski, who admits that Jesus could not have spoken of 'the Church' in its later meaning 'even if only for the reason that no such word or concept existed in Israel at the time'. He too mentions the fact that even this word appears only twice, and is combined with the commission to 'bind and loose'. And the devout author asks the painful question: 'Not even here does Jesus refer to the Church by name. Nowhere does he say Church, as nowhere does he say Christ. He does not wish to say it, or cannot say it. But why? For the two thousand year duration of Christendom none has ever asked' (*Jesus Manifest*, pp.252/3). May not the reason be that both concepts were alien to Jesus?

Beware of false prophets

Jesus suspected that false prophets would arise to confuse the innocent and simple in heart. He even knew that some would come in his name, with his words on their lips. 'Beware of false prophets.' he exclaimed, 'which come to you in sheep's clothing, but inwardly they are ravening wolves' (*Matthew* 7:15). With equal emphasis he said: 'Take heed that no man deceive you. For many shall come in my name, saying, I am *Christ*, and shall deceive many' (*Matthew* 24:4). In the same sermon we find 'There shall arise false Christs, and false prophets . . . insomuch that if . . . possible, they shall deceive the very elect' (*Matthew* 24:24). We find the warning also in Mark's Gospel: 'False Christs and false prophets shall rise and shall . . . seduce if . . . possible even the elect' (*Mark* 13:22). In Luke's Gospel we read: 'Take heed that ye be not deceived: for many shall come in my name saying: I am *Christ* . . . go ye not after them' (*Luke* 21:8). These references to 'Christ' should not confuse the reader, they are printed in italics to indicate that the words are the translators' insertions.

Wanting to find the origin of these sayings, we do not have to look far. We can find them in the Old Testament: The warning against false prophets is explicit in *Deut* 13:1 to 3, *Jer.* 14:14, 23:21 and 25, *Micah* 3:5, and *Zech* 10:2. The prototype of 'many shall come in my name'; is to be found in Jeremiah: 'Thus saith the Lord of hosts, Hearken not unto the words of the prophets . . . they make you vain: they speak a vision of their own heart, and not out of the mouth of the Lord' (*Jer.* 23:16) and 'That prophesy lieth in my name' (*Jer.* 23:25). [I am aware that the Bible prints 'prophesy lies in my name' but in the context this makes no sense and I believe it is a mistake.]

Before I consider the sayings themselves, I must make clear that contrary to the New Testament the texts quoted above (Authorised Version), Jesus did not refer to himself as 'Christ', and the term printed in italics does not appear in the Greek original. Indeed, I believe that the text read originally: 'Many shall come in the name of God', 'I am' being used as the name of the Almighty.

The first question we have to answer is: what is meant by 'false prophets' and by 'false teachers'? Catholic theologians are fond of quoting the saying: 'Verily, verily, I say unto you, He that entereth not by the door into the sheepfold, but climbeth up some other way, the same is a thief and a robber' (*John* 10:1). According to this, the false prophet is he who 'climbeth up some way', since the 'door', 'God's Church, cannot become corrupt because He [Jesus] promised to preserve it from error' (*QB*, p.134). Thus the Catholic faith becomes an impregnable fortress: freedom from error is divinely granted to the Catholic Church.

However, the problem who these false prophets were to whom Jesus referred, occupied the Christians' mind throughout history. The *Didaché*, a book of orders and regulations which was discovered towards the end of the 19th century, contains a clear indication of the character of the false prophet. It discusses the way in which itinerant prophets should be treated. It requires the believer to give them 'honour and hospitality for one or two days, but if he remains three days, he is a false prophet'. The most important test, however, is whether he does as he preaches. In chapters 11 and 12 of the *Didaché* we read: 'If a prophet, claiming to speak in the spirit, orders a table and a meal to be set before him, he is a false prophet. If he asks for money, he is a false prophet. If a wanderer comes to the congregation and wishes to settle there, if he has a trade let him work and eat. If he has no trade, consider in your wisdom how he may live with you as a Christian in idleness . . . But if he will not do this, he is a trafficker in Christ. Beware of such!' (Quoted from Barclay, *The Gospel of St. Matthew*, I, p.287). Some Protestant theologians believe that Jesus referred to miracle-workers and faith-healers. Dummelow, however, comes nearer the truth when he claims that Jesus did not mean Pharisees or heathens but 'Christian' false prophets and teachers. According to him, by 'sheep's clothing' Jesus understood the hypocritical professions and the outward display of piety of the false teacher.

Comparing the teaching of Jesus with the doctrines of the Christian churches, may I suggest that the 'false prophets and ravening wolves in sheep's clothing' are none other than (or rather most) Christian theologians who come in the name of Jesus or of God and 'produce a religion which consists mainly in the observance of externals . . . prohibitions . . . and divorce religion and life . . . are arrogant and separatist'. These words are borrowed from one of the theologians,

Professor Barclay, who himself described very aptly the characteristics by which false prophets and teachers can be recognised.

It is instructive to confirm Jesus' words with a passage from Paul's Epistle to the Corinthians: 'For such are false prophets, deceitful workers, transforming themselves into apostles of Christ. And no marvel; for Satan himself is transformed into an angel of Light. Therefore it is no great thing if his ministers also be transformed as the ministers of righteousness; whose end shall be according to their works' (*2 Cor.* 11:13/15). It could not have been put better.

Ye shall know them by their fruits

Jesus answers all the arguments about what he 'meant', and how his warning was to be understood: 'A good tree cannot bring forth evil fruit, neither can a corrupt tree being forth good fruit . . . Wherefore by their fruits shall ye know them' (*Matthew* 7:18/20). Very similar utterances can be found in *Matthew* 12:33 and *Luke* 6:43/4. 'Ye shall know them by their fruits' (*Matthew* 7:16) is the simple and infallible yardstick by which we are able to recognise true teachers and false teachers, true friends and false friends. In other words, Jesus is saying that a good attitude of mind will produce good actions, while an attitude of mind which is corrupt will produce corruption and deceit. With astonishing singlemindedness, Christian thinkers do not seem ever to have considered the possibility that this yardstick could be applied to their religion and to their organisations. On the contrary, they appear to find a good deal of selfjustification in these words. Barclay apparently considers it a passage with which to beat the Roman Catholics: 'The teaching which declares that any Church or any sect has a monopoly of the grace of God is false teaching, for Christ is not the Christ who divides, He is the Christ who unites' (*The Gospel of St. Matthew*, II, p.293). The saying about the tree and its fruits was a widespread metaphor in the antique world, and Seneca himself used it declaring that good cannot grow from evil any more than olives from a fig tree. Christian commentators mostly use it to justify Christian attitudes towards non-believers. Of all the apologists I have read, Fenton alone has the humility simply to say: 'Love or good works are the test for distinguishing the true from the false teachers' (*Commentary to St. Matthew*, p.113).

This is indeed the core of the teaching, and any attempt to disguise or misrepresent it, merely distorts the image of Jesus.

Provide neither gold nor silver

To the disciples sent out to teach his doctrine, Jesus addressed the words: 'Provide neither gold nor silver nor brass [i.e., no money of any kind] in your purses' (*Matthew* 10:9/10). In Mark's Gospel it is recorded that he 'commanded them that they should take nothing for their journey, save a staff only; no scrip, no bread, no money in their purse' (*Mark* 6:8). And Luke quotes: 'Take no money for your journey . . . neither bread, neither money; neither have two coats apiece' (*Luke* 9:2).

These texts are elaborations on Jesus' fundamental approach to spiritual gifts: 'Freely ye have received, freely give' (*Matthew* 10:8). No attainment of the mind, of human understanding, should be the object of barter; advice, doctrine, compassion and love must be the fruits of man's attitude and not of his needs. The sayings are probably talmudic quotations; according to Barclay the Talmud teaches that 'no one should go to the Temple Mount with staff, shoes, girdle of money or dusty feet' (*The Gospel of St. Matthew*, I, p. 378). The Old Testament also has related passages, such as the story of Gehazi and Naaman: 'Went not mine heart with thee? . . . Is it time to receive money, and to receive garments and olive-yards? . . . (*2 Kings* 5:26)'. In another book we read: 'I will love them freely' (*Hos* 14:4).

The problem revolves around the question whether a teacher should expect and accept payment, or not. Much is made of Jesus' saying that 'the worker is worthy of his meat' (*Matthew* 10:10). Professor Barclay argues, 'It is true that a rabbi might not accept payment, but it is also true that it was considered at once a privilege and an obligation to support a rabbi, if he was truly a man of God' (ibid., I, p. 378).

Walsham How recognises the potential danger involved when he is at pains to explain that 'it would show ignorance to take these commands as a rule for Christ's ministers, except in the general sense to avoid all worldly cares and anxieties, and to be content with what God provides'. R.M. Wilson, too, comes near to understanding the saying: 'The missionaries,' he writes, 'are to be like an invading army and live on the country; their business brooks no delay. Of the message with which they were entrusted nothing is said, but it must have related to the imminence of the kingdom . . . It was the reading of the Mission Charge that inspired Francis of Assisi to embrace "the Lady Poverty"' (*PC*, p. 805).

The Church has gone a long way from considering the words of the man it claims to be its Master. Its enormous properties and revenues, its financial transactions and extractions are rationalised by the need of 'the missionaries' to make a living.

The blind lead the blind

Speaking of hypocritical leaders and teachers, Jesus said: 'Let them alone; they are blind leaders of the blind. And if the blind lead the blind, both shall fall into the ditch' (*Matthew* 15:14). The Gospel according to Luke puts it less harshly: 'Can the blind lead the blind? shall they not both fall into the ditch?' (*Luke* 6:39). We find the origin of this saying in Isaiah: 'For the leaders of this people cause them to err and they that are led of them are destroyed' (*Isaiah* 9:16), and, 'O my people, they which lead thee, cause thee to err, and destroy the way of thy paths' (*Isaiah* 3:12). On other occasions, too, Jesus upbraided the hypocritical teachers, calling them 'blind guides' (*Matthew* 23:16 and 24).

What was meant by this reference to the blind? Graves and Podro shed light on the problem by reformulating the saying: 'To be blind is no sin, but to be blind and say: "We see, let us guide thee", the same is deceit and sin (*NGR*, p. 194). Blindness is obviously meant metaphorically: indifference or even contempt for truth. The blind who pretend to be leaders, show disregard for the will of God, as revealed through the teaching of Jesus, and thereby they steer straight for the ditch. In Matthew the image is uncompromising and direct, the dupes of the counterfeiters are also destined for perdition. Luke is somewhat more lenient: putting the saying in the form of a question, he allows a ray of hope for the misled.

To the same category belongs the bleak statement in Mark's Gospel: 'Making the word of God of none effect through your tradition, which ye have delivered: and many such things do ye' (*Mark* 7:13). The will of God can only be discerned by man through his reaction to every situation as it arises. Tradition replaces free choice with rigid patterns of the law according to the letter, and thus tradition can blind man to God's will. When Christianity developed into a complex of rigid traditional laws and rites instead of the free acceptance of Jesus' teaching, its leaders became the blind guides of the Gospels.

Why call me Lord, Lord

To these blind guides and their dupes are directed his words: 'Why call me Lord, Lord, and do not the things which I say?' (*Luke* 6:46). The origin of this saying is possibly the passage in Malachi where the Lord

(God) complains that men call him Father and Master, yet do not seem to honour him (*Mal.* 1:6ff). It is conceivable that the saying (*Luke* 6:46) also spoke in the name of God, and stated that many call upon the Lord, but ignore his will. Or else, Jesus may have chided those of his disciples who called him their teacher ('master'), yet did not follow his words. This mighty saying which challenges the right of most Christians to call themselves followers of Jesus, is practically ignored by the commentators. Caird used it as an occasion to meditate upon the significance of the expression 'Lord' (*Gospel of St. Luke*, pp. 106/7), and Lampe merely remarks that 'Jesus warns us against false disciples' (*PC*, p. 830).

Jesus is recorded to have put this text in the negative on another occasion: 'He that loveth me not keepeth not my sayings: and the word which ye hear is not mine by the father's which sent me' (*John* 14:24). This seems to confirm the view that he regarded his teaching as an expression of God's will, and reproached several of his disciples for the lack of real love and concern by disregarding the teaching which reflects the will of God. Jesus presented this view with yet greater emphasis when he said: 'My doctrine is not mine, but his that sent me' (*John* 7:16). 'I do nothing of myself but as my father has taught me, I speak these things' (*John* 8:28); and, 'For I have not spoken of my self; but the father which sent me, he gave me a commandment, what I should say, and what I should speak' (*John* 12:49). The evangelist who recorded this last passage may have had in mind a saying of the Old Testament: 'I will raise them up a prophet from among their brethren . . . and will put my words into his mouth, and he shall speak unto them all that I shall command him' (*Deut.* 18:18). Another source of inspiration may have been the text in Ezekiel: 'They hear thy words, but they will not do them' (*Ezek.* 33:31).

In this connection we may also quote another of Jesus' sayings: 'He that heareth you, heareth me: and he that despiseth you, despiseth me: and he that despiseth me despiseth him that sent me' (*Luke* 10:16), paralleled by passages in *Matthew* 10:40, *Mark* 9:37 and *John* 13:30. The fact that each one of the evangelists recorded this saying shows the importance attached to it by the early disciples. They saw themselves as carrying the message of Jesus into the world, and the message was a reflection of this will of God. It is significant how the latter-day vicars of Jesus see this passage: Walsham How, himself Canon and Rural Dean, whose book was published by the S.P.C.K., remarks with blissful ignorance: 'How careful should this make us not to despise the message of those who bear Christ's commission and speak in His name.' Lightfoot sees in this text a further affirmation of Christ's closeness to, and oneness with, the Father. I have not found one commentator who realised that it contains an overriding obligation of the disciple to heed the words of Jesus, because in these words he saw the revelation of the divine message.

Where two or three are gathered in my name

Many commentators take refuge in the saying of Jesus: 'Where two or three are gathered in my name there am I in the midst of them' (*Matthew* 18:20). The invocation of the name seems to them a proof of Jesus' presence in their midst. What Jesus probably said was that when two or three gather in the name of God ['I am'], God's spirit is in their midst. However, I should not base my argument on speculation, and have to accept the saying in its present form. In any case, two or three gathered together for any purpose do not add up to a congregation, a religious community, let alone a mighty organisation. To quote these words as a proof of the Church's relation to Jesus, is ludicrous. Even in its accepted form, the text merely states the old claim that the spirit of a personality or idea is present when invoked by two or three people. Words attributed to R. Hanina ben Teradion express the view that 'when two sit, and there are between them the words of the Torah, the Shekinah rests between them' (*Pirke Aboth* 3:3). Yet this deeper meaning of the words has been ignored or forgotten. The Christian clergy regards them as a hint concerning the significant part the Church was to play as Christ's representative on earth. 'The saying . . . is clearly meant as a promise that Christ himself is acting with the Church,' comments Professor Stendahl (*PC*, p.789). Dummelow comes nearer the truth, but frightened, withdraws immediately into his orthodox niche: 'Christ gives reasons why God will grant such prayers. It is that He himself, the great Intercessor is personally present in every worshipful assembly of Christians, and presents their prayers to the Father. The passage is particularly true of assemblies of the Church . . . A convincing proof of Christ's divinity may be drawn from this promise' (*OVBC*, p.687).

Many Christian theologians feel entitled to claim that the Church represents the forces of good described in the parables of Jesus in *Matthew* 13:11 and 24/41, *Matthew* 13:47/50, 25:1/12, and others: in all the parables where Jesus spoke of the kingdom of Heaven.

What is this kingdom of Heaven or kingdom of God which is at the core of the message of Jesus? And where one, only one, is inspired by the will of God, it can be said that the kingdom of Heaven is within him or her.

What is to become of the kingdom within us if we are to regard the posturing of powerful institutions around us as 'the kingdom'? The very comparison prompts us to distrust or reject altogether the Church's authority and interpretations. If the Church is, as it claims, the kingdom of Heaven, will on the Day of Harvest the wheat be burnt and the tares be gathered into the Barn of God?

Index of Names

ABELARD, Pierre, French scholastic, 1079–1142   *146*
AELIANUS, Claudius, Latin author and rhetorist, early 3rd c.   *97*
AGRIPPINA the Younger, wife of Emperor Claudius, 16–59   *214*
AKHENATON or Edinaton, Egyptian Pharao   *286*
ALBERTUS, Magnus St., German Dominican scholastic, 1193–1280   *146*
ALEXANDER, the Great, king of Macedonia, 336–232, b.356 BC   *161*
ALEXANDER, St., trinitarian bishop of Alexandria, 312–326   *136–7, 140*
ALEXANDER VI Borgia, Pope 1492–1503, b.1431   *229*
ALMOS, brother of King Stephen I of Hungary, rebel leader, d. early 11th c.   *226*
ALTIZER Thomas, US professor of comparative religion, b.1926   *87*
AMBIBULUS Marcus, Roman procurator of Judaea, 10–13   *13, 195*
AMBROSE St., Latin church father, bishop of Milan, 340–397   *55, 177, 187, 255, 277*
ANDREWES Lancelot, Anglican bishop, 1555–1626   *188*
ANNIUS Rufus, Roman procurator of Judaea, 13–14   *198*
ANNIUS of Viterbo, Italian theologian, d.1502   *13, 324, 336*
ANSCAR St., 'Apostle of the North', 801–865   *226*
ANSELM St., Italian scholastic, Archbishop of Canterbury, 1093–1109   *146*
ANTONINUS Pius, Roman emperor 138–161, b.86   *4*
APPOLLONIUS of Tyrana, Pythagorean miracle worker, 3BC–97AD   *162*
AQUINAS Thomas St., Dominican scholastic, 1225–1274   *87, 101–2, 141, 187, 218, 231*
ARISTEAS, alleged author of OT apocryphal book, between 200–50 BC   *265, 272*
ARISTIDES, Athens, Christian philosopher, 2nd c.   *182*
ARISTOTLE, Greek philosopher, 384–322 BC   *146, 212, 231, 272*
ARIUS, presbyter of Baucalus, opponent of trinitarians, 280–336   *41, 50, 83, 140–1*
ARNOLD of Brescia, enemy of established Church, 1090–1155, executed   *227*
ARTAXERXES I (Hashayasha), king of Persia, 465–425 BC   *197*

ARTAXERXES II Mnemon, king of Persia, 405–359 BC   *119*
ASHOKA (Ashokavardana), Indian ruler, Buddhist, 273–233 BC   *269, 284*
ASSURBANIPAL, king of Assyria, 669–626   *268*
ATHANASIUS St., trinitarian church father, 295–373   *46, 80–1, 108, 136, 141–2, 183*
ATIA, mother of Emperor Augustus, niece of Caesar, d.43 BC   *162*
AUGUSTINE St., bishop of Hippo, Latin theologian, 354–430   *41, 46, 55, 145–6, 177, 183, 185*
AUGUSTINE St., of Canterbury, 'apostle of Britain', England 597, d.604   *225*
AUGUSTUS Caesar Octavius, Roman emperor, 31BC–14AD, b.63BC   *162*

BALTHASAR, king of Babylon, dd.530 BC
BARCLAY William, Scottish professor of theology, 1907–1978   *128, 171, 180, 201–2, 208, 237, 241, 244, 250, 260,   262, 270, 272, 276,   341, 351, 353–4, 355*
BARNES Ernest William, bishop of Birmingham, 1874–1953   *70, 79, 99, 151, 215, 283*
BARRETT, C. Kingsley, Durham professor of theology, contemporary   *40, 46, 70, 276–7*
BARTH Karl, Swiss protestant theologian, 1886–1968   *42, 59, 88, 112, 153, 283*
BASIL St., Greek church father, 329–379   *40, 62, 142, 255–6*
BASILIDES of Alexandria, Christian gnostic, 2nd c.   *82*
BAUER Bruno, German theologian, 1886–1968   *21–3, 29, 34, 36, 68–70, 126, 205, 215*
BEA Augustine, German Jesuit cardinal, 1881–1968
BEASLEY—MURRAY Dr. George, Anglican theologian, 20th c.   *48*
BELLARMINE Robert St., Italian Jesuit cardinal, 1542–1621   *231–2*
BENEDICT XIII, Avignon Pope, 1394–1424   *229*
BERDYAYEV Nicolas, Russian Christian philosopher, 1874–1948   *151*
BERGUER George, Swiss author, 19th c.   *62, 79, 328*
BETTENSON Henry, author, contemporary   *137, 143*
BEVENOT Maurice, Jesuit Oxford professor, 20th c.   *109*
BIRD T.E., RC theologian, 20th c.   *324–5, 347*
BJÖRN, king of Sweden, around 830   *226*
BLACK Matthew, Anglican scholar, orientalist, 20th c.
BLASS Friedrich, German professor of classical philology, 1843–1907   *336*
BOËTHIUS, Roman philosopher, poet and statesman, 470–525   *146*
BONAVENTURA St., Italian cardinal, theologian, 1217–1274   *193*
BONHOEFFER Dietrich, German theologian, killed by SS, 1906–1945   *88*
BONIFACE VIII, Pope, 1294–1303   *228*
BOUQUET Alan, protestant theologian and author, 1884–?   *160*
BOUSSET William, German theologian, 1865–1920   *31, 65*
BRAMHALL John, Irish prelate, 1594–1663   *188*
BRANDES George, Danish critic and author, 1842–1953   *25*

BRIGHTMAN Edgar S., US philosopher, 1884–1953 *151*
BRUCE Frederick F., C of E professor of theology, 20 c. *51*
BRUEGHEL Pieter the Older, Dutch painter, 1525–1569 *238*
BRUNNER Emil, Swiss professor of theology, 1889–1966 *42, 62, 88, 112*
BUDDHA, Gautama Siddharta, Indian religious teacher, c.560–480 BC *27, 198, 269*
BULL George, Anglican bishop, 1634–1710 *48*
BULTMANN Rudolf, German protestant theologian, 1884–1976 *42–3, 112, 294*

CABOT Richard Clarke, US protestant theologian, 1868–1939 *282*
CAIRD George Bradford, Oxford professor of theology, 1917–1984 *59, 97, 238–9, 244, 250, 327, 357*
CALIGULA Gaius Julius, Roman emperor, 37–41, b.12 *214–5*
CALVIN Jean, Geneva leader of Reformation, 1509–1564 *59, 147–8, 188, 212, 230*
CANUT I (Knud), king of Denmark and England,   1017–1035 *226*
CARPOCRATES, Alexandrian gnostic mentioned by Irenaeus, 2nd c. *330*
CAUSSIN Nicolas, French Jesuit, 1675–1751
CERINTHUS, 'judaizing' Alexandrian gnostic, about 100 *82*
CHADWICK Henry, Anglican Oxford professor of theology, b.1920 *131*
CHARLEMAGNE (Charles I) Frank–Roman emperor, 768–814, b.742
CHRYSOSTOM St., bishop of Constantinople, 347–407 *2, 4, 40, 45–6, 48, 55, 69, 184*
CHWOLSON Daniel, Russian–Jewish scholar, 1819–1911 *245*
CICERO Marcus Tullius, Roman orator & lawyer, 106–43 BC *4*
CLAUDIUS Tiberius Drusus, Roman emperor 41–54, b.10 BC *4, 214–5, 221*
CLEMENT of Alexandria St., Christian apologist, c.150–215 *182–3*
CLEMENT of Rome, apostolic father, end of 1st c.
CLEMENT V (Bertrand de Got), Pope 1305–1315, b.1264 *228*
CLEMENT VIII, anti-pope 1592–1605, b.1536 *229*
CLOVIS I (Chlodwig) king of Franconia, 481–511, b.465 *224*
CONFUCIUS (kung–fu–tse) Chinese philosopher, 551–479 BC *222*
CONRAD Noel, sometime vicar of Thaxted, 20 c. *257*
CONSTANS I, Roman emperor, 337–350, b. c.320 *141*
CONSTANTIA, sister of Constantine I *141*
CONSTANTINE I, Flavius Valerius, Roman emperor 296–337, b.274 *80–1, 137–9, 140, 204, 222*
CONSTANTINE II, Roman emperor 337–340, b.316 *141*
CONSTANTINE V, emperor of Byzantine (Eastern Roman) empire 741–775, b.718 *225*
CONSTANTIUS Chlorus, Roman emperor 305–306, b.250 *137*
CONSTANTIUS II, Roman emperor 350–361 *141–2* (also Eastern emperor from 337)
CONYBEARE Fredrick, US author, 1856–1924 *62, 78, 178*
COPONIUS, Roman procurator of Judaea, 6–9 *13, 198*

CORBISHLEY T., Jesuit professor of theology, b.1909 54
CORSWANT W., French professor of archaeology, 20th c. *334, 341*
CROSSLEY R.S., sometime curate of Beckenham, 20 c. *89, 131, 150–1*
CUMONT F., Belgian professor of archaeology, 1868–1947
CURTIUS Quintus Rufus, Roman historian, 1st c. *5*
CYPRIAN St., Latin church father, bishop of Carthage, 200–158 *133–183*
CYRIL St., of Alexandria, patriarch 412–444, b.376 *332*
CYRIL St., of Jerusalem, bishop of Jerusalem, 315–386 *40–46, 183*
CYRUS (Koorosh), founder and king of Persia, 560–529 BC *197*

DAGOBERT, king of Franconia, 623–632 *225*
DAMASUS St., Pope 366–384, b.304 *143*
DANIELOU Jean, French Jesuit theologian, 1905–1974 *95, 180*
DARIUS I (Daryush), king of Persia 560-529 BC *197*
DAUBE David, Jewish scholar and author, 1909–1971 *99, 121, 127*
DECIUS, Roman emperor 249–251 *221*
DEMETRIANUS of Antioch, author of Christian apocrypha, time unknown
DEMETRIUS of Phalerum, Greek historian, 345–283 BC *157*
DIBELIUS Martin, German theologian, 1883–1947
DIDEROT Denis, French author, 1713–1784 *24*
DIOCLETIAN, Roman emperor, 285–305 *137, 221–2*
DIONYSUS, bishop of Alexandria, 190–264 *136*
DIONYSUS, bishop of Rome, 259–268 *136*
DOGDUYAH (Dughdova), virgin mother of Zarathustra
DOMITIAN, Roman emperor 81–96 (b.51) *215, 221, 329*
DORNER Isaac August, German theologian 1809–1884 *77*
DOSTOJEVSKI Fjodor Mihaylovitch, Russian novelist, 1821–1881 *199*
DREWS Dr. Arthur, German bible scholar and writer, early 20th c. *52, 78*
DUMMELOW J.R., Anglican cleric and commentator, early 20th c. *41, 50–1, 87, 97, 101, 128, 131–2, 172, 188–9, 200, 206, 237, 239, 251, 260, 263, 266–7, 279, 326, 333–4, 340, 344, 358*
DUNS John Scotus, scholastic, opponent of Aquinas, 1274–1308 *146, 187*
DUPUIS Charles François, writer on comparative religion, 1742–1809 *25*

EGBERT, king of West Saxons (Wessex), 802–839 *225*
ELIZABETH I, queen of England, 1558–1603, b.1533 *234*
EMERIC St., son of king Stephen of Hungary *226*
EMERSON Ralph Waldo, US author, 1803–1882 *28, 148*
EPIPHANIUS St., Greek Chruch Father, 310–403 *33, 136, 186, 177, 189, 330*
ERASMUS Didier of Rotterdam, Dutch philosopher and writer, 1467–1536 *106, 133*
ERIC, joint king of Denmark with Harald I, about 820 *226*
ETHELBERT, king of Kent, about 620 *225*
ETHELWULF, king of England, son of Egbert, 839-858, *225*

EUGEN III, Pope, 1145–1153   *227*
EUGENIUS, bishop of Carthage, 5th c.   *133*
EUSEBIUS, bishop of Caesarea, church historian, 265–339   *1–2, 4, 80, 83, 136, 139*
EUSEBIUS, bishop of Nicomedia, protector of Arius, d.342   *180, 222, 323, 328–330, 334*

FAUSTA, wife of Emperor Constantine I, daughter of Maximian   *138*
FENTON John, Anglican theologian and commentator, b.1921   *59, 125, 172, 178, 202, 237, 243, 257, 260, 266, 270, 276, 326*
FLEG Edmond, French author, 1874–1963   *41*
FLINDERS-PETRIE Sir W.M., English egyptologist, early 20th c.   *159*
FOSTER R.J., RC theologian, now Monsignor in New York   *213*
FRANCE Anatole (Anatole Thibault), French author,1844–1924   *14*
FRANK Mark, Anglican theologian, 17th c.   *127, 151, 188*
FRAZER Sir James George, anthropologist and author, 1854–1941   *123, 159*
FREDERICK I Barbarossa, German emperor, 1152–1190, b.1123   *1*
FREDERICK II the Great, king of Prussia 1740–1786, b.1712   *123*
FREUD Siegmund, psychologist and author, 1856–1941   *112, 115*
FRIEDLAENDER M., Hungarian-Jewish theologian, 1831–1908   *245*
FROMM Eric, US/German psychologist and author, 1900–1980   *253*
FULGENTIUS St., bishop of Africa, theologian, 468–533   *133*

GALERIUS, Roman emperor 306–311   *138, 212*
GALLUS Gaius V., half-brother of Emperor Julian, d.354   *142*
GANDHI Mahatma (Mohandas Karamchand), Indian nonviolent resister, 1869–1948   *284*
GELIMER, last king of Vandals, supporter of Arianism, 532–534   *145*
GELLIUS Aulus, Latin author, 130–180   *346*
GENEBRARD Gilbert, bishop of Aix, 1537–1597   *66*
GEORGE V, king of England 1910–1936, b.1865   *257*
GHILLANY Friedrich Wilhelm, German Protestant theologian, 19th c.   *62*
GIBBON Edward, English historian, 1737–1794   *2, 3*
GIBSON Mrs., discoverer of Sinai manuscripts, 19th c.   *328*
GINNS R., English professsor of RC theology, now in New York   *54, 174, 23, 240, 243*
GISELA, Bavarian wife of Stephen I of Hungary, around 1000   *226*
GLOVER T.R., Anglican theologian, 1869–1943   *88*
GORE Charles, Anglican bishop and theologian, 1853–1932   *88*
GORM The Old, king of Denmark, 855–939   *226*
GRAETZ Heinrich, Jewish historian, 1817–1891   *6*
GRATIANUS, Roman emperor, 375–383   *224*
GRAVES Robert, English poet and author 1895–1986   *41, 45–6, 50, 60–1, 128, 173, 180, 196, 205, 236, 300, 322, 329–30, 334, 339–40, 345, 351, 353*
GREGORY, St. of Nazianzus, Greek Church Father, 330–390   *56, 142*
GREGORY, St. of Nyssa, brother of St. Basil, Church Father 340–400   *142*

GREGORY V, Pope 996–999   *227*
GREGORY VII, Pope, 1073–1085 (Canossa 1077), b.1021   *227*
GREGORY IX, Pope, 1227–1241, b.1148   *225*
GRIFFITH-THOMAS W.H., British theologian, 19/20th c.   *66, 85, 87, 94, 108, 132, 149, 191–2, 235, 270–2, 279–81, 348*
GROTIUS Hugo, Dutch theologian, 1583–1645   *66*

HADRIAN, Roman emperor 117–138, b.76   *4, 5, 222, 253, 343*
HADRIAN IV, Pope 1154–1159, English-born 1021   *227*
HALL Joseph, Anglican bishop of Norwich, 1574–1656   *188*
HARALD I, joint king of Denmark with Eric, about 820   *226*
HARALD II, king of Denmark, 939–985   *226*
HARNACK Adolf, German professor of theology, 1851–1930   *42, 80–1, 108, 146*
HEGEL Georg Wilhelm Friedrich, German philosopher, 1770–1831   *39*
HELENA St., mother of emperor Constantine I, 247–327   *138*
HELVIDIUS, 'heretic' Latin theologian, 4th c.   *176–7, 179*
HENRY II St., German emperor 1002–1024, b.973   *227*
HENRY IV, German emperor, 1056–1106 (Canossa 1077), b.1050   *227*
HERACLITUS of Ephesus, Greek philosopher, 576–480 BC   *67–69*
HEROD, king of Judaea, 30BC to 4AD   *206*
HILARY St., bishop of Poitiers, Church Father, 303–367   *69, 206, 250*
HILDEBRAND, monk, later Pope Gregory VII   *227*
HILLEL, Jewish teacher and sage, 70BC–10AD   *202, 242, 272, 314, 345*
HIPPOLYTUS of Rome, Church Father, 170–236   *79*
HITLER Adolf, German dictator 1933–1945, b.1889   *204*
HOSIUS, bishop of Cordoba, 257–357   *140–1*
HUEGEL Baron Friedrich von, German philosopher, 1852–1925   *151*
HUGO of St. Victor, scholastic, 1097–1141   *145*
HUNNERIC, Vandal king 477–484   *133*
HUTTEN Ulrich von, German reformation, 1488–1531   *147*
HUXLEY Thomas Henry, English biologist, 1825–1895   *36*

IGNATIUS St. of Antioch, bishop & apostolic father, 1st c.   *79, 182*
INCHOFER, Viennese Jesuit, d.1648   *7*
INNOCENT I St., Pope 402–417   *218, 227*
INNOCENT II, Pope 1130–1143
INNOCENT III, Pope 1198–1216, b.1160   *218, 227*
IRENAEUS St., Church Father, bishop of Lyons b.130   *39, 82, 109, 182, 330*
IRENE, empress of Byzantium, 780–802 (b.752?–d.803)   *187*

JACKSON, F.F.J., British church historian, 1855–1941   *112*
JASPERS, Karl, German professor of philosophy, 1883–1969   *19*
JENS Hermann, German author, 20th c.   *160*
JEROME St., Latin Church Father, Bible translator, 347–420   *5, 176–7, 179, 183–5, 336*
JOHN XVII, Pope 1003   *227*

JOHN XXIII (the first), anti–pope 1410–1415, deposed   229
JONES, A., RC British professor of theology, b.1934   *81, 101, 237, 241–3, 249, 259, 262–3, 336, 347*
JOSEPHUS Flavius, Jewish Greek-writing historian,37–95   *1–2, 21, 98, 158, 173, 205–6, 316, 318, 345*
JOVIAN, Roman emperor 363–364   *142*
JOWETT B., Master of Balliol, classics scholar, 19th c.   *154*
JUDAH the Galilean, Jewish rebel leader, c.4 BC   *205*
JUELICHER Adolf, German theologian, 1857–1938   *52*
JULIAN the Apostate, Roman emperor 361–363, b.332   *79, 142, 222–4*
JULIUS Africanus, Christian writer, about 160–240   *323*
JUNG, Carl Gustav, Swiss psychologist & author, 1875–1961   *77, 114–6, 152–5, 191–3*
JUSTIN St., (Justin Martyr), Church Father, about 100–163   *4, 61–2, 79, 182, 206,315–6, 330*
JUSTINIAN I, Eastern Roman emperor 527–565, b.483   *187*
JUSTINIAN II, Eastern Roman emperor 685–695, Roman emperor till 711   *225*
JUSTIN Marcus J., Roman historian, 3rd c.   *5, 315, 318*

KAMAL-UD-DIN, The Kwaya, professor of history, 20th c.   *62, 77*
KANT Immanuel, German philosopher, 1724–1804   *39*
KAUTSKY Karl, Marxist theoretician, 1854–1938   *253*
KENYON Sir Frederick George, English theologian, 1863–1938   *328*
KEYSERLING Graf Hermann, German philosopher, 1863–1952   *34*
KIERKEGAARD Søren, Danish Christian philosopher, 1813–1855   *88*
KLAUSNER Joseph, Jewish professor and author, 1874–1958   *4, 7, 9, 14–5, 17, 46, 56, 60, 66, 71, 170, 180, 201, 246, 269, 274, 301, 313, 330, 342*
KLEIN Samuel, Jewish biblical scholar, 1886–1940   *6*
KLEOBULOS, tyrant of Rhodos, sage of the 'Golden Age', 5th c. BC   *269*
KUPA, Hungarian rebel against forcible Christianisation, d.999   *226*

LACEY Thomas Alexander, Anglican canon of Worcester, 1853–1931   *109, 137, 146*
LACTANTIUS, Christian apologist, 260–330
LAGRANGE Marie-Joseph, French Dominican bible scholar, 1855–1938   *208*
LAMPE Geoffrey, Anglican professor of theology, 20th c.   *55, 174, 239–40 ,243*
LAO-TZU, Chinese philosopher, author of Tao-te-king, about 600 BC   *119*
LATTEY C., English Jesuit professor of theology, 20th c.   *48–49*
LEAHY, James, professor of theology, contemporary   *213*
LE CAMUS Etienne, French cardinal, 1632–1707   *200, 324*
LENTULUS Publius, fictitious procurator of Judaea   *13*
LEO I St., Pope 440–461, b.c.400   *166, 186*
LEO III St, Pope 795–816 born 750   *195*
LEO XIII (Joachim Pecci), Pope 1878–1903, b.1810   *255*

LEO II, emperor of Byzantium 717–741   *225*
LEONARD W., Australian RC professor of theology, 20th c.   *40, 45–6, 70, 277*
LESSING Gotthold Ephraim, German author and playwright, 1729–1781   *36*
LEWIS John, Cambridge professor of theology, 20th c.   *253*
LICINIUS, Roman emperor 307–323, d.324   *137–139, 222*
LIETZMANN Hans, German professor of church history, 1875–1942   *52, 61, 66, 179*
LIGHTFOOT Robert Henry, Anglican theologian, 1883–1953   *41, 45, 46, 177, 276, 326, 189*
LOISY Alfred Firmin, French scholar and writer, 1857–1940   *6, 24, 25, 97*
LUCIAN, Greek satirist, 117–180   *5*
LUNN Brian, English author, Luther biographer, 20th c.   *218*
LUTHER Martin, Augustine monk, leader of German reformation, 1483–1546   *84, 110–1, 147, 188, 205, 211, 218–9, 220, 230, 254–5, 273*

MACCABAEUS Judah, leader of Jewish rebellion, ruler of Judaea, d.160   *197*
MACEDONIUS, bishop of Constantinople, deposed 360, d.362   *108*
MACKINTOSH Hugh Ross, Moderator of Church of Scotland, 1870–1936   *150*
MANSON Thomas W., Anglican theologian, 20th c.   *214, 274*
MARCION, gnostic 'heretic' in Asia Minor, c.100–165   *48*
MARCUS Ambibulus, Roman procurator of Judaea 10–13
MARCUS AURELIUS, Roman emperor and philosopher, 161–180, b.121   *5, 222*
MARTIN V, Pope 1417–1431, restored papal unity, b.1368   *229*
MATTHEWS W.R., sometime dean of St. Paul's, 1881–?   *112, 151, 157*
MAXENTIUS, Roman emperor 306–312   *138*
MAXIMIAN, Roman emperor 286–305, d.311   *138*
MAY Herbert G., US professor of theology, 20th c.   *271*
MELA Pomponius, Latin geographer, about 40AD   *5*
MELANCHTON (Philipp Schwarzerd) German reformation leader, 1497–1560   *147, 230*
MENDELSSOHN Moses, German Jewish philosopher, 1729–1786   *123*
MEREZHKOVSKI Dmitri Sergeyevitch, Russian novelist, 1865–1941   *29, 295, 351*
MESSALINA, first wife of Emperor Claudius, d.48   *214*
METHODIUS St., 'apostle to the Slavs', Thessalonian, 826–885   *80*
MICHAEL III, Byzantine emperor 842–867   *225*
MILL John Stuart, British philosopher, 1806–1873   *28*
MONTEFIORE Claude, English-Jewish theologian, 1858–1938   *17, 77*
MOULE Charles F.D., Cambridge professor of theology, b.1908
MULACK Dr. Christa, German theologian, contemporary   *296*
MURATORI Lodovico Antonio, Italian theologian, 1672–1750
MURRY John Middleton, British author and scholar, 1889–1957   *257*

NEBUCHADNEZZAR II, king of Babylon, 605–562 BC   *196–7*
NERO, Roman emperor 54–68 b.37   *3–4, 214–5, 221*
NESTORIUS, Syrian Church Father, excommunicated, d.451   *182*
NEUBAUER Adolf, Oxford librarian, orientalist, 1831–1907   *6*
NEWMAN John Henry, convert to RC, cardinal and author, 1801–1890   *71*
NIEMOJEWSKY Andrzej, Polish author, 1864–1921   *25, 78*
NIETZSCHE Friedrich, German philosopher, 1844–1900   *10, 19–21, 81, 216*
NINEHAM Dennis Eric, Cambridge professor of theology, b.1921   *203, 208–9, 243, 250*
NOVATIAN, influential 'heretic', trinitarian, c.200–258   *135–6*

OCCAM William, British Franciscan monk, scholastic, 1285–1347   *146*
O'FLYNN John A., Irish American professor of RC theology, 20th c.   *54, 249*
OLYMPIAS, mother of Alexander the Great   *161*
ORCHARD Dom Bernard, British lecturer in RC theology, 20th c.   *329*
ORIGEN, theologian and apologist, later rejected by Church, 185–254   *2, 14, 79–80, 109, 183, 166, 179, 183, 206, 330*
ORWELL George (Eric Blair), English author, 1903–1950
OTTO I, German emperor 936–973, b.912   *227*
OTTO III, his grandson, German emperor 983–1002, b.980   *227*

PADEREWSKI Ignace Jan, pianist, President of Poland, 1859–1938   *342*
PATERCULUS VELLEIUS, Latin historian, hist. of world, 19BC–32AD   *215*
PAUL III (Alexander Farnese), Pope 1534–1549, Trent, b.1468   *147*
PAULUS Heinrich Eberhard Gottlob, German theologian, 1761–1851   *66*
PAUSANIAS, Greek historian and traveller, 143–176   *5*
PERICTIONE, mother of Plato   *161*
PEARSON John, English bishop, 1613–1686
PFLEIDERER Otto, German Protestant professor of theology, 1839–1908   *68, 162*
PHILIP II, king of Macedonia 360–336 BC, b.382 BC
PHILIPPE IV, king of France 1285–1314, b.1268   *228–9*
PHILO the Jew, Alexandrian Greek philosopher, about 25BC–50AD   *21*
PILATE Pontius, Roman procurator of Judaea 26–36   *7, 14, 73, 211, 215, 217, 221*
PINCHES Theophilus G., German professor of archaeology, 19th c.   *117*
PIUS IX (Mastai-Ferreti), Pope 1846–1878, b.1792   *190*
PIUS XI (A.A.D. Ratti), Pope 1922–1939, b.1857   *271*
PIUS XII (Eugenio Pacelli), Pope 1939–1958, b.   *190*
PLATO, Greek philospher, 429–347 BC   *151, 153–4, 161, 269, 272*
PLINY Gaius Publius (the Elder), Roman writer and naturalist, 23–79   *5*

PLINY Gaius Caecilius (the Younger), Roman writer, 62–114 *5, 221*
PLUTARCH, Greek historian and philosopher, 46–120 *79, 97, 154, 346*
PODRO, Joshua, Jewish scholar and author, 20th c. *41, 45–6, 56, 60–1, 125, 173, 180, 196, 236, 300, 322, 329–330, 334, 339–40, 345, 351, 353*
POLANYI Michael, Hungarian–born British scientist and author, comtemporary 1891–1976 *212*
PORPHYRY, Alexandrian Greek neo-platonist philosopher, 232–303 *146*
POWELL Gordon, British author of evangelical Christian tracts, 20th c.
POWER E., Irish Jesuit professor of archaeology, 20th c. *271*
PRAXEAS, Greek 'heretic', Rome, end of 2nd c. *83, 134–5*
PRINGLE-PATTISON A,S., Scottish professor of theology, 1856–1921 *76*
PRISCILLIAN, Spanish Manichaean 'heretic', beheaded 386 *133*
PROPERTIUS Sextus, Roman poet, 50–15 BC *47*
PTOLEMY I, king of Egypt, 323–282 BC *157*
PTOLEMY II, king of Egypt, 283–246 BC, commissioned Septuagint *157, 341*
PYTHAGORAS, Greek philosopher and mathematician, 582–493 BC *162*

QUINTILIANUS Marcus Fabius, Roman rhethoretician, 35–100 *5*
QUIRINUS, Roman governor of Syria, about 4 BC *196*

RAMSES II, king of Egypt, 1317–1250 BC *114*
RANKE Leopold von, German historian, 1795–1886
READE Winwood, English traveller and author, 1838–1875 *35–6*
REIMARUS Hermann Samuel, German scholar and author, 1694–1768 *29, 36*
REINHARD Franz Volkmar, German theologian, 1753–1812 *28*
RENAN Ernest, French author, *Life of Jesus, 1823–1892* *28–9, 39*
REVILLE Albert, French Protestant theologian and author, 1826–1906 *6*
RIPLEY Francis J., head of Missionary Society RC, 20th c. *152*
ROBERTS R.C., US professor fo theology and philosophy, b.1942
ROBERTSON Archibald, English author, 1886–? *48, 78*
ROBERTSON John M., English author, early 20th c. *27, 160*
ROBINSON A.T., bishop of Woolwich, theologian, 20th c. *61, 69, 112*
ROOSEVELT Theodor, US president 1901–1909, b.1858–d.1991 *233*
ROSE Hugh James, Cambridge scholar (Oxford Group), 1795–1838
ROUSSEAU Jean-Jacques, French philosopher, 1712–1778 *232*
ROYCE Josiah, US philosopher, 1855–1916 *33*
RUFINUS of Aquilea, Latin theologian, 345–410 *185*
RUSSELL Earl Bertrand, English philosopher, 1872–1970 *27*
RUSSELL R., RC theologian, 20th c. *109*

SAADIYAH Gaon, Jewish theologian, 882–942   *122*
SABELLIUS, outstanding 'heretic', monarchism, early 3rd c.   *41, 135*
SALVADOR Joseph, French Jewish scholar, 1796–1873
SANDAY Dr. William, Anglican theologian, 1843–1920   *134, 329*
SANDMEL Samuel, US Jewish professor and bible scholar, 1911–1979
   66, 313, 336, 346
SANTAYANA George, US philosopher, 1863–1952   *26–7*
SATURNINUS of Antioch, gnostic teacher, 2nd c.   *81*
SCALIGER Joseph Justus, French Calvinist scholar, 1540–1609   *6*
SCHILLEBEECKX Edward, Dutch theologian, b.1914   *42*
SCHLEIERMACHER Friedrich Ernst, German theologian, 1768–1834
SCHOEPS Hans-Joachim, German Jewish professor and author, b.1909
   133, 179, 313
SCHOLEM Gershon G., Israeli professor Jewish mysticism c. 20th.
SCHUERER Emil, German professor and bible scholar, 1844–1910
SCHWEITZER Albert, French/German theologian, philosopher,
   1875–1965   *7, 21, 29–30, 33, 67*
SCIPIO Africanus, Roman general v. Hannibal, 235–183 BC   *162*
SCOTUS John Erigena, scholastic, 810–877   *147, 187*
SCRIVENER Frederick Henry, Cambridge professor of philology, 19th c.
   133
SENECA Lucius Annaeus, Roman philosopher, 2BC–65AD   *354*
SERVETUS Miguel, Spanish anti-trinitarian philosopher, 1511–1553
   147–8, 230
SERVIANUS, Emperor Hadrian's brother-in-law, c.40 to 130   *5*
SHAMMAI, Jewish religious teacher, opponent of Hillel, 1st c. BC
   351
SHAW George Bernard, Anglo–Irish playwright, 1856–1951   *32, 70–1,
   252*
SIGURD Ring, king of Denmark, c.700   *226*
SIMPLICIUS St., Pope 468–483   *137*
SISEBUT, king of the Visigoths 612–621   *225*
SMITH-LEWIS Mrs., co-discoverer of Sinai manuscripts, 19th c.   *328*
SOCINUS (Lelio Soccini), Italian unitarian, 1525–1562   *148*
SOCRATES, Greek philosopher, 468–399 BC   *27*
SOCRATES, Greek church historian, 380–450   *84, 141*
SPENCER Herbert, English agnostic philosopher, 1820–1903   *146*
SPINOZA Baruch, Dutch-Jewish philosopher, 1632–1677   *39*
SPIRE Johannes de, Venetian printer/publisher, 15th c.   *3*
STALKER David M.C., Scottish cleric and bible scholar, 20th c.   *263*
STAUFFER Ethelbert, German bible scholar, b.1902   *208*
STENDAHL Krister, US protestant professor of theology, 20th c.   *55,
   59, 101, 125, 237, 241, 257, 263–4, 265, 270, 274, 325, 338, 350*
SUAREZ Francisco de, Spanish Jesuit theologian, 1584–1617   *232*
SUETONIUS, Roman historian, 75–160 (Gaius Suetonius Tranquillus)
   4–5, 21, 162, 205, 214, 222
STRAUSS David Friedrich, German theologian, 1808–1874   *23, 39*
STEPHEN I, king of Hungary 997–1038 (St. Stephen apostolic king)   *226*

TACITUS Publius Cornelius, Roman historian, 55–120   *3, 4, 21, 221*

TAYLOR Robert, Cambridge professor, anti-Christian author, early 19th c.   *12, 160*
TAYLOR Vincent, Protestant commentator and author, 1887–1968   *244*
TEMPLE William, archbishop of Canterbury, 1881–1944   *42*
TERTULLIAN, Carthage apologist turned 'heretic', 150–222   *3, 78, 83–4, 109, 133–5, 182–4*
THEISSEN A., German professor of theology, 20th c.   *51–2*
THELWULF, king of the Angles 839–858   *226*
THEODORA, dowager empress of Byzantium, Regent, 842–867   *225*
THEODORET of Cyrrhus, Greek church historian, 393–458   *8, 108*
THEODOSIUS I, Roman emperor 379–395, b.346   *143*
THEODOTUS of Byzantium, gnostic adoptionist 'heretic', 2nd c.   *83*
THEOPHIL, bishop of Antioch, Church Father, d.190   *5, 69*
THYRA, mother of Danish king Harald II   *226*
TIBERIUS (Tiberius Claudius Nero), Roman emperor 14–37, b.42 BC   *3, 7, 205, 214–5, 277*
TILLICH Paul, US German theologian, 1886–1965   *67, 111–2*
TISCHENDORF Constantin von, German theologian, 1815–1874   *52*
TRAJAN (Marcus Ulpius Trajanus), Roman emperor 98–117, b.53   *221*
TROKI Isaac, Jewish scholar and writer, 1553–1594   *123, 316, 318*

VALENTINIAN I, Roman emperor 364–375, b.321   *142*
VALENTINIAN III, Roman emperor 425–455, b.419   *224*
VALERIAN (Publius Licinius Valerianus), Roman emperor 252–260, b.193   *221–2*
VALERIUS Gratus, Roman procurator of Judaea 14–25   *13, 198*
VANOZZA Rosa, mistress of Pope Alexander VI, mother of his children   *229*
VERMES Géza, Hungarian-British historian/theologian, b.1924   *267, 346*
VESPASIAN (Titus Flavius Vespasianus), Roman emperor 69–79, b.7
VIGILIUS, Pope 537–555   *133*
VOLNEY Comte Constantin de, French writer, 1757–1820   *25, 78*

WAIK, name of King Stephen of Hungary before baptism   *226*
WALKER Williston, US professor of church history, 20th c.   *135, 142*
WALSHAM HOW W., Anglican rural dean, commentator, late 19th c.   *87, 100, 201, 270, 276, 326, 329, 339, 355–7*
WAMBA, king of the Visigoths 672–680   *225*
WATTS Alan W., US philosopher, 1915–1973   *86, 152, 189–190*
WEISS Johannes, German professor of theology, 1863–1914   *31, 316, 328*
WELLHAUSEN Julius, German theologian and orientalist, 1844–1918   *245*
WELLS G.A., London professor and writer, contemporary   *27*
WELLS Herbert George, English novelist, 1866–1945   *36*
WELSH Claude, US professor of protestant theology, 20th c.   *145*
WIDUKIND, Saxon leader, vanquished by Charlemagne 785, d.807   *225*

WILLMERING John H., US RC theologian, now living in Honduras
132, 222, 243
WILSON Robert McL., Scottish Protestant theologian, 20th c.   *55, 101, 243, 270, 274, 276, 355*
WINTER Dr. Paul, German-Jewish scholar, 20th c.   *18*
WIRGMAN A. Theodor, Anglican author, d.1917   *191–2*
WORDSWORTH Christopher, Anglican bishop of Lincoln, 1807–1850
46, 51–2, 65–6, 134, 239, 257, 271, 336
WORDSWORTH William, English poet, 1770–1850   *189*
WREDE Wilhelm, German professor of theology, 1859–1906   *33–4*

YEARSLEY Macleod, Scottish bible scholar and author, 20th c.

ZARATHUSTRA (Zardtosht), Medo-Persian religious leader, 628–551 BC
78
ZENO of Citium, Greek philosopher, influence of Stoics, 342–270 BC
69
ZENO, Eastern Roman emperor 474–491   *186–7*
ZWINGLI Ulrich (Huldreich), Swiss leader of Reformation, 1484–1531
147, 230

(This index does not include biblical or mythological figures)

Bibliography

General Literature
BARCLAY William, The Gospel of St. Mark, Edinburgh 1965
 The Gospel of St. Matthew, Edinburgh 1959
BARNES E.W., The Rise of Christianity, London 1948
BARTH Karl, The Faith of the Church, London 1960
BERGUER Georges, The Life of Jesus, London 1923
BETTENSON Henry, Documents of the Christian
 Church, London 1944
BIRD T.E., A Study of the Gospels, London 1961
BLASS Friedrich, Philology of the Gospels, London 1898
BLUNT J.J., Coincidences of the Old and New Testament,
 London 1865
BRUNNER Emil, Unser Glaube, Zurich 1963
BULTMANN Rudolf, Das Urchristentum, Hamburg 1963
CAIRD G.B., Saint Luke, Harmondsworth 1965
CHWOLSOHN Daniel, Das letzte Passamahl Christi, Leipzig
 1908
CONYBEARE F.C., The Historical Christ, London 1914
CORSWANT W., A Dictionary of Life in the Bible Times,
 London 1960
CRAWLEY Ernest, Oath, Curse and Blessing, London 1934
CROSSLEY R.S., The Holy Trinity, London 1965
DANIÉLOU Jean, Théologie du Judéo-Christianisme, Tournai
 1958
DAUBE David, The New Testament and Rabbinic
 Judaism, London 1956
DUMMELOW J.R., A Commentary on the Holy Bible, London
 1915
FENTON J.C., Commentary to St. Matthew, Harmondsworth
 1963

FISON J.E., The Faith of the Bible, Harmondsworth 1957
FOERSTER Werner, Palestinian Judaism in New Testament Times, London 1964
FRAZER Sir James George, Magic and Religion, London 1945
FROMM Erich, The Dogma of Christ, London 1963
FURNEAUX Rupert, The Empty Tomb, London 1963
GASTER T.H., The Dead Sea Scrolls in English, New York 1957
GRAVES Robert & Joshua Podro, The Nazarene Gospel Restored, London 1953
GRIFFITH THOMAS W.H., The Principles of Theology, London 1945
HAMMOND C.E., Outlines of New Testament Textual Criticism, Oxford 1890
HARNACK Adolf, History of Dogma, London 1893
    What is Christianity, London 1958
HOLMES-GORE V.A., Christ or Paul? Ashingdon 1946
HOSKYNS Sir Edwyn & Noel Davey, The Riddle of the New Testament, London 1958
JENS Hermann, Mythologisches Lexikon, München 1958
JUNG C.G., Psychology and Religion: West and East, London 1958
KENYON Frederic G., The Text of the Greek Bible, London 1937
KLAUSNER Joseph, Jesus of Nazareth, London 1947
LACEY T.A., Essays in Positive Theology, London 1931
LIETZMANN Hans, The Founding of the Church Universal, London 1963
    The Era of the Church Fathers, London 1963
    From Constantine to Julian, London 1960
LIGHTFOOT R.H., A Commentary to St. John's Gospel, London 1957
LOISY Alfred, The Birth of the Christian Religion, London 1948
LUNN Brian, Martin Luther, London 1934
LUTHER Martin, The Large Catechism, Philadelphia 1959
    Luther in Gespräch, Stuttgart 1938
McCABE Joseph, The Social Record of Christianity, London 1935
MERESHKOVSKY Dmitri, Jesus Manifest, London 1935
MULACK Dr.C., Die Weiblichkeit Gottes
NIETZSCHE Friedrich, Der Antichrist, Stuttgart 1964
NINEHAM D.E., Saint Mark, Harmondsworth 1967
OSBOURNE H. (editor), Whom Do Men Say That I Am? London 1932

PFLEIDERER Otto, The Early Christian Conception of Christ, London 1905
PHYTHIAN ADAMS W.J., Mithraism, London 1915
PINCHES T.G., The Religion of Babylonia and Assyria, London 1906
RENAN Ernest, Vie de Jésus, Paris
REYNOLDS Alfred, Pilate's Question, London 1982
RIPLEY F.J., The Blessed Trinity, London 1959
ROBERTSON A., The Bible and its Background, London 1942
Jesus: Myth or History, London 1949
ROBERTSON J.M., Pagan Christs, London 1911
ROBINSON J.A.T., Honest to God, London 1963
ROYSTON PIKE E., Ethics of the Great Religions, London 1948
RUSSELL Bertrand, Why I am not a Christian? London 1967
SANDMEL Samuel, A Jewish Understanding of the New Testament, New York 1956
SCHOEPS Hans Joachim, The Jewish–Christian Argument, London 1965
SCHOLEM Hershom G., Jewish Mysticism, London 1955
SCHWEITZER Albert, The Quest for the Historical Jesus, London 1954
SCRIVENER F.H., Criticism of the New Testament, London 1874
SHAW George Bernard, Androcles and the Lion, London 1918
STAUFFER E., Die Botschaft Jesu, Bern 1959
ST.CLAIR TISDALL W., Mythic Christs and the True, London 1909
TAYLOR Robert, The Diegesis, Boston 1883
TILLICH Paul, Theology of Culture, New York 1959
The Shaking of the Foundations, Harmondsworth 1962
VERMES G., The Dead Sea Scrolls in English, Harmondsworth 1962
WALSHAM HOW W., Commentary to the New Testament, London 1878
WEISS Johannes, Earliest Christianity, New York 1959
WELLS Herbert George, The Outline of History, London 1924
WINTER Paul, On the Trial of Jesus, Berlin 1961
WIRGMAN A.T., The Blessed Virgin, London 1905

Reference Books
The Bible Handbook, London 1953
The Cambridge History of the Bible, Cambridge 1969

The Catholic Commentary on Holy Scripture, London 1954
Christianity and the Social Revolution, London 1935
The Didaché, London 1957
Everyman's Talmud, London 1943
Halley's Bible Handbook, Grand Rapids, Mich. 1957
Helps to the Study of the Bible, Oxford
The Holy Koran, New York 1963
Peake's Commentary on the Bible, London 1964
Philosophers Speak of God, Chicago 1953
The Question Box (Roman Catholic), New York 1929
Religious Systems of the World, London 1908

Scripture Used
English Bibles
The Holy Bible – Authorised Version (Wordsworth), Oxford 1880
The Holy Bible – Revised Version (O.U.P.), Oxford 1885
The Holy Bible – Authorised Version (O.U.P.), New York
The Holy Bible – Catholic R.V. Edition, London 1966
The New English Bible–New Testament, Cambridge 1961
The Parallel New Testament, Cambridge 1882
The Triglott Evangelists–Interlinear A.V., London 1834

Other Bibles
The 24 Books of the Holy Scriptures – Masoretic Text, New York 1914
The New Testament – Received Greek & English AV, London 1957
Novum Testamentum Graecae (Nestle), Stuttgart 1963
Old Testament in Greek (Septuagint), Amsterdam 1725
Biblia Sacra (Vulgata), Rome 1956
Die Heilige Schrift (Luther), Stuttgart 1941
La Sainte Bible (Protestant), Paris 1954
La Sacra Bibbia (Protestant), Roma
La Santa Biblia (Protestant), Madrid 1919
Bibeln (Protestant), Stockholm 1950

Other Books
The Book of Common Prayer – C.o.E., London
The Apocrypha – Old Testament (O.U.P.)
The Apocryphal New Testament, Oxford 1960

Glossary

ABSOLUTE – Something which must be accepted without reservation or qualification; self-evident knowledge which embraces its object fully and with finality. From Latin absolute = perfectly, completely.

AEON – Eternity, unlimited duration, cosmic period. From Greek αἰών, αἰώνος.

ANTHROPOMORPHIC – Possessing human qualities, attributes or characteristics; 'in the form of man'. From Greek ἄηθρωπος = man and μορφή = form.

APOCALYPSE – revelation, last book of New Testament. From Greek ἀποκαλύπτω = disclose, uncover. (Apocalyptic)

APOCRYPHA – hidden writings; books of the Bible excluded from Canon, official recognition. From Greek ἀποκρύπτω = hide away. (Apocryphal)

APOSTASY – abandonment of religious faith. From Greek ἀπόστασις = defection. (Apostate)

APOLOGETICS – Defence of the faith, substantiation of various tenets of religious doctrine. From Greek ἀπολογέομαι = to speak in defence. (Apologist)

APOTHEOSIS – deification, deified ideal. From Greek ἀποθεόω = to deify.

ARCHETYPE – original model. From Greek ἀρχέτυπον = model. (Archetypal)

ASCENSION – ascent of Christ on the fortieth day after the resurrection. From Latin ascensio.

ASCETIC – severely abstinent, non-indulgence in and avoidance of all forms of physical pleasure. From Greek ἄσκησις = practice, exercise. (Asceticism, an ascetic)

ASSUMPTION – reception of Virgin Mary into heaven. From Latin assumptio.

ATHEISM – without God, the rejection of any kind of God-idea. From Greek.

ATTRIBUTE – belonging or appropriate to, characteristic quality. From Latin attribuere = assign. (attributable)

AXIOM – Established principle, maxim, self-evident truth. From Greek ἀξίωμα. (Axiomatic)

CANON – List of writings accepted and authenticated by Church or religious body. The first Canon was drawn up by the 'heretic' Marcion. The most important Canon still acknowledged is the 'Muratori Fragment' first published by Bishop Muratori in 1740 based on a Milan manuscript probably from 2nd century. The actual organisation of the New Testament is attributed to Eusebius, ratified by Council of Carthage in 397. Jewish Canon is held to originate from Ezra. Josephus thought it was drawn up in the time of Artaxerxes. From Greek = reed, ruler. (Canonical)

CATECHISM – Instruction by question and answer; published instruction by Church in this form. From Greek κατηχήτικος = oral teacher. (Catechetic)

CONSENTIENT – Agreeing, concurrent. From Latin consentire = agree.

CONSUBSTANTIAL – of the same substance, the three Persons in the Godhead. From Latin consubstantialis.

CORPOREAL – Bodily, material, tangible. From Latin corpus = body.

COVENANT – Agreement between Jehovah and Abraham *(Gen.* 15), i.e. God and the Israelites. From Latin convenire = assemble, agree.

CRITICISM – (Higher) Discovering as much as possible of the original wording of the New Testament. (Lower) Tracing the history and development of the New Testament throughout the centuries and the effect of external circumstances. From Greek κριτικός = critical. (Critic, critical)

DIATRIBE – Crude and bitter criticism, invective. From Greek τρίβω = rub away.

DOCTRINE – Teaching, body of instruction. From Latin doctrina. (Doctrinal)

DOGMA – Article of faith which must be accepted by the believer. From Greek δόγμα = opinion, that which one thinks true. (Dogmatic, dogmatism)

EMANATION – issuing or proceeding from a source. From Latin emanatio, manare = flow.

EMPIRICAL – based on experience and observation, not on theory.

From Greek εμπειρια = experience. (Empiricism, empiricist)

EPISTEMOLOGY – investigation of the origins of knowledge and the methods of obtaining it. From Greek ἐπιστήμη = knowledge. (Epistemoligical)

EPISTLE – Letter, especially Letters from apostles. From Greek ἐπιστολή.

ESCHATOLOGY – The doctrine of final things: death, the Kingdom of God, the Last Judgment, the Second Coming, heaven and hell. The belief in events which accompany God's final intervention. From Greek ἔσχατος = last.

EUCHARIST – Bread and wine changed into the body and blood of Christ. From Greek εὐ- = well, happily, and χάριζ favour, grace.

EXEGESIS – Explanation of the meaning of scriptural texts. From Greek ἐξηγέομαι = to expound, interpret. (Exegetic)

GEMARAH – commentaries on the Mishnah. Written in Aramaic.

GNOSTIC – having esoteric spiritual knowledge. Also early Christian heresy. From Greek γνῶσις = knowledge. (Gnosis, gnosticism)

HELLENIC – Greek

HYPOSTASIS – Personal manifestation of the Godhead. From Greek μπὸστᾶσις.

HYPOSTATISE – to give personal substance to something which does not possess it.

HYPOTHESIS – Supposition upon which reasoning is based. From Greek μπόθεσις = foundation.

IDEA – mental concept without direct relation to experience. From Greek ἰδέα = form, appearance, kind.

IDEAL – A person's highest conception, a state or thing aimed at.

IDEOLOGY – System of ideas based on a central proposition with corresponding subsidiary propositions.

IGNOMINIUS – humiliating, sometimes bordering on infamous. From Latin ignominia. (Ignominy)

IMMACULATE – pure, spotless, faultless, unsullied. From Latin macula = spot.

IMMANENT – fully contained within itself. From Latin manere = remain. (Immanence)

IMPASSIBLE – Incapable of emotion, not subject to suffering. From Latin passibilis. (Impassibility)

INCARNATION – embodiment in flesh, especially of Christ. From Latin carno, carnis. (Incarnate)

IPSO FACTO – by that very fact (Latin).

LOGIC – science of art of reasoning, consistent chain of reasoning.

Greek λογῐκη. (Logical, logician)

MASORETIC TEXT – Second century text of Jewish scriptures, preserved almost unchanged by Jewish scholarship.

METAPHYSICS – Study of that reality which cannot be recognised by the senses. From Greek τὰ μετὰ τα ψῦσικα (Aristotle). Works placed after the 'Physics'. (Metaphysical, metaphysician)

METATRON – The occupant of the throne next to God's own, the Chief Angel, Christ. From Greek μετα = by, beside, and ἱρόνος = throne.

MIDRASH – Rabbinic literature on Old Testament material.

MISHNA – First part of Talmud, also called Second Law.

MONOTHEISM – The belief that there is only one God, that God is One. From Greek μόνος one, alone, single, and θεός God. (Monotheistic)

MYSTICISM – Claim to an awareness of the ultimate reality revealed only to the second sight of the initiated. From Greek μυστικός mystical, secret. (Mystic, mystical)

MYTH – Fictitious narrative involving supernatural persons. From Greek μῦθος = legend, fable. (Mythical, mythology, mythological)

OBJECTIVE – Dealing with external things, independent of personal thought and feeling, generally communicable. Misused Latin. (Objectivity)

OBTUSE – stupid, slow of perception. From Latin obtusus. (Obtuseness)

ONTOLOGY – The doctrine of existence per se, seen in separation from the content of being. The objective existence of a thing is assumed by giving content to conceptual entities. From Greek τὰ ὄντα = things which actually exist, reality. (Ontological)

PARADOX – Seemingly absurd though possibly well-founded statement, conflicting with preconceived views. Greek παράδοξοω. (Paradoxical)

PARAPHRASE – Free rendering of a text. Greek παραφράσις.

PAROUSIA – The 'coming', usually of Christ. Greek.

PREMISE or premiss – Starting statement from which another is inferred, basic proposition. From Latin praemittere = from preceding to send.

PRINCIPLE – fundamental truth as basis of reasoning, the foundation of attitude. From Latin principium = beginning. (Principled)

PROSELYTE – Convert from one opinion, faith, ideology to another. From Greek προσέρχομαι = to come forward, to draw nigh. (Proselytize)

PURIFICATION – Cleansing, cleansing of a woman after childbirth under the Jewish Law. From Latin purus = clean. (Purify)

QUATERNITY – Extension of the Trinity to a Foursome by addition of another Person.

RATIONALISM – The belief that reason can find most answers and only those answers can be trusted which reason supplies. From Latin ration = reason.

REVELATION – Knowledge disclosed by divine agency, last book of New Testament. From Latin revelo = uncover, lay bare.

SACRAMENT – ritual ceremonial act which the Book of Common Prayer defines as an outward and visible sign of an inward and spiritual grace: baptism, confirmation, eucharist, penance, extreme unction, orders and matrimony. From Latin sacramentum = military oath.

SCHOLASTICISM – Theological trend attempting to provide exact definitions and exposition of doctrine and dogma. From Greek σχολάζω = to have leisure, to devote oneself to something. (Scholastic)

SIFRA – Book (Hebrew)

SOLSTICE – Time when the sun is farthest from the earth, 21st June summer-solstice, 22nd December winter-solstice. From Latin solsticium.

SOPHISTRY – Fallacious and dishonest reasoning intending to deceive, quibbling. From Greek σοφός = clever, prudent, wise.

STATUS QUO -- unchanged condition. Latin.

STIGMA – Mark branded on slave, stain on one's good name. From Greek στίγμα = mark, spot, brand-mark, puncture. (Stigmatize)

STIGMATA – Marks corresponding to the crucifixion wounds developed by believers.

SUBJECTIVE – Dealing with personal experience or point of view, communicable only to those who share or at least consider the particular view or experience. Misused Latin. (Subjectivity)

SUPPLICATION – Humble petition. From Latin supplicare.

SUBSTANCE – Essential nature underlaying a thing or idea: that part which, if it were not present, the entity could not exist. From Latin sub = under, beneath, and stare stand. (Substantial, substantiate)

SYLLOGISM – Arriving at a conclusion from two given propositions. From Greek συλλογίζομαι to reckon together, to infer.

SYMBOL – Typifying something or recalling something by association in fact or thought, conventional sign. From Greek συμβολέω = throw together, to relate, to join. (Symbolic, symbolism)

SYNOPTIC – Giving a summary survey, those gospels which give a mutually related view of the life of Jesus, ie., Matthew, Mark and Luke. From Greek συνοράω = to see together at the same time. (Synopsis, synoptical)

TALMUD – Record of Jewish customs, traditions, historical events, fables, anecdotes and interpretations of Scripture, collected from 2nd c. onward on the basis of oral tradition. From Hebrew lamad = teach.

TANNAIM – teachers of the torah (Hebrew).

TELEOLOGY – Doctrine that events and entities are due to the final cause or design that is served by them. From Greek τέλος = end.

TETRAGRAMMATON – The four-letter symbol YHWH (Yahwe) for God. From Greek τετρα- = four and γράμμα written character.

THEISM – belief in personal God who is the creator, sustainer and ruler of the universe. From Greek θεός = God. (Theist, theistic)

THEOCRACY – State governed by religious leaders on behalf of God.

THEOLOGY – Study of the teachings concerning the nature of God as revealed to men. (Theologian, theological)

THEORY – Supposition purporting to explain both the factual and hypothetical phenomena relating to a problem. (Theorist, theorise, theoretical) From Greek θεωρέω = behold.

THEOTOKOS – God-bearer (Greek). Title of the Holy Virgin.

THOMISM – Theological teachings of Thomas Aquinas, of predestination and grace.

TORAH – Mosaic Law, the revealed will of God (Pentateuch). From Hebrew torah = instruction.

TRANSCENDENTAL – Meaning differs in various philosophies. Christian definition: The view that God stands above and beyond the world (Professor Claude Welsh). In Kantian terms, understanding of a priori character, presupposed in and necessary to experience. Others, explaining phenomena as products of the subjective mind. Transcendental concepts cannot be ascertained empirically. From Latin trans = across and scandare = to climb.

TRANSSUBSTANTIATION – The change of bread and wine of the eucharist into the flesh and blood of Christ.

TRIUNE – Three in One. (Triunity)

UNITARIAN – Christian who does not accept the trinitarian concept of God. From Latin unus = one. (Unitarianism)

UNSUBSTANTIATED – Statement or claim for which no good grounds are given.

VEDIC – from Veda, ancient Hindu legends and hymns. From Sanskrit Veda = knowledge).

VULGATE - Latin translation of Greek Bible, attributed to Jerome. It became the official Bible of the Western Church. From Latin vulgus = common people, later   vulgare = make public.

ZODIAC – Constellation of the sky, divided into 12 equal parts called signs of the zodiac. Greek ζωδιακόζ.

Index of Biblical Passages

Matthew

1:1	(254–5)(321, 323)	5:24	(303)
1:7	(6,166)	5:25	(302)
1:16:25	(145, 170, 172, 175) (254, 259, 266–267, 320, 324, 327–8)	5:28	(303)
		5:30	(303)
		5:32	(260, 303)
1:18	(172, 181)	5:33	(256, 303)
1:23	(10, 170, 337)	5:34	(303)
1:31	(8, 37)	5:35	(303)
3:11	(98–9)	5:39	(266, 280)
3:16–25	(120, 127)	5:41	(265)
3:21–22	(126)	5:42	(304)
4:4	(201, 302)	5:43	(264, 266)
4:7	(302)	5:44–45	(304)
4:8-10	(199)	5:48	(266, 304)
4:10	(302)	6:1–4	(304)
4:16–17	(302)	6:2	(304)
5:3	(278, 302)	6:3	(304)
5:4	(236, 302)	6:4	(304)
5:5	(302)	6:5–6	(298)
5:6	(234, 237) (302)	6:7	(9, 298, 304, 342)
5:7	(302)		
5:8	(302)	6:9	(304, 342)
5:9	(237) (302)	6:10–12	(303, 343)
5:13	(303)	6:13	(303, 343)
5:14	(303)	6:16–19	(298, 305, 340)
5:17	(303)		
5:18	(245, 303)	6:17	(305)
5:17–19	(298, 303, 316)	6:19–20	(239)
5:20	(245, 266)	6:24	(240)
5:21–22	(263)	6:25–26	(305)

6:30–31	(305)
6:33–34	(255, 305)
7:1	(217, 305)
7:3	(305)
7:6	(305)
7:8	(306)
7:11	(99)
7:12	(272, 306)
7:15–16	(306, 352, 354)
7:18–20	(354)
7:23	(306)
7:29	(8, 300)
8:4	(293, 318)
8:17	(306)
8:20	(66)
8:24	(306)
9:3	(306)
9:6	(299)
9:13	(299)
9:18	(292)
9:27	(321)
9:30	(318)
10:5–6	(9, 22, 124, 297)
10:6	(306, 316)
10:8–14	(306, 355)
10:18	(306)
10:19	(306)
10:21–22	(307)
10:24	(251)
10:28	(307)
10:34	(259)
10:35	(307)
10:40	(357)
11:3	(22)
11:5	(307)
11:10	(307)
11:14	(307)
11:18–19	(307)
11:23	(307)
11:25	(307)
11:29–30	(308)
12:3–4	(308)
12:5–8	(308)
12:18–21	(308)
12:31	(92–100)
12:33	(354)
12:46–50	(169)
13:10	(308)
13:11	(358)
13:13	(308)
13:22	(241, 298)
13:35	(309)
13:47–50	(358)
13:55–56	(6, 169, 175, 328, 333)
14:18	(309)
15:8–9	(309)
15:14	(309)
15:19	(309)
15:22	(9)
15:24 16:16	(70, 71, 318, 349, 351)
16:17–18	(349)
16:20	(37, 318)
16:27	(309)
17:5	(309)
17:11	(309)
18:5	(266)
18:9	(309)
18:15–16	(309)
18:17	(9)
18:20	(358)
18:21–22	(278)
18:25	(177)
19:4–5	(310)
19:9	(310)
19:12	(10, 291)
19:14	(310)
19:17	(43–5, 231, 235) (39, 55, 300)

19:19	(310)
19:20	(249)
19:23	(310)
19:26	(310)
20:15–16	(310)
20:23	(54, 56)
20:25–28	(202, 210)
20:31	(342)
21:3	(64)
21:5	(310)
21:13	(310)
21:16	(310)
21:19	(310)
21:42	(310)
22:15–22	(204)
22:37	(311)
22:41–44	(298)
22:44	(322)
23:3	(311)
23:6	(298)
23:9–11	(242)
23:12	(311)
23:14	(311)
23:23	(299, 311)
23:24 (and 16)	(354)
23:25	(311)
23:37–38	(311)
24:2	(311)
24:4	(352)
24:6	(56, 275)
24:7	(311)
24:8	(311)
24:24	(252, 358)
24:28–30	(312)
24:36	(54, 56, 312)
24:41	(312, 358)
25:1–12	(312)
25:32	(312)
25:34–6	(300)
25:36	(300)
25:41	(312)
25:46	(312)
26:11	(312)
26:28	(312)
26:39	(340, 342)
26:42–44	(340, 342)
26:52	(269, 270, 312)
26:53	(55)
26:63	(347)
26:64	(59)
26:73	(6)
27:32	(266)
27:46	(51, 54, 55, 312–3)
27:56	(169)
28:6	(64)
28:18	(124)
28:19	(91)

Mark

1:7–11	(98)
1:8	(99)
1:10–11	(120, 126)
1:22	(8, 300)
1:23	(10)
1:25	(318)
1:34	(318)
1:35	(340)
1:44	(299, 318)
2:7	(298)
2:10	(299)
2:27	(8, 10)
3:2	(318)
3:5	(317)
3:29	(92, 100)
5:19	(64)
5:43	(318)
6:3	(6, 169, 175, 328, 333)
6:7	(22, 316)
6:8	(353)

6:46	(340)	1:15	(106)
7:13	(356)	1:19	(95)
7:25	(316)	1:26–38	(163, 170)
8:27	(22)	1:27	(329)
8:29	(34, 70–1, 350)	1:31	(8, 175)
9:37	(357)	1:32	(96, 321, 325)
10:8	(300)		
10:12	(295)	1:33	(96)
10:18	(54)	1:34–37	(337)
10:20–27	(249)	1:35	(91, 96)
10:42	(202, 210)	1:36	(166, 331)
11:3	(64)	1:45–55	(164)
11:17	(341)	1:67	(106)
11:25–26	(270, 271, 27)	2:4	(321)
12:10	(100)	2:5–7	(138, 258) (165, 172, 326)
12:13–17	(204)		
12:16	(318)		
12:29	(248, 300)	2:11	(70–1)
12:35–37	(322)	2:21	(4, 173)
12:38–40	(242–3)	2:25	(106, 174)
13:6	(74)	2:27	(171)
13:8	(275)	2:33	(327)
13:20	(64)	2:41	(328)
13:22	(352)	2:41–43	(328)
13:26	(66)	2:48	(171, 328)
13:32	(54–56, 300)	3:14	(270)
14:17–50	(283)	3:16	(98)
14:32	(340)	3:21–22	(98, 120)
14:34–35	(340)	3:23	(7, 328, 338)
14:39	(340)		
14:62	(59, 61)	3:31	(170, 324)
14:70	(6)	4:1	(106)
15:11	(317)	4:4	(201)
15:15	(317)	4:6	(214)
15:40–41	(169)	4:15–16	(341)
16:15	(124)	4:32	(8)
16:19	(59, 64)	4:34–35	(318)
		4:41	(318)
		4:44	(341)

Luke

1:5	(6, 166)	5:14	(298, 318)
		5:16	(340)

5:21	(299)
5:24	(299)
6:12	(340)
6:20	(236)
6:24	(239)
6:27–28	(266)
6:31	(354)
6:37	(217)
6:39	(266)
6:43–4	(354)
6:46	(356)
7:31	(63)
7:34	(66)
8:19–21	(169)
9:1	(316)
9:2	(22)
9:13	(99, 299)
9:20	(71, 350)
9:56	(273)
10:1	(63)
10:8	(215)
10:16	(357)
10:27	(300)
10:38	(293)
11:13	(107)
11:20–28	(294)
11:39	(66)
11:42	(242, 243, 249)
12:10	(92, 100)
12:21	(240)
12:31	(256)
12:33–34	(240)
12:51–53	(258)
13:10	(341)
16:13	(240)
16:17	(298)
17:1	(276)
17:3–4	(278)
17:5	(63)
18:6	(63)
18:19	(54, 55, 300)
18:21–27	(249)
19:8	(63)
20:20–26	(204)
20:39–44	(322)
20:46	(242–3)
21:8	(74, 352)
21:10	(275)
22:25–26	(202–210)
22:31	(63)
22:36	(274)
22:38	(228, 274)
22:41	(340)
22:69	(59)
22:70	(61)
23:2–5	(211, 317)
23:23	(317)
24:47	(124, 316)

John

1:1–4	(69)
1:3	(89)
1:4	(69, 89)
1:5–7	(91)
1:19	(127)
1:26–34	(98, 127)
1:30–37	(99, 120, 126)
1:42	(251, 351)
1:45	(327)
1:51	(66)
2:1–4	(168)
3:8	(110)
3:17	(273)
4:2	(125)
4:26	(74)
5:22	(89)
5:30	(41, 300)
5:44–45	(314)
6:15	(127)
6:42	(169, 327)
6:59	(341)
6:69	(350)

7:16	(40, 357)		19:10–11	(217)
7:41–43	(321)		19:25–27	(7, 169, 176–7)
8:24	(74)		20:17	(141)
8:28	(74, 300, 357)		20:8	(38)
8:43–44	(314)		20:17	(54)
8:57	(7, 202)		20:18	(54, 141)
8:58	(74)		20:22	(114)
10:1	(353)		20:27	(46)
10:8	(2, 117)		21:7	(64)
10:30	(38, 40, 41, 87)		21:12	(64)
10:33	(40)		21:25	(64)
10:38	(40)			
11:41–42	(340)			
12:27–28	(340)			
12:31	(210)		**Acts**	
12:47	(273)		1:5	(99)
12:49	(321, 357)		1:8	(316)
13:4	(202)		1:14	(169)
13:19	(74)		2:17	(107)
13:30	(357)		2:21	(107)
14:1–7	(54, 87)		2:22	(57, 67)
14:6	(38, 44, 102, 111)		2:24	(57)
14:9	(38, 45, 329)		2:30	(321)
14:10	(40)		2:36	(57)
14:11	(40)		2:38	(106, 125)
14:16-17	(92, 103, 109, 120)		2:44–45	(251)
14:24	(357)		3:15	(58)
14:26	(91, 103)		4:6	(58)
14:28	(54)		4:8	(106)
14:30	(210)		4:10	(58)
15:26	(91, 103–4)		4:26	(58)
16:7	(104–5)		4:32–35	(252)
16:11	(210)		5:4	(255)
16:13	(91, 104, 105)		5:30–31	(58)
16:33	(276)		5:32	(106–7)
17:1–26	(276, 340)		6:3–5	(106)
17:21	(40)		7:55–56	(59)
18:19	(74)		8:16	(125)
18:20	(241)		8:17	(107)
18:36	(276–7)		10:44	(107)
18:38–40	(317)		10:45	(106)
19:4–6	(317)		10:48	(125)

11:1	(125)
11:16	(99)
11:19	(125)
11:24	(106)
11:29	(252)
12:17	(180)
13:22	(337)
13:23	(321)
13:52	(106)
15:8	(107)
15:11	(217)
16:3	(318)
16:37	(280)
18:12	(4)
19:5	(125)
19:6	(107)
21:18	(180)
22:25–28	(230)
23:5	(209)
26:19	(47)

Romans

1:3	(217, 321)
1:3–4	(57, 99, 323)
1:4	(126)
1:7	(59)
1:9	(347)
3:13–17	(273)
4:13	(315)
6:3	(125)
6:4	(57)
8:11	(57)
8:14	(107)
8:34	(59)
9:5	(38, 51)
9:14	(280)
9:27	(316)
9:31	(314)
10:1	(284)
10:3	(314)
10:21	(314)

10:38	(57)
11:1–4	(314)
11:25	(316)
12:2	(282)
12:20	(264, 273)
13:1	(209)
13:1–7	(210, 212)
13:4	(219)
14:11	(49)
14:17	(107)
14:19	(274)
15:16	(120)

1 Corinthians

1:3	(59)
1:7	(287)
1:13	(125)
6:14	(57)
6:19	(107)
8:6	(57, 80, 130)
9:20	(316)
10:32	(315)
11:3	(57, 130, 288)
11:14	(12)
15:5–8	(47)
15:21	(57)
15:24	(57)
15:28	(57)

2 Corinthians

1:3	(57)
1:23	(347)
5:1	(323)
5:10	(89)
5:17	(78)
11:4	(5)
11:13–15	(283, 254)
11:31	(59, 347)
13:14	(120)

Galatians
1:1	(57)
1:8	(76)
1:9	(283, 347)
1:10	(241)
1:12	(180)
1:19	(186)
1:20	(347)
2:9–12	(180, 316)
3:27	(125)
4:4	(172, 228)
6:16	(315)

Ephesians
1:1–3	(59)
1:17	(58)
2:14	(316)
2:18	(120, 131)
5:20	(59)
5:23	(234)
6:5–8	(209)
6:23	(59)

Philippians
1:2	(59)
1:8	(347)
2:6	(38, 48, 337)
2:9	(59)
2:10–11	(38, 49, 89)
2:5–11	(49)
2:6–7	(58, 130)
2:11	(58)

Colossians
1:1	(58)
1:2–3	(59)
1:16–17	(89)
2:2	(54)
2:9	(35, 88)
3:1	(58)
3:11	(213, 284)
3:17	(59)
3:18	(59)
3:22–24	(209)

1 Thessalonians
1:1	(58)
1:3	(59)
2:15	(314)
3:11	(59)
3:13	(59)

2 Thessalonians
1:1–2	(59)
2:13–14	(120)
2:16	(59)

1 Timothy
1:1–2	(58–9)
2:1–2	(209, 213)
2:5	(57, 130, 144, 289)
3:16	(39, 53)
6:10	(241)
6:17	(241)
9:15	(288)

2 Timothy
1:14	(107)
2:8	(331, 336)
4:1	(89)

Titus
2:9–10	(209, 213)
3:1	(209, 217)

Hebrews
1:3	(8, 59)
1:8	(39, 50)
2:18	(200)
4:15	(200)
6:16	(347)
9:24	(58)
10:12	(59, 130)
12:23	(58)
13:20	(58)

James
1:1	(58)
1:10–11	(247)
2:3–6	(243, 247)
2:10	(9)
4:4	(241)
5:12	(345)

1 Peter
1:2	(120)
1:3	(58)
2:9–10	(315)
2:13–17	(208, 210, 213)
3:1–6	(289, 315)
3:22	(59)
5:3	(283)

2 Peter
1:2	(58)
2:9–10	(210, 212)

1 John
2:4	(283)
2:15	(241)
2:16	(201)
5:6	(91)
5:7	(91, 120, 133)
5:10	(54)

2 John
3	(58)

Jude
4	(58)
7–8	(210, 213)

Revelation
2:2	(283)
5:5	(321)
5:7	(54)
5:13–14	(89)
7:10	(59)
9:14	(130)
10:12–15	(130)
13:10	(269, 283)
17:5–6	(215)
22:16	(321)
22:18–19	(76)